Theology and Down Syndrome

Theology and Down Syndrome

REIMAGINING DISABILITY IN LATE MODERNITY

AMOS YONG

BAYLOR UNIVERSITY PRESS

Cover Design: Stephanie Blumenthal

Unless otherwise noted, the scripture quotations contained herein are
from the New Revised Standard Version Bible, copyright © 1989 by
the Division of Christian Education of the National Council of the
Churches of Christ in the U.S.A., and are used by permission. All rights
reserved.

Library of Congress Cataloging-in-Publication Data

Yong, Amos.
  Theology and Down syndrome : reimagining disability in late modernity / Amos Yong.
      p. cm.
  Includes bibliographical references (p.   ) and indexes.
  ISBN 978-1-60258-006-0 (pbk. : alk. paper)
  1. People with disabilities--Religious aspects--Christianity. 2. Down
syndrome--Religious aspects--Christianity. 3. Church work with people
with disabilities. I. Title.

  BT732.7.Y66 2007
  261.8'322--dc22
                                    2007028566

Printed in the United States of America on acid-free paper with a minimum of 30% pcw recycled content.

To Mark and Eben

I dedicate this book to my two brothers. Mark, you know who's "the man"—you are! Eben, I am proud to be your older brother. Mark and Eben, I love you both!

Contents

Preface   ix

PART I
Anticipating Down Syndrome and Disability

1. Introduction   3
   Narrating and Imagining Down Syndrome and Disability

2. The Blind, the Deaf, and the Lame   19
   Biblical and Historical Trajectories

PART II
Down Syndrome and Disability in the Modern World

3. Medicalizing Down Syndrome   45
   Disability in the World of Modern Science

4. Deconstructing and Reconstructing Disability   79
   Late Modern Discourses

5. Disability in Context   117
   Feminist, Cultural, and World Religious Perspectives

PART III
Reimagining and Renewing Theology in Late Modernity: Enabling a Disabled World

6. Reimagining the Doctrines of Creation, Providence, and the *Imago Dei*   155
   Rehabilitating Down Syndrome and Disability

7. Renewing Ecclesiology   193
    Down Syndrome, Disability, and the Community
    of Those Being Redeemed

8. Rethinking Soteriology   227
    On Saving Down Syndrome and Disability

9. Resurrecting Down Syndrome and Disability   259
    Heaven and the Healing of the World

Epilogue   293

Notes   297

Abbreviations   339

References   341

Scripture Index   433

Name Index   436

Subject Index   442

Preface

Upon beginning my research for this book, I quickly discovered the complexity of the category "disability." This is the case not only for physical disabilities but also for those with intellectual disabilities. The proper language to use has always been contested—hence the wide range of nomenclature, each one succeeding the previously accepted terminology—and this is all the more the case in the politically correct times of late modernity. Since I have chosen to retain the language of "disability" (and "intellectual disability") throughout this volume, I need to enter at least three caveats in defense of my choice.

First, I am writing principally for colleagues in the Christian theological academy, seminarians and graduate students in theology and religion, and pastors and theologically interested laypeople. (As a Christian in a world of many faiths, I hope that theologians and intellectuals from other faith traditions will also find something of value in this book—I certainly have benefited from consideration of resources in other religious traditions in working out my own thinking, as the following will show—but the reader should beware that I am writing theology from an explicitly Christian point of view.) While this audience needs to be informed about the terminological debates in the various fields and disciplines associated with disability (and I do some of that in the pages to come), as a theological text it is less confusing to use a recognized and standard vocabulary. The category "disability" suits my purposes. My goal, however, is to point out just how complex its theological and religious meanings really are. Yet, in the end, I hope that the language of disability will be deconstructed, transformed, and perhaps redeemed.

Second, the people most likely to pick up this book will also be those with and without theological education who probably either have disabilities themselves or have friends or family members with disabilities. While I use people-first language through most of this book—for example, "people with disabilities"—in order to accentuate that we are all people qualified in various ways, including disabilities, at times I will reference "the disabled," usually although not always in quote marks. This is not meant to deny the fullness and richness of the lives of people with disabilities. Rather, aside from stylistic variation (in a long book, repetition can get rather monotonous), language about "the disabled" is also designed to remind us about the subtle yet undeniable ways that people with disabilities continue to be objectified and thereby experience the world through discrimination at the hands of the "nondisabled." For educated laypersons, I try to minimize the theological jargon or at least provide a brief explanation when that is unavoidable; but you might also find something like the *Westminster Dictionary of Theological Terms* (Westminster John Knox Press, 1996) helpful while working your way through at least part 3 of this book.

Third, in part because I write out of a secondhand rather than a more in-depth firsthand experience of disability, as an older brother to a younger brother with Down Syndrome, I will quote and cite many other sources in the following pages. And since these sources derive from many time periods and different disciplinary perspectives, a wide range of language reflecting those times and viewpoints will be evident. This should remind us that no one nomenclature captures the full extent of the complexity of the phenomenon of "disability," "intellectual disability," or "Down Syndrome."

Some final points about usage. "People with disabilities" in this book will refer first and foremost to people with Down Syndrome or people with intellectual, cognitive, and developmental disabilities, and only secondly to people with sensory-motor and physical disabilities.[1] The one clear exception will be in chapter 4, at which point I will remind the reader of this adjustment. On other occasions, "people with disabilities" may be more inclusive, referring to those both with physical and with intellectual disabilities, but on those occasions, the context should make these more inclusive references clear. Also, the phrases "severely disabled" or "profoundly disabled" (or "severely and profoundly disabled") will refer usually to people with intellectual disabilities (as will be clarified in chap. 3, pp. 57–60). Finally, I will also use "nondisabled" oftentimes as a contrast to "disabled," especially for the purpose of creating cognitive dissonance among readers who think of themselves as self-sufficient and who are used to characterizing people with disabilities as "others" who are lacking something.

My hopes for this book are threefold: that you, the reader—whether theologically educated or not—may be edified; that the discipline of theology will be affected in such a way that things will not go on as usual, in general ignorance of the experience of disability; and that this book can contribute in some small way toward the healing of the world so that it becomes a more hospitable place for all people, especially those with disabilities.

The seeds for this book were sown on March 16, 1975, when my youngest brother, Mark, was born to Reverend Joseph and Irene Yong in Kuala Lumpur (KL), Malaysia. My parents were successful pastors of a vibrant Assemblies of God church in Petaling Jaya, a suburb of KL, and they already had two sons: me (almost ten), and my brother Ebenezer (age six). Mark's young life was filled with complications, though he was not diagnosed with Down Syndrome until after we moved to the United States in late 1976. After Mark came along, I spent the next nine years of my life with him in the home—doing all the things that other brothers do with their disabled youngest siblings—before heading off to college.

While at college, I would return home every few weeks (it was only a two-hour drive). Four years later, however, I got married, and a year after that, we moved from our apartment an hour away from home to my wife's hometown, two states away. We kept moving after that, but always farther and farther away, except for one semester (the spring of 1999) after completing my Ph.D., when we rented an apartment two miles away from home while I commuted two hours one way to teach at my undergraduate alma mater. Other than this one semester, I have seen Mark only sporadically since 1988, perhaps, on average, one week every other year. Over time, while we try to maintain regular telephone contact, I have understood his verbal communications less and less, having been disattuned from his habits of speech. All the while, Mark has remained at home with our parents, to the present.

After publishing my first book, I struck up a conversation with my mother during the Christmas season of 2001 about someday writing the story of how God has blessed our lives with Mark. In one sense, this book is the product of that conversation, as I will tell more of the story of Mark and our family in the introductory vignettes to the chapters that follow. In fact, it has been precisely in and through the research and writing of this book that I have come to a much deeper understanding of and appreciation for my brother, and a much better sense of his habits, sensitivities, characteristic features, and needs. I feel like I have become a better brother to him, at least that is what I hope and pray has been part of the result of this work.

All the same, my training was in systematic theology, and I have therefore sought to think through the theological loci from out of my experience of growing up with Mark. Hence, this book is not just about Mark, although his life is certainly the inspiration behind it. The family vignettes beginning each chapter are designed not only to provide some concrete detail of a life with intellectual disability but also to serve as narratives on which theology engages and reflects.

There are innumerable individuals who have helped me with various tasks in the research and writing of this book. To begin with, I wish to acknowledge support from the Louisville Institute Christian Faith and Life grant, which made possible a full sabbatical over the academic year 2005–2006, during which period the first draft of this book was written. Thanks also to the administration of Regent University and dean of the School of Divinity Vinson Synan (now dean emeritus) and his staff for inviting me to join the divinity faculty while honoring and funding part of this sabbatical leave.

I am also grateful to the following persons for giving me the superb feedback that made my proposal sufficiently competitive so as to be awarded one of the Christian Faith and Life grants: Eben Yong, Harold G. Koenig, William C. Gaventa Jr., J. Ruth Nelson, Kathleen McGillivray, David Kling, Richard Sherry, Christian T. Collins-Winn, and David W. Anderson. In addition, I received two research grants from Bethel University (St. Paul, Minnesota): from the Bethel Alumni Association in the spring of 2004 when I first began my research; and the Edgren Scholarship for the summer of 2005, which funded my collaboration with Jason Berger, then a senior student in the business and political science programs at Bethel, who helped me better understand issues in the politics of disability.

In November 2005 I presented a paper to the Religion and Disability Group of the American Academy of Religion titled "Disability, the Human Condition, and the Spirit of the Eschatological Long Run: Toward a Pneumatological Theology of Disability" (published in 2007 in the *Journal of Religion, Disability & Health*), which included some of the main ideas developed at much greater length in this book. I am grateful for the comments and questions from the audience, as well as the more formal response from John Swinton, and a lengthy e-mail response from Nancy Eiesland, all of which combined to shape my thinking about disability and theology.

I also owe a debt of gratitude to the following who have given me invaluable feedback on the penultimate draft of the manuscript: Eben Yong, David W. Anderson, John W. Nelson, M. Miles (with Christine

Miles), Christopher Newell, Thomas E. Reynolds, William C. Gaventa Jr., Hans Reinders, and Debbie Creamer. In addition, the following students in my Further Readings in Theology doctoral seminar in the summer of 2006 at Regent University read the manuscript and provided thoughtful responses: Horace Shelton "Skip" Horton-Parker, Daniel Alvarez, and Benjamin Robinson. My two graduate assistants, Christopher Emerick and Raiford Doc Hughes, also read through the manuscript as well as provided all of the various kinds of support that make it possible for professors to research and write books. Finally, an anonymous reader for Baylor University Press gave me very helpful input that has made this book better. Of course, stubborn and fallible as I am, not all of the advice provided has been heeded, and none of the above should be held responsible for any infelicities and errors of fact and interpretation that remain.

Words also cannot express how deeply I appreciate the library staffs, especially those working in the interlibrary loan sections, of the following institutions: Betty Bond and her team at Bethel University, where I was teaching when I began research on this book; Xavier University (Cincinnati, Ohio), where I spent the fall semester of 2004 as the Edward Brueggemann Visiting Professorial Chair in Theology and Dialogue and researched and drafted the grant proposal; and Patty Hughson and her team at Regent University, where I completed my research and wrote the book during the academic year 2005–2006.

I am also grateful to my student, Bradford McCall, for his assistance in compiling the indexes.

Lastly, "thank you" to Carey Newman, director of Baylor University Press, for believing in the original proposal, and working with me through the details of publishing a book that attempts to break new dialogic ground between disability studies and theology. Thanks also to Myles Werntz, editorial assistant to Carey, Diane Smith, production manager, and Ellen Condict, book production assistant, who have worked with me in various ways to improve the manuscript and move it through the publication process.

PART I

Anticipating Down Syndrome and Disability

Part 1 of this book introduces its methodological and theological background. The first chapter on methodology focuses especially on the theoretical framework underlying the book and provides an apologetic for why a nondisabled person like me can and should write about disability and theology. As we navigate our way through questions regarding methodology, however, it will be clear that we can distinguish preliminary and prolegomena concerns from substantive considerations of disability and theology only artificially. In that sense, issues of method are always already intertwined with matters of content.

While both chapters 1 and 2 anticipate our formal discussion of disability and theology, chapter 1 does so by focusing on methodological deliberations and chapter 2 does so by overviewing the history of the Christian theological tradition. There is not much the Christian theological tradition says specifically about Down Syndrome for the simple reason that this label itself derives from a physician and researcher, J. Langdon Down, who lived in the nineteenth century. To shift to the broader category of "disability" risks being completely anachronistic if applied to the biblical texts and much of the history of the Christian tradition since, as I will show in part 2, our contemporary views about disability are distinctive to the modern experience. Yet, of course, the Bible does speak about the blind, the lame, and the deaf, and the Christian tradition does feature scholars like Didymus the Blind and others who may or may not have been impaired in some respect but either reflected

1

theologically on these bodily conditions or worked to serve persons who were blind, lame, or deaf. Hence I suggest that our survey of how the biblical and theological traditions understood such bodily experiences serves less as data or resources for a contemporary theology of disability than as background perspective for such an undertaking. In that sense, then, chapter 2 will explore the history of Christian beliefs and practices vis-à-vis the blind, the lame, and the deaf in anticipation of the theology of disability to be developed in part 3 of this book

I

Introduction

Narrating and Imagining Down Syndrome and Disability

[T]he challenge of learning to know, to be with, and care for the retarded is nothing less than learning to know, be with, and love God. God's face is the face of the retarded; God's body is the body of the retarded; God's being is that of the retarded. For the God we Christians must learn to worship is not a god of self-sufficient power, a god who in self-possession needs no one; rather ours is a God who needs a people, who needs a son. Absoluteness of being or power is not a work of the God we have come to know through the cross of Christ.

—Hauerwas 1986, 178

Mark was born with some serious physical complications, including an ongoing fever and leukemia. Mom recalls wondering why he was rushed off by the medical staff, and why she was not allowed to hold him. She did know that he was born with an extra thumb, and when a nurse brought a document by for Mom's signature, she thought it referred to the surgical removal of the extra thumb (which actually remains with Mark to the present). During these early days, Mom and Dad named their son Mark—after the gospel "evangelist"—due to his standing in the balance between life and death. On the fifth day, the doctors explained that Mark was very sick and his prognosis for life was not good.

Unable to suckle or feed himself, Mark was incubated (for twenty-one days) and fed intravenously (for the first two months of his life). Daily, his parents and church friends would visit him, fasting and praying for his recovery. No clear diagnosis was given to Mom and Dad at this time (remember, this was in Kuala Lumpur, West Malaysia, in 1975). Mark was finally released after about two months, with the doctors saying, "If he's still alive in two weeks, bring him back for a checkup and other tests."

During the first year of Mark's life, feeding was very arduous. Over the next few doctor's visits, numerous tests were performed, and one of the diagnoses regarding his morbid eyes was that Mark was blind. Mom discontinued taking him to the doctor's after a few months because they kept drawing blood without any satisfactory explanation (for her), and because Mark became too sickly after each time blood was drawn. At one point, Mom noticed that Mark's thick tongue was dangling out of his mouth, so she prayed, speaking to him to pull in his tongue (she did not recognize nor was she told at this time that this was a characteristic of Down Syndrome, although she insists his tongue ceased falling out after a few months). Both parents recognized that Mark was not "normal" (compared with their other two boys), since he did not feed well (it would take Mark two hours to finish two ounces of milk) and did not take in solid food (for years), did not hold up his head on his own for the first time until after he turned one year old, did not gain more than twenty pounds of weight during the first three years, did not begin crawling until well after his fourth year, and did not begin walking until after five years of age.

Mark said his first intelligible string of words at the age of fourteen. Even today, unless someone works closely with Mark on a day-to-day basis, it is very difficult to understand him. Further, Mark rarely initiates conversation. He seems, however, to understand much more than what his speech reveals. Mark communicates affectionately, expressively, and kinesthetically rather than verbally or propositionally. When I recently asked him what he would like others to know about his life story, Mark answered, "I am fine!"

Stanley Hauerwas's claim that "God's being is that of the retarded" may or may not be the conclusion reached in this book. To reach any conclusion about God and "the retarded," however, requires us to attain a measure of understanding about God, about "the retarded," and about how to construe the relationship between the two.[1] The first two concerns are fraught with methodological difficulties. On the one side is the complex set of contested questions surrounding how best to understand God and things divine, while on the other side is the equally disputed set of issues about how best to understand retardation and disability. In this chapter we will deal first with the latter before turning our attention to the former. The rest of the book will sort out the various ways to make connections between the two.

Narrating Down Syndrome and Disability

It does not take long after beginning research in Down Syndrome to come to the realization that its experts can be found in different fields of inquiry. There are doctors who specialize in the care of people with Down Syndrome, special educators whose expertise is in early intervention, and social service professionals who work with issues ranging from housing to employment and beyond. Each of these groups of persons is informed by different disciplinary perspectives, utilizes different discursive categories, and is concerned with different issues. If we turn from Down Syndrome to disability, this diversity of approaches and methods only multiplies exponentially. At the pragmatic level, besides concerns with health, education, and housing already mentioned, disability has economic, legal, and political dimensions that need to be addressed from those vantage points. In addition, the emerging field of disability studies has identified theoretical levels of concern, wherein the experience of disability begs for phenomenological, social, and cultural analysis.

The approach to Down Syndrome and disability adopted in this book will draw from all of these approaches. Research in Down Syndrome and disability is at least interdisciplinary insofar as many different fields of inquiry, each with its own set of methodologies, contribute distinctive perspectives, and multidisciplinary insofar as these various perspectives combine to shape a common framework of understanding and action (Orelove and Sobsey 1991: 13–14). Beyond this, however, the dynamic nature of contemporary research means that our approach will also be transdisciplinary insofar as many disciplines—in this case, all of the above plus theology—cross-fertilize and produce wholly new approaches, beliefs, and practices relevant to the challenges we face today.

At one level, then, our methodological commitments—to an inter-, multi-, and transdisciplinary approach—have already been laid out. At another level, however, our focus on Down Syndrome requires that we address more specifically the question "Who Speaks for the Retarded?" (Rothman 1982). While some might dismiss this as just another ideological question motivated by the politics of identity, I suggest that important methodological issues will be neglected if we do not pause to examine this matter.

"Who Speaks for the Retarded?"

The question Who speaks for the retarded? itself has a history. In the past, people with intellectual disabilities have been, generally speaking, objects of pity, of scorn, or of charity. In each of these cases, "the retarded" were reduced to one-dimensional creatures that lacked personal subjectivity and interpersonal agency.[2] Later on we shall see why it is unsurprising that the earliest scholarly life portraits of the "feebleminded" were by medical professionals (e.g., Goddard 1912), and that for a long time, the common understanding of such persons was shaped predominantly by the narratives of medical doctors (see Smith 1985).

Of course, the intellectually disabled have all had parents, and many were raised at home. Contrary to the myth perpetuated by the narratives of medical institutions, not all parents abandoned their children out of convenience. While this very complex story will be unfolded later, suffice it to say that most if not all parents who have placed their children in institutional care have done so only after a prolonged process of decision making. Pearl Buck's *Child Who Never Grew* (1950) was one of the first of its kind in providing a parent's perspective on the challenges involved in raising an intellectually disabled child, and in detailing the agony involved in the institutionalization process.[3] This book accomplished at least two things. First, it was a kind of "coming out" that confronted the stigma associated with being a parent of a child with intellectual disability. Second, it provided legitimation for the voices of parents of such children to be heard.[4] These parental perspectives were crucial in opening up space for narratives of intellectual disability that oftentimes countered the dominant medical accounts. From the parents' perspectives, no one other than they could speak with more authority on behalf of their children.[5]

However, the claim that *only* parents can speak for their retarded children is problematic in part because many are overprotective. Further, parental narratives remain about themselves and inevitably provide windows into the lives of their children from "the outside." Hence more recently, researchers such as Dorothy

[handwritten marginalia: Problem - researchers may project their ideas into those w/ intellectual disabilities]

Atkinson have insisted on adopting a life history approach whereby people with intellectual disabilities collaborate with research partners to develop their own life narratives.[6] Involving reminiscence, guided conversations, archival research, photographs, and family/community informants, a life history approach allows the memories, perspectives, and hopes of people with limited communicative abilities to be registered. Atkinson suggests (2000: 158), "The life story is the ultimate means of self-representation. It allows otherwise oppressed and powerless people to speak for themselves, to reclaim their past and, in so doing, to rediscover their identity."

[handwritten marginalia: Positive side of life story]

Self-Advocacy, Intellectual Disability, and Personal Narrative

This conviction regarding listening to people with disabilities has contributed to the emergence of their personal narratives. Within the wider disability movement, such autobiographical narratives have become standard following the mantra "nothing about us without us" (Charlton 1998).[7] Methodologically, the main question here is: who are the real knowers about the experience of disability if not people with disabilities themselves (cf. Vlachou 1997: 174; Fiser 1994)? This ideal is especially challenged, however, when dealing with people with intellectual disabilities.

[handwritten marginalia: Belgium - self - advocate]

Up until a generation ago, it was assumed that the "retarded" lack the historical agency and personal subjectivity required to tell their own stories. Gradually, however, these individuals have emerged into the public consciousness in various ways. To be sure, advocacy groups have worked with people with intellectual disabilities to ensure that their needs, desires, and perspectives are taken into consideration (see Williams and Shoultz 1984; Longhurst 1994). Over time, individuals with Down Syndrome have come to publish accounts of their own lives.[8] The most famous of these, so far, has been Jason Kingsley and Mitchell Levitz's *Count Us In: Growing Up with Down Syndrome* (1994).

Kingsley and Levitz's book consists mostly of interviews conducted with their mothers, Emily Perl Kingsley and Barbara Gibbs Levitz, between 1990 and 1992. Emily Kingsley was one of the staff writers for *Sesame Street*, and they were already talking about including disabled children on the show when Jason was born. Jason debuted on *Sesame Street* when he was fifteen months old and occasionally thereafter while growing up. He also starred later in *The Fall Guy* with Lee Majors.[9] Jason and Mitchell agreed to call their condition "Up Syndrome" rather than Down Syndrome (1994: 44). In their book, they chat not only about having Down (Up!) Syndrome, but also about friendship, school, recreation and fun/play times, girls and sex, marriage and children, becoming independent, and future plans. There are also conversations between Jason and his grandfather, as well as discussions about the Jewish beliefs and traditions of their families. Both boys embraced their Jewish faith in God, in Jason's case despite his mother's questioning the traditional notions of God and of God's existence. In the midst of the 1992 U.S. presidential race, Jason advocated for the Clinton-Gore ticket while Mitchell supported Bush-Quayle, with both showing a good deal of familiarity with the issues.

The emergence of the voices of people with Down Syndrome in the public square means that their perspectives can no longer be ignored. This is the case not only in terms of their participation in public affairs (e.g., Carabello and Siegel 1996), but also with regard to theological reflection, the main task of this book. For this reason, each of the chapters begins with the thoughts and ideas of people with intellectual disabilities (although not exclusively, as there are a few occasions when quotations from people with physical disabilities are reproduced), followed by the Yong family vignette. These words and expressions both set the tone for the discussions to follow and serve up symbols designed to give rise to theological thought.[10]

But even if we do agree that people with intellectual disabilities need to be consulted in order to adequately name and understand this experience (Luckasson 2003), what happens when such disabilities are so encompassing that the persons are unable to communicate either on the physical or the cognitive level? While many people with Down Syndrome are as fluent and conversant as Kingsley and Levitz, those who are severely and profoundly retarded are also physically disabled and verbally inarticulate. In some of these cases where we remain unsure about what level of self-consciousness actually exists, we remain reliant on their caregivers or other advocates (most often parents).

Other-Advocacy and Emancipatory Witness

Against this backdrop, it is important for us to confront the question of what right I as a nondisabled individual have to write a book about Down Syndrome in particular and about disability in general. The force of the question hits me quite directly since I agree with Robert Perske, who argues (in Gaventa and Coulter 2003: 39–41) that to think theologically about anything or anyone we need to enter into their world; but I have not had extensive interaction with people with Down Syndrome other than growing up as a sibling of a younger brother.

There are two distinct methodological issues behind this concern. The first is the familiar question of insider-versus-outsider perspectives. A radical disability rights position would insist that only people with disability can speak for or about disability matters. Of course, the question of how to handle the case of people with severe and profound cognitive disability elicits no clear response from this standpoint. Further, the reality is that the lines between disability and nondisability are much more ambiguous than assumed, not only because of technological advances (e.g., a person may be legally blind but still sighted with the proper eyewear) or the at-times fluid relationship between illness and disability, but also because of more recent attempts to de-essentialize disability and define it as a sociopolitical construct. Finally, of course, to hold fast to the "insiders only" position would have implications for what it means about who gets to teach religion, culture, or any of the vast number of other subjects in the humanities that few, if any, would be willing to argue for in current academia (see Creamer 2004a, 2004b: 10–16).

The other methodological question has to do with whether or not disability researchers are merely either "gazing" or "eavesdropping" on the lives of people with disabilities or are engaging in emancipatory advocacy. Because the former approach is at best rude and at worst an uncalled-for invasion of privacy, there are a growing number of theorists arguing that disability research must serve to address the discrimination, marginalization, and oppression experienced by people with disabilities, and to empower such persons and groups of persons to transformative and liberative action

(Johnson and Walmsley 2003: 10; Oliver 1996a, 1999b). Attached to this is an ethical question regarding whether researchers are merely opportunistic voyeurs who stand to gain from reporting on the "mentally retarded" or whether their work contributes to the emancipation of an oppressed group of persons (Ramcharan, Grant, and Flynn 2004).

I view my own work as contributing to social change indirectly more through the raising of public (especially ecclesial) consciousness than through working directly with people with intellectual disabilities (see Kitchin 1999: 225). Though I am not an activist and have little extended contact with people with disabilities (other than my brother), I see my work as representing a stance that is in solidarity with emancipatory researchers and people with disabilities (and their caregivers) in their resistance toward a form of discrimination called ableism perpetrated, mostly unconsciously, by the nondisabled majority.[11] Hence, I agree with how Jennie Block characterizes her own book (2000: 12): "At one level, I speak reluctantly for I believe it is essential that people with disabilities take the lead and speak of their own experiences. At another level, I believe that my perspective is valuable and worth sharing; however, I speak for myself."[12] At the same time, it is precisely through lifting up and making known the voices and experiences of people with intellectual and physical disabilities that I hope to effect transformation in the church, and through that, in society as a whole. So I agree with Jewish thinker David Blumenthal (1993: 237–39), who suggests that theologians are advocates of a peculiar sort: representing God to the world on the one hand, and the world to God on the other.

Theological Method and the Pneumatological Imagination

But can theologians really be advocates of the kind Blumenthal suggests, especially with regard to people with intellectual and physical disabilities? While in a real sense it will take me the rest of this book even to begin to respond adequately, let me comment in a preliminary sense by addressing the concerns behind this question related to theological methodology. In brief, I suggest that an approach to theological reflection informed and shaped by the Christian experience of the Holy Spirit provides what I call a "pneumatological imagination" that not only opens up space for the possibility of a dialogue with experiences of disability but also, arguably, requires such a conversation for Christian theology to maintain its credibility and plausibility in the twenty-first century.

The Pneumatological Imagination

Elsewhere, I have discussed the pneumatological imagination at length (Yong 2002: pt. 2). In brief, the pneumatological imagination can be said to be an epistemic posture shaped in part by the biblical narratives of the Holy Spirit and in part by the Christian experience of the Spirit. From the biblical text, I draw especially from the account of Pentecost in the second chapter of Acts:

> All of them were filled with the Holy Spirit and began to speak in other languages, as the Spirit gave them ability. Now there were devout Jews from every nation under heaven living in Jerusalem. And at this sound the crowd gathered and was bewildered, because each one heard them speaking in the native language of each. Amazed and astonished, they asked, "Are not all these who are speaking Galileans? And how is it that we hear, each of us, in our own native language? Parthians, Medes, Elamites, and residents of Mesopotamia, Judea and Cappadocia, Pontus and Asia, Phrygia and Pamphylia, Egypt and the parts of Libya belonging to Cyrene, and visitors from Rome, both Jews and proselytes, Cretans and Arabs—in our own languages we hear them speaking about God's deeds of power." (Acts 2:4-11)

From this narrative, I have argued that the many tongues of Pentecost signify both the universality of the gospel message and its capacity to be witnessed to by those who derive from the many nations, cultures, ethnicities, and languages of the world (see also Yong 2005a: chap. 4). The significance of this pneumatological imagination, I suggest, is at least threefold. First, it provides an explicitly theological framework for thinking about the perennial metaphysical and philosophical question concerning the one and its relationship to the many. Second, and building on the first more explicitly for the purposes of this volume, it provides a theological rationale for preserving the integrity of difference and otherness, but not at the expense of engagement and understanding. Finally, it alerts and invites us to listen to the plurality of discourses and languages in the hope that even through "strange tongues," the voice of the Holy Spirit may still speak and communicate.

How this pneumatological imagination "works" might be more clearly seen in the concrete case of theology's engagement with the sciences, as will unfold in the pages to follow. Now some might say that the language of spirit is obsolete in the modern world dominated by science. Even if there are voices in late modernity that suggest the "end of science" (e.g., Horgan 1997), the presence of modernity remains palpable in our midst, especially in our experience of being dependent on and often dominated by scientific technology. In this environment, science is chastened, but nevertheless ubiquitous. Theology in the late modern world therefore cannot avoid science but needs a specifically theological rationale for engaging with science. I suggest that the pneumatological imagination provides such a rationale for the dialogue with science since, in a late modern context, the many languages of the Pentecost narrative can be understood to include the diversity of academic discourses and scientific disciplines (Yong 2005b). The credibility of any contemporary theology of disability rests in large part on its capacity to engage both the broad spectrum of the humanities—and the various social, cultural, economic, political, and philosophical discourses of disability—and the wide range of medical, biogenetic, and evolutionary sciences, all of which continue to shape our understandings of disability. A pneumatological imagination alerts us to seek out, listen to, and discern the presence and activity of the Holy Spirit even in the "tongues" of the sciences, of modern technology, and of humanistic scholarship.

But beyond the sciences, as we have already discussed, the voices of people with intellectual and physical disabilities, and of all those who care for them, also need to be heard. This is the narrative dimension of Down Syndrome and disability so important for our understanding. I suggest that the tongues of Pentecost can be understood to include not only the diversity of academic discourses and scientific disciplines but also the emergent cultural traditions formed by new configurations of human interactions in our late modern world. This includes the postcolonial voices of women and persons of color from outside the Euro-American West, as well as those of people with disabilities (e.g., Deaf culture or disability culture). Again, the pneumatological imagination provides a theological rationale for engaging the (auto)biographies of people with Down Syndrome and other disabilities and invites us to pay attention to these experiences so as to discern how the Holy Spirit is present and active beyond our assumptions. In this case, the pneumatological imagination validates the conviction growing in theological circles that theology is rooted fundamentally in biography and narrative as much as it is in Scripture and tradition (McClendon 1974).

Pneumatological Theology and Emancipation

So far, however, we have been concerned only with how the pneumatological imagination functions as an epistemology in terms of its securing input for theological reflection from the sciences and from personal narratives. Yet, the fact that the pneumatological imagination is grounded in the Pentecost narrative means that its epistemology is but part of a "larger" soteriological vision. There are both performative and redemptive aspects of this pneumatological soteriology that need to be mentioned in connection with issues of theological method under discussion.

First, because the Scriptures attest to the Holy Spirit as the Spirit of Jesus the Christ, the pneumatological imagination also inspires and shapes the body of Christ, the church. In this sense, the pneumatological imagination is never only of epistemic import but is always connected to the life of the church. An ecclesial theology of disability cannot be concerned with mere description but is always motivated by how the church's understanding, beliefs, and confessions can and must shape her practices. To be sure, the discussion in the following pages will include both metaphysical and theological speculation, but these are for the purposes of (re)shaping the Christian imagination and for (re)ordering ecclesial practices. At this level, we might say that the pneumatological imagination serves to empower the church's performative engagement with the world.[13] In this case, the theology of disability to be developed in this book is also a *performative theology* that informs, shapes, and guides the practices of the church.[14]

But to what ends are the church's performative engagement with the world directed? With regard to the topic of this book, we might say that the pneumatological imagination empowers Christian witness to establish a more peaceful and just society for all people, especially those with disabilities. Because the Holy Spirit empowers human witness, I claim that the pneumatological imagination not only enables human knowing but also directs liberative human activity. Again, our knowing by the Spirit is never only for knowing's sake but always correlates with the larger purposes of God's redemptive work in the world. The pneumatological imagination therefore serves not only the task of theological description, but also that of performative prescription. In other words, the empowering of the Spirit enables human witness both in word (testifying to the truth) and in deed (living the truth), so that we might work to establish righteousness, peace, and justice, and in that way participate in the redemptive work of God in the world. At this level, we might say that the pneumatological imagination serves to inform and transform the church so that her members can bear emancipatory witness to the gospel in our late modern world.

Overview of the Volume

In this chapter, I have proposed the pneumatological imagination as central to the methodology of this book on disability in theological perspective. As I have defined it, the pneumatological imagination allows the church to be shaped by the work of the Holy Spirit, and to participate in the redemptive work of God in the world. For this reason, epistemology (and methodology) blends into soteriology, and the theological argument in this book is understood to be performative in terms of wishing to shape the emancipatory witness of the church. In this framework, the pneumatological imagination is constituted by the many tongues of Pentecost, which signal the diversity of witnesses to the redeeming activity of God. In our late modern context, I have suggested, the many tongues of Pentecost might include the narratives of people with disabilities and the many professional, scholarly, and scientific discourses that illuminate the experience of disability. The pneumatological imagination not only allows but in some way demands we heed all of these witnesses. Over the course of this book, these methodological commitments will be fleshed out, and in the process we will need to discern the wheat from the chaff, discarding the latter, but redeeming the former as part of the redemptive work of God.

We will develop the remainder of our argument as follows. Chapter 2 provides the biblical, historical, and theological background in the West against which any theology of disability must work, surveying developments through the eighteenth century. We will explore how images of disability in the biblical canon— the blind, the lame, the deaf—have been interpreted throughout the history of the church to exclude people with disabilities from participation in the community of faith. The goal in this chapter is to identify some of the theological sources of the oppressive discursive practices that continue to inform contemporary (mis)understandings of disability, especially in Western culture.

The three chapters of part 2 focus on the transformation of disability during the last two centuries as a peculiarly modern phenomenon. Chapter 3 presents a brief history of what we now call Down Syndrome, beginning with its continually changing nomenclature (idiot, moron, feebleminded, mongoloid, retard, developmentally disabled, cognitively disabled, intellectually disabled), and then explicating its institutional histories and the movements to deinstitutionalize people with Down Syndrome and mental retardation in the last forty years. The emphasis in this chapter will be on illuminating how medical science and the medical industry have come to dominate our thinking about Down Syndrome, not only in terms of treating its many cognitive and physical side-effects, but also in terms of educating people with Down Syndrome and, most importantly, of the practices and assumptions surrounding prenatal testing for its chromosomal conditions.

Chapter 4 examines the various late modern and postmodern attempts to destabilize the hegemony of the medical discourses of disability that our generation has inherited. Central to the postmodern counterdiscourses is the idea that disability is a social, political, and cultural construct. Medical perspectives are not thereby unimportant, but they provide only limited insight into why people with disabilities are stigmatized, marginalized, and oppressed. We need instead, disability rights activists insist, economic, geographic, and legal analyses that can expose and transform the structures of discrimination erected against people with disabilities. The concluding section of this chapter applies postmodern arguments to the phenomenon of cognitive disability, asking specifically about whether or not mental retardation is a social construction, and examining some of the practical and political implications of that claim.

Chapter 5 shifts the focus from the modern West to the global situation. We examine first how the voices of women with disabilities from around the world both complement and challenge feminist critiques of the disability rights movement, and we then turn to explore how issues of disability in general and cognitive disability in particular are emerging and being transformed in the developing world by processes of urbanization, industrialization, and modernization. Focusing our discussion on the cultural and religious factors specifically at work in the Indian scene introduces the role played by the religious traditions of the world in the lives of people with physical and cognitive disability. The goal of this chapter is twofold: to situate the developments of the modern West, including its postmodern counterperspectives, in a global context, and to sketch the multicultural and multireligious background against which the arguments of contemporary Christian theology must be made.

The four chapters of part 3 are concerned with sketching a constructive theological vision in light of the modern and postmodern experiences of disability. Chapter 6 is a discussion of the human condition whereby the traditional theological doctrines of creation, providence, and theological anthropology are revisited in light of changing modern understandings of intellectual disability specifically and disability generally. We deal here with two major questions: How can Down Syndrome be understood within traditional construals of the doctrines of creation and providence (e.g., Calvinism, Arminianism, Open Theism), and How can we understand the doctrine of the *imago Dei* in light of our experience of disability in the modern world? Central to our response to both questions is another look at Jesus Christ as the humiliated and suffering servant whose resurrected body retained the historically contingent marks of his impairment borne for the healing of the world. From this, we develop resources in dialogue with disability perspectives to rethink (and renew) our understanding of the human image of God as embodied, interdependent, and relational.

Chapter 7 turns from theological anthropology to ecclesiology, emphasizing the church as the community of members of the broken body of Christ who *are being* redeemed. Here, ecclesiologies of inclusion need to be renewed in light of the human experience of disability so that they are also ecclesiologies of physical, affective, and cognitive accessibility, all of which are especially important for people with Down Syndrome. We explore how people with the full range of physical and cognitive disabilities can participate in the catechisms, sacraments, and liturgies of the church, and how the church as the fellowship of the Holy Spirit is not only empowered on behalf of such persons but is also empowered precisely because such persons are active ministers within and beyond the community of faith who exemplify the anointed witness of Jesus Christ through weakness.

Chapter 8 revisits traditional formulations of the doctrine of salvation such as the *ordo salutis* and the healing of the body. While I will argue in light of the preceding and concluding chapters that these are only aspects of a full Christian soteriology, I nevertheless realize that any theology of disability must render accounts of how people with cognitive disability can be saved (if justification and conversion come by hearing and confessing the word of God), and why people with physical (and intellectual) disability are not healed (if the gospels communicate that the healings of Jesus are normative signs of the in-breaking kingdom of God). I conclude this chapter with a sketch of a holistic doctrine of salvation that both includes people with disabilities and specifies what it means to talk about the multidimensional healing (salvation) of the world.

The final chapter extends this vision for the healing, salvation, and renewal of the world to the doctrine of eschatology. I claim that it is precisely our eschatological notions that often dictate how we organize, structure, and live in this world. Hence, eschatological images that exclude what we call disabilities sustain exclusionary practices in the here and now. But how can we reimagine the eschatological glory of God as revealed in weakness? Drawing from Gregory of Nyssa's eschatological vision of being transformed eternally "from glory to glory," and from the biblical insights regarding the nature of the spiritual body, I develop a dynamic and pneumatological theology of life after death that includes all people with varying degrees of dis/abilities, and suggest how such an eschatological understanding both preserves the continuity of

II

The Blind, the Deaf, and the Lame
Biblical and Historical Trajectories

Religin [sic] is all over me. It means something; it means my life. They call it the Pentecost movement. The Bible talks about it. All the prophets and the apostles and Jesus got together in the upper room for the Last Supper. There was a break-out, speaking in tongues—in each person's own language. They started talking to the Lord in his tongues. This is His gift to us. When you cry or you ask Him for the gift, He gives it to you. This is what the Pentecost movement is. It is experiencing a lot of things. It is experiencing the speaking of tongues. If you can speak in tongues you also can interpret it. The interpreter gives the message to the believers.

—Pattie Burt, in Bogdan and Taylor 1994: 186–87

The Bible uses deafness as a metaphor for spiritual defect. . . . Without hearing, education was thought to be impossible; and without hearing and reading, one could not receive the Word. We [deaf persons] were exempt from evangelization and its purported benefits. . . . For me, the biblical images of deafness applied ironically to my students. Nothing I said about historical and cultural context sank into some heads. They just knew what it meant, as effortlessly as hearing people hear.

—Raphael 2005: x

[T]he worldview reflected in the Bible is more than 2,000 years old and in need of critique. In assessing the Bible's understanding of disability (as well as its understanding of science, medicine, astronomy, geology, homosexuality, geography, and other fields), the reader must understand that we are dealing with an ancient understanding of the natural world. . . . [Insofar as] inclusion has replaced healing as the indicated treatment and desired outcome, biblical healing narratives become irrelevant. They may be useful as inspirational words of hope, but they are not helpful for those of us who choose to see our disabilities as an integral aspect of our identity.

—Molsberry 2004: 98

Mark loves reading the Bible. Over the years, oftentimes long into the night and into the wee hours of the morning, he has gone through all of his many personal Bibles, marking and highlighting them from cover to cover with pens and markers of all colors. Because of his impaired vision—Mark's eyesight last tested at 20/200, but he has perennially resisted wearing his eyeglasses—he assumes a posture hunched over the sacred text, with his face just a few inches from the biblical pages. What exactly does Mark understand? We know that during years of Sunday school and other venues, Mark has memorized large portions of Scripture. His favorite Bible stories involve Jesus, even as he knows many, if not all, of the biblical books by name. When I recently asked Mark why the Bible was important, he answered that it was because it had the stories of Jesus and the disciples, and told of how to "walk the gospel," saying, "That's me!"

Christian theological reflection, at least in the Protestant tradition (where I find myself), has long sought to begin with the biblical witness. The problem for our purposes is that the Bible talks about the blind, the deaf, and the lame, among other impairments and impeding conditions, but not about "Down Syndrome" or even about "disability." In fact, researchers who set out looking for a biblical theology of disability will be quickly disappointed because our contemporary notions of disability are for the most part foreign to the worldview of the biblical authors. Yet people with intellectual and physical disabilities have long had to deal with the legacy inspired by the biblical references to the blind, the deaf, and the lame. Hence any theological exploration about Down Syndrome will need to come to grips with what the Bible says about these matters, and how these texts have been interpreted and understood by the church. In fact, it is precisely by confronting this history that the need to rethink our theology of disability will impress itself on us.

In this chapter, then, we will overview traditional readings of the biblical references to the blind, the deaf, the lame, and other related conditions; survey the history of the church's beliefs and practices regarding these categories of persons; and summarize the tradition of biblical and theological thinking about "disability" that remains widespread in the popular Christian imagination. Our focus throughout is descriptive: we will look at the effects of images of "disability" in the biblical canon—the blind, the lame, the deaf—not only on the history of the church but also on the wider society.[1] By the end of this chapter, we should be able to identify the theological logic and ecclesial practices that have shaped and continue to inform contemporary notions of disability.

Our goal, however, is not only understanding, but an intellectual and even affective conversion toward a posture that insists traditional understandings of disability cannot go unchallenged in our time. The reader should be warned that some of what follows may be discouraging and even depressing, especially when read by a person with disability looking for biblical edification. However, theologians of disability can neither simply give up on the Bible nor allow traditional interpretations of disability to be perpetuated in our churches. For this reason, we need to feel the full force of previous theologies of disability so that we will be motivated to rethink the issues. When we proceed to do so (in pt. 3), we will then retrieve some of the more hopeful interpretations of disability in the history of Christianity excluded from this chapter.

The Hebrew Bible and the Christian New Testament

The Bible does not say anything about what we today call intellectual disability.[2] What we do have, however, are catalogues of various motor-sensory conditions that are recognizably disabling.[3] In the following survey of such conditions in the biblical narratives, we will not treat each and every reference but will categorize them under a few more general headings.

"Disability" in Ancient Israel

One of the first biblical references connects blindness, deafness, and muteness to the sovereignty of God: "And the LORD said unto him [Moses], Who hath made man's mouth? or who maketh the dumb, or deaf, or the seeing, or the blind? have not I the LORD?" (Exod 4:11). While the logic of divine sovereignty in this verse points to God as the originating source of these disabling conditions (cf. Ruconich and Schneider 2001: 196–97), this announcement actually served to encourage a fearful Moses in his calling with his stuttering to represent the people of Israel before Pharaoh. In this context, God's creative sovereignty over the human body is only part and parcel of God's creating the world and ordering its nations. At the same time, however, the explanation for "disability" is found in the inscrutable will of God.[4]

A second influential text that has informed Christian beliefs and practices about "disability" throughout the centuries derives from a discussion of rules regarding the Levitical priesthood:

> And the LORD spake unto Moses, saying, Speak unto Aaron, saying, Whosoever he be of thy seed in their generations that hath any blemish, let him not approach to offer the bread of his God. For whatsoever man he be that hath a blemish, he shall not approach: a blind man, or a lame, or he that hath a flat nose, or any thing superfluous, Or a man that is brokenfooted, or brokenhanded, Or crookbackt, or a dwarf, or that hath a blemish in his eye, or be scurvy, or scabbed, or hath his stones broken [NRSV: "crushed testicles"]; No man that hath a blemish of the seed of Aaron the priest shall come nigh to offer the offerings of the LORD made by fire: he hath a blemish; he shall not come nigh to offer the bread of his God. He shall eat the bread of his God, both of the most holy, and of the holy. Only he shall not go in unto the veil, nor come nigh unto the altar, because he hath a blemish; that he profane not my sanctuaries: for I the LORD do sanctify them. (Lev 21:16-23)

Clearly this text meant to exclude persons whom we would recognize as disabled today from approaching the sanctuary of God and making the sacrificial offering (note, however, that priests could eat of the sacrificial bread).[5] Yet these prohibitions should be understood within the wider framework of the Levitical purity code (chaps. 11–24), which also excluded certain kinds of blemished animals from being sacrificed (Lev 22:19; cf. Deut 15:21; Mal 1:8; see Hentrich 2003). Ancient Israel was less concerned with what we late moderns would call discrimination against people with disabilities and more concerned with ordering an impure world through proper rituals, a recognizable symbol system, bodily hygiene, and social practices (Douglas 1966: chap. 3). Further, however, the same holiness code warns, "Thou shalt not curse the deaf, nor put a stumbling block before the blind, but shalt fear thy God: I am the LORD" (Lev 19:14; cf. Deut 27:18).[6] People with "disabilities" are therefore made special objects of divine care, often in connection with the poor, the oppressed, and the marginalized (Job 29:12-17; Jer 31:8; Zeph 3:19). For these reasons, few Christians (we will look at Jewish interpretations later) today would agree that these criteria should remain in effect, especially as it seemed they were revised in the postexilic period when emphasis was placed on social integrity and devotion to God—for example, clean hands and a pure heart (see Bergant 1994: 28–29)—and when the eunuch (the one with "crushed testicles") was pronounced clean and included in the activities of the temple of YHWH (Isa 56:3-5).

However, these exclusive texts have not been so easily dismissed precisely because they are set within a worldview deeply shaped by dualistic notions of purity and defilement. To argue that the priestly proscriptions against serving the sacrificial offerings represented ancient Israel's view of YHWH as a transcendent and holy God who was alone able to provide for the "perfect" priesthood (McCloughry and Morris 2002: chap. 4) leaves intact the idea that people with "disabilities" represent all that is unholy and imperfect before the eyes of this same God.[7] In fact, this has been historically understood to have been an association made in the covenant itself: that disobedience would bring upon the people of Israel all manner of plagues, pestilence, consumption, disease, (chronic) illness, madness, blindness, and other bodily afflictions (Deut 28:15-68; cf. Zeph 1:17).[8] Israel knew that their sin brought about divine disfavor and trouble instead of healing (Exod 32:35; Jer 14:19). The penitential psalms reflect throughout the sorrow of Israel in repenting of sin and pleading for healing from the hands of God (e.g., Ps 6, 32, 38, 51, 102, 143; see Deland 1999: 54). It is precisely at this point that Israel's monotheistic

framework operated unlike the polytheistic Grecian and Meso-
potamian healing cults that provided multiple diagnoses and prescriptions; instead, for ancient Israel, all sickness and "disability"
was the instrument of YHWH, whether directly or indirectly, "to
enforce covenants made with humans" (Avalos 1995: 242).

Israel did anticipate full healing, in the coming day of YHWH.
Throughout Isaiah, we hear the prophet's proclamation: "[I]n that
day shall the deaf hear the words of the book, and the eyes of the
blind shall see out of obscurity, and out of darkness" (29:18), and
"Then the eyes of the blind shall be opened, and the ears of the
deaf shall be unstopped. Then shall the lame man leap as an hart,
and the tongue of the dumb sing: for in the wilderness shall waters
break out, and streams in the desert" (35:5-6). In second Isaiah, the
servant of YHWH is called "for a light of the Gentiles; To open the
blind eyes, to bring out the prisoners from the prison, and them
that sit in darkness out of the prison house" (42:6b-7), and YHWH
will "[b]ring forth the blind people that have eyes, and the deaf
that have ears" (43:8). But while it is important to note that such
pronouncements have been the source of hope to many people
with "disabilities" throughout the centuries, they also reinforce an
ableist notion of embodiment that suggests both that people with
"disabilities" are less than whole, and that bodily "disabilities"
must be cured before such persons can be fully included in the
kingdom of YHWH (cf. Melcher 2004). Alternatively, as Rebecca
Raphael (2003) has noted, other passages in the prophets include
the blind and the lame in the final restoration without specifically
mentioning their healing (Jer 31:8-9; Mic 4:6-7; Zeph 3:19; Isa
33:23b). But still the question needs to be posed: what about the
status of such people with "disabilities" before that final day of
YHWH? Is theirs solely an eschatological expectation without any
hope for the present life?

"Disability" and the Early Church

The idea in the prophets that people with "disabilities" can be
included in the reign of God only after they are healed persists
albeit in modified ways in the early church's understanding of the
miraculous healings of Jesus. While we will provide alternative disability readings of the healings of Jesus in chapter 8, a few comments should be noted here.

First, Jesus' healing of the blind, the lame, the deaf-mute, and other "disabilities" may serve to confirm a number of traditional stereotypes regarding people with "disabilities," chief of which is that they are passive and pitiable objects of historical forces dependent fully on God's redemptive healing by the power of Jesus. According to an in-depth study of the gospel of Luke, S. John Roth (1997) argues that the blind, the lame, and the poor are not characters per se—they have few character traits, are often without points of view, and rarely initiate activity—but are a literary representation of the class of persons who are wholly at the mercy of others. The paralytic is carried to and then healed by Jesus (Luke 5:17-26); the son of the widow of Nain and Jairus's daughter are raised from the dead (7:11-17, 8:51-56); the boy with epilepsy is delivered (9:37-43); the crippled-over woman is straightened up (13:10-13); lepers are cleansed (17:11-19); and the blind man receives his sight (18:35-43). Yet in each case the point made is Christological: that Jesus is the one who is to come since through his ministry, "the blind see, the lame walk, the lepers are cleansed, the deaf hear, the dead are raised, to the poor the gospel is preached" (7:22b). Roth (1997: 141) concludes that these are "character types who are standard, conventional recipients of God's favor. Often they are almost romanticized, because their future is ultimately secured by God, and indeed, by God alone." The result is at least threefold: (1) that healing came to be seen as the ultimate sign of divine favor upon people with disabilities; (2) that the church, the body of Christ empowered to carry out his work in his absence, was encouraged to look upon and minister to such helpless persons; and (3) that people with "disabilities" came to internalize a self-identity of passive resignation and adopt a posture of patient suffering while awaiting either the gifts of healing mediated through the church or the eschatological healing of God.

Second, Jesus' healing narratives served to perpetuate, at least implicitly, the ancient Hebraic beliefs regarding the connections between "disability" and sin, impurity, and disorder. Now to be sure, this assumption was explicitly rejected by Jesus in the episode involving the man born blind: "And his disciples asked him, saying, 'Master, who did sin, this man, or his parents, that he was born blind?' Jesus answered, 'Neither hath this man sinned, nor his parents: but that the works of God should be made manifest in him'" (John 9:2-3). But even if we grant for the moment that Jesus' response definitively breaks the causal connections between sin and "disability," other difficult questions arise, such as the theological issue of God being the "cause" of this man's congenital blindness, or the ethical matter of this man's blindness being merely instrumental for other divine purposes.[9] However, the association between sin and "disability" is not so easily dismissed in John in light of what Jesus said after healing the paralytic at the pool: "Behold, thou art made whole: sin no more, lest a worse thing come unto thee" (John 5:14).[10] I need to be clear that I am not arguing the theological case for attaching disability to sin. I am only pointing out that ideas from the Hebrew Bible persisted during the early Christian period, and that they continued, as we shall see in the next section, to shape the church's attitudes toward people with disabilities.

The third point to be made about the healing narratives in the gospels is the emerging association between "disability" and evil spirits. The basis for such a demonological etiology for "disability" derives from the gospel authors' discussion in the same breath of Jesus exorcising evil spirits and curing physical and mental infirmities and "disabilities" of all sorts (e.g., Matt 4:24, 8:16; Mark 1:32-34; Luke 7:21; Acts 8:7). Even more damaging are explicit statements that certain "disabilities" were brought about by specific demons, or that "disabilities" were cured through exorcisms rather than medical treatments. Thus we have references to "one possessed with a devil, blind, and dumb" (Matt 12:22), a mute possessed by a demon (Matt 9:32-33; Luke 11:14), a crippled woman "which had a spirit of infirmity" (Luke 13:11), and an epileptic boy with a "dumb and deaf spirit" (Mark 9:14-29, esp. 25; cf. Matt 17:15-18).[11] Finally, in another connection it is said of Jesus: "He hath a devil, and is mad; why hear ye him? Others said, 'These are not the words of him that hath a devil. Can a devil open the eyes of the blind?'" (John 10:20-21). The implications of this Johannine reference are twofold: that devils can only cause blindness (rather than heal them, as Jesus did by the power of God) and that lunacy is attributable to demonic possession. All together, however, the links between "disability" and evil spirits are clearly established in the gospel narratives.

People with "disabilities" are marginalized in the gospel accounts through their portrayal as dependent on God's healing power, through the continuation of the idea that "disability" is related to sin, and through a new association (not present in the Hebrew Bible) between "disability" and evil spirits. But what about the parable of the great banquet where the maimed, the lame, and the blind are invited to attend such as they are (Luke 14:12-24)? Yet, even here, traditional interpretations emphasize not this point, but focus instead on who is excluded and why, or on who the rich or well-to-do should invite to their banquets and why (the motivation should not be on expecting recognition and repayment in this life), or on the issue of discipleship (Carey 1995). These readings remain problematic from a disability perspective since they assume the secondary status of people with disabilities who were invited only after the other guests rebuffed the invitation.

Yet the pejorative use of "disabilities" functions not only in the gospel narratives, but also in the metaphors involving disability that are found throughout the New Testament. One of the ambiguous elements of the story of the man born blind in John 9 is the question of who is really blind: the man who was blind but now can see, or the Pharisees who can see but do not believe in Jesus.[12] The blindness of the Pharisees is elsewhere associated with their hypocrisy, dishonesty, and folly (Matt 23), even as the metaphors of blindness and deafness are repeatedly explicated in the Bible in connection with spiritual hardness of heart, moral obduracy, and even wickedness (Rom 11:7, 25; Eph 4:18; 2 Cor 4:4; 2 Pet 1:9; 1 John 2:11; Rev 3:17; Isa 56:10; and Isa 6:9-10, alluded to in John 12:40 and Acts 28:26-27). On one occasion (Heb 12:12-13), lameness is used metaphorically to warn about what might happen to those who do not suffer hardship patiently as if enduring divine discipline. Clearly, then, "disability" in the New Testament functions rhetorically to call attention to negative realities such as sin, evil spirits, spiritual degeneration, and moral reprobation.[13]

"Disability" in the History of Christianity

The power of the biblical narratives to shape attitudes, beliefs, and practices regarding the blind, deaf, and lame should not be underestimated. In this section, we will trace the effects of the biblical

witness about "disability" as manifest in the history of Christianity.[14] We begin with ancient Greece and Rome not only to provide some additional background to the ideas of the early church,
but also to note the dialectical interaction between "secular" and
"biblical" notions of "disability" that played out in the Western
world.

Background: Ancient Greece and Rome

While we are far from able to provide any exhaustive account of
"disability" in ancient Greece and Rome,[15] a number of summary
statements may be proffered. On the positive side, the Greeks
understood disability as a family and civic matter, negotiated on a
case-by-case basis within various sectors and arenas. In a few cases,
city-states made financial provisions for the aged and "disabled"
(Jeffreys and Tait 2000). In other cases, the military included a
wide range of people with "disabilities" (Edwards 1996), and some
blind persons even served as judges and held senatorial rank (Gardner 2002: 158). But because deafness was often understood by the
ancients more in terms of intellectual than sensory impairment,
deaf persons were assumed incapable of bearing legal responsibility and politically marginalized (Edwards 1997).

With regard to what we call intellectual disability today, "it
is likely that cases of at least mild mental retardation have always
been a part of human history" (Berkson 2004: 198). However,
explicit references to this phenomenon did not appear until the
second millennium B.C.E., and even then, they are few and far
between. Various explanations have been suggested for why mention of intellectual disability is so rare—for example, the high mortality rate for such infants; intellectual disabilities as recognized but
simply not thought worthy of mention by those who could write;
or people with mild retardation were functional in their societies
(see pp. 133-37) and therefore no mention was warranted (Berkson
2004: 203)—but among these reasons must surely be the fact that
the difference between dementia or mental illness and intellectual
disability was slow to emerge in the ancient Greek world. It would
not be until the Christian era when such a distinction was made,
and it would have to wait until the Renaissance and early modern periods when the fool as a metaphor is distinguished from the
fool as an intellectually disabled subject and when focused research

on congenital intellectual disability commenced (Stainton 2004; Berkson 2006).

Returning to ancient Greece, since the god of fire, Hephaestus, was a cripple whose disability was compensated with magical powers to infuse life into inanimate objects and to create incomparably excellent armor, people with "disabilities," though marginalized, were also thought to possess extraordinary abilities. Given this possibility of heightened powers, some Greco-Roman physicians were committed to treating and at least alleviating if not fully correcting congenital deformities of the body. Yet there were also less optimistic diagnoses: that "disabilities" were thought to result from environmental factors (e.g., climate and quality of water for drinking), complications in the pregnancy (e.g., frightening maternal impressions, traumatism, uterine irregularities, and postnatal injury),[16] or adverse influences at the time of conception. From the religious point of view, deformed and disabled children were either the product of the sins of parents, or omens and signifiers of religious pollution. For the Romans, "monstrous births"—from the Latin *monstrum*, etymologically derived from *monere*, "to warn"— were signs "that the sacred *pax deorum* or 'covenant with the gods' had been broken" (Garland 1995: 67). If deformed infants were not killed,[17] that was because they were somehow "saved" from being sacrificed, and therefore still belonged to the gods as holy or consecrated (Stiker 1999: 51). Of course, the gods were able to cure "disabilities" through magical incantations, prayers, amulets, charms, votives, and potions (Vlahogiannis 2005).

Still, deformed and disabled persons were often derided and scorned. Their representations in artistic portraits and images signified fear, loathing, contempt, and pity. These negative perceptions no doubt were fueled in part by the Greek philosophical tradition. In his *Generation of Animals*, for example, Aristotle argues that monstrosities—he names extra feet or extra heads— were the unfulfilled potential of nature's causes (IV.4; 1943: 425). If excesses that depart from the mean are deficiencies and marks of vice, then deformities that depart from nature's general cases are signs of uncompleted pregnancies (IV.6; 457). Although deformities happen more in males than females, "we should look upon the female state as being . . . a deformity, though one which occurs in the ordinary course of nature" (IV.6; 461).[18] Finally, most pertinent to intellectual disability, Aristotle posited a hierarchy of the human species based on the degree to which individuals possessed rationality. Combined with the Platonic emphasis on the ideas or forms as the highest exemplars of the true, the good, and the beautiful, reason came to demarcate human difference and value over and against other creatures in the animal kingdom (see Stainton 2001a: 453–54). If Whitehead is correct that philosophy in the western tradition is not much more than a set of footnotes to Plato, then ideas about deformity, disability, and human rationality in Western civilization may be an extension of Plato through Aristotle's long-lasting legacy.

The Patristic and Medieval Periods

The absence of references to intellectual disability in the Bible is almost replayed in the premodern history of the church.[19] Some historians of mental retardation have cited traditions about Saint Nicholas Thaumaturgos (the Wonder-worker) being the protector of the feebleminded (Kanner 1964: 3),[20] even as others have called attention to the history of medieval court jesters as almost certainly including persons who were at least mildly mentally retarded (Wolfensberger 1982). Yet this same silence also applies to the history of disability in general. There is reference to Zotikos, a fourth-century martyr who rejected the practice of infanticide and cared for discarded children, of whom it was said: "[H]e exonerates God of these malformations and he relieves humanity of its fear" (Stiker 1999: 76). There were also those who started homes and hospitals for orphans, the sick (including disabled), and especially the impoverished, although the major motivations here were the alleviation of poverty and the fulfillment of the Christian duty to provide charity (Stainton 2001b). Our discussion will focus on Saint Augustine and a number of medieval saints.

If Aristotle insisted that deformities did not violate the natural causes of the world, then it was left to theologians like Augustine to argue that these also did not escape the sovereign ordering of God. What for the ancient Greeks and Romans were *prodigia*, *portenta*, and *monstra* was for Augustine *miracula*, and demonstrated that "God will bring to pass what He has foretold regarding the bodies of men, no difficulty preventing Him, no law of nature prescribing to Him His limit" (*City of God* 21:8; 1994a: 460). Augustine's was hence a theological explanation that connected the Neoplatonic idea of the completeness of Creation with the medieval doctrine of the Great Chain of Being: God in God's infinite wisdom brought forth a diversity of creatures to manifest his glory and power. "For God, the Creator of all, knows where and when each thing ought to be, or to have been created, because He sees the similarities and diversities which can contribute to the beauty of the whole" (*City of God* 16:8; 1994a: 315). Yet, Augustine also thought that the "monstrous races" might be counted as human in some respect: "But whoever is anywhere born a man, that is, a rational, mortal animal. . . . [E]ither these races are non-existent or, if existent they are non-human, or, if human they are Adam's descendants and rational" (*City of God* 16:8; 1994a: 315).

While this criterion of rationality would formally exclude people with intellectual disability from the human family for the next millennium, yet in his *De Peccatorum Meritis et Remissione* (*On the Merits and Forgiveness of Sins*) Augustine describes a simpleton (*moriones*) "of so highly meritorious a character as to entitle him to a preference in the award of the grace of Christ over many men of the acutest intellect" (1994c: 28). Later on in this same treatise, however, he notes without castigation that persons whom commoners call moriones fetched prices for the amusement of the sane (1994c: 41). So while Augustine included people with "disabilities" in his theological scheme of things, he is still driven less by issues of inclusion and equality than by a theological vision of God as omnipotent creator.[21]

A number of saints also illuminate the church's beliefs and practices regarding "disability." Saint Dymphna (see Lovasik 1971) allegedly lived in the seventh century and sought refuge from her father at a convent in Gheel (later Ghent, now Belgium). She suffered martyrdom at the hands of her insane father (who wanted to marry her because he could find no other suitably beautiful woman to replace his deceased wife), but tradition further has it that Dymphna's body did not decompose in her coffin. Her grave became a site of pilgrimage where miraculous healings occurred, especially for those suffering from nervous ailments and mental afflictions. By the thirteenth century, Gheel had developed a tradition of caring for the mentally ill, and it became a model site for other homes and hospitals that focused on meeting the needs of the poor, the

sick, and the "disabled." In 1431 Dymphna was canonized by Pope
Eugenius IV after becoming widely recognized as patron saint of
the mentally ill.

The medieval mystic Hildegard of Bingen (1098–1179) also
appears to have been, to use contemporary diagnoses, chronically
ill (see Betcher 2000: 94–96). She wrote in the conclusion of *The
Book of Divine Works*:

> From the very day of her birth this woman has lived with painful
> illnesses as if caught in a net, so that she is constantly tormented by
> pain in her veins, marrow, and flesh. . . . This vision has penetrated
> the veins of the woman in such a way that she has often collapsed out
> of exhaustion and has suffered fits of prostration that were at times
> slight and at other times most serious. Therefore, her way of life dif-
> fers from that of others. She is like a child who is too immature to
> know how people live. For she is under the inspiration of the Holy
> Spirit in a life of service. She derives her bodily makeup from the
> air. And thus illness is stamped on her from this airy sphere by rain,
> wind, and every change in the weather to such a degree that she has
> no stability of body. If things were otherwise, the inspiration of the
> Holy Spirit could not dwell in her. At times the spirit of God awakens
> her from this mortal illness with the great power of its kindness as if
> with a refreshing dew, so that she can continue her life of service to
> the inspiration of the Holy Spirit. (Fox 1987: 265)

Hildegard's life became a vivid example of how trials and tribula-
tions could work patience and hope (according to Rom 5:3-4).

If Dymphna was noted for her miraculous cures and Hildegard for her virtuous suffering, these were combined in the life of
Margaret of Castello (1287–1320), a limped, hunched, blind, and
dwarfed woman who was rejected and abandoned by her family.
However "little Margarita" gave herself wholly to God, cheerfully
fasting and continually mortifying her body for the sake of experiencing the presence of Jesus. She accomplished more than two
hundred miracles during her lifetime and was beatified in 1609 (see
Orsi 1997: 39–42).

While not formally a saint, Teresa de Cartagena (b. ca.
1415–1420) also deserves mention. Already marginalized because
her family converted from Judaism to Christianity in fifteenth-
century Spain, Teresa became completely deaf in her late teen

years. After 1450 she wrote her spiritual autobiography, *Arboleda de los enfermos* (*Grove of the Infirm*), and an apology for the earlier work, *Admiración operum Dey* (*Wonder at the Works of God*), wherein she constructs herself "as one of the admirable works of God" (Seidenspinner-Núñez 1998: 138). Her books reflect the classic spiritual interpretation of illness, disability, invalidity, and suffering as the "exilic" means through which God purifies and sanctifies the understanding (of self-pride), memory (of self-esteem), and will (of self-dependence) so that God's children develop patience and the full range of virtues necessary for the afterlife. The motif of God disciplining those God loves (Heb 12:4-13) is central to Teresa's work. Still, her writings provide a lens into the experience of spiritual turmoil and socioreligious estrangement that no doubt characterized the lives of women with disabilities in medieval Christianity (see Juarez 2002; Castro-Ponce 2003).

A number of themes stand out in this brief overview of Christian views regarding "disability" in the patristic and medieval periods. First, nothing escapes God's sovereignty, not even "monstrous births." Deformities and disabilities exhibit the wide range of God's creative works. Second, while people with "disabilities" lived difficult lives, such were necessary to cultivate holiness. Physical suffering thus served the larger purposes of God. Finally, the church should enact works of charity toward and on behalf of people with "disabilities," but such works were only temporary measures that anticipated the miraculous power of God to heal either in this life or in the life to come.

Throughout, there is little discussion of intellectual disability as a distinct medical or psychological category. To be sure, there were "simpletons," "idiots," and "natural fools," but these were based on commonsense observations (rather than medical diagnoses) and were used to establish the rights and responsibilities of those considered mentally deficient. So the thirteenth-century *Prerogativa Regis* states in its eleventh chapter: "The King shall have the Custody of the lands of natural fools, taking the Profits of them without Waste or Destruction, and shall find them their Necessaries, of whose Fee soever the land be holden. . . . And after the Death of such Idiots he shall render it to the right Heirs, so that such Idiots shall not aliene, nor their Heirs shall be disinherited" (quoted in Stainton 2001b: 21).

The Reformation and Early Modernity

It was during and after the Reformation that advances on the medical front led to more focused discussion of intellectual disability.
While the major threads of this story will be woven in the next
chapter, here I want to focus specifically, albeit briefly, on the views
of Luther, Paracelsus, Ambroise Paré, Paulus Zacchias, and John
Locke.

While Reformers such as Calvin retained the Augustinian idea
of all deformity displaying the glory and grace of God (see his *Institutes*, 2.2.17; I, 267–77), it is Luther's suggestion to drown a mis-
shapen boy, also identified as being demonically possessed, which
has gathered the most attention in histories of mental retardation.
His *Table Talk* from September 1540 records: "In Dessau there was
a twelve-year-old boy like this: he devoured as much as four farmers did, and he did nothing else than eat and excrete. Luther suggested that he be suffocated. [Why?] He replied, 'Because I think
he's simply a mass of flesh without a soul. Couldn't the devil have
done this, inasmuch as he gives such shape to the body and mind
even of those who have reason that in their obsession they hear,
see, and feel nothing? The devil is himself their soul'" (Luther
1967: 396–97).

We have already seen in the pages of the New Testament that
epileptic children were understood to be possessed by demons. By
the time of the Renaissance, this idea had developed through a
number of tortuous twists and turns so that some malformed children (perhaps with subnormal intelligence) were thought to have
been changeling victims of demonic activity (Eberly 1991). It is
against this background of demonological ideas—which included,
for Luther, connections between the papacy and the devil—that
Luther's views regarding changelings need to be understood
(Colón 1989: 78–80; Goodey and Stainton 2001: 230–32). Hence,
Luther was circumspect about baptizing infants with deformities (1967: 44–45, 58). Yet, as M. Miles has argued (2001: 27–28),
Luther's longtime personal assistant, Wolf, appears to have been
mildly disabled. Further, following Jerome rather than Augustine,
Luther insisted that the deaf "hear" and receive the gospel since it
is not ears that are important but God's illumination of the heart,
and since all are "spiritually deaf" apart from regeneration (Miles

2001: 24).[22] Given these further considerations and the wider set of personal, ecclesial, and social contexts, it is wiser to see the Dessau account as reflecting a contextual understanding rather than as the standard view of Luther's.

At about the same time, Luther's contemporary Paracelsus (1493–1541) wrote *De generatione stultorum*, one of the earliest learned treatises devoted to the etiology of "foolishness."[23] In contrast to Luther's comment about the boy from Dessau being without a soul, Paracelsus notes that fools are redeemed by Christ even if there is no account of Christ restoring fools in the gospels. In fact, in the tradition of northern Renaissance humanists like Erasmus, whose *In Praise of Folly* was a satire on human wisdom, Paracelsus suggests that "all of us in our wisdom are like the fools. . . . Therefore the fools, our brethren, stand before us" (Cranefield and Fedorn 1967: 59). Yet within a Neoplatonic framework, Paracelsus assumed that only in their mortal minds are humans fools, even while their immortal souls remain holy, uncontaminated by the effects of sin and the Fall. This allows, occasionally, for a purity of wisdom or divine truth to be expressed through the unpolluted vehicle of the fool.[24] At the same time, a variant of the changeling idea was presented to explain infant deformities and mental deficiencies. While human beings sow the seed of their children, the germination and formation of some of these pregnancies is marred in the hands of mediatorial creators—these "vulcani," are described as "heavenly apprentices and immature master craftsman" (1967: 63)—who shape the seed in the womb.[25] In the end, Paracelsus assumes the medieval idea of a perfect paradise and concludes that divine salvation includes the eventual restoration of the mind and body to their pre-Fall condition. Therefore in eternity there will be neither the crippled nor the fool (1967: 74).

After Paracelsus, the "science" of teratology—from the Greek *teras* (genitive *teratos*), meaning "monster"—arguably reached its zenith with the publication of *Des monstres et prodiges* in 1573 (1982) by a French surgeon, Ambroise Paré (ca. 1510–1590). This encyclopedic treatise summarizes the common beliefs about "disability" in the sixteenth century. Most important for our purposes is Paré's discussion of physical and moral monstrosities in humans and animals. He presented twelve causes of deformities and monstrosities as:

1. resulting from God, intended for God's glory
2. emanating from the wrath of God
3. emerging from too great a quantity of seed, or
4. too little a quantity of the same
5. being misshapened by the imagination of the pregnant mother
6. by the narrowness/smallness of the womb
7. by a traumatic pregnancy, or
8. by the mother's fall
9. deriving from other hereditary mechanisms or accidental illnesses
10. rotten or corrupt seed
11. or the improper mingling/mixture of seed
12. being changelings of the devil

While Paré's etiology includes some rather extraordinary fictions when compared to later medical explanations, Rosi Braidotti is correct to point out (1999: 291) that "these fictions are embedded in some of the most serious canonical texts of Western theology and biology, mostly based on Aristotle."

A generation after Paré, Paulus Zacchias (1584–1659) was a papal physician whose *Quaestiones Medico-legales* (1621) was "the first modern treatise devoted to medicolegal problems" (Cranefield and Federn 1970: 3). Like Paracelsus, Zacchias also took notice of the fool and the deaf-mute (questions VII and VIII). He identified a wide range of people with intellectual deficiencies. "Slow learners" were those who can marry and even be held legally accountable for at least some of their actions; "fools" can be barely instructed and permitted to marry, but only by judges; and the "stupid" or "mindless" are excused from penalties of the law and cannot marry, primarily because they cannot understand or receive the sacraments.[26] About the dumb and deaf, he confessed, "we cannot correctly include them among the mindless or among the fools, and yet it cannot be truly affirmed that they are of sound judgment" (1970: 14). In Zacchias's work, the medieval notion of "foolishness" as primarily a quasi-legal term used to establish the parameters of responsibility for the mentally deficient is expanded to include the diagnoses made possible by advances in early modern medicine.

Alongside these advances on the legal and medical front were changes in the philosophical and theological climate. Some of these developments can be seen in John Locke's *Essay Concerning Human Understanding* (1690).[27] Locke followed Aristotle, Augustine, and even Descartes in defining human beings as creatures who were rational, but he specified more clearly that this meant the ability to think in abstractions (2.11.12). Those unable to do so are unreasonable creatures: "[H]erein seems to lie the difference between Idiots and mad Men, That mad Men put wrong *Ideas* together, and so make wrong Propositions, but argue and reason right from them: But Idiots make very few or no Propositions, and reason scarce at all" (2.11.13; 1975: 161).[28] Because idiots do not have innate ideas/knowledge, they only give the appearance of being human. Locke argued that if we assume bodily defects make monsters (which all of his contemporaries agreed), all the more should we assume that mental or rational defects exclude one from being considered human (4.4.16). So against Paracelsus, who advocated that fools nevertheless have unsoiled souls, Locke insisted that idiots, perhaps like changelings (whom Locke understood in terms of natural history; see Goodey and Stainton 2001: 237), were neither moral nor soulish creatures (4.4.13–14, 3.3.17).[29] Infanticide is therefore justified (so as not to give room to the devil) (3.6.26, 39), even as idiots are not expected to partake in eternal life (since this follows not the bodily shape but the reasonable soul) (4.4.14–15).

Locke's concern in the *Essay*, it must be remembered, was to establish the parameters of what it meant to be human within a natural history framework. More specifically, he was interested in a definition that could include the insane. This led him to the argument that the mad were those who were capable of abstractions (unlike idiots or brutes), but who had been misled by their imaginations. The result, however, was the exclusion from the human family of those incapable of abstract thought and communication. Yet, as C. F. Goodey notes (1996 and 2001), Locke must be understood at least in part against the backdrop of the debates among seventeenth-century theologians. While Locke himself had come to reject the Calvinist doctrine of predestination by the time he wrote the *Essay*, his own solution was but a logical extension of earlier attempts to distinguish between the elect and the reprobate. Whereas Arminians insisted that even the reprobate must have had the ability to believe in order to be culpable for their unbelief, the perennial Calvinist response was to distinguish between intellectual ability and moral depravity. But what about those without natural intellectual potency? While even moderate Calvinists still tended to lump these among the reprobates, for Locke idiots were by definition incapable of reason and therefore not reprobate but simply excluded from the class of those capable of an afterlife. Similarly, with regard to the debate about whether or not the Lord's Table should be open only to the elect (Calvinists) or to all would-be communicants (Arminians), Locke's suggestion shifted the terms of the conversation from the elect to those incapable of receiving the grace of Holy Communion.

Looking Backward, Looking Ahead

Our very brief survey of the biblical material and of "disability" in the history of Christian thought no doubt leaves much unsaid. Recall, however, that our purpose is not to provide exhaustive coverage of these matters, but to get some sense of what has gone before so that we can better discern the task that lies ahead. In the last few pages of this chapter, we will sketch the basic contours of the theology of disability assumed in the popular Christian imagination and identify what this means for those attempting to renew theology in disability perspective today.

The Legacy of the Biblical and Theological Traditions

The preceding survey has identified all of the main elements that continue to inform the theology of disability operative not only among lay Christians today but also in the wider society. In brief, such a theology consists of three basic notions: (1) that disabilities are either ordained or permitted by God for God's purposes; (2) that people with disabilities are encouraged to hope and trust in God's plan for their lives; and (3) that the church (and society) is to meet the needs of people with disabilities. Let me briefly unpack these ideas.

First, disabilities are part of God's plan. This is an explicitly theological statement that flows out of the overall portrait of divine sovereignty found in the Bible, and elaborated on systematically by theologians like Augustine. It also means, according to Joni Eareckson Tada (a leading spokesperson for people with disabilities in the North American evangelical community), that "God does not create accidents" (Tada and Newman 1987: chap. 1). Rather, since all history is ordained by God, even disabilities play a role in the wider scheme of things. Sure, disabilities may be the result of the devil's activity or the consequences of our personal sin—both are biblical notions, as we saw above—but either happen within the parameters previously established by God and therefore reside at least within God's permissive will. And in all cases (whether resulting from God's active or permissive will), God uses disabilities to accomplish myriad purposes—whether to reveal God's healing power, to test believers, to shape saintly lives, or any number of other divine intentions—and ultimately, God's justice and glory will be revealed in the lives of people with disabilities.

Second, people with disabilities are to endure patiently the outworkings of God's inscrutable plan, given the hope that God's ultimate intentions include their well-being and vindication. This is an existential statement designed to encourage persons who are both suffering and doubting God's goodness. Christian hope is grounded in the healing narratives of the Bible, which promise healing perhaps in the present life, but surely in the life to come when the perfect (Adamic) image of God will be restored to all persons. But, as important, if physical healing is not experienced in this life, suffering is God's instrument that leads to repentance (for the unbeliever) or nurtures holiness (for believers). Now even if people with intellectual disabilities might never be able to understand the rationale for why they need to respond to life's challenges in this way, their caregivers can find comfort and hope along these same lines in working with them. For the non-intellectually disabled, such "holy innocents" or "blessings in disguise" are signs (portents, as the ancients said) from God for the rest of us, either warning us to holiness (lest something worse befall us) or testing our resolve and commitment. In any case, "[e]very disabled individual is a person of dignity and worth, has a soul with an eternal destiny, and is beloved by the sovereign God. Therefore, realizing that God does know and care, the parents can take the youngster as he or she is and learn to know the child as a unique self" (Carder 1995: 59).

Finally, the injunction to the church that its members are to meet the needs of people with disabilities is a practical exhortation

designed to mobilize the body of Christ to enact the love of God
for the less fortunate who are dependent on the goodwill and charity of others. To be sure, in many cases, people with disabilities are
excluded from some or other aspect of the community of faith
(especially from its positions of leadership or ministry) according to the biblical purity laws. However, people with disabilities
are always included as recipients of divine favor with others: the
poor, widows, orphans, and strangers sojourning in a far-off land
(see Exod 22:21-24; Lev 19:9-10; Deut 24:17-18; cf. Klages 1999:
214n3). The models of charitable witness are Job in the Hebrew
Bible—who said: "I was eyes to the blind, and feet was I to the
lame. I was a father to the poor: and the cause which I knew not
I searched out" (Job 29:15-16)—and the Good Samaritan in the
New Testament. Further, if the life of Jesus is paradigmatic for the
ministry of the church, then the ministry or sacrament of healing
becomes central to the witness of the body of Christ. The hos-
pice at Ghent was only one of innumerable homes and hospitals
serviced by Christians who cared for the sick, the poor, and the
"disabled." Christian doctors not only cared for the bodies of their
patients, but also ministered to their souls. Historically, then, people with "disabilities" have been made, with all good intentions,
the objects of charity by the church. At the level of being recipients of the church's ministry, there has always been a place for less
fortunate people with intellectual and physical disabilities.

Disability and Theology: Toward a New Vision

I began this chapter with quotations from Pattie Burt (a pseud-
onym) and Robert Molsberry. Labeled "retarded" in part because
of IQ scores from the low 60s to low 70s (Bogdan and Taylor 1994:
24), Burt was nevertheless able to articulate her own ideas about
her life, her "retardation," and even her religion. As intimated
from what I reproduced, Burt's religious background includes
experiences in Pentecostal Christianity. We might quibble with
her understanding of Pentecostalism, of the baptism in the Holy
Spirit, of the experience and significance of speaking in tongues,
and so on, but we cannot deny that Pattie Burt has her own distinctive religious and even theological views. Sure, such views derived
from her interaction with Christian (Pentecostal) churches and
their members. But Burt didn't just believe what her pastors and

friends believed; rather, she sorted out what she received from them, embraced some of it, revised other ideas, and rejected the rest.[30] Still, for reasons to be discussed in the next chapter, people with intellectual disability are more apt to develop fairly conventional religious beliefs, especially if these are shown to be derived from their religion's sacred text(s).

But here we encounter a dilemma. On the one hand, if we embrace conventional theological views about disability, we will be burdened with many of the ideas already presented in the preceding. On the other hand, if we proceed to rethink our theologies of disability—as the quotation from Robert Molsberry suggests—then we run the risk of ignoring the conventional views of people with disabilities like Pattie Burt. The latter horn of the dilemma is especially egregious in a book whose author is committed to retrieving and heeding the voices of people with intellectual disabilities. The former horn of the dilemma is that we cannot challenge many of the contemporary practices that need to be challenged without also at the same time revising at least some of our conventional beliefs. How then do we proceed?

One way forward involves the possibility of rereading the biblical canon closely in search of positive presentations of disabilities and of people with disabilities. For example, biblical scholar Kerry Wynn (2003) has presented a new reading of Jacob that contests the "normate" or "ableist" hermeneutic presumed for the biblical text. In this conventional reading, the limping Jacob is considered "subnormal" at best and "abnormal" at worst. But if we bracket such "normate" assumptions, then Jacob's limp is "noticeable" at worst and even "extraordinary" at best. In this case, rather than being seen as a tragic hero, Jacob's "disability" becomes instead a sign of the covenant with God. The limp is no longer a pathological wound but a distinguished mark of Jacob's new identity. Similar rereadings might be suggested with regard to other biblical "heroes" such as Isaac (with his blindness), Leah (and her "weak eyes"), Moses (and his stuttering), Zechariah (and his muteness), and Paul (first with his blindness and then with his "thorn in the flesh").[31]

This strategy, however, involves reading beneath, between, and even against the ableist assumptions at the surface of the biblical text. This is much easier said than done since we are dealing not with any book, but with a sacred text. Nevertheless, we might take some cues from recent interpretations of folklore informed by disability perspectives. In her survey of more than four thousand folktales, Adele McCollum (1998) shows that while the plain sense of many of these stories may be discouraging and even offensive to people with disabilities, yet their subtexts speak of tolerance, empathy, and modest inclusiveness vis-à-vis disabilities. The paradigmatic figures in our folktales include blind men who are insightful (like Tiresius); retarded people who exhibit honesty and innocence; "not quite human" stories of courage and character (applied to hunchbacks, dwarfs, etc.); disabled persons who improvise in order to overcome hurdles and meet the crises of life; and so on.[32] On the surface, arguably, these tales perpetuate stereotypes of people with disabilities, but they can also be read subversively and "redemptively" so that disability is no longer the only or predominant feature of these characters.

Similarly, I suggest that any theology of disability for the twenty-first century will have to acknowledge and confront the conventional understandings of disability manifest in the biblical text (which we have done in this chapter), but yet proceed to subvert conventional antidisability readings of the Bible by reading beneath and between its lines (which we will do in part 3 of this book).[33] So on the one hand, a redemptive theology of disability for today cannot ignore what people like Pattie Burt have to say, even while recognizing that Burt's perspective is contestable even from the perspective of other people with intellectual disabilities. On the other hand, a redemptive theology of disability for our time has to go beyond a merely surface reading of scriptural texts on disability (because the plain interpretation of such texts has over the centuries been oppressive to people with disabilities), and set them within a wider biblical and theological—even pneumatological—horizon. The challenge will be to redeem these texts and the people to whom they have so often been tragically applied, rather than to continue ignoring them in the hope that things will just take care of themselves; the process will involve reading these texts amidst other texts from disability perspectives. The result, I hope, is the renewal of theology in late modernity.

PART II

Down Syndrome and Disability in the Modern World

A number of promissory notes were issued in the first part of this book, especially with regard to the claim that Down Syndrome in particular and disabilities in general are distinctively modern experiences that cannot be easily equated with anything we find in the biblical and Christian theological traditions. In this part of the book we attempt to make good on these promises. Our argument in chapter 3 in particular is devoted to the phenomenon of Down Syndrome. I suggest that the biblical and theological emphasis on healing has shaped modern traditions of medicine in general and of mental health and well-being in particular such that our contemporary medical understandings of Down Syndrome and related forms of intellectual disabilities are fundamentally based on theological presuppositions. Hence, I suggest that the history of Christian perspectives on "disability" has colluded with modern medicine, even if unintentionally, in producing what might be called a "medicalized" notion of intellectual and physical disability. In this framework, Down Syndrome and other disabilities are medical problems to be addressed with medical prescriptions and technologies.

Understood in this way, however, the problem of Down Syndrome is individualized, and the wider social aspects of intellectual and physical disability related to Down Syndrome are inadequately acknowledged. Chapter 4 will therefore interrogate this medical definition of Down Syndrome and intellectual disability as unnecessarily limited at best and deceptively misleading at worst. If

modernity medicalized disability, then postmodernity has socialized and politicized it. But if in our late modern context both
modern and postmodern discourses are being contested, the way
forward, I propose, is to adopt the strengths of both the medical
and social models of disability while avoiding their weaknesses.

Chapter 5 will provide us with further critical perspective in
order to accomplish this task, since it leverages the medical and
social models of disability by locating them in world context.
Women's experiences, non-Western worldviews, and world religious perspectives on disability are introduced into the discussion.
If theological discourse in a late modern world is said to be pluralistic, then the Anglo-American models of disability, whether
medical or social, will need to be contested in global context. Further, Christian theology negotiated in dialogue with the world's
religions means that we cannot summarily dismiss traditional or
conventional interpretations of disability as being merely "premodern" without confronting the postcolonial critique.

In a sense, then, the end of part 2 will bring us back to the question we asked in the last few pages: where do we go from here if
we cannot ignore traditional religious and theological perspectives
but at the same time need new attitudes and practices to engage
the phenomenon of disability in the twenty-first century? The difference is that we will have expanded our frame of reference to
include the late modern world cultural and religious context and
will have gained, so I am betting, critical perspective and helpful
resources for the theological task. Our goal is to set a proper stage
so that the constructive work of part 3 will be more socially alert,
globally situated, and temporally relevant for our late modern, scientific, and multireligious world.

III

Medicalizing Down Syndrome
Disability in the World of Modern Science

I've got four handicaps. I've got Down's syndrome, special needs, learning disability and a mental handicap.

—Anonymous, in Marks 1999: 150

We're all human beings. Some of us are a little slower than others. You remember that and you'll get along fine, you'll see. . . . I haven't got too many years left, so I have to work hard and play hard to make up for everything I missed when I was a boy! They say institutions are better now. . . . But . . . it's still not the same as being free.

—Ted McQuaid, in Schwier 1990: 159

I am retarded. . . . My wife and I have been married for four years. When we got married nobody wanted us to and people were mad. But we had each other so it didn't matter. Now her family likes me and mine likes her. I go around and talk to social workers about being married. . . . I want to make it so that people who are born like me have a better life. I want them to have it easier than I did. Me and my wife want to make a difference.

—Phil Allen, in Hingsburger 1990: 6–7

Scott and me do okay. We can't buy pork chops or bacon because we got no deep freezer. We eat a lot of macaroni and cheese. I make a casserole. I get $410 a month and the rent is $325 and it's going up, so it's pretty tough.

—Neil Mercer, in Schwier 1990: 127

My parents were in the process of moving from Malaysia to the United States (to pastor a church among Chinese-speaking immigrants) when Mark was born. Because he could not be vaccinated for smallpox, our move was delayed until October 1976. Shortly after arriving in Stockton (California), social workers from the Valley Mountain Regional Center Inc. (serving the San Joaquin Valley area) came to conduct a home visit for Mark. They recommended that Mark enroll in the Walton Developmental Center for the most severely handicapped children, and Mark proceeded to attend Walton for a few years. They also recommended doctors for Mark and referred our family to the State of California's Crippled Children's Services (CCS) for medical coverage.

Over the course of the first few months in the United States, Mark was diagnosed with Down Syndrome, a double murmur in his heart, flat-footedness (for which operations, like those related to his extra thumb, were recommended, scheduled, postponed, and have never taken place, leading Mom to recollect the scripture text: "He keeps all their bones; not one of them will be broken"; Ps 34:20), vision impairment (including prescription eyewear), and deafness (Mark's repeated ear infections at one point brought a prescription for a hearing aid, which he has also resisted wearing). A heart cauterization was recommended soon after the diagnosis of the murmurs, and medication was prescribed. Year after year, the cauterization was recommended but postponed as the risks seemed to Mom to outweigh the benefits (given Mark's precarious condition). When Mark was six, the doctors decided that they could not delay the cauterization any longer, and Mark had successful open-heart surgery—in two and a half rather than the expected six hours—in the fall of 1981. He was blessed with a swift recovery, released by the doctors from his heart medications, and discharged after nine days.

Throughout this period of time, my parents came to a slow awareness of what Down Syndrome meant for Mark. However, their main concerns were not his mental handicap, but his overall health and physical condition, including his heart, sight, hearing, and feet. In retrospect, all Mom could see, instead of his mental handicap, were miracles—e.g., the successful heart surgery, Mark getting along just fine without his eyeglasses, his ability to hear (albeit selectively, when it comes to what is being said or asked of him, of course!), and his mobility to the point of participating in relay races in the Special Olympics. From a physical point of view, Mark has lived a relatively healthy life since his open-heart surgery more than twenty-five years ago. When I asked Mark recently how he felt, he said, "healthy," but (at that moment) with a "sore throat."

What does it mean to say that Down Syndrome is a distinctively modern phenomenon? While the following pages will attempt to answer this question at some length, it is important here to clarify that I am not saying intellectual disability itself is merely a modern construct. We have already seen that the ancients were well aware of people with diminished intellectual capacities and even talked about them using a wide-ranging vocabulary.[1] My claim, however, is that social and theoretical perspectives have not remained static, and there have been substantial shifts in how intellectual disability has been conceived, examined, discussed, and engaged (see Goodey 2005). The onset of modernity transformed these matters in significant ways, and that transformation is what we will be presenting here.

The anonymous quotation beginning this chapter—where a perceptive individual identifies his or her Down Syndrome as consisting of having "special needs, learning disability and a mental handicap"[2] —introduces the basic categories that structure the following discussion. We begin with an overview of the history of the family of labels associated with Down Syndrome as told from the perspective of the modern medical institution, then focus on three of the specific categories of analysis and practice that have dominated the twentieth-century medical discussion (the intelligence quotient, the human genome, and prenatal testing), and conclude by sketching the emergence of the professional industry that now services the needs of people with Down Syndrome, emphasizing social inclusion but also using the latest advances in science and technology.

Our goal is to provide a broad introduction to Down Syndrome as a product of modern science, medicine, and technology. While this exercise will aid us in our task of formulating a Christian theology of Down Syndrome, it will also highlight two other considerations: how modern medicine has preserved and even extended the lives of people with Down Syndrome on the one hand, but also, paradoxically, how modern technology has more recently come to threaten even the very existence of such people on the other. This latter realization, along with other related concerns, reveals the limitations of a solely medicalized approach to Down Syndrome and invites the postmodern critique (chap. 4).

Down Syndrome and the Medical Institution: A Brief History

The basic histories of Down Syndrome are usually told as part of the history of intellectual disability in general.[3] Many of these histories are told from the perspective of the medical establishment. While we will retell this story from other points of view in the next chapter, here we will overview the history of intellectual disability and its relationship to the medical institution. I will divide this narrative into three periods: the period of institutional emergence and development (the nineteenth century), the period of what I will call sociomedical control (the first half of the twentieth century), and the period of deinstitutionalization and independent living (since the 1960s).

The Emergence of the Institution for the Mentally Defective

By the early nineteenth century, hospices like that at Ghent, which had spread all over Europe and America, had been transformed and in many places replaced by asylums (at worst) and almshouses (at best) that either contained or sought to meet (sometimes attempting both) the needs of a wide range of impoverished people, including those with intellectual and physical disabilities. Yet advances had nevertheless been made through the work of educators or physicians like Vincent de Paul (1581–1660), Philipe Pinel (1745–1826), Jean Etienne Dominique Esquirol (1782–1840), and Jean-Marc-Gaspard Itard (1774–1838).[4] By the mid-nineteenth century, a student of Itard, Edouard Seguin (1812–1880), had become convinced that even the most defective or mentally deficient child could understand and learn. His work teaching retarded children over the years led him to develop a fourfold classification: idiocy, imbecility, feeblemindedness, and simpleness. Seguin has since come to be known as the father of special education, as his work and ideas have influenced social reformers like Samuel

Gridley Howe (1801–1876), physicians like John Langdon Down (1826–1896), and educators like Maria Montessori (1870–1952).

J. L. Down, after whom the syndrome is named, was superintendent of the Earlswood Asylum for the mentally defective in Surrey, England, from 1858 to 1868. A rising young physician at the time of his appointment, Down continued his research at Earlswood as he observed and cared for hundreds of children during his tenure (Wright 1996). His convictions that insanity should be distinguished from learning disability and that physical and mental defectiveness did not equate with moral darkness motivated his work. In 1866 he published a paper, later included in his *Mental Afflictions of Children and Youth* (1887), describing what is today known as the Down Syndrome phenotype: flat occiput (head), slanting eyes, malformed ears (small or absent lobule), flat nasal bridge, broad and short neck, underdeveloped male genitalia, hyperextensible joints (in extremities), gap between the first and second toes, smaller skull or head (taking up to nine years to reach the size that a normal baby develops in one year), and accompanying motor, cognitive, linguistic, and social behavioral patterns. Idiocy (a term that Down disliked) was reclassified into three etiological categories— congenital (idiots), accidental (idiots and feebleminded), and developmental (feebleminded)—and explicated with a new evolutionary hypothesis: that such children were "Mongoloids," "a product of the spontaneous reversion by Caucasian children to an earlier, 'less developed' race" (Borsay 2005: 101).[5] By the late 1870s Down had by and large discarded this hypothesis because he opposed slavery and the antiabolitionist arguments (see Ward 1998: chap. 14). However, as anthropological theories of racial degeneration were widely circulating in Europe, Great Britain, and North America in the mid-nineteenth century (Wright 2001: 156), "Mongolism" stuck and served to fuel the ethnic/racial hypothesis for idiocy long into the twentieth century. This interpretation was finally and decisively discredited only by statistical research in the 1930s, but it was not until 1961, when the American Association on Mental Retardation proposed to shift the terminology from Mongolism to Down Syndrome, that Down's contributions were definitively acknowledged.

By the end of the nineteenth century, however, the euphoria over the pioneering research of individuals like Seguin and Down had abated. The initial optimism that all children with intellectual disabilities could be educated and even cured had disappeared as a growing number of "unteachable idiots" populated the asylums. But as institutions like Earlswood expanded their services to accommodate and deploy the feebleminded within their walls, the demand for physicians like Down and their staff also increased. The result was that the "major development in the area of mental retardation in the last half of the nineteenth century was not the triumph of custodialism but its medicalization. . . . This, in turn, was intimately associated with the rise of a new professional class of institutional experts, and its quest for respectability as a medical specialty" (Ferguson 1994: 160).

But the medicalization of mental deficiency was also reinforced by parallel social developments. Socially, the turn of the century was marked by delinquency, deviancy, prostitution, alcoholism, and pauperism, and blame for these ills was increasingly shifted onto the feebleminded.[6] Books like *"The Jukes": A Study in Crime, Pauperism, Disease, and Heredity* (1875) and *The Kallikak Family: A Study in the Heredity of Feeble-mindedness* (1912) confirmed the suspicions of the masses that innocent women had to be protected from feebleminded men, and feebleminded women needed to be protected from illicit sexual activity, and unwanted and unneeded pregnancies; that the feebleminded had more offspring on the average than the non-feebleminded; and that left unchecked, feeblemindedness would destroy civilized society. As a result, the asylum was slowly transformed from being a symbol of the "Age of Improvement" motivated by visions of therapeutic and educational progress to being a symbol of national degeneration hounded by the "menace of the feebleminded" (Tyor and Bell 1984: 71; Wright 2001: 194–200).

The emerging challenge of moral imbecility would prove to be as intractable as mental imbecility. If moral imbeciles could not be deterred by punishment (since they lacked the kind of abstract thinking that could make connections, follow out consequences of their actions, or learn from past mistakes), then asylums needed to develop alternative means of social control. The medicalization of the feebleminded would soon turn in increasingly ominous directions with the development of "scientifically legitimated programs" of intelligence testing, sterilization, and eugenics designed to deal with the problems of imbecility.

Sociomedical Control and the Feebleminded

The idea of an intelligence test originated with Alfred Binet (1857–1911), a researcher in physiological psychology at the Sorbonne. During the first few years of the twentieth century, Binet and his student Theodore Simon (1873–1961) devised tests to identify and classify the feebleminded for special class placement, and they formally introduced these measurement devices in 1905. From an educational perspective, Binet and Simon posited three levels of feeblemindedness: *idiots*, who could not communicate either verbally or in writing; *imbeciles*, who could speak, but not read or write; and *morons*, who were delayed in school studies by a few years, never attaining to much higher than a twelve-year-old level of intelligence. Meanwhile, a German psychologist, Louis William Stern (1871–1938), revised the Binet-Simon test and introduced a "constant" intelligence quotient (IQ) that correlated the mental and chronological ages of the test-takers. Once such a practically given test was made available, it was widely accepted, given the confidence in science during this period of time, to compare, correlate, and measure changes of intelligence. Still, Stern "unwittingly encouraged the simplification of the extraordinarily complex concept of intelligence . . . [since such tests] assumed that the intelligence quotient was analogous to, if not synonymous with, native intelligence" (Blatt 1987: 52).

On the American front, Henry H. Goddard (1866–1957), director of the research department of Vineland Training School for Boys and Girls in New Jersey and author of *The Kallikak Family* mentioned earlier, was already convinced that human abilities could be anthropometrically measured when he learned about the Binet-Simon test while traveling in Europe in 1908. Goddard worked with the Binet-Simon test to develop a similar tripartite division of Vineland inmates, which became standard in the field of mental retardation: *idiots* were those with a mental age of under two years; *imbeciles* ranged from two to seven years; *proximates* (later *morons*) were ages eight to twelve. This classification was given further specification through an adaptation of the Stern IQ by Lewis Madison Terman (1877–1956) when Terman published a revision of Binet's intelligence test in 1916:

Above 140, near genius or genius
120–140, very superior intelligence
110–120, superior intelligence
90–110, normal or average intelligence
80–90, dullness, rarely classifiable as feeblemindedness
50–70, morons
20 or 25–50, imbeciles
Below 20 or 25, idiots

(cited in Scheerenberger 1983: 144).[7]

Terman's IQ test, also known since as the Stanford-Binet Test (Terman was head of the Stanford University Department of Psychology from 1910-1930), has been revised periodically over the years, but basically remains in effect even today.

But just when psychologists and psychiatrists in the growing field of mental hygiene were exerting their influence in the institutions for the feebleminded, physicians reasserted themselves with a strategy developed from heredity studies: sterilization. Set within the wider context of the eugenics movement at the beginning of the twentieth century, sterilization (implemented in tandem with restrictive marriage laws in some states) was designed to provide added assurance that the institutionalized feebleminded would not reproduce their kind.[8] Although castrations and ovary removals were conducted (illegally) as far back as the 1890s, it was not until after one of the early presidents of the American Association on Mental Deficiency, Martin Barr (1863–1938), publicly argued that the implementation of sterilization in the institutions for the feebleminded would result in "improvement mental, moral, and physical" (1904: 197) that the first laws were passed. "By constructing sterilization as a tool for institutional survival and control, superintendents made it a day-to-day part of the life and meaning of the institution. As such, the control became increasingly routine, ordinary, and hence, self-regulatory. After all, the most effective social controls are often those that give the appearance of being day-to-day care" (Trent 1994: 224).

The legal case *Buck v. Bell* concerned Carrie Buck (1906–1983), a resident at the Virginia State Colony for Epileptics and Feebleminded. The argument for Buck's sterilization was that her mother was a feebleminded with a mental age of eight and a record of immorality and prostitution, that she was incorrigible, and that she had already had an illegitimate daughter by the age of eighteen.[9] Buck's guardians challenged the application of Virginia's sterilization law and appealed the ruling all the way to the U.S. Supreme Court. In his opinion upholding the decision to sterilize in 1927, Justice Oliver Wendell Holmes wrote these famous words: "It is better for all the world, if instead of waiting to execute degenerate offspring for crime, or to let them starve for their imbecility, society can prevent those who are manifestly unfit from continuing their kind. The principle that sustains compulsory vaccination is broad enough to cover cutting the Fallopian tubes. . . . Three generations of imbeciles are enough" (in Trent and Noll 2004: 12).[10] Within a decade after *Buck v. Bell*, which coincided with the onset of the Great Depression and increased fears about feebleminded individuals on parole, thirty states passed sterilization laws similar to Virginia's, and many of these statutes remained in effect well into the 1960s. During the four decades of the 1930s–1960s, four thousand persons were sterilized at State Colony, now Central Virginia Training Center (until 1972), eight thousand in the entire state of Virginia, and more than fifty thousand overall (Smith and Nelson 1989: 181).

But if positive eugenics looked to populate the world with the "fit" and negative eugenics sought to limit the propagation of the "less fit," then the eugenic logic pushed to its most radical conclusions resulted in a movement focused on eliminating the "unfit." By the early decades of the twentieth century, the ancient practices of infanticide were being rehabilitated by appeals to social Darwinist theories (see Schwartz 1976) and applied to deformed infants through the "science" of eugenics. Harry J. Haiselden (1870–1919), head surgeon of Chicago's German-American Hospital, was one of the first to publicize the "letting die" of severely deformed newborns beginning in 1915. While opposition to such practices came from within the ranks of the medical profession itself (see Pernick 1996: 105–9), it was during Haiselden's generation that a scientific movement supposedly devoted to fighting hereditary diseases converged with other race, class, ethnic, and gender hatreds and devolved into a policy to justify genocide.

This genocidal impulse was most concretely enacted in Nazi Germany. A new academic discipline of "racial hygiene" based on the ideology of social Darwinism had already been in the works since the mid-1890s, with its theoretical justification clearly laid out in the 1920 volume *Die Freigabe zur Vernichtung lebensunwerten Lebens, ihr Mass und ihre Form* by psychiatrist Alfred Hoche and jurist Karl Binding. The authors advocated "compassionate" and "healing killing" of terminally ill people on the basis that they were entitled to "death with dignity" from "the legally acknowledged right to the complete relief of an unbearable life," and averred that because of the heavy burden on families and the state, maintaining idiots whose lives were "completely useless" was not cost-effective (Hoche and Binding 1975).[11] By the time the first eugenic laws were enacted in the mid-1930s, German racial hygienists and advocates of eugenics were appealing further to American applications of eugenic theory to public policies, including citing *Buck v. Bell* as "precedent for Nazi race hygiene and sterilization programs" (Smith and Nelson 1989: 183; cf. Pernick 1996: 163–64). The Law for the Prevention of Genetically Diseased Offspring and the Law against Dangerous Habitual Criminals passed in July 1933 targeted people with congenital mental defect, schizophrenia, manic-depressive psychosis, hereditary epilepsy, chorea, blindness, deafness, deformity, and alcoholism (Müller-Hill 1988: 28). While the Nazi regime proceeded to sterilize more than two million "defective" persons (Smith 1985: 156), this was not the worst thing that happened. Extermination campaigns began secretly in 1939 among the mentally and physically disabled as the war brought on extreme measures, and more than 275,000 were killed during the next few years (Gallagher 2001: 97; cf. Mostert 2002). Such "sanitation" procedures were advocated for the "public health" (Hubbard 1997: 195).

While clearly the Nazi example is an extreme, nevertheless it reveals "abuses of power in the name of science and social necessity" (Smith 2003a: 58). This is seen today not only in contemporary practices surrounding prenatal testing but also in the debates surrounding euthanasia.[12] While we will return to these issues in the next two sections, suffice it to note here that people with intellectual disabilities were at the mercy of "experts" (physicians, psychologists, scientists, etc.) so long as they were institutionally confined. Slowly but surely after the war years, questions began to arise about whether or not the medical institution was the best place for people with intellectual disabilities.

Deinstitutionalizing Down Syndrome

Institutional life for people with intellectual disabilities has not always been horrendous. To be sure, new initiatives, programs, and facilities often begin afresh and are committed to doing things better than ever before. Inevitably, however, funds are cut, quality control becomes sloppy, and conditions deteriorate. All of this had definitely intensified during the 1950s when, due in part to the "coming out" narratives of individuals like Pearl Buck and Dale Evans Rogers (see pp. 6–7), "inmate" populations experienced their fastest rates of increase ever (Trent 1994: 241–42), and the supply could not keep up with the demand. Making matters worse, however, was that institutional staff worked in maintenance mode, rather than in educational or rehabilitational mode since there was little hope by this time that mentally retarded people were capable of making a contribution to society (Shorter 2000: chap. 1). Hence there was limited consensus regarding treatment goals and means. Often staff was overworked, underpaid, and overwhelmed numerically; 50 percent of adult patients did nothing all day and were referred to and treated as "children" by staff; and hospitals (and patients) were isolated both geographically and socially (Morris 1969).

The result was that patients internalized a self-identity of dependency on staff and the institutional structure. Worse than isolation and routinization was the loss of privacy, punitive framework, and in some cases, mortification, stripping, and hazing—these were the day-to-day means through which control was enacted over the population of retarded individuals (see Vail 1966: pt. 1). Institutional life resounded with barrenness, dreariness, and a palpable sense of abandonment and hopelessness. The mentally retarded housed (incarcerated!) within institutions represented the "dejectedness" of humanity and the "brokenness" of creation (Blatt and Kaplan 1974). Out of this sense of desolation arose an outcry against these dehumanizing structures and policies: "We must evacuate the institutions for the mentally retarded. There is no time any more for new task forces and new evaluation teams. The time is long past for such nonsense" (Blatt, Ozolins, and McNally 1979: 143).

The wheels of change had begun to turn, even if slowly, as illustrated by the case of Willowbrook School on Staten Island (see Rothman and Rothman 1984). Beginning in 1965, exposés raised public awareness of the atrocious conditions and led, in 1972, to a class action lawsuit by the New York State Association for Retarded Children. The state agreed to close Willowbrook, but the process of closure was arduously sluggish. In May 1975 a consent decree was entered requiring a phaseout of the Willowbrook population from 5,400 to 250 by 1981 and their placement in a "least restrictive" alternative environment. Even then, only about 50 percent were transitioned into new communities by 1982. At the same time, this series of events resulted in the reformation of the entire system of caring for the mentally retarded. Deinstitutionalization was now in full force, motivated by the conviction that "*all* people are equally valuable and deserve to be part of a normal world" (Blatt 1987: xv, italics in original).

The transitional process was difficult for numerous reasons, not the least of which was the self-internalized dependency of individuals who had been institutionalized for years if not most of their lives. The deinstitutionalized, like Ted McQuaid quoted at the beginning of this chapter, had to be resocialized about how to live outside of the institutional framework. But too many failed to make any kind of smooth transition. There are also too many structured relationships, behavioral patterns, social constraints, and environmental barriers that complicated and compromised independent living for intellectually disabled persons (Barnes 1990). Even for those who were placed in residential homes, the criterion of "least restrictive setting" was difficult to determine, and there was always the cost factor for the various supports that were needed (Halpern 1980). While living outside was better than living inside, for most the realities did not match up to the hopes of the intellectually disabled or to the lives that most non-intellectually disabled folk live. Social isolation remained for most people with intellectual disabilities even in their new residential communities (Smith 1995). The difference was that they had traded in the control of lockdowns and "incarcerations" for the control of individualized educational programs (IEPs) and "rituals of assessment and strategic placement" (Johnson and Traustadóttir 2005b: 21).[13]

Now deinstitutionalization had made it possible for people with intellectual disabilities to establish a sense of personal self-identity and to be empowered as individuals with responsibility (Nosek 1982; Gadacz 1994). At the same time, given the challenges faced by people with intellectual disabilities, it was essential that this new paradigm emphasized social services (Mansell and Ericsson 1996), professional support networks, and most importantly, the cultivation of genuine friendships (O'Brien and O'Brien 1996; Morris 1993).[14] Herein lay a tension between a focus on individualized and personal supports on the one side and an emphasis on social participation and community development on the other. We will see in the next two sections how these divergent emphases have played out during the last generation.

From the IQ to the Human Genome:
The "Problem" of Down Syndrome and Its "Solution"

In the preceding we have sketched but some of the highlights of the history of intellectual disability in general and of Down Syndrome in particular, focusing on the medicalization and institutionalization that has dominated the story up until recently. In the following, we want to focus on the shifting scientific discourses and practices that have been shaped by the processes of deinstitutionalization. Whereas previously the mentally retarded were subjected to whatever procedures institutional superintendents wished to experiment, the reach of medical and scientific technology is less encompassing, invasive, and insidious now that most people with intellectual disabilities are not residentially confined. However, medical science remains pervasive in the individual lives of such persons. While the next section will seek to uncover the subtle control that science retains in the daily lives of people with Down Syndrome and other intellectual disabilities (as it does in all of our lives), here we will focus on the more recent research on mental retardation in professional organizations and in the biomedical sciences.

Defining Mental Retardation

Unsurprisingly, the question of how to assess mental ability has been a perennial point of debate. The emergence of the IQ test provided one avenue of quantifying such assessments in what was thought to be a scientifically rigorous way. Yet, the IQ test itself has always had its detractors. As early as 1919, Lewis Terman himself came to see that IQ was not static but dynamic, even changing by as much as 20 points or more in some individuals (Scheerenberger 1983: 180).[15] Further questions were raised when over 50 percent of all immigrants tested as feebleminded,[16] when successful Iowa farmers tested as morons, and when 47.3 percent of white and 89 percent of black World War I army draftees also fell into that category (Tyor and Bell 1984: 121; cf. Noll 1995: 31)! The army soldiers were not summarily dismissed, however, and many of these became efficient and productive workers (Tyor and Bell 1984: 214–15).[17] Obviously cultural elements had to be considered and the difference between "test smarts" and "street smarts" had to be factored in.

Deinstitutionalization provided a broader context (communities rather than residential hospitals) within which to reassess the meaning of mental retardation. Changes in the definitions of disability and mental retardation during the last generation have reflected these developments. The most important clarifications to have emerged have been promulgated by the World Health Organization (WHO) and the American Association on Mental Retardation (AAMR).

Two publications of the WHO are especially pertinent for our purposes. In 1980, WHO's *International Classification of Impairments, Disabilities, and Handicaps* set forth the following definitions: an impairment "is any loss or abnormality of psychological, physiological, or anatomical structure or function" (1993: 27); a disability is "any restriction or lack (resulting from an impairment) of ability to perform an activity in a manner or within the range considered normal for a human being" (28); and, finally, a handicap is "a disadvantage for a given individual, resulting from an impairment or a disability, that limits or prevents the fulfillment of a role that is normal (depending on age, sex, and social and cultural factors) for that individual" (29). Thus, *impairments* are understood primarily in organic or biomedical terms, *disabilities* are functional or practical limitations according to what is considered normal, and *handicaps* involve an axiological dimension (a "disadvantage") that is contextually determined vis-à-vis social expectations. We will see in the next chapter how these WHO definitions were significantly influenced by the new social model of disability.

Five years later, WHO published *Mental Retardation: Meeting the Challenge* (1985). Mental retardation, WHO stipulated, involves four levels—mild, moderate, severe, and profound—and includes two essential components: "(a) intellectual functioning that is significantly below average, and (b) marked impairment in the ability of the individual to adapt to the daily demands of the social environment. There is now widespread agreement that *both* intellectual functioning and adaptive behavior must be impaired before a person can be considered to be mentally retarded. Neither low intelligence nor impaired adaptive behaviour alone is sufficient" (WHO and JCIAMR 1985: 8). In this case, IQ tests should be "appropriate to the area where they are performed (the local culture), administered by persons specifically trained in their use, and regularly repeated, since experience has shown that increased opportunities and higher levels of demand and stimulation can change the IQ score" (9). Hence, "IQ is not necessarily constant during an individual's life-time, social adaptation may also change; a poorly adapted adolescent may become a normal citizen a decade later" (10).

Of the four levels of retardation identified by WHO, the vast majority—from 75 up to 90 percent—fall into the first category of mildly retarded (IQs from 50/55 to 70). The moderately retarded (IQs from 35/40 to 50/55) number between 5 and 15 percent, while the severely retarded (IQs from 20/25 to 35/40) about 3.5 to 5 percent, and the profoundly retarded (IQs below 20/25) approximately 1.5 to 5 percent (see WHO and JCIAMR 1985: 9). Although the last three categories include only a minority of persons classified as "retarded," it is precisely at these levels that the most pronounced differences are to be found, differences that will often challenge any generalizations made about retardation as a whole. These differences should be kept in mind for the remainder of this book, although I will try to be as specific as possible if I am referring to the moderately and especially severely and profoundly disabled.

The WHO's definitions shaped the work of the AAMR (formerly the American Association on Mental Deficiency).[18] The ninth edition of the AAMR's *Mental Retardation: Definition, Classification, and Systems of Supports* proffered: "*Mental retardation* refers to substantial limitations in present functioning. It is characterized by significantly subaverage intellectual functioning, existing concurrently with related limitations in two or more of the following applicable adaptive skill areas: communication, self-care, home living, social skills, community use, self-direction, health and safety, functional academics, leisure, and work. Mental retardation manifests before age 18" (AAMR 1992: 5). Building on the WHO understanding of disability and mental retardation, this definition was set in a framework that assumed a relational rather than a deficit model of individual disability prominent in the previous editions. Consequently, valid assessment of retardation took into account cultural/linguistic and communication/behavioral factors. Further, limitations in adaptive skills had to be measured within the social context of the individual's community and against peers, taking into account individualized needs for supports. Finally, adaptive limitations could coexist with strengths in other areas, while sustained and appropriate supports would improve life functioning capacities.

Whereas the IQ test was thought to measure individual intellectual capacity, it slowly became apparent that intelligence or cognitive retardation was a relational and transactional phenomenon negotiated by persons interacting in changing environments (Rapley, Kiernan, and Antaki 1998; McConkey 1997: 77). Hence, the AAMR definition included intellectual functioning and adaptive skills, psychological and emotional considerations, health and physical aspects, etiological elements, and environmental dynamics. In this framework, the IQ test becomes only one of a number of different measurements of mental retardation, and even then, has to be used critically with recognition of its limitations. So while the science of cognitive intelligence testing has come a long way since Binet, it remains a central form of assessment for mental retardation and is the primary tool for applying the labels of mild, moderate, severe, or profound retardation. But these labels tell us much more about "the retarded" than that they have cognitive limitations.

Down Syndrome: Recent Biomedical Research

The more severely or profoundly disabled the individual, the more likely he or she is to have additional physical, affective, emotional, and behavioral complications. Whereas the "cure" for mental

retardation and its effects had earlier been thought to be education or eugenic control, more recent scientific research has been
motivated by the possibility of finding other biomedical solutions.
In what follows, we shall briefly examine the genetic, etiological,
and biological research on Down Syndrome.[19]

Whereas J. L. Down had described the phenotype of the syndrome given his name, Dutch geneticist Petrus Johannes Waardenburg (1886–1979) suggested (in 1932) that what Down portrayed
might be the consequence of a chromosomal aberration. In 1959,
French pediatric researcher Jérôme Jean Louis Marie Lejeune
(1926–1994) and his colleagues confirmed that Down Syndrome
derived from a mutation of the twenty-first chromosome. Instead
of the twenty-three chromosomes from the male sperm and female
egg paired together, the twenty-first chromosome multiplies abnormally either prior to or at conception, resulting in three instead of
a pair (hence trisomy). So when most human beings have forty-six
chromosomes in each cell, the initial trisomy produces forty-seven
chromosomes instead. After Lejeune, the good news is that "Down
Syndrome is no longer associated with atavistic regression, parental sin, alcoholism, congenital syphilis, maternal tuberculosis, or
even bad thinking during pregnancy" (Rondal 2003: v).

Still, are trisomic cell divisions purely random mutations or are
they caused by other factors? There have been suggested connections between trisomy 21 and occupational/environmental expo-
sures (e.g., pesticides, heavy metals, toxic waste, electromagnetic
fields), medical technologies (e.g., X-rays, anesthetics), reproductive "drugs" (like oral contraceptives, spermicides, fertility drugs),
habituating agents (e.g., tobacco, alcohol, caffeine), and intrinsic
predispositions (like age of father, parental consanguinity, thyroid
autoimmunity). Yet, "it is important to stress that none of these
factors has ever been proved to be associated with trisomy. Indeed,
despite exhaustive study there remains only one factor that is incon-
trovertibly linked to trisomy, namely increasing age of the woman"
(Hassold 1998: 73; cf. Hassold and Sherman 2002: 296–98).

While most trisomic zygotes do spontaneously abort,[20] about
10 to 20 percent of them survive resulting in from 1 in 700 to 1 in
1,000 live births (Hook 1982: 35; Bellenir 1996: 19). It was estimated at the turn of the twenty-first century that there were more
than 350,000 people with Down Syndrome in the United States,

and about 5 million worldwide (Massimini 2000: 53; Perera 1999: 230). Modern medicine has enabled older women to bear children successfully, and fragile fetuses and infants to survive conditions that they previously could not.[21] In at least both of these further senses, it can be said that Down Syndrome is a distinctive product of modernity.

When trisomy 21 is carried to full term, it generates the Down Syndrome phenotype and intellectual disability.[22] In fact, Down Syndrome is by far the most common genetic disorder associated with intellectual disability,[23] constituting up to 30 percent of all cases of severe or profound retardation (Moser 1995: 4–6). In addition, other congenital malformations appear in part because of the production of either too much or too little protein to regulate all the genes and ensure stable cell divisions (Hawley and Mori 1999: chap. 9; Shapiro 2003). So although trisomy 21 is often known as the "Prince Charming syndrome" (Rondal et al. 2004: 26), in some cases of moderate retardation and in most cases of severe and profound retardation it brings with it much higher incidences of potentially fatal conditions like cardiovascular diseases, pulmonary vascular abnormalities, hematologic (blood-related) and gastrointestinal disorders, leukemia, pneumonia, diabetes (and all of its side-effects), thyroid disease, epileptic seizures, osteoporosis (bone fragility), and insomnia (which deprives the victim of the sleep essential for daily functioning).[24] In fact, these complications often are cumulative such that the more retarded "may have multiple disabilities, such as epilepsy, cerebral palsy, speech or physical impairment" (Gething 1997: 208; cf. Richardson and Koller 1996: chap. 11), as well as be at greater risk of autism (Capone 2002; Sigman and Ruskin 1999). Last but certainly not least, the severely and profoundly retarded may also exhibit behavioral disorders that provide further challenges for caregivers.[25]

Given the complexity of diseases and disabilities generated by trisomy 21, more recent biomedical research has been motivated to find genetic solutions to Down Syndrome. Is medical knowledge and technology sufficiently advanced so that we can now repair or replace the affected genetic material? Strategies have been suggested in two directions: somatic cell therapy that is focused on correcting or replacing defective genes in somatic tissue, and germline modification that is designed to insert new genetic sequences into the human genome that are then passed on to future generations (Moser 2000). We are at the point where individual somatic cell therapy is advanced enough—for example, in cancer, metabolic disease, infectious diseases such as AIDS, and neurological disorders—that we need to begin in earnest the ethical discussion about germline modification for subsequent generations (de la Cruz and Friedmann 1995). But the problem when dealing with Down Syndrome or mental retardation is that neither are single gene disorders, and even when they might be—a subset of perhaps one-fourth of the more severe forms of mental retardation—in those cases the clinical symptoms are detectable too late (during the postnatal period) for any substantive genetic adjustments to be made (Moser 1995: 5). Thus, while research continues at a frenzied pace on the genetic makeup of Down Syndrome and forms of intellectual disability, at best we may be able to ameliorate some of the accompanying conditions, but not the syndrome itself. As pediatric specialist Charles Epstein (1995: 245) summarizes, "Reduction in the rate of non-disjunction leading to trisomy 21 is not likely to occur. At present, there does not exist a conceptual understanding of meiotic errors that would permit us to visualize an approach to reducing this frequency. This is unfortunate, since this is where the ultimate solution to Down Syndrome resides."

Prenatal Testing for Down Syndrome

But if we cannot prevent the conception of fetuses with trisomy 21, can we not prevent their births? Whereas previous generations focused on educating the feebleminded or curing imbecility and current energies are being directed toward exploring intellectual disability in light of the Human Genome Project, might the "solution" to Down Syndrome be as simple as application of our sophisticated prenatal testing instruments?

Of course, our discriminative procedures are (allegedly) much more enlightened than the infanticide practiced by our forebears: we have genetic counseling sessions and modern technology for "safe abortions" that the ancients lacked (Gardner and Sutherland 1996). Yet such counseling, while supposedly nondirective, is generally biased and prejudiced against deformed or handicapped babies.[26] Further, while up to 80 percent of HMOs cover prenatal testing for Down Syndrome, that genetic counseling "is not generally covered except through hidden charges in the physician's fee" (Powell 2000: 49) suggests that emphasis is placed more on selective abortion than on serious exploration of the potentialities ahead of such lives and the possibilities available to their parents. The most blatant stance to take is that advocated by radicals like Peter Singer who argue that since fetuses projected to be severely or profoundly handicapped will never attain to full human status anyway, their infanticide is ethically justified (Singer 1994: 210–17; Singer and Kuhse 1985; cf. Fletcher 1979: chap. 11). While most counselors working in the medical community do not adopt this extreme position, yet a subtle if not even at times overt ableism is communicated to parents expecting handicapped children, so that it is only "bad mothers" who choose to keep their "defective" children (Carlson 2001: 140). Unsurprisingly, when presented with this kind of "guidance," since 1989 70 to 90 percent of Down Syndrome fetuses have been aborted by prospective parents (Shuman and Volck 2006: 81, 154n7).[27]

The solution in a liberal society is not to prohibit genetic screening but to interrogate our biases, assumptions, attitudes, and practices (see Mason 2004: 79–83; Louhiala 2004: chap. 7). The "arguments" that people with Down Syndrome and other disabilities lead lives of needless suffering or are a burden to their families or to society as a whole reflect more our existential fears and ignorance than they do facts. In the first place, there is a strong counterargument that the "suffering" of people with disabilities stems less from their intellectual or physical impairments than from the social prejudices, environmental inaccessibility, and lack of supportive networks.[28] Second, from a parental point of view, while some have admitted they might have decided to selectively abort a fetus if given the choice through genetic testing, almost all affirm they have been transformed by the experience of parenting a mentally retarded child in such a way that they came to see their child as a gift. Hence, "these parents no longer identify with their 'old' self. The choice for prevention no longer is a possibility that they find relevant to contemplate for themselves" (Reinders 2000: 192; cf. Asch and Wasserman 2005). Third, the argument about social and economic cost assumes a zero-sum perspective when in reality there is plenty of money channeled to the military as well as tax breaks given to the wealthy. "If a majority of American citizens decided to revise their political priorities, there would be more than enough in national and state budgets to provide housing, health care, and education for everyone, with and without disabilities" (Wong 2002: 95). Fourth, there is always the potential of false diagnoses, but even if a fetus was accurately identified as having trisomy 21, the severity of disability will not be known until (sometimes long) after birth (Kennedy 1988: 156; Hubbard 1997: 197–98).[29] Fifth, what about the counterquestion that human beings are intrinsically rather than only instrumentally valuable? Yes, "it is right to regard cognitive disability in the abstract, in isolation, as negative in value, but it is [also] right to regard the concrete whole who is the child (the person) with the disability as of intrinsic, compelling worth" (P. Byrne 2000: 102). This argument will gather increasing force since more sophisticated technology will unearth previously hidden deficits in our bodies (Silvers 2005). Lastly (for the moment), isn't it presumptuous to think that we can eliminate intellectual and physical disability through abortions? This question is especially pertinent if technological interventions such as prenatal testing followed by abortions are not the answer to "problems" of "handicap" and "impairment" that are socially and environmentally caused (Reinders 2000: 81–83).

But what about newborns who are severely disabled? The case of "Baby Doe" sparked a national debate (see Hentoff 1987; Verhey 1987; Koop 1991: chap. 10). Born with spina bifida, cerebral palsy, congenital heart disease, Down Syndrome, and esophageal aresia in a Bloomington, Indiana, hospital in April 1982, Baby Doe was given (by one opinion) only a 50 percent chance of surviving the esophagus surgery. The state Supreme Court refused to override the parents' decision not to proceed given the circumstances and the child died of starvation after six days. The issues were, indeed, wide ranging: parental autonomy; state responsibility; legal aspects of withholding treatment; medical ethical issues such as the distinction, if any, between "passive euthanasia" and selective nontreatment; the rights of infants; socially weighted benefit or burden calculus; the value of human life; the capacity to measure the quality of life, and so on.[30]

Now while it is certainly possible to resist the abortion of fetuses with Down Syndrome and to affirm extraordinary means on behalf of such vulnerable infants from religious and theological points of view, there are also arguments on these issues from specifically disability perspectives.[31] Chief among them is that the social values underlying prenatal testing and selective abortion are expressed in discriminatory structures and practices against people with disabilities. Even those who defend a pro-choice perspective on abortion recognize that prenatal testing is at least implicitly oppressive of people with disabilities in that it communicates they are not wanted if their conditions were to have been diagnosed before birth (Morris 1991: chaps. 2–3). Further, even if we can identify a subgroup of cases projected to have a low quality of life,[32] the causes of such may not be particular traits like trisomy 21. Finally, the whole idea of prenatal testing begs the question of what kind of criteria inform the selection of fetuses kept versus aborted. In fact, it seems that proponents of selective abortion not only could opt for children with certain features but would also "see nothing wrong with sex selection" (Wong 2002: 97). Rather than selecting abortions driven by economic circumstances, commercial influences, sociopolitical pressures, Darwinian views regarding the "survival of the fittest," and a laissez-faire system of human reproduction, we should instead value the wide range of humanness marked by intellectual and physical differences.

This is not to say that we should not seek to prevent intellectual disability. On the contrary, we can and should strive to reduce alcohol consumption and cigarette smoking during pregnancy, introduce seat belts and helmets to protect against head injuries that cause retardation, forestall premature births (and low birth weights), provide early interventions for environmental stimulations to families in lower socioeconomic classes (e.g., Head Start), reduce lead in paints and in gasoline, and make widely available vaccines for measles (rubeola), smallpox, polio, and other diseases that can cause retardation (Alexander 1998). Similarly, the "solution" to Down Syndrome is not the technology of selective abortion but early interventions, educational programs, and environmental modification. Yet, even though we have implemented many programs in response to Down Syndrome along these lines, science and technology remain omnipresent not only in terms of the possibilities they introduce to better the lives of people with Down Syndrome but also in terms of the threats they continue to pose.

Down Syndrome: Professional Industry and Technology across the Life Span

I now want to pick back up where we left off earlier on the story of Down Syndrome after deinstitutionalization. I said then that in the era after deinstitutionalization, science and technology may be (with the exception of abortion of unborn fetuses) less violently imposed, but they are for that reason no less pervasive and intrusive. We also indicated that independent living after deinstitutionalization resulted in a tension between fostering individual competences on the one hand, and yet nurturing social support systems on the other. If biogenetic research, neuroscience, and prenatal technology represented attempts to provide scientific "solutions" to Down Syndrome considered as a medical "problem," the following discussion of Down Syndrome across the life span—particularly with regard to special education, adulthood, and aging and dying—will highlight the increasing realization that Down Syndrome is also a social and even spiritual phenomenon.[33]

Early Interventions and Special Education

In many ways, people with Down Syndrome are living more productive and fulfilling lives than ever before. Early diagnosis usually brings with it extensive multidisciplinary interventions including but not limited to special education, counseling, health and medical services, and nutrition recommendations and provisions (Ramsey and Ramey 1999). Yet there remain challenges and disagreements on specific strategies for improving the quality of their lives.

One area extensively debated in the 1980s was cosmetic surgery (see Bass 1978; May 1988; Feuerstein and Rand 1997: chap. 12; Goering 2003: 178–83). Given the specifics of the Down Syndrome phenotype, the argument was made that advanced medical operations could eliminate some of the more obvious features of "Mongolism"—for example, reshaping the wedge portion of tongue (partial glossectomy); adjusting the epicanthal folds (at the margins of the eyes) via raising the nose bridge through silicone inserts or cartilage taken from other parts of the body; straightening the oblique eyelid axes; augmenting the receding chin; raising the flat cheeks (again, through silicone or cartilage inserts); repairing the lower hanging lip; correcting the ear position and size;

widening the nostrils (to improve ease of breathing); removing fat from the upper neck and lower half of the face—and thereby also alleviate much of the social stigma encountered by these children during their formative years. Objections included the obvious one that such procedures inflicted unnecessary suffering and the message communicated to Down Syndrome children that they are unacceptable as they are. Yet, by and large this practice had fallen out of favor by the 1990s because "the postsurgery photographs were found to be less attractive . . . [and] there has been no evidence that children who have undergone plastic surgery have achieved greater skills, integration, or happiness than those without surgery" (Cooley 2002: 265).[34]

A response less drastic but no less debated has been the attempt to educate children with Down Syndrome. Deinstitutionalization meant that the days of segregated education were numbered. In 1975 Congress passed the Education for All Handicapped Children Act (PL 94-142)—renamed the Individuals with Disabilities Education Act (IDEA) in 1990—which involved three basic commitments: (a) that students with developmental delays (a sociobehavioral issue) and learning disabilities (an educational issue) should be integrated into regular schools and classroom environments whenever possible; (b) that separated special educational classrooms, when necessary, were to be structured according to the principle of the "least restrictive environment" so as to continue to allow interaction between disabled and nondisabled students; and (c) that all students needed to be assessed and educated according to an "individualized educational plan" (IEP) so that their strengths and weaknesses could be adequately taken into account (Fleischer and Zames 2001: chap. 11). For some special educators, PL 94-142/IDEA has evolved from integration into regular classrooms in the 1970s (with some separated special education classes as necessary) to full "inclusion" in the 1990s, whereby children with disabilities are educated with their nondisabled peers (with special services provided where appropriate).[35]

In a sense there has been a renaissance of the optimism of Itard, Seguin, and Down regarding the educability of these children, especially when interventions occur earlier in life, and this optimism is manifest in the inclusive education movement. The basic idea is that if people with Down Syndrome, developmental delays, and other learning disabilities are going to be fully accepted and if such individuals are to reach their full potential, then their education needs to take place within inclusive and integrated communities since it is only in such communities that mutuality, reciprocity, interdependence, and friendships can be cultivated between people with and without disabilities (Kliewer 1998: chap. 7). The more successful cases involve skillful teachers, nondisruptive students, and parents who come to appreciate the learning possibilities of an inclusive environment (Falvey, Rosenberg, and Falvey 1997).

On the other side, there have been counterarguments that full inclusion is more an ideological position than an adequate pedagogical program (Sykes 1996: chap. 14). Practically speaking, how are teachers to work with children with severe or profound handicaps and exceptional or gifted children all in the same inclusive classroom (Howe and Miramontes 1992)? Realistically speaking, is not inclusion flawed in assuming that severely and profoundly disabled children are educable and can be fully integrated into society with special considerations?[36] Philosophically, politically, and legally speaking, if "integration—in the sense of positive intergroup relations—cannot be legislated" (Murray-Seegert 1989: 105), then is PL 94-142/IDEA the way forward even if we agree with the basic concept?[37] Then there is empirical evidence that some believe suggests the following (Mostert and Kavale 2003: 197–99): that teachers are generally much less enthusiastic than administrators (who are farther away from the "trenches") about full inclusion; that students who have been harassed by other kids have themselves favored pull-out programs; and that parents have only favored inclusion if (a) their child's disability was not severe, (b) they thought their children would be challenged by higher expectations and by exposure to nondisabled peers, (c) it was clear that inclusion of their child would not overburden teachers, and (d) there were indications that their child would be welcomed by his or her classmates.[38]

One of the issues being debated concerns the question of the difference involved. In the case of Down Syndrome children: are they just slower learners or is their form of learning fundamentally different? Linguistic studies suggest, on the one hand, that while children and people with Down Syndrome have a difficult time mastering complex sentences and communicating using abstract ideas (here confirming Locke's hypothesis) or symbolic representations (to use the language of contemporary cognitive science), they are able to use language pragmatically.[39] From this perspective, Down Syndrome presents a developmental delay rather than a fundamentally different mode of learning. On the other hand, neuroscientific studies are not only suggestive regarding hypotheses about the diminished capacity for abstract thinking (Nadel 1986: 246), but they have also identified morphological differences in terms of brain size and shape, dendritic and synaptic operations, and brain circuit and neuronal network formations.[40] These findings would sustain the claim that Down Syndrome learning is qualitatively rather than just quantitatively different.

Further supporting the neuroscientific data is the evidence regarding savant syndrome.[41] Researchers of moderately retarded savants with demonstrated unusual skills in calendar calculation, artistic production, feats of memorization, and playing music (especially the keyboard) have presented various theoretical explanations: the role of hereditary factors; the presence of eidetic or photographic memory; the emergence of concrete reasoning capacities to compensate for the lack of ability to reason abstractly; the concentrated development of one or two skill areas in response to sensory deprivation in other areas; or processes of social reinforcement at a young age (see Cheatham et al. 1995). While there is no doubt that some and perhaps even many of these factors contribute to the emergence of savant syndrome, more recent theories have relied on brain research. Besides the suggestion that savants have compensated for an underdeveloped left-hemisphere with right-hemisphere capacities (Treffert 1989), there is also the growing realization that human cognitive capacities may operate independently in certain cases. Whereas human brains usually access different functions and perform multiple tasks simultaneously, in the case of people with intellectual disability neural dysfunctions do not allow for this kind of coordination or accessibility, thus requiring some capacities to operate independently (Howe 1989: 84–88).[42] Put alternatively, savant behavior may represent "the operation of normative or conventional modes of information processing, but in a relatively limited domain" (Miller 1989: 178).

If these findings hold up, the program of inclusive education would need to be modified in the direction of a more gradualist and contingent approach that is able to take into account the particular strengths and needs of the wide range of learning and developmentally disabled children and adults (Gerber 1996). The basic idea of inclusion itself, however, seems intact. This is especially the case given the emergence of computers and other kinds of technological aids as educational media.[43] These new technologies can now enhance the ways in which students learn, so long as teachers are skillful enough to utilize various teaching methods for the different learning styles/abilities (Shogren and Rye 2005: 49). If this happens, scientific technologies will not only have prolonged the lives of children born with Down Syndrome, but also have provided them with educational opportunities unavailable to previous generations.

On Work, Marriage, and Children

Of course, technological supports are available not only in classrooms but also after graduation into communities and workplaces (McMurray 1987; Roulstone 1998). In the decades since deinstitutionalization, people with Down Syndrome or mild mental retardation are increasingly able to find work in their communities. Although their experiences are shaped in many ways by the central themes of the independent living movement—autonomy of decision making; going beyond paternalism; human dignity; self-identity, responsibility, and agency; and quality of life (Nosek et al. 1982)—people with Down Syndrome or mental retardation often are in a situation called supported employment. These supports include technological aids as well as social services, transportation, job training, and when necessary, personal assistance, all of which combine—with the collaboration of family members, social service professionals, and employers—to enable people with intellectual disabilities to earn an income and contribute to society (see Wehman et al. 1997; Riggar and Riggar 1980: chap. 10; Mackelprang and Salsgiver 1999: chap. 8). In most instances, supported employment comes as part of a more comprehensive support plan for residential or independent living.

Deinstitutionalization has also opened up the possibility for friendships and relationships with the opposite sex prohibited within the regimen of the mental asylum. If the prevailing assumption is that people with disabilities in general are either sexually unattractive (at best) or without sexual desires (at worst),[44] then people with intellectual disabilities are thought to be either wholly asexual (without even any sexual needs) or sexually dangerous (at least previously). In fact, rather than being predatory, people with intellectual disabilities are especially vulnerable to being physically and sexually abused.[45] While these violated individuals need special counseling and rehabilitation, others with intellectual disabilities are sexual beings with similar ranges of sexual needs and desires as among the nondisabled (see Hingsburger 1991; Schwier and Hingsburger 2000). As reported by those who have worked closely with this population: "The saddest stories come as quiet longing from people who find themselves isolated, protected by family or staff from the risks of daily life, guarded from the risk of exploitation, denied their sexuality, or simply not encouraged or supported to make friends because that category doesn't appear on an Individual Program Plan. It is difficult to think that for many people, loneliness is ensured every day for a lifetime" (Schwier 1994: 190–91).

Increasingly, people with intellectual disabilities are finding relationships with the opposite sex, with a few cases proceeding to marriage and even children.[46] An early study of thirty-two deinstitutionalized married couples in the 1960s concluded that "paired, many of them were able to reinforce each other's strengths and established marriages which, in the light of what had happened to them previously, were no more, no less, foolish than many others in the community, and which gave them considerable satisfaction" (Mattinson 1973: 185). With the kinds of professional, social, and community supports available today, there should be no objection to intellectually disabled couples who desire to marry, all else being equal. To be sure, many challenges remain, but advocates say that these pose no insurmountable obstacles if the proper support systems are in place (Murphy and Feldman 2002). Couples like Neil and Scott Mercer, or Mr. and Mrs. Phil Allen, both of whom were quoted in the chapter introduction above, are a testimony to the resilience of people with intellectual disabilities in their efforts to lead fulfilling married lives.

Marriages do lead to children, however, and the assumption persists either that people with intellectual disability will have retarded children or that they will be inadequate parents.[47] It has been especially at this level that old habits die hard. Even in the 1970s, ethical arguments (as in Bass 1978 and Macklin and Gaylin 1981) insisted that the rights of people with intellectual disability to bear children must be weighed against their ability to care for these children, the rights of grandparents not to have to raise grandchildren, and the rights of a community (i.e., the state) not to have to be financially responsible for such children. If the mildly disabled can give informed consent and want to marry, then why could they not assent voluntarily to sterilization, especially when welfare laws—then—stopped including birth control? As late as 1986, a member of the state of Virginia Board of Social Services even went so far as to suggest that welfare mothers be sterilized; to be sure, this caused an outcry and the official apologized, but still said that he received many favorable letters about this idea (Smith and Nelson 1989: 252–53). This reveals that when push comes to shove, even "civilized Westerners" fall back on scientific rationality and technological instrumentality to "solve the problem of the retarded."

The issues here are complex (see Field and Sanchez 1999), and I have no major proposals to resolve them. Yet the point to note in this regard is that given the medicalization of intellectual disability since the mid-nineteenth century, medical solutions such as prenatal screening, selective abortion, and sterilization are all too frequently entertained when thinking about intellectual disability. At the same time, medical technology has also made it possible for infants with Down Syndrome to survive the trauma of birth and then live reasonably healthy and even productive lives. Further, we have come a long way in terms of transforming the social conditions that nurture the lives of people with and without disabilities together. Have we come far enough so that our medical technology will preserve rather than end prematurely the lives of an increasingly elderly population of intellectually disabled persons?

On Aging and Dying

Greater biomedical knowledge, advances in public health care, and technological developments have made it possible for people with Down Syndrome in developed countries to live to an average age of fifty-five (Massimini 2000: 57). Growing older brings with it a distinctive set of challenges for people with disabilities. I will discuss briefly issues related to aging, and to death and dying. We will conclude this chapter with some observations about bereavement and the place of spirituality in the support systems of people with intellectual disabilities.

Aging is disabling for all persons, even those without intellectual or physical disabilities. Yet most elderly do not identify themselves as disabled or associate themselves with the politics of disability since they see their condition as due to the "normal" impairments of old age rather than resulting from an ableist society (Monteith 2005: 58; cf. Overall 2006). We pause here to note, however, that all nondisabled people, who do not die young, will eventually taste disability in some way. Still, on top of such "normal" impairments (if these could be identified as such), older persons with disabilities often point to additional frustrations and challenges such as the lack of general understanding of the medical and physical dimensions of aging with disabilities, of unsuitable or unacceptable living options, of inadequate health benefits and other supports, and of inaccessible information and unavailable choices. What are the "answers" toward which we should work? A "supportive environment" that provides information, user-led personal supports, financial resources, and security; that recognizes and values difference; and that secures rights, empowers choices, and seeks creative solutions to the challenges of growing old with disabilities (Oliver and Zarb 1993: chaps. 6–7; cf. Iris 2003).

Older persons with intellectual disabilities desire and are due no less than this (Edgerton 1991), even if their main concerns remain meaningful activities and personal friendships (Boyd 1997; Krentel 1986). Other age-related problems include depression, further sensory impairments, increasing weight (problematic for people with Down Syndrome, who are generally overweight to begin with), further sleep and appetite disturbances, or thyroid dysfunction (Holland 1999). In addition, however, one out of four older persons with Down Syndrome—versus 6 percent of the general population—are likely to experience the onset of Alzheimer's disease after they turn thirty-five (Massimini 2000: 61; cf. Berg, Karlinsky, and Holland 1993).

People with disabilities are also at greater risk of various complications in the dying process than most other people. These complications are exacerbated by social prejudices. In part because elderly people with disabilities do not fit into the rehabilitation and cure framework of the medical establishment, their lives are often devalued at these most vulnerable periods of old age and dying (see Wolfensberger 1992, 2005: esp. 3–15). A logic similar to that operative in the practices of prenatal screening comes into play in end-of-life situations involving people with severe physical and intellectual disabilities: whereas selective abortions are implicitly advocated in the former case, the "right to die" with physician assistance—euthanasia, to be explicit—is assumed in the latter case where a diminished quality of life is assumed.[48]

We have already discussed the eugenically justified infanticide of Haiselden and his colleagues, and the Nazi program of euthanasia. Yet the euthanasia of the mentally retarded occurred not only in Germany but also in the United States. During the first half of the twentieth century when the medical institution possessed unparalleled powers over the lives of its patients, the euthanasia of sick and older mentally retarded people was explicitly advocated and, in some cases, even implemented, albeit without public knowledge (Elks 1993: 203–6).[49] Have attitudes changed after deinstitutionalization so that people with intellectual disability are also allowed to die with dignity as valued members of the human community? Advocates, guardians, and especially family members need to be especially vigilant in end-of-life situations that involve not only the terminally ill or persons in comas but also people with intellectual disabilities. Because in some cases people with intellectual disabilities may not be able to communicate clearly their feelings and desires, the physical presence of family members or caretakers who have established interpersonal relationships and moral bonds with such persons is crucial for end-of-life decisions (Jordan 1985: chap. 6). These are often ambiguous situations where trust and compassion become most important for helping us decide not only what to do, but also "how to be" (Reinders 2005a: 47; cf. Turnbull 2005).

Yet there is one other end-of-life situation demanding special consideration with regard to people with intellectual disabilities: that involving the death of a family member or loved one. At one point it was assumed that people with intellectual disability were unable to grieve, but later, institutions did not allow them to attend the funerals of their friends because that was assumed to be upsetting to the families of the deceased.[50] The capacity of people with intellectual disability to comprehend death and to grieve should not be underestimated. Rather, those working with people with intellectual disabilities and their families should attend to two questions upon the death of a loved one: "how can we make sure that the tender feelings of people with learning difficulties, and their families, and their staff, are treated with sensitivity? And how can we plan services so that they do not make sad people sadder?" (Oswin 1991: 16). Insofar as people with intellectual disability have an aptitude for matters pertaining to the spiritual life, to that same extent they are able to grieve the loss of loved ones, and should be supported appropriately through that grieving process.

This issue of the spirituality of people with intellectual disabilities is one that has slowly begun to receive attention. Whereas throughout most of the twentieth century it was assumed either that people with intellectual disabilities had limited if any comprehension of spirituality-related matters or that if they did, that was their own private affair, more recently there has been a realization not only that people with intellectual disabilities are concerned with spirituality, but also that this is an area in which support services could and should also be provided (Gaventa and Peters 2001; Gaventa and Coulter 2001a). As with all other people, spirituality helps those with intellectual disabilities and other illnesses to find meaning and purpose in their lives, to give and receive love, and to be hopeful and even creative. Hence, spirituality is a powerful coping mechanism, especially in enabling relationships with God and providing support networks with faith communities (Kaye and Raghavan 2002; McNair and Swartz 1995). Service providers and professionals who are concerned with "values-based services" (Pengra 2000) should be especially focused on integrating spirituality into the support systems for people with intellectual disabilities.

Our overall objective in this chapter has been to present the case for understanding Down Syndrome as a distinctively modern phenomenon (Judge 1975: 26–27). Positive and negative conclusions can be drawn anticipating the rest of this book. With regard to the latter, we cannot but observe in the most forceful of terms the injustice perpetrated against people with intellectual (and physical) disabilities over the last 150-plus years, much of it with the backing of the medical establishment. Whether discrimination based on IQ testing, eugenic movements, forced institutionalization (or incarceration), prenatal testing leading to abortions of fetuses identified with trisomy 21 or other genetic or chromosomal mutations, or other inequitable treatments proposed and implemented by modern medicine, the rights and privileges of people with Down Syndrome have been routinely violated. The modern Enlightenment was anything but kind to those who did not measure up to the alleged standards of universal reason. The religious and theological establishments, however, cannot be too self-righteous about this whole affair simply because of their complicity in the modern medical prognoses and prescriptions. Part of the reason for writing this book is to expose this history of medical (and religious and theological) discrimination against people with intellectual and physical disabilities, and to suggest how we might avoid these past mistakes in our present and future endeavors.

Positively, however, we have also seen in this chapter that modern medicine has illuminated the phenomenon we call Down Syndrome in various ways. On the one hand, the cognitive, biological, and genetic sciences have explicated and then provided treatments for the challenges peculiar to this syndrome. But while scientific research on Down Syndrome and other congenitally related intellectual disabilities shows no signs of abating (Parmenter 1999; cf. Harris 2006), the last generation has seen the emergence of another approach to intellectual and physical disabilities to confront this medical paradigm that has been dominant for the last century. Its proponents call it the social model of disability. What is or is not at stake in this new development for our understanding of Down Syndrome and for people with Down Syndrome?

IV

Deconstructing and Reconstructing Disability
Late Modern Discourses

D[on]. Let's talk a little bit more about Down Syndrome. You say
you like it. What do you like about of [sic] it?

B[eth]. It's just a part of me. That's what I like about it.

D. If you could get rid of your Down Syndrome, would you?

B. No.

D. Do you really want it to be part of you for the rest of your life?

B. Yes. Anyway, I can't get rid of it because I was born with it.

D. But if you could, would you want to?

B. No, it's just a part of me, it's a part of my life, and I want to be
a part of it.

—Don Bakely and Beth Bakely, in Bakely 2002: 182

Retarded is just a word. We have to separate individuals from the
word.

—Ed Murphy, in Bodgan and Taylor 1994: 92

Handicapped people, you know, whether we can talk or not, you
gotta give us credit. We're here and that's that. We're human
bein's [sic] just like everyone else, and we have rights. You know,
some of us are cool and some of us are not.

—Michael Dalziel, in Schwier 1990: 44

I work, I pay taxes and I vote! I think I probably know a lot more
about candidate positions than voters who vote straight party
ticket, vote for someone on the advice of a friend, or vote for a
candidate because they like their ad.

—Peder Johansen, in Johansen 2004: 9

*Moving to the United States from Malaysia turned out to be a blessing
for Mark and our family. California's CCS (Crippled Children's Services)
put Mark in school and provided educational and social opportunities for
him that he would not have had if our family had remained in Malaysia.
Although his teachers were concerned about his passivity in the face of being
bullied by other kids in school, Mark has always been a good student, making adequate progress and participating in activities with other students.*

*After he turned eighteen, Mark continued in school for a number of
years. At various points, he was given opportunities for vocational training.
However, these never translated into employment for Mark in part because
his skill set never matured to the point where placement was warranted,
but also in part because his parents never saw the need to push him in that
direction.*

*Yet the school environment gives Mark some important outlets. He
learned to use the computer at school, and this resulted, at one point, in
his being quite the video game player at home (his favorite game then
was Super Mario Bros.). Mark has also made some school friends; his best
friends are Rita and Stephanie (his teachers), Mark McCann, and "everybody!" (including church friends). But most importantly in recent years for
Mark are the bimonthly bowling events. Even long after he lost interest
in going to school—and Mark can be quite obstinate with regard to doing
things he doesn't want to do, especially after he was recognized by his teacher
to be a capable and intelligent adult, and then encouraged to be more independent[1]—he still looks forward to the second and fourth Thursdays of each
month when he aims to beat his high score (as of July 31, 2006) of 118!*

If Down Syndrome were a medical condition that was "fixable,"
then why would individuals like Beth Bakely (above) not want to
be without Down Syndrome? But if Down Syndrome was also a
product of social relationships and we could see that Beth thrived
socially, perhaps we might understand her perspective. In this
chapter we explore disability informed by a social model approach.
In brief, this viewpoint argues that disabilities are as much, if not

more, social, cultural, economic, and political constructions as they are biological, cognitive, and genetic conditions.[2] We will examine each aspect of this constructivist argument in turn before asking in the last section of this chapter about how applicable it is to the experience of intellectual disability. Because the social model has been developed by people with physical disabilities and disability rights activists, the voices and perspectives of people with intellectual disabilities will be basically absent from my exposition of the model. However, I believe it is worth our while to proceed carefully through the social model in part because of its many ramifications for any theology of disability, and in part because we have already established that Down Syndrome and other intellectual disabilities are almost never devoid of accompanying physical impairments.

Our objectives here are twofold. First, we want to highlight the differences between modern and postmodern or late-modern approaches to disability in general and intellectual disability in particular. Whereas modernity adopted a medical model, late modernity has shifted toward social perspectives on disability. I will argue in the end that these approaches are complementary even as they provide critical perspectives we should heed. Second, we hope to show how late modern discourses about disability illuminate the phenomenon of disability against a wider set of concerns. This complicates our established (medicalized) notions of disability but also invites responses to the challenges posed by intellectual and physical disability that will help us reconstruct our theology of disability on a more just foundation.

One final caveat before proceeding. Those of my readers who have worked in or contributed to the field of disability studies will probably feel most at home with the terminology and arguments of this chapter, even if my methods and analyses might be contested from any number of perspectives that constitute the field. I do not pretend to have mastered the increasingly voluminous literature that disability studies scholars have developed. I am convinced, however, that the theology of disability will remain impoverished and even impotent so long as disability scholarship is ignored. This volume is motivated in part by the need to bring these discourses into conversation.

Disability as Social and Cultural Construction

What does it mean to say that disability is a social and cultural construct? I will explore this question by focusing on sociological and disability studies of freaks, deviance, and normalcy and then probe the question about whether or not we can speak coherently about a "disability culture." Our goal is to illuminate the social aspects of disability on the one hand even as we see how disability perspectives might reconstruct such realities on the other.

On Freaks and Deviants: Stigma as Social Construct

In chapter 2 we introduced the idea that for the ancients, *monstra* were in some instances understood to be either signs of the gods or malformations of demons (Warkany 1977: 7; cf. Warkany 1971: chap. 2; Friedman 1981; Wilson 1993). In the Christian view of things, *monstra* even as hypothetical entities generated debate about whether or not such creatures had souls (were fully human) or could be converted. If Rome or Athens was considered the center of civilization, the *monstra* were, like the biblical Cain and his descendants, cast out to inhabit the world's outer edges. Hence, the Great Commission to take the gospel to "every creature" (Mark 16:15, KJV) was argued by some to include the *monstra*. During the early modern period, the *monstrum* was slowly transformed into the "noble savage" or "natural slave" who was not quite beast, but not fully human either. As European travelers to the "New World," "darkest Africa," and the "Far East" brought back stories, curiosities, and memorials of their findings, members of learned societies were busy updating ancient supernaturalistic explanations with "natural histories" and "natural theologies" of such fascinating (or horrendous) exotica. The results, however, were a mixed bag from a contemporary disability perspective: if on the one side materialized the classifications of the modern scientific disciplines, on the other emerged the freak show of the nineteenth and twentieth centuries.[3]

During the heyday of the freak show, human "monstrosities" were paraded in circuses, fairs, carnivals, and amusement parks throughout the Euro-American West before the gawking eyes of those curious, amused, and horrified all at the same time.[4] The public was enticed through (many false) advertisements to view dwarfs, giants, the ugly, feral children, hermaphrodites, Siamese twins (who were allegedly found in the exotic land of Siam), amputees, hirsute persons, the extraordinarily obese or anorexic, microencephalitics (probably individuals with intellectual disabilities), albinos, aborigines, wild men from Africa or Borneo, Amazon women, Circassian beauties and slaves, and other human and "extrahuman" oddities. Later on, after the medical profession began to institutionalize people with starker physical differences, "self-made freaks" like tattooed persons, sword swallowers, and snake charmers were hired to fill the void, and the freak show industry turned increasingly to deception in order to perpetuate its revenues.

One of the most famous "freaks" was the "Elephant Man" (Montagu 1971; Howell and Ford 1980; Shapiro 2002). Joseph Merrick (1862–1890), who may have had either neurofibromatosis (the tendency to develop tumors in nervous tissues) or Proteus syndrome (gigantism in various bodily organs and appendages), was on display during the 1880s and became the epitome of the "freak." Merrick labored under this burden. Abandoned by his father and then left alone after his mother's death, he longed for friendship and for relationships with women. Merrick even seems to have experienced Christian conversion in some respect, knowing both the Bible and the Prayer Book (Graham and Oehlschlaeger 1992: 48). Yet the freak show objectified human beings like Merrick: "Freaks and prodigies were solely bodies, without the humanity social structures confer upon more ordinary people" (Thomson 1997: 57).

More recently the freak show and its legacy have been reassessed in part through the theory of stigma and deviance. As classically expressed by sociologist Erving Goffman (1974), stigma denotes the dynamic relationship between discredited and marginalized groups of persons and the norms of the dominant society. Deviations from the norm are marked so that individuals may feel different levels of stigmatization with respect to a wide range of social views and values. Historically, groups such as heretics, homosexuals, Jews, and witches were marginalized when the language of stigmatization was controlled by clergy and the church. However, with the shift of authority in modernity to new institutions and discourses such as therapeutic medicine, social science, and criminal justice the newly stigmatized groups became the insane, alcoholics, the poor, and criminals (Solomon 1986).

Building on Goffman's hypothesis, Irwin Katz (1981) has argued that stigma applies not only to racial and ethnic minority groups but also to people with disabilities. Among Katz's findings pertinent to our study is that unintentional harm-doers will more likely denigrate or respond negatively to either blacks or disabled persons than to whites or the nonhandicapped. Interestingly, people are also more likely to help blacks or handicapped victims than whites or nonhandicapped persons. Yet, handicapped persons with desirable traits were less likely than handicapped persons with nondesirable traits to get help from the majority group, perhaps because handicapped persons are not supposed to possess or exhibit desirable traits. On the whole, then, Katz's study advances the further hypothesis that stigmatization involves two elements (1981: 18-23): (a) the perception of a negative attribute, and (b) a devaluation of a person with such an attribute. In this framework (a) and (b) could be independent variables. More often, however, either (a) causes (b) or vice versa, but both exemplify the social model of disability in operation.

On Normalcy and Difference: Deconstructing Disability

The work of sociologists like Goffman and Katz is suggestive for our purposes on a number of levels. Looking back at the history of disability, the social model interrogates our received ideas of monstrosity, freakery, and disability. The term *monstra*, a social approach suggests, tells us less about those who are so labeled than it does about the dominant majority doing the labeling (Jo Cohen 1996; Beal 2002; Mitchell 2002; Shildrick 2002). The "monsters" of the Western culture have represented its internal crises and vulnerabilities, its deepest fears, its enemies, the strangers in its midst, and the borders demarcating the unfamiliar, unknown, and incomprehensible that have lurked within (e.g., Crawford 2005). As Richard Kearney puts it (2003: 4), the "[u]nnatural, transgressive, obscene, contradictory, heterogeneous, mad . . . , are, deep down, tokens of fracture within the human psyche. They speak to us of how we are split between conscious and unconscious, familiar and unfamiliar, same and other. And they remind us that we have a choice: (a) to try to understand and accommodate our experiences of strangeness, or (b) to repudiate it by projecting it exclusively onto outsiders." Hospitality results when the former approach is adopted, but monstrosity the latter.

Similarly, the freak unveils social attitudes, fears, and prejudices. Robert Bogdan writes (1988: 267): "A freak was defined not by the possession of any particular quality but by a set of practices, a way of thinking about and presenting people with major, minor, and fabricated physical, mental, and behavioral differences." Hence freak shows are less about individuals on display than they are about organizations, social values, and the perspectives of the majority. Even if we are sympathetic to the concerns of one of the last "freaks"—Otis "the Frog Man" (with poorly functional underformed limbs), whose exhibition was curtailed in the mid-1980s by objections against exploiting the disabled (Bogdan 1988: 279–81)—that his freedom to earn a living was being taken away, a social approach to freakery would suggest that the historical and social oppressiveness within which "freaks" like Otis have lived their lives undermine the notion that they had genuine choice (Gerber 1992). "Freaks" are being displayed rather than engaging in active performance because of social constraints that inhibit the exercise of their freedoms. Hence, "freaks" are stigmatized objects of curiosity, pity, ridicule, and maybe even charity, but not subjects and agents in the making of their own histories.

From this, disability is now defined by social relationships rather than in biomedical terms. On the one hand, the social model of disability exposes false assumptions about disability: that it is located solely in biology (without other variables); that it is impairment that causes all the problems disabled persons encounter or experience (ignoring the fact that social factors could be just as much the cause of the problems of disabled persons); that disabled persons are "victims" (with all the psychological baggage accompanying such a self-concept); that disability is the central or only element of a disabled person's self-identity; and that disabled persons need help and social support, and cannot live independently or be a source of help themselves (Fine and Asch 2000). On the other hand, the social model places the responsibility for the negative attitudes of the majority on sociocultural conditioning and childhood influences; on psychodynamic mechanisms such as fear of ostracism combined with the attendant need to develop and enhance a socially acceptable self-concept; on socioreligious notions of disability such as punishment for sin or as reminder of death; on socially homogeneous ideas about bodily integrity and aesthetics; on concerns about minority group incompatibility often enacted within an intergroup conflict or competition model; and on demographics and other issues of personal identity (Livneh 1991; Mason et al. 2004). Reinforced by social Darwinist conceptions of progress, individualism, and responsibility, these factors have conspired to "*force* handicapped individuals into a position of deviance" (Liachowitz 1988: 5, italics in original; cf. Gliedman and Roth 1980: chap. 1). As Rosemarie Garland Thomson summarizes (1997: 31–32): "The process of stigmatization thus legitimates the status quo, naturalizes attributions of inherent inferiority and superiority, and obscures the socially constructed quality of both categories. . . . [S]tigma theory reminds us that the problems we confront are not disability . . . ; they are instead the inequalities, negative attitudes, misrepresentations, and institutional practices that result from the process of stigmatization."

But if monstrosity, freakery, and disability are socially negotiated, then is not "normalcy" also socially formulated? In his book *Enforcing Normalcy: Disability, Deafness, and the Body* (1995), literature professor and disability theorist Lennard Davis points out that the word "normal"—meaning "standard, regular, usual"—appeared in England 150 years ago and in France 200 years ago. It was during this period of industrialization and the consolidation of bourgeois power that novels began to represent disabled characters with ideological markings signifying connections with disease, accident, moral ambiguity, and sexual illicitness. Whereas the "ideal" had previously functioned Platonically as an aesthetic standard that no one met, the appearance of the "normal" transformed the "ideal" into a concrete expression of a positive deviation from the norm. On the other side, the "grotesque," which before referred to the common life and to common folk, now came to signify a negative deviation from the norm. A bell curve emerged whereby ideal bodies were exalted—for example, the "Cult of Slimness" or the "Cult of Eternal Youth"—and normal bodies had begun to exercise a tyranny that not only displaced but also excluded and marginalized disabled or fragmented bodies (Fiedler 1996: 147–55; cf. Donley and Buckley 1996). The disabled individual had become the excluded stranger. Davis, who writes from the liminal experience of being a CODA—"Child of Deaf Adults"—presents examples of people in the legal, judicial, and penitential systems who because of their profound deafness and without American sign language skills have never been tried but have been incarcerated, sterilized, or committed to mental institutions—or all of the above (1995: 167–71).

In our late modern context, however, the voices and perspectives of those previously on the margins have begun to be heard. So if the notions of normalcy and disability have been deconstructed as self-reiterative categories of experience and exposed as sets of social constructions—so people with disabilities are "disabled" in certain relational contexts but not in others (see Price and Shildrick 1998: esp. 230–42)—is it not possible, even desirable, to reconstruct disability in ways that eliminate the stigma, prejudice, and discrimination it often brings? What has recently emerged, then, is discussion about "disability pride" and "disability culture" (Fleischer and Zames 2001: 201).

Disability Culture and Media: Reconstructing Disability

Unlike ethnic cultures, of course, "disability culture" is usually not transgenerational (although this may change given the emergence of genetic technologies). Rather, people with disabilities have similar experiences that provide a strong sense of group identity for those who are able to connect with one another.[5] After deinstitutionalization, communities emerged wherein people with disabilities began collectively to construct a way of life more suited to their needs, desires, and capabilities. It is at this point in our thinking about disability as a cultural construction that it might be helpful to observe the commonalities but also differences between the "disability experience" and the "deaf experience."

One of the issues debated is whether "deafness" is a "disability" or an expression of cultural and linguistic difference. Advocates of Deaf culture have long argued both that there is an entire way of life (beliefs, practices, and communicative expressions) that is particular to people with hearing impairments and that those who identify with such a way of life see deafness not as a disability but as the common feature of a distinctive form of social organization. The classic case is that of the island of Martha's Vineyard, where, from the eighteenth to early twentieth centuries, the remarkably high percentage of deaf people among the population—one in 155 on the island versus 1 in 5,728 Americans in the nineteenth century—resulted in sign language becoming common currency (Groce 1985: 3). This large number of deaf persons mitigated prejudice against deafness so that even after deafness disappeared from the island in 1952, people continued to sign while speaking. In contrast, during the same period of time the wider society witnessed a protracted debate between oralists and manualists (Davis 1995: 50–72; Baynton 1997; Burch 2001). The former were primarily hearing educators of deaf persons who advocated lip-reading and lip-communicating based on the assumption that speech was the defining aspect of human rationality and that deaf people with these skills were better able to adapt and be integrated into society. Manualists, however, consisted of deaf persons who found themselves in solidarity with one another in subaltern communities (e.g., the schools for the deaf), and who resisted being subsumed under the dominant modes of communication imposed by society. Against the attempts to "mainstream" deaf persons into a hearing framework, Deaf culture advocates insist that natural languages (like manualism) are much less arbitrary and much more natural, universal, lucid, and fluid; that signs are more spatial/embodied; and that signing is more concrete, precise, subtle, and flexible (see Rée 1999: chap. 21).

While the manualists have since won the pedagogical and philosophical debate, the problem for Deaf culture is at least threefold. First, it is rarely passed on from generation to generation (nine out of ten deaf children have hearing parents, and deaf parents have hearing children eight out of ten times) and hence is perpetuated through family traditions only in a few cases. Second, it does not have a "written culture" that can be easily transmitted from generation to generation and hence cannot imbibe the wisdom of past generations (the sign languages of the ancient world, for example, are irretrievably lost). Finally, it is transmitted by schools, which are public institutions that are much more subject to historical forces than are family institutions. Do not even more severe challenges confront other minority disability groups that do not have even a common communicative system around which to rally?

In addition to the problems identified by advocates of Deaf culture is the fact that disabilities come in an innumerable variety of forms that do not translate into very many similar experiences. But there is one type of experience that might bind people with disabilities together: that of social stigmatization and marginalization. If the challenge is that of generating a social medium for creating, maintaining, and perpetuating a disability culture, then the question for disability culture may be: how can cultural representations of disability—for example, the arts and the humanities (see Devlieger, Rusch, and Pfeiffer 2003: 14-15)—be transformed so that people with disabilities are no longer stigmatized, marginalized, and oppressed on account of their bodily (or intellectual) differences?

It is here that the emergence of disability perspectives on cultural media such as literature, art, theater, and film has begun to make an impact.[6] From a representational standpoint, media portrayals have historically all too often perpetuated problematic stereotypes of people with disabilities as saints, martyrs, tragic victims, helpless burdens, charity cases, pathetic, pitiable, isolated, abhorrent, disgusting, shitty, dribbling and drooling, better-off-dead, maladjusted-own-worst-enemies, sinister, objects of violence or of ridicule, asexual or sexually abnormal, or even survivors against all odds. Perhaps this is to be expected as portrayals of disability have inevitably been produced by those who have not critically questioned their able-bodied points of view. Hence ableism subtly but assuredly distorts the experiences of people with disabilities.

To be sure, times have begun to change and we are seeing fewer negative portrayals of people with disabilities in the media. Yet, further critical questions remain. For starters, why is the ordinary day-to-day life of people with disabilities still missing in large part from media representations? Disabilities continue to be featured in crime and thriller films, or in special achievement shows and medical news reports, but not in the dramas and soap operas that portray "regular" life (see Cumberbatch and Negrine 1992: 135–38). Further, when are people with disabilities going to appear realistically rather than continue to be represented through dominant images that are "crude, one-dimensional and simplistic" (Shakespeare 1999: 165)? Finally, even though there is a proliferation of disability in some TV and film circles, more often than not these are reruns that perpetuate ancient plot lines. Part of the process of constructing a disability culture includes interrogating historical representations of disability production in dialogue with people with disabilities, formulating principles that will eliminate ableist biases and imagery, and empowering disability activism so that such misrepresentations can be corrected (for books, films, videos, broadcasts, print media like newspaper and magazines, and advertisements).

One way forward is to involve people with disabilities in the various aspects of media production from screenwriting to performance so that insider perspectives and concerns can be accurately depicted (see Kuppers 2001, 2004; Goodley and Moore 2002). People with disabilities are increasingly resisting being limited to performances in the medical arena (where they take painkillers) or the social sphere (where they use disabled parking plates). On stage or camera, performers with disabilities resist objectification and become agents of their own representation. Through their own enactments, disability is discursive, contested, and multiple, even as normalcy is deconstructed and social certainties are challenged and upset. This is not to deny that disabled persons' knowledge about disability oftentimes only with difficulty translates into knowing how to communicate such in writing scripts or acting them out. It is to say that the emergence of a disability culture is possible if people with disabilities are involved in its construction.

This task of disability cultural construction is now being undertaken even by those who are profoundly disabled. The London-based arts company Entelechy employs "enablers" who work with the profoundly disabled to stimulate artistic creativity and expressions through dance, movement, and music (Nash 2005; cf. Benjamin 2002). What goes on in Entelechy workshops is a shift from performance as viewed to performance as participation. Adopting multisensory interactive experiences such as tactility, contact improvisation, and mirroring, the lines between spectator and performer and between disabled and nondisabled are blurred since all involved "experience the world as intersubjective and intercorporeal beings" (Nash 2005: 199). Yet, in all of this cultural representation, we need to ask: "how can we give up these stable categories without denying the existence of current realities of oppression, division, subjugation and exclusion?" (Kuppers 2004: 51). Entele-chists respond that while they do not claim to be therapists or heal-ers, they are agents of liberation who through the transformative medium of the performing arts "inculcate changes at individual, cultural, and societal levels" (Nash 2005: 191).

Disability as a Political and Economic Construct

In the preceding we have overviewed the argument that disabil-ity is a social construction mediated through historical stereotypes and cultural representation. In this section I wish to expand on this argument by delineating the political structures and economic forces undergirding the modern conception of disability. Again, we will see how late modern perspectives can shed light on disabil-ity as a historical construction on the one hand and yet point ahead to liberative possibilities for the future on the other.

Destructuring and Restructuring Disability: The Discourses of Law and Politics

There have always been laws addressing cases of people with dis-abilities, including those suffered during war or those that are work related.[7] Yet, by and large, disability has been politically framed in terms of services rather than of rights. In an individualistic society, people with disabilities have been considered less than equal. The success story of President Franklin D. Roosevelt is an exception that proves the rule.[8] After being struck by polio in 1921, Roos-evelt nevertheless rose to attain the presidency from 1933 to 1945. Yet, because his success was dependent on a public portrayal of his abilities, his disability was intentionally masked. One of his biographers rightly says Roosevelt "dominated his times from a wheelchair yet he was simply not perceived as being in any major sense disabled. . . . The strategy [to minimize his handicap] was eminently successful, but it required substantial physical effort, ingenuity, and bravado. This was FDR's splendid deception" (Gal-lagher 1985: xiv). In Roosevelt's life, we see the pressure of tra-ditional society to construct ability by masking disability and to construct disability by masking ability. In this framework, there is no room to ask about the rights of "the disabled" (see Colker 1996: esp. chap. 6).

The height of the civil rights era in the 1960s, however, brought in its train not only the feminist movement but also the disability rights movement.[9] Over the last forty years, disability rights activists and advocates have worked to pass a number of landmark statutes addressing disability concerns related to the accessibility of public spaces, transportation, employment, and health care (see Eisenberg, Griggins, and Duval 1982: pt. 2; Rothstein 1997). The most important have been the Architectural Barriers Act in 1968, the Rehabilitation Act in 1973, the Education for All Handicapped Children Act in 1975 (renamed the Individuals with Disabilities Education Act in 1990), the Civil Rights of Institutionalized Persons Act in 1980, the Fair Housing Act in 1988, a number of voting statutes (the Voting Accessibility for the Elderly and Handicapped in 1984, the National Voter Registration Act in 1993, the Help America Vote Act in 2002) (see Schriner and Ochs 2000), and most importantly, the Americans with Disabilities Act (ADA) in 1990. Due to constraints of time and space, we will focus briefly on the legislation and implementation of the Rehabilitation Act and the ADA.

There were four major sections (501, 503, 504, and 508) to the Rehabilitation Act that prohibited discrimination on the basis of disability in programs conducted by federal agencies. The statute focused on programs receiving federal financial assistance, federal employment, the employment practices of federal contractors with contracts of more than $10,000, and electronic and information technology developed, maintained, procured, or used by the federal government. With this act, the federal government led the way by holding itself to these new standards for treating people with disabilities.

The implementation of the Rehabilitation Act in 1973 was a long-drawn-out process (Percy 1989: chaps. 4–5; Scotch 2001). Hundreds of protests over the next fifteen-plus years took up various funding and service-related causes associated with the statute (Barnartt and Scotch 2001). Protesters adopted a wide range of strategies—marches, demonstrations, rallies, takeovers, lockouts, sit-ins, chainings, vigils, chantings, strikes (hunger, rent, boycott), blockades, crawling exhibitions—at various state, federal, and local governmental agencies, public buildings, transportation facilities, and educational institutions. Some were impairment-specific protests, but others involved persons from across the disability spectrum. While most of these contentious activities were successful in terms of procuring enforcement of the Rehabilitation Act, they also gave visibility to the disability rights movement and raised awareness of the need for more sweeping legislation.

After almost twenty years, the passage of the ADA expanded the range of the Rehabilitation Act and provided a clear and comprehensive national mandate to end discrimination against people with disabilities. The statute applies to employers, services, and programs of state and local governments and impacts public accommodations, communication, and transportation providers, regardless of whether they receive or benefit from federal funding. The ADA's comprehensiveness can be seen both in its definition of disability and in the areas for which protection against discrimination is provided. Definitionally, Congress proceeded broadly, finding some 54 million Americans (one in six, according to census estimates of that time) have one or more physical or mental impairments. This was based in part on an understanding of disability as referring to anyone (a) with a physical or mental impairment that substantially limits one or more major life activities (e.g., someone in a wheelchair); (b) with a record of having such an impairment (e.g., someone whose disabling cancer is in remission); or (c) regarded as having such an impairment (e.g., a person who is HIV-positive). This broad definition was intended by Congress to include and therefore protect a large number of American citizens from discrimination.

In addition, the ADA was divided into five titles that targeted four key areas of discrimination: employment, public services, public accommodations, and telecommunications. While the ADA adopted the standards for determining employment discrimination under the Rehabilitation Act, the ADA went further to state that no covered employer shall discriminate against any qualified person with a disability in regard to all terms, conditions, or privileges of employment. A covered employer is a private employer with fifteen or more employees or a state or local government employer regardless of the number of employees. A qualified individual with a disability is one who, with or without a reasonable accommodation, can perform essential functions of the job under consideration. Discrimination in employment also includes not making reasonable accommodations to the known limitations of a qualified person with a disability, unless the employer can demonstrate that the accommodation would impose an undue hardship. While the majority of accommodations that employers make are relatively inexpensive, they do provide access for people with disabilities.

Implementation of the ADA has been arduous and contested, with some even perceiving the emergence of a "backlash against the ADA" (Krieger 2003).[10] Perhaps reacting to various public concerns bemoaning the "crisis" of the welfare state—for example, benefits are too high or are being paid to those who are undeserving (not truly disabled); there is too much fraud and not enough rehabilitation or work incentives; the "culprits" are the users and the "accomplices" are the administrators of the system (Stone 1984: 171)—the courts have applied a narrow definition of "disability" to begin with so that individuals have to show they are disabled before they can bring suit. Hence, plaintiffs have found themselves in a quandary: either claim themselves as disabled in order to qualify for coverage under the ADA but then risk the assessment that their disabilities inhibit their participation in whatever they are suing for, or insist that they are fully qualified and capable to participate in whatever they are suing for except for existing discrimination and risk their case being dismissed as unqualified for ADA coverage. Besides the legal issues, people with disabilities have had to confront the fact that lawmakers negotiated broad coverage at the expense of stronger enforcement options (e.g., plaintiffs can sue only for injunctive relief, not for monetary damages).[11]

Part of the reason for the "backlash," I suggest, is that the ADA marks a shift to a social understanding of disability that has not yet been fully embraced by those who believe disability is primarily a biological, cognitive, or individual affair (see Schriner and Scotch 2003). So long as disability is defined primarily by the medical model, it will belong in the domain of charity and services rather than that of rights. Against this view, activists and advocates are arguing that disability is politically constructed. This means that society's biases against people with disabilities are institutionally organized and legally constituted. Hence the demographics of disability—that 29 percent of disabled persons live in poverty (under $15,000 annual income), versus 10 percent of the nondisabled population; that 22 percent fail to graduate from high school, versus 9 percent of nondisabled; that only 12 percent graduate from college, versus 23 percent of nondisabled; that 28 percent cannot afford basic health care, versus 12 percent of nondisabled; that 30 percent have transportation problems (e.g., inaccessibility), versus 10 percent of nondisabled, and so on (Colker 2005: 69)—must be engaged at least on the legal and political fronts. If a people's values are enshrined in their laws, then talk about a democratic society must deconstruct laws that are discriminatory and reconstruct ones that preserve the rights of historically marginalized and oppressed persons.

Fracturing and Manufacturing Disability: The Discourses of Geography and Economics

There are two specific areas of disability law that I now want to address: accessibility and employment. With regard to issues of accessibility, the three major domains are transportation, public buildings, and housing. Each domain raises questions concerning what is called the geography of disability.

The issues of public buildings and transit are interrelated. The debates about remodeling and redesigning have always been between accessibility perspectives on the one side and cost-efficiency and budgetary constraints on the other (Katzmann 1986; Johnson and Shaw 2001). The argument remains now, as then, both that this issue involves prioritizing a society's values to include all persons and that universal accessibility benefits all people, not only a minority group of persons (Hastie 1997: 122). With the passage of the ADA, residential and private housing issues entered the discussion (Lanspery and Hyde 1997). Various housing adaptations are now available, especially in community residential homes, with individualized modifications also increasingly widespread.

The practical issues regarding accessibility are now being theorized under a geographic perspective that understands disabilities as embodied experiences, and embodied creatures (whether disabled or not) as environmentally situated.[12] Insofar as "normalcy" and "deviancy" have been architecturally, topographically, and geographically constructed (Gleeson 1999: chaps. 6–7; Anderson 2005), we need to interrogate the ableist assumptions on which they have been erected. Only in this way can we see that "western cities are characterized by a 'design apartheid' where building form and design are inscribed with the values of a society which seeks

to project and prioritize the dominant values of the 'able-bodied'"
(Imrie 1996: vii–viii). From here comes the awareness that disability is not merely an individual matter, but is a relational concept
including family, institutions, communities, political structures,
topographical spaces, and physical environments (Brandt and
Pope 1997: chap. 6; Freund 2005). While we realize that some
geographic conditions such as dry climates are beyond our control,
our built environments can and should feature flat terrains, clear
paths, ramps, adequate lighting, Braille signage, and assistive technology. If these elements are to become standard, people with disabilities should participate in the processes of designing universally
accessible devices, spaces, and environments.[13]

Related to the issue of accessibility is that of economics. Here
our focus is not only on the cost of modifications (even if that is an
important issue), but on the fact that the modern industrial city is
itself constituted by modes of economic production, and its social
spaces exclude people with disabilities (Gleeson 1999: chaps. 4–5).
In contrast, feudal and preindustrial societies were more inclusive
precisely because there was much more vocational flexibility for
people with differing abilities in close-knit communities. Industrialization during the nineteenth century, however, fractured the
communal networks that had previously served the needs of families and their disabled children (e.g., Hirst and Michael 2003). The
emergence of the factory and the new labor market resulted in
displaced occupations for people with disabilities (who could work
on farms, but could not compete in the new capitalistic environment) as well as in the rupture of their support systems (because
now their parents or guardians were at work). It is no wonder that
asylums, during this period, became "dumping grounds" for epileptics, syphilitics, comsumptives, diabetics, victims of lead poison-
ing, the malnourished, the unemployed and underemployed, the
simpleminded, and those who "failed to conform to the economic
regime of an increasingly industrialized society by participating in
the labour market" (Borsay 2005: 77, 79). In time, overpopulated
asylums became economic burdens shouldered by the emerging
welfare state.

In his book on mental deficiency and social order, Mathew
Thomson summarizes (1998: 293): "[S]ince the theory of citizenship underlying the Welfare State was premised on notions

of social responsibility, it maintained (perhaps even confirmed) mental defectives in the position of second-class citizens, and paid little attention to the special needs and rights of those who lay outside the boundaries of 'social citizenship'. From the perspective of mental deficiency, therefore, the advent of the welfare state was a mixed blessing."[14] This "mixed blessing" applied also to people with physical deficiencies. On the one hand, the welfare state provided relief for those who were unable to participate competitively in the labor market. On the other hand, "disability" came to be equated with the incapacity to be gainfully employed, and compensation laws and social status began to reflect this understanding. Hence, the welfare state became a need system for those who were categorically exempted from the labor market: people receive benefits, privileges, and exemptions if they fit the appropriate category of aged, sick, or disabled.[15] But if one was categorically disabled, then people with disabilities "had been defined, de facto, as nonworkers by disability policies that paid them for not working and explicitly declared them unable to work" (Barnartt and Scotch 2001: 28). Herein emerges a catch-22: if one tried to work, this placed one's benefits in jeopardy; yet the benefits were hardly ever sufficient for the needs of people with disabilities. Even in the present, unchecked laissez-faire capitalism exploits people with disabilities through "sheltered workshops" that pay less than minimum wages (e.g., Goodwill Industries since 1938), by having them sequestered under segregated and inhospitable working conditions, and via employment practices that grant little or no opportunity for challenge and advancement (Johnson 2006: 48–49).

One response to the "crisis" of the welfare state was aided by the deinstitutionalization movement in the 1970s and 1980s. In this case, the economy was given a boost by the emergence of the "disability business" and the "rehabilitation industry" (Albrecht 1992). The transition into residential communities meant that new systems of support networks and delivery services had to be developed. In this process, disability became a commodity that was produced, advertised, and distributed by the market system (DePoy and Gilson 2004: 46–49). This was "big business," indeed, since as of the early 1980s, 12.3 million of 22 million disabled adults were unemployed, receiving annually $70.6 billion in cash transfer payments and $114 billion in health care (this total of $184.6 billion was 6.28 percent of

GNP) (Rogers 1987: 117). People with disabilities had thus become consumers whose demand impacted the market supply, but the line between users (the disabled) and providers (the nondisabled) was reinforced. Insofar as human worth remains measured according to work in a capitalist society, those unable to contribute to the economy actively are commodified into clients and the mechanics of oppression is perpetuated (Russell 1998: pt. 2; Wilton 2006). The nonworking disabled remained unproductive (and unhappy), even as employers and taxpayers remained disgruntled.

All along, of course, there have been efforts to rehabilitate "the disabled" so they could be vocationally employed (O'Brien 2001). But what if some could not be fully rehabilitated either because of congenital impairments or because the appropriate technological aids had not yet been developed? Only in the most dire of situations such as national wars would this "industrial reserve army" comprised of marginal groups of persons be activated to perform routine jobs not regarded by the market capitalist system as deserving of the prevailing wage (Hahn 1997: 173–74). But with the emergence of the disability rights movement, the issue of vocational rehabilitation was reframed so that employment was no longer only an opportunity but actually a right for handicapped persons (Percy 1989: chap. 9).[16] In this new situation, the emphasis was placed on accessibility, supports, and reasonable accommodations.[17]

There remain, however, a number of unresolved issues. At the practical level, there are issues of accommodation costs that some claim are counterproductive to the rights of people with disabilities to employment (Weaver 1991: pt. 1). At the theoretical level, some have countered that anti-discrimination and reasonable accommodations legislation will not accomplish the needed wealth and income redistribution. At the end of his study of employment discrimination laws, University of Chicago economist Richard Epstein writes (1992: 505) of being persuaded about "the bedrock social importance of the principles of individual autonomy and freedom of association. Their negation through the modern civil rights law has led to a dangerous form of government coercion that in the end threatens to do more than strangle the operation of labor and employment markets. The modern civil rights laws are a new form of imperialism that threatens the political liberty and intellectual freedom of us all."

Any adequate response to these issues will be complex and far beyond my expertise.[18] However, two points should be noted here. First, there is the social justice argument that given the history of prejudice against "the disabled" in the workplace, antidiscrimination laws are necessary even if economically costly. Second, there are also some convincing arguments that it will be more costly for us not to work toward a fully inclusive society. If the social problems of major import for the twenty-first century are poverty, burdensome government, and the increasing number of the elderly with longer life expectancy, the single thread to dealing with all of these challenges is disability. Frank Bowe suggested (1980: ix–xi) that the cost of fully implementing a social vision inclusive of people with disabilities will be approximately $22 billion a year for about ten years; but if we don't spend this money to deal with these problems, the cost will exceed $150 billion a year in the long run. If disability is an economic construction in the sense delineated in the preceding, then perhaps it can also be reconstructed on a more just and equitable basis.

Disability and Late Modernity: Identity, Criticism, and Phenomenology of the Body

I have argued in this chapter that disability is a discursive construction of the social, cultural, political, and economic forces that constitute the modern world. At the same time, if this thesis is true, then our late modern experience can just as well transform these discourses so as to create a more just and inclusive society. Now I need to be clear that in making this argument I am neither reducing disability to any or all of these categories nor saying that the solution to disability is simply to talk differently about it. In the first place, disability is much more complex than even these four discourses can adequately comprehend, and in the second place, revisions of the medical model of disability in the direction of a phenomenological approach to the disabled body will continue to remind us not to neglect the particularity of embodied experiences that inform and shape the disability construct. My argument so far can be summarized thus: whatever else disability is, it is also the experience of discrimination, marginalization, and exclusion from the social, cultural, political, and economic domains of human life; and part of the solution to disability is to overcome the barriers to full participation in these arenas (see Bowe 1980). In part, given the development of enabling technologies (discussed in the previous chapter), even the most severely impaired individuals are now able to be included in ways that were impossible a generation ago.[19] To reimagine, reenvision, and reconstruct our lives in a way that "includes disabled people on equal terms with full participation is to envisage a society which has redefined its relationship to welfare, work and citizenship in ways that would benefit all other marginalised and oppressed groups" (Priestley 1999: 214).

In a sense, this process has been well under way over the last forty years. The preceding analyses have emerged in our late modern situation precisely because people with disabilities across the spectrum have had opportunities to be educated, to speak out, and to be heard. Their experiences, perspectives, and critical insights have illumined how the medical construct has dominated the discussion about disability and how the airing of other perspectives, including their own, is imperative for a more just and inclusive society. In other words, discourses *of* people with disabilities are now correcting and filling out (ableist) discourses *about* people with disabilities.

Disability perspectives have increasingly expanded from applied, professional, and service-related arenas into more theoretical domains. This is evidenced by the number of disability studies programs that have begun to appear across the Anglo-American academy. There are a number of noteworthy features of this new field of study.[20] First, disability is conceived of both as a subject of inquiry and as a methodology and category of critical analysis. As a subject, disability is positioned as part of the liberal arts curriculum, as an academic discipline in its own right. As a category of analysis, disability provides an epistemological, rhetorical, and methodological vantage point that is experientially grounded and that is able to inform the wide spectrum of studies in the humanities, the social sciences, and increasingly, the natural sciences. This means, second, that disability studies is intrinsically interdisciplinary, drawing as much from the fields of philosophy, literature, and women's studies as from politics, geography, and economics. Third, disability studies scholars not only seek to integrate disability into their teaching but also to conduct emancipatory criticism of the assumptions, symbolic representations, and practices of ableism in social institutions, such as church and academy. Finally, disability studies works to retrieve disability identities from the margins of society, to destabilize ableist or normative notions of social uniformity, and to champion diversity and inclusion.

One of the more specific but noteworthy projects within disability studies circles is the formulation of a new theory of aesthetics. At one level, the argument can and has been made that social movements are driven by aesthetic considerations—witness, for example, Haiselden's eugenic science and the Nazi program of euthanasia (Pernick 1997). At this level, the goal of disability studies is an aesthetic that appreciates novelty rather than normalcy, that is subversive of the dominant market and cultural conceptions of beauty, and that openly embraces the richness and diversity of human lives (Silvers 2002: 239–40; Hahn 1990). Long after minority group politics runs its course, an aesthetic that understands disability as human variation will continue to influence social attitudes and structural policies (Scotch and Schriner 1997). It is fair to say, then, that the work of disability scholarship is "to critique the politics of appearance that governs our interpretation of physical difference, to suggest that disability requires accommodation rather than compensation, and to shift our conception of disability from pathology to identity" (Thomson 1997: 137).

Clearly disability studies is a peculiar product of the postmodern (late modern) academy. But in this context, identity politics is precarious even if extolled. As philosopher Shelley Tremain notes (2001: 635), "a disabled people's movement that grounds its claims to entitlement in the identity of the subject ('people with impairments') can expect to face similar criticisms from an ever-increasing number of constituencies that feel excluded from and refuse to identify with those demands for rights and recognition; in addition, minorities internal to the movement will predictably pose challenges to it, the upshot of which are that those hegemonic descriptions eclipse their respective particularities." While Tremain's first point about external criticism is important (and we will return to it in the next chapter), her second reference to internal dissension needs to be expanded on.

In the last ten-plus years, there have been important reminders in the field of disability studies about the embodied nature of disability. These disability studies voices have advocated, variously, feminist, materialist, and phenomenological approaches to disability (see Davis 1995: 50–72; Baynton 1997; Burch 2001). While recognizing that there is a wider social context within which disabilities are constituted, and while granting the importance of disability perspectives for cultural and social criticism, there is also increasing acknowledgment that disability theory needs to account for the phenomenology of the disabled body. Simply put, there are objective aspects to the phenomenon of disability and subjective experiences of impairment that cannot be ignored (Crow 1996; Jeffreys 2002). Disability pride, for example, "is not just an attitude determined by the experience of the social forces of oppression: it is a carnal style, a way of being in the world that embodies resistance to the tyrannies of aesthetics" (Hughes and Paterson 1997: 337; cf. Paterson and Hughes 2000). Thus, there is concern that the standard distinction between impairment and disability (see pp. 58–60 above) perpetuates the perennial dualism (since Descartes) between body and mind or culture. In this case, not only is the domain of the medical model simply shifted to that of bodily impairments, but the medical model itself remains immune from social criticism in general and disability criticism more specifically.

So what we need is a new social model of impairment that neither separates body and culture nor relinquishes control of bodily impairments back to the medical sciences (again!). In this view, impairments are both biological facts and discursive products emergent from the welter of experiences negotiated by individuals even as disability is constituted both by social forces and by the vast diversity of corporeal forms. By contrast, the medical body is simultaneously individual and social, even as medical practices are corporeally and socially constituted. At the end of the day, we need both medical sociology and disability theory working collaboratively and in conjunction with other disciplines in order to engage, diagnose, treat, and emancipate the experience of disability (see Williams 1996, 1998). This collaboration is essential when we are dealing specifically with the phenomenon of intellectual disability.

Implications and Applications for Intellectual Disability

If disability is a social, cultural, political, and economic construct in the sense explicated thus far, can the same be said about intellectual disability? In asking this question, we should note that disability rights rhetoric and advocacy has, by and large, proceeded on two tracks: the more widely known and publicized disability movement involving people with physical and sensory disabilities, and the smaller and less well known groups associated with people with intellectual disabilities who "will not cease to be dependent and will never live independently" (Barnartt and Scotch 2001: 54). Further, are not intellectual disabilities such as Down Syndrome biogenetic and chromosomal conditions rather than discursive phenomena? Finally, if we were to take seriously the need to allow people with intellectual disability to represent themselves, we do not hear too much from them about their experience as being mere social constructs (Gothard 2002: 6). I want to suggest that both biomedical and social models are helpful for understanding intellectual disability today. I will prosecute this hypothesis in three steps: by discussing normalization theory, by surveying the proposals about intellectual disability as a theoretical construction, and by focusing on two sets of experiences of people with intellectual disabilities.

Intellectual Disability, Stigma, and Normalization

At a number of levels, intellectual disability can be examined from any of the perspectives previously introduced in this chapter. At the juncture of economics and geography, for example, there has been research exploring the economic structure and environmental shape of institutions and residential homes for the intellectually disabled (Laws and Radford 1998; Park and Radford 1999; Takahashi 1999). Further, historical studies have rooted contemporary legislation regarding people with intellectual disabilities in idiocy laws in colonial New England that structured the transfer of property to idiots, exonerated them from responsibility for capital crimes, and provided relief for the impoverished (Wickham 2001). At the same time, these laws also stigmatized idiocy with stereotypes that have continued to influence contemporary discussions of the rights of people with intellectual disabilities (Hudson 1988). This raises the question: how does stigma theory as presented above illuminate the experiences of people with intellectual disabilities?

One of the first to confront this question head on was anthropologist Robert Edgerton (1967). In his ethnography of forty-eight deinstitutionalized individuals in the mid-1960s, Edgerton observed that a great deal of energy was expended on "passing" as nonretarded in "normal" circles. Most of these mentally retarded individuals experienced a sense of vindication when released from the institution and preferred to explain their "hospitalization" to be the result of "nerves," mental illness, alcoholism, epilepsy, sexual delinquency, criminal offenses, physical illnesses, a need for education, or abandonment by parents or relatives (Edgerton 1967: 148–50). "Benefactors" were nonretarded individuals whom deinstitutionalized persons were reliant on for help with passing even as they attempted to demonstrate the ability to live independently. In short, the stigma of being labeled mentally retarded was an intensely motivating factor for people with intellectual disabilities (Dudley 1997).

Two questions arise in light of Edgerton's study. The methodological question is this: if Edgerton wished to allow the group of persons labeled as mentally retarded to speak for themselves (and he does), then how could he identify subjects for ethnographic observation if their own perspectives rejected that labeling? Edgerton could therefore proceed with his study only if he adopted "outsider" labeling devices that already "named" such persons as "mentally retarded" (Luckin 1986). The other set of questions concerns passing. To the extent that an intellectually disabled person succeeds in passing, he or she will end up denying him- or herself many of the benefits and supports that are available. Further, since passing is a comparative exercise, those who attempt it inevitably adopt wider social conventions about "normalcy" and perceptions about "retardation," even as they devalue and hence intensify the stigmatization of others who are less capable passers than they (Gibbons 1986). Finally, "at what point does successful passing become no longer a masquerade, but the basis of a newly authenticated self?" (Gerber 1990: 14).

These questions about passing and stigma can be further pressed by examining the "normalization" movement of the 1970s and 1980s (Flynn and Lemay 1999). Developed originally in Sweden in the 1960s by social work theorist Bengt Nirje, the normalization principle was designed to aid the transition of mentally retarded people from institutional to community life. In 1976 Nirje succinctly defined the principle as follows: "making available to all mentally retarded people patterns of life and conditions of

everyday living which are as close as possible to the regular circumstances and ways of life of society" (Nirje 1976: 231). This
included the normalization of daily, weekly, and yearly rhythms of
the life cycle from childhood through school age and adulthood,
and of economic and environmental standards. The focus was on
changing individuals as well as the environments into which they
were being integrated.

Nirje's ideas shaped and informed the work of psychologist Wolf
Wolfensberger. In the American context, Wolfensberger defined
the principle of normalization as follows: "Utilization of means
which are as culturally normative as possible, in order to establish
and/or maintain personal behaviors and characteristics which are
as culturally normative as possible" (1972: 28). Normalization was
possible even for the profoundly mentally retarded (1972: chap.
9) and could be activated through a variety of strategies: physical
therapeutics, a movement-oriented education curriculum, developmental materials and special learning environments, emphasis
on early interventions, focus on developmental role perceptions,
and sensitivity to interrelationship between various activating
measures. For Wolfensberger, "deviance" was always understood
to be an attribute of persons that lies not in them but in the eyes
of "beholders." Hence, the principle of normalization provides
the conditions that permit persons to function as normally as they
desire to, while at the same time advocating tolerance for those
who look or act differently.

A number of critical questions, however, were quickly raised
regarding the normalization principle. First, at a practical level,
what did it mean to say that people with intellectual disabilities
were leading "normal" lives? Jean Vanier, founder of L'Arche, an
international organization that establishes residential communities
for people with intellectual disabilities, made this observation:

> I met men and women with mental handicaps living in their rooms or
> individual apartments with their own television and bottles of beer!
> This was presented to me as the height of successful normalization
> and integration! They were certainly better off than the people in
> the big institutions and psychiatric hospitals . . . , but somehow life
> seemed no longer to flow in them. Shut off in their lonely rooms,
> they seemed sad and introverted, psychologically cut off from life.

... I am told that in Paris 40 per cent of people live alone. All these
people are forced to protect themselves. They have to defend themselves against all society's hostile influences. (Vanier 1997a: 177; cf.
Spink 1991: 187)

At a more theoretical level, does not normalization perpetuate
the normal-abnormal dichotomy, whereas the discourses of late
modernity have gone beyond such dualism toward an emphasis on
difference (Oliver 1999a)? Even the binary nature of retarded-non-
retarded has been exposed. Increasingly, mental retardation itself
is being recognized as a category that is heterogeneous, unstable,
and able to generate prototypes (Carlson 2003).

In part in response to some of these criticisms, Wolfensberger
developed the idea of "Social Role Valorization" (SRV), which was
based on the realization that people are devalued insofar as they
are not seen as having or fulfilling social roles. Any attempt to
revalue people, then, proceeds along two lines: first, to "reduce or
prevent the differentness or stigmata ... which may make a person
devalued in the eyes of observers," and second, "to change societal
perceptions and values in regard to a devalued person or group so
that a given characteristic or person is no longer seen as devalued"
(Wolfensberger 1983: 235). These two responses can be retheo-
rized in terms of enhancing the self-perception of "the disabled"
along with the "social image" or perceptions of others about people with disabilities, and of enhancing the "competencies" of "the
disabled." SRV is further premised on a few assumptions:

- Valued persons have more access to more of the good life,
  however this may be defined, so that improving the estimation
  of other persons' evaluation of disabled people is what enables
  the latter group of persons to access life's goods
- Negative evaluations are almost always unconscious or sub-
  conscious as opposed to positive evaluations
- Devalued persons often have hurtful experiences because of
  their being devalued
- People often are related to and evaluated according to their
  social roles rather than because of their inherent values.

Wolfensberger thus adapted the French term *valorisation sociale*
because it indicated value and worth, and unlike "normaliza-

tion," it was a technical notion devoid of meaning for most people even while carrying all the implications and inferences regarding valuation.

Still, the critical responses to SRV have been predictable. Most pointedly, SRV seems to assume a "largely homogeneous society with a set of values that are 'given.' It is difficult to see in a pluralistic and diverse society how SRV can be generalizable to all nations of the world" (Parmenter 2001: 277). Further, both normalization and SRV appear to accept social conventions of normality rather than challenge the status quo. This is problematic in our late modern situation if normality is equated with goodness, and difference is devalued (Nind 2003: 70–71). Inclusion, on the other hand, celebrates difference (rather than apologizes for it).

Intellectual Disability as a Theoretical Construct: Argument and Counterargument

There are indications, however, that our society has yet to come to terms with intellectual (and physical) difference. In this section we examine this matter by looking at the claims that mental retardation is a pejorative theoretical construct. Our question is whether these claims level out the ontological differences between retardation and nonretardation, in which case they seem to reject or deny rather than embrace difference.

It is interesting to note that there is plenty of discussion about "mental retardation" as a social construct (see Bogdan and Taylor 1992; Cocks et al. 1996; Jenkins 1998), but not about "intellectual disability" as a social construct.[21] Might this simply be a case of reacting to the prejudice and discrimination that has accumulated around the label of retardation, but not yet accrued around the newer nomenclature of intellectual disability (or cognitive, developmental, or learning disability, for that matter)? If so, then the claim about mental retardation as social construct is concerned precisely with the negative sociohistorical effects of that label, especially with how the baggage of the past might shape the future lives of persons so labeled. Let me elaborate on this claim by talking about three distinct moments of the fluid circle through which mental retardation is socially constituted.

At the first moment, an individual is identified as possibly retarded because he or she does not conform to social conventions and behaviors. At this moment, "retardation" has not yet been formally defined, and so refers not to an individual's cognitive capacities but to how he or she functions in the world, or relates to others. So individuals are picked out as different depending on their social ineptness or incompetence—e.g., not keeping up with classmates, not interacting appropriately with peers, or not holding down a job (Angrosino 1998). Cultural and social context is essential in this process. Therefore, even concepts like intelligence and autonomy are relative notions when applied in different contexts (see Gottlieb 2002a: 191–95). There are large numbers of cases (usually of those labeled mildly retarded) classified as "situational retardation" (Mercer 1973: chap. 6) wherein the "retarded" live "normally" outside institutions, either at home or in their neighborhoods, but attend schools or other organizations where they are labeled retarded and there play out those roles. In societies where classification is more ad hoc and the process less institutionalized, more opportunities are opened up for individuals with less competence to succeed. In Greece, for example, successful adults marry and have families. "It is sometimes possible for 'incompetent' people to live up to these expectations. We thus see, ironically, that in a country where formal interest in, and care of, incompetent people is minimal, incompetent people, because of local social and economic structures and a different model of competence, do have a chance to be a part of their society" (van Maastricht 1998: 152). All of this suggests that retardation is a fluid social and cultural notion rather than a biological and cognitive phenomenon, and individuals who are able to survive or even pass as nonretarded will finally escape being saddled with that label.

But once so identified, an individual enters in the second moment into an institutionalized industry that actually creates retarded identities. Through day-to-day interactions with service caregivers, medical experts, and professional assessors (occupational therapists, physiotherapists, and speech therapists, to name just a few) these persons come, inevitably, to internalize the retarded identity (Edgerton 1986; Rapley 2004). At this level, two processes are occurring simultaneously. On the one hand, the system is "producing" the "retarded" through IQ tests and other allegedly objective standards of measurement (Ryan and Thomas 1987: 21–22), and people are trained to perform according to scripts devised by the medical and health care industries, by asylums and other facilities, by funded research projects, and by the wide range of service professions, all of which have come to represent the industry of retardation over the last century.[22] On the other hand, certain beliefs and practices have been instilled through these interactive performances so that those labeled retarded come to see the world and themselves through that categorical lens. They have lost their sense of self-identity and have become devalued even in their own eyes (McCullough 1984). Theirs is the ultimate catch-22: their rejection of the retarded label is proof to others of their incapacity to understand their plight, condition, and needs, even as their accepting the label perpetuates their oppression in a society often inhospitable to people like them.

The third moment consists of selling the retarded identity back to the wider society. At this moment, the language of "mental retardation" perpetuates, even if unconsciously, mistaken stereotypes about people with retardation—for example, that they do not have a self-understanding of their circumstances; are inarticulate about their dislikes, wants, or needs; are oblivious of their stigma/label; or are lacking completely in the potential for creative expression (Lea 1988). The label now sustains and even creates new forms of oppression and marginalization and comes to represent a society's ignorance and fears about a certain group of people (Ferguson 1990) more than it is an objective description about them. Here, new understandings of language as speech-acts that are not only descriptive but also performances through which human beings get things done have illuminated how the label of mental retardation functions to structure human relationships, institutional operations, and social projects. Think, for example, about the ways in which the word "retarded" is used in daily speech: "What does she know? She's retarded"; "You're so retarded"; "I must be retarded. . . . I always burn my finger on this thing"; "Don't tell him to do that. He looks retarded when he does that" (see Danforth and Navarro 1998). These sayings call attention to how nonretarded people orient themselves to those whom they perceive as retarded (e.g., clumsy, look a certain way), and how they should posture themselves and act toward those who bear that label (e.g., because of the special treatment occasioned by the ignorance or social naiveté of "the retarded"). Once society has bought into these ideas about retardation, then they are applied to the next generation of incompetent individuals who become candidates for treatment and services.

It is precisely because we now realize the mechanisms through which "mental retardation" is socially constructed that some have called for its eradication. The weaker version of this call insists on a moratorium on the terminology and label. For those who oppose the use of this label, retardation is a myth that exists especially in our typologies (Smith 2003b: 359, 361; cf. Smith 2000). If so, then "mental retardation is an invented disease whose cure lies with those who invented it—civilization itself" (Blatt 1987: 358). To conquer retardation, then, means not ridding society of "the retarded" but ridding society of negative attitudes toward retardation; not only educating "the retarded" but educating all persons; not changing "the retarded," but changing society as a whole. The stronger version also argues for a moratorium on the language of retardation but goes further to insist on full inclusion. Those opposed are charged with being interested only in perpetuating all the oppressive -isms of our time—whether racism, classism, sexism, or now, ableism. The word "retarded" has done nothing but destroy lives, and so the first step toward rehabilitating these people and healing our societies of this ill is to do away with this human construction.

But in the end, "mental retardation" appears to have survived, even if under other constructs like intellectual disability. This is because the differences that these various labels try to name, whether phenotypical, genotypical, or behavioral, do not disappear just because we no longer name them.[23] Those working in the "harder" sciences are more apt to dismiss the social constructionist argument as flawed either because of implications regarding cultural relativism or because it cannot account for the very real cases of organic brain damage and of severe and even profound intellectual disability (see Gordon 1980a, 1980b; P. Byrne 2000: 27–34). But even educators are countering that the full inclusion posture has been turned into an ideology that not only denies real differences but also dismisses the sciences as no more than ideological constructions (see Mostert, Kauffman, and Kavale 2003). In our late modern context, differences are valued and embraced, and so people with intellectual disabilities ought to be accepted as they are rather than labeled something they are not in the interest of political correctness.

The position I wish to defend agrees with that of Robert Hayman Jr., who argues (1998: 119–22) that mental retardation is a theoretical construction reflecting social values and social practices. But, and this is important, such a view does not deny the very real differences between those with and those without intellectual disability. It acknowledges that intellectual disability is *also* a theoretical construction in terms of the prejudices against persons in that category that are embedded in our cultural systems. In the next section, I will argue this point with reference to the criminal justice system and the phenomenon of disability sports.

Reconstructing Intellectual Disability: Two Specific Domains

A number of questions arise when we consider the claim that intellectual disability is a theoretical construct in the context of the criminal justice system.[24] To begin, there is the assumption carried over from turn-of-the-twentieth-century rhetoric that lower levels of intelligence correlate with higher levels of delinquency and criminal behavior. Although this has not been borne out in the research (Menolascino 1974), people with intellectual disability still seem to be accused of criminal wrongdoing at a much higher rate than the general population. One study has shown, for example, that 12 to 13 percent of the prison population has intellectual disability versus only 2 to 3 percent of the general population (Byrnes 1999: 313).[25] Now it may be the case that people with intellectual disability are more prone to break laws, especially when they do not understand those laws to begin with. In that case, not prosecuting them would neither uphold the standard of the law nor recognize them as individuals with (in many cases) the competence to be held accountable (Byrnes 1999: 321). My point is not to absolve individuals with intellectual disability from responsibility for their actions, but to probe and assess the mechanisms of the criminal justice system with regard to such persons.

When we begin to look beneath the surface to how people with intellectual disabilities are finally imprisoned, we find justice may be lacking in the criminal justice system. This is especially clear when we review the rights that pertain to people who are accused of criminal wrongdoing: the right to informed consent;

the right to refuse treatment; the right to be free from discrimination; the right to treatment/services; the right not to incriminate oneself; the right to an adequate defense (Levy and Rubenstein 1996). With respect to these rights, people with intellectual disabilities are at a distinct disadvantage. First, there is no clear distinction made in most jurisdictions between intellectual disability and mental illness, with the latter category providing the dominant perspective on both groups of persons. Second, in many cases, a significant period of time lapses before intellectual disability is properly identified, resulting in the intellectually disabled being provided with an inadequate defense.

Third, even if a person's intellectual disability were identified early in the questioning process, most law officers are uninformed about how to interact with such people.[26] People with intellectual disability have shorter attention spans compared to the duration of most interrogations; have restricted vocabularies, impaired judgment, real memory gaps, and the inability to reason abstractly (always important in identifying cause-and-effect sequences); are incapable of clear communication either conceptually or verbally; abhor the language of "mentally retarded," so may attempt to pass as nonretarded even in the context of a criminal investigation; are very influenced by authority figures and are thereby more likely to follow the clues or cues given them; typically answer questions in ways they believe will please their interviewer/interrogator; do not understand their rights—hence do not know how what they say "may be used as evidence against them"—the meaning of court proceedings, or the concept of punishment; are quick to take the blame; are easily frightened and thus more likely to opt for short-term solutions (e.g., confess and go home) without comprehending long-term implications of their responses; and in some cases may be able to bluff greater competence than they possess. Unsurprisingly, people with intellectual disabilities make for great scapegoats, and many find themselves incarcerated, yet not because they have had a fair trial.[27]

Fourth, once imprisoned, the fate of people with intellectual disabilities often depends on chance circumstances, and most are not able to "work the system" in order to create a "good time" account. Further, they are often placed in the same institutions designed to deal with the mentally ill where the presumption is that the former are not as pliable for rehabilitation as the latter. At the end of the day, the biggest problem remains, however, that "[w]e do not know how retardation affects culpability and competency" (McAfee and Gural 1988: 11).

The most problematic issue concerns capital punishment of intellectually disabled offenders (see Perske 1991, 1995). As of the late 1990s, only twelve of thirty-eight death penalty states have laws against executing a person who is intellectually disabled (Perske 2000: 403). On the one side, the argument is that the equal rights of people with intellectual disability to independent living and entitlements goes hand in hand with their having responsibilities like everyone else. Thus, to exempt people with intellectual disabilities from capital punishment is to commit the fallacy of categorical assumptions; instead, culpability and punishment need to be determined on a case-by-case and situation-specific basis (see Calnen and Blackman 1992). On the other side, to say that people with intellectual disabilities are entitled to jobs or housing does not mean that they are entitled to any or all jobs or houses; similarly, "Just as an individual who happens to have mental retardation is not entitled to every job, that individual is not *entitled* to every criminal penalty" (Celeste 1992: 565). Further, no expert can access the mental state of persons with intellectual disability to determine his/her strengths, limitations, and so on, and hence, no adequate defense can ever be mounted on behalf of those with intellectual disability (Field 1992). Finally, the intellectually disabled should be exempted from capital punishment not because of their condition, "but because of their history of vulnerability to abuse by the criminal justice system, their exposure to harsh treatment, and a tendency to not exercise their legal rights" (Schalock 1992: 571).

This discussion establishes the following two important points in the debate about intellectual disability as a theoretical construct. On the one hand, because historical views about intellectual disability have survived to the present, knowledge that someone is intellectually disabled generally results in a prejudiced perspective against them (e.g., the presumption of guilt, even when the ability to recognize guilt may not be present). On the other hand, not knowing detainees are intellectually disabled may result in dire consequences for them. Hence, intellectual disability is *not* just a theoretical construct; rather intellectual disability is a difference that makes a difference, with (perhaps dire) implications for the fate of people with intellectual disabilities who find themselves caught up in the criminal justice system.

Turning briefly to a discussion of disability sports will also help us to identify intellectual disability as a difference that makes a difference, albeit in another key. Disability sports have become a booming industry during the last few decades (see DePauw and Gavron 1995; Paciorek and Jones 2001). For people with intellectual disabilities, the Special Olympics (S.O.) has become the primary venue of sports expression since its founding in 1962 (see Shorter 2000: chap. 5). What began as a program to deal with weight problems, poor physical development, and the lack of focused activity in institutions has evolved to such an extent that S.O. is not just about sports, but about sharing and celebrating life with others (Corman 2003). Yet, sports skills are also being cultivated. People with intellectual disability (and Down Syndrome) have engaged in alpine skiing, aquatics, badminton, basketball, bowling, cross-country skiing, cycling, equestrianism, figure skating, floor hockey, football, golf, gymnastics, powerlifting, roller skating, sailing, softball, speed skating, table tennis, team handball, tennis, and volleyball at increasing levels of skill and intensity. Given these developments, some have argued, "Athletes with Down Syndrome, when provided proper training, ample competition opportunities, and good coaching, continue to expand the limits (implying a traditional stigma) that have been associated with the disorder. In fact, no limits are appropriate at all" (Songster et al. 1997: 349).

Yet, there have been a number of criticisms of S.O. (Storey 2004). Pragmatically, there is the question of whether or not S.O. cultivates the necessary functioning skills often lacked by people with intellectual disabilities, or whether S.O. provides age-appropriate divisions for its wide range of athletes versus "infantilizing" adult athletes. Economically, does S.O. promote corporations and their public-relations projects who support/finance S.O. rather than the people it is designed to serve (witness the high financial salaries of the top S.O. executives who make upwards of $200,000 per year plus perks)? Ideologically, does S.O. foster an "us against them" attitude, since it is a segregated rather than integrated event? Is not the organization paternalistically structured from the top down (unlike Deaf Olympics or ParaOlympics, which are "governed" by the deaf and by paraplegics, respectively)? Does it not "retard" the normalization process in terms of not allowing the "dignity of risk"? And, finally, does it not promote negative media images and handicappism that is focused on disability rather than on persons?[28]

The most helpful responses to these critical questions are those that have emphasized the goal of accepting differences. This is being accomplished by including the nondisabled in the competition in an effort to promote sports partnerships, involving people with intellectual disabilities more in community-based recreation programs, offering more activities that are integrated in more localities, and expanding S.O.'s program to include lifetime leisure sports, rather than just one-day events/activities (Block and Moon 1992). The fact of the matter is that people with intellectual disabilities in general and with Down Syndrome in particular are different enough so that they cannot compete in the Olympics or other like sports events. The claim that intellectual disability is merely a theoretical construct does not do justice to these facts. At the same time, people with intellectual disabilities do compete at various levels in events like S.O. On this point, the denial that intellectual disability is in part a social construction will paralyze us from working together to create a more just and hospitable world.

In this chapter we have found that late modern discourses have indeed unveiled "disability as an unstable category" (Davis 2002: chap. 1), even as they have also shown that the ideology of ableism has constructed a prejudiced and discriminatory world hostile to the flourishing of people with disabilities. At the same time, we have discovered that intellectual disability resists being reduced to any one category of analysis, whether social, cultural, political, or economic. And we shall further expand and perhaps even complicate our analysis in the next chapter by drawing on feminist, intercultural, and comparative religious theories.

But before doing so, we must ask if the social model of disability has been any kinder to people with Down Syndrome than the medical model? To be sure, we have already noted that the social model works much more easily with physical disabilities than with intellectual disabilities. Insofar as people with intellectual disabilities do not fit as well into the social approach, to that same degree they remain marginalized, but this time by those who they thought were their coadvocates rather than their oppressors. This is not to say that the social model is to be jettisoned entirely in the remainder of our analysis. Rather, the social model, like the medical one, is an essential albeit incomplete tool for understanding people with intellectual disabilities and interacting with them. Hence, our religious and theological proposals will certainly draw from the best insights of the social model of disability, but I will also suggest that the latter needs the former to ensure the full inclusion of people with intellectual disabilities in the project of social liberation.

V

Disability in Context
Feminist, Cultural, and World Religious Perspectives

[Jennifer] is a survivor, but she is not strong. Both of us know that. What has been harder for both of us to learn is that I too am not strong. . . . As I have come to terms with these facts, I have learned to live outside of illusion of self-sufficiency and to accept help. I no longer expect reciprocity, nor do I train Jennifer for it. Real acceptance of her particular disabilities includes acceptance of an unequal, uneven relationship . . . Jennifer taught me the limits of her life—and mine.

—Hillyer 1993: 247–48

When I'm at home I do cleaning. . . . We have to keep things quiet during the Mosque prayers.

—Nadia, in Turner et al. 2004: 165

My disability is a sign of destiny. In the past, I used to climb the baobab tree to pick up some fruits and everything went fine. My disability occurred the day it should have occurred, that is on Sunday, 19th or 20th of March, 1995, when I fell off the baobab. This was the fasting period, I was not fasting and Sunday is a day for rest, I was not supposed to work. So, when I fell, I immediately knew that it was a punishment from God.

—Anonymous, in Gbodossou 1999: 76

It was at this moment I learned the message that needs to be sent to the seventh generation. It is that my disability makes me a healer.

—Cynthia Gere, in Gere and Gere 2000: 145

When Mark was born, it took him quite a while to take his first breath (even if that did not quite translate into a full newborn's cry), and so the medical staff was unsure about his health. Then later, the nurse showed Mom Mark's extra thumb and, from Mom's perspective, seemed to shove him onto her as if saying, "Here is your deformed child!" At that point, Mom's birthing experience turned from one of joy to fear. She recalled sensing and "seeing" a demonic figure in her hospital room mocking her, "Where is your God?" For the next few moments, Mom hated Mark, her eleven-fingered boy, not knowing how her Christian friends would react to her newborn baby. Then Mark was taken from her, and she was sent to the maternity ward. For the rest of that day, Mom experienced a deep pain in her heart, a longing for her newborn, and even felt a kind of numbing paralysis throughout her body. She was both traumatized by her experience—without yet knowing the full extent of Mark's "abnormality" (i.e., his Down Syndrome)—and even ashamed of it (a normal reaction within our Chinese culture of shame).

Dad came in the evening to visit and pray for Mom. After he left, she continued to pray, and then heard a voice, "Do you know who you are? You are the daughter of the King of Kings. You have the authority in Jesus' name." When the same demonic figure she had seen before reappeared, she rebuked it in Jesus' name, and found authority, relief, strength, and healing. At that moment, a divine love flooded Mom's heart for Mark. Still, for the next four days, she wondered why her baby had not been brought back to her (the medical staff said nothing to her), all the while worrying that something was desperately wrong.

If we had remained in Malaysia, I am unsure that Mark would have received the medical care, especially the heart cauterization, he needed. In that sense, I am unsure that Mark would have lived to adulthood, much less that he would have remained with us until today. Mark probably would not have been placed in school. More than likely, he would have remained in a back room of the house, the usual place for all children with intellectual and/or physical disabilities in developing countries like Malaysia. Perhaps at some point, my parents might have begun taking him to church, but this would have happened only after he reached his teen years (even after we moved to the United States, for years I stayed home on Sunday mornings to take care of Mark while my parents fulfilled their pastoral ministry at church), and there is no guarantee that Mark would have survived to that age.

Anne Gere and Cynthia Gere are both Native Americans. Anne adopted Cindy at age three, long before Cindy's diagnosis of fetal alcohol syndrome (FAS). The voice of their essay alternates between mother and daughter. Cindy ends the essay telling of how her "testimony" in Anchorage led a Native American healer to say after her talk that if he had a child with FAS, he would send the child to Cindy. The quotation above reflects Cindy's realization of a new self-identity: that of disabled healer.[1]

Cindy's story introduces us to the main themes of this chapter: women's perspectives and other cultural and religious perspectives on disability. We will take up each in order in the three sections that follow. As the pivot point of this book, this chapter is intended to accomplish the following two objectives. First, if late modernity signals the end of modernity's positivistic rationalism and opens up to the various voices of the post-Western world, then the medical, political, economic, and cultural analyses of the previous two chapters need to be themselves situated in global context. When so located, these various discourses are neither dismissible nor embraceable as wholes; rather they are complicated and transformed by the discourses of women, of postcolonial resistances, and of the various cultural and religious narratives of the East and the global South.

Second, because we have gone out of our way in the last two chapters to ensure that our theological reflections are adequately grounded in disability scholarship, we need to begin reengaging the topics of religion and theology. In particular, we are extending the cultural model of disability developed in chapter 4 in dialogue with feminist, indigenous, and world religious perspectives on disability. Further, our survey of disability in world religious context will also reconnect with the theological ideas in the history of Christian thought introduced in chapter 2, revealing continuities and discontinuities, even as it blurs the lines between premodernity and postmodernity, between East and West, and between culture and religion. Finally, when set in religious context, discussion about disability inevitably raises questions about healing and salvation, as Cindy Gere's self-reflections reveal. These are central to the project of thinking Christianly and theologically in global context, the task of part 3 of this book.

Women and Disability: Local and Global Perspectives

The experiences of women with disability have not been specifically noted thus far. In this section, we will complicate our discussion from the perspectives of women's experiences in general, especially in the West, feminist criticisms and theories of disability, and non-Western women's voices. My goal is to interrogate the preceding accounts in terms of the challenges pertinent to that half of the human race that, as we previously saw, Aristotle considered to be deformities according to the ordinary course of nature.[2]

A number of caveats, however, should be registered before proceeding. First, the following discussion is not intended to minimize the oppression and marginalization experienced by disabled men. Further, naming and identifying the oppression and marginalization of disabled women, especially in the developing world, is not meant to deny that there have been significant strides made with regard to social attitudes and practices related to women. Finally, I should also admit that my representation of the experiences of women (with and without disabilities) in the developing world is viewed through a Western lens, often through feminist perspectives, and for purposes most directly related to thinking about a theology of disability in the Western context. All of these qualifications mean that any conclusions drawn from the following discussion are tentative, limited by our methodological and perspectival approach, and subject to revision as new light illuminates the issues.

Disability in the Experiences of Women

The literature on women and disability in the West has documented a number of issues that may be specific to women.[3] In the first place, it needs to be explicitly stated that everything we have discussed thus far about the challenges encountered by people with disability are arguably multiplied in the lives of women. Women with disabilities experience a "double handicap"—on account of being a woman and then on further account of being disabled—with regard to the economic, social, and political disparities we have outlined (Schur 2004; cf. Deegan and Brooks 1985). Lower levels of education, lower employment rates, lower incomes, higher poverty rates, greater social isolation, less autonomy in decision making—these factors are aggravated in the lives of women with disabilities. Further, if media images of people with disabilities generally evoke pity or aversion, or are designed to elicit sympathy or charitable action, such images are even more damaging for women in Western culture where the ideal feminine forms are elevated as sexual objects of male desire (Hall 1992). Finally, insofar as women's disabilities are just as, if not more, apt to be hidden or invisible to the public eye—whether because of greater susceptibility to chronic illness, or other complications specific to the biological and physiological constitution of women (see Wendell 2001; Eisenberg, Sutkin, and Jansen 1984; Hey, Kiger, and Seidel 1984; Rotholz 2002)—there is the added challenge of negotiating social relationships in the public domain where individuality and autonomy are operationally assumed (see Lonsdale 1990: chap. 4). In all of these areas, disabled women's experiences of marginalization and oppression are more intensified when compared with those of men or of nondisabled women.

Second, there is the entire range of complications related to sexuality. We have already touched on issues related to the physical and sexual abuse of women, as well as on the history of enforced sterilization. Beyond these matters are also issues related to reproduction, childbearing, and parenting.[4] If "normal" childbearing is itself a strenuous and intricate process, it is much more so for women with disabilities. So if women with intellectual disabilities have been forcibly prohibited from bearing children, women with physical disabilities have not been supported in their desire to have children, have even been prevented from doing so (albeit through less forcible means than sterilization), or discriminated against during the process of childbearing. For those women who are unable to conceive or carry pregnancies to full term, there are additional challenges associated with the use of new technologies, adoption, or other parenting alternatives (Jacobsen 1999). And, of course, for those who do succeed in having children, the nature of their disabilities will additionally complicate the already difficult tasks of parenting. Without the experience of having and raising children, not only are the desires of many women unfulfilled, but according to certain traditional conceptions of womanhood as being completed by parenthood, issues of female identity are also at stake.

Third, women's perspectives on disability derive both from women with disabilities and from women as caregivers of people with disabilities. Here the issue is that a vast majority of long-term caregivers of people with disabilities are mothers, spouses, and female family members. Depending on the severity of the disability, caregiving may be a 24-hour-a-day, 365-day-a-year job. Women as caregivers experience isolation and loneliness; lack of physical support and financial resources; and resistance from the medical, educational, and social service establishments that think they know better than caregivers (Tamler 1993; Iozzio 2005a). For spouses of men who are disabled, there are additional issues connected with the presence of children in the family, respite or residential care, separation or divorce, and sex and sexuality.[5] Most importantly, women who have devoted their lives to caring for disabled family members often forgo education and in doing so are less employable and more financially dependent later in life.

Finally, specifically pertinent to women's experiences of disability are the challenges of aging. Here again, a number of issues are peculiar to women. Barbara Simon (1988: 224) notes, "The aging process creates a large caste of women into which never-married women merge after decades of social isolation." For these women, there are problems related to the provision of basic economic needs, health care, and personal quality of life (see Walsh and LeRoy 2004). The vulnerability of disabled women with regard to end-of-life stages puts them, arguably, at greater risk than men or nondisabled women in similar situations.

From the perspective of women, then, the challenges of living with disability—whether the disability belongs to themselves or to loved ones—are "doubled" in terms of the discrimination that is confronted and the hurdles that must be overcome. Of course, these difficulties regarding childbearing, parenting, and aging are vastly multiplied in the cases of women with intellectual disabilities. While "caught in a paradoxical web of good intentions" (Weinberg 1988: 287), women with intellectual disabilities are vulnerable since they are subject to the whims, expertise, and concerns of the multitude of "caregivers" (personal, social, and supportive) engaged in their lives. Their needs and desires, however, may not be much different from those of other women and hence should not be ignored. Yet attempts to factor the experiences of women with intellectual disabilities into the equation remain complicated even today.

Whereas the foregoing has been largely descriptive, in the next section, we interrogate more normative issues in dialogue with feminist philosophers who think out of their experiences with disability.[6] Certainly feminists with disabilities address the patriarchalism, misogynism, and androcentrism prevalent in most discussions of disability, even as they complicate our understanding of the medical and social models of disability. Yet, at the same time, feminists working explicitly from the standpoint of disability perspectives also raise a number of critical questions for nondisabled feminist discourse.[7] We shall see that feminists with disabilities have found their "double handicap" exacerbated by their marginalization even from their feminist colleagues who cannot (or will not) identify with the experience of disability.

Feminism and Disability

To begin with, whereas feminists have long emphasized the autonomy of women over and against the heteronomy of men, feminists with disabilities have recently begun to articulate instead a relational, interdependent, and interpersonal understanding of what it means to be human. This threatens, however, to weaken the traditional feminist cause because it tends to associate disability, illness, invalidity, weakness, and neediness with femaleness.[8] In part for this reason, "nondisabled feminists are reluctant to engage with disabled women, namely because they perceive them not as powerful, competent, and appealing females but instead as dependent, passive, and needy" (Silvers 1998: 337). Feminists with disabilities have responded by criticizing nondisabled feminists for colluding, even if unintentionally, with the patriarchal regime by pointing out that the traditional feminist platform not only continues to function oppressively for women but also perpetuates the Aristotelian assumption about the inferiority of women (see Silvers 1996). On the other side, however, overemphasis on interdependence may be counterproductive for women with disabilities insofar as they risk being reduced to being passive objects of care, are obligated to render compliant behavior in order to continue receiving care, or place themselves at the mercy of the kinds of help that caregivers are willing to give. In each of these cases, the strategy of emphasizing an ethic of care may be detrimental to the experiences of women with disabilities in terms of submitting them to the forces of oppression again. From this perspective, the way forward for women with disabilities is a fine line between an ethic of autonomy on the one side and an ethic of care on the other.

This fine line continues with regard to the question about feminist epistemology. Insofar as traditional feminist thought has long sought to legitimize itself by adopting rationalist modes of argumentation prevalent in the (male-dominated) discourse of the Western philosophical tradition, the emergence of feminists with disabilities threatens to reintroduce subjectivity, the affections, empathetic thinking, and the centrality of embodiment into the conversation. Precisely for this reason women with disabilities have therefore felt the pressure (even if unspoken) to distance themselves from these elements in order to enter into the feminist conversation. On this point, however, feminists with disabilities have sided with those working in the areas of medical sociology and the sociology of impairment (see chap. 4) and reminded their colleagues that all critical thinking is conducted by feeling bodies that are also socially and environmentally shaped.[9] In this case, recognition of the interpersonal, affective, and embodied rationality derived from the experiences of women with disabilities serves to illuminate the epistemological shortcomings of both patriarchal and nondisabled feminist thinking.

There are also concrete and practical issues at stake. With regard to sexual reproduction, whereas feminists fought for the rights of women to control their own bodies and not to be subjected to carrying unwanted pregnancies to full terms, feminists with disabilities have argued for the rights of disabled women to have babies and to be parents, even as they have argued against selective abortion solely on the criterion that the fetuses are expected to have disabilities (see Asch 1989, 2003; Asch and Fine 1988). Extended to the experience of parenting and caregiving, the emphasis on normalization has also been critiqued. In reflecting on her experience of caring for her profoundly disabled daughter, philosopher Eva

Kittay insists that the dominant "normalization" model is inadequate since this group of persons can never live independent lives. On the contrary, "normalization" discourse continues to privilege the traditional, abstract, Western model of the individual human being and, in the process, leaves the profoundly retarded on a level that is still "less than fully human" (Kittay 2002: 115). Therefore, normalization theory must be critically engaged since "'normal' women's lives are often oppressive" (Hillyer 1993: 8).

Many of these threads are woven together by Susan Wendell, a philosopher with chronic fatigue immune dysfunction syndrome, in her book *The Rejected Body: Feminist Philosophical Reflections on Disability* (1996). Wendell argues that disability emerges where individual embodied experiences intersect with social expectations and environmental constraints. Caregiving and the receiving of care are thus both materially and socially negotiated. The challenge is to recognize that interdependence—which characterizes *all* human relationships, not just those involving people with disabilities—must acknowledge the tendencies toward domination that can emerge on either side of the relationship, even as each party remains sensitive to the wants and needs of the other (caregivers have needs as well).[10]

Wendell further suggests that a feminist posture informed by disability perspectives would accentuate human variation not in terms of stigma but in terms of difference. This difference manifests itself epistemologically and ontologically.[11] The politically correct notion of "differently-abled," however, does not do justice to the special challenges many disabled persons face (Wendell 1996: 79). Rather, the difference that makes a difference involves both acceptance of human variation and a new social orientation accompanied by new social practices:

> What would it mean, then, in practice, to value disabilities as differences? It would certainly mean not assuming that every disability is a tragic loss or that everyone with a disability wants to be "cured." It would mean seeking out and respecting the knowledge and perspectives of people with disabilities. It would mean being willing to learn about and respect ways of being and forms of consciousness that are unfamiliar, and it would mean giving up the myths of control and the quest for perfection of the human body. (Wendell 1996: 84)[12]

Finally, and perhaps most importantly for our purposes, Wendell shines a critical light on current philosophical and disability reflections on embodiment. From a disability perspective, the body is paradoxically both accepted and yet rejected. There is an acceptance of its variation, of its being a site of a distinctive epistemological standpoint, and of its ontological givenness. Yet there is also a rejection of the idealizations of embodiment promoted by both male and nondisabled female discourses given the sense that the disabled body is itself reacting to and even rejecting itself. Wendell writes (1996: 93), "Until feminists criticize our own body ideals and confront the weak, suffering, and uncontrollable body in our theorizing and practice, women with disabilities and illnesses are likely to feel that we are embarrassments to feminism."

Engaging the conversation at this level leads Wendell to philosophize about the transcendence of the body. Although we begin with the suffering, limited, painful, fragile, and vulnerable body, we soon realize that paying too much attention to these aspects of the body is debilitating, and that we must learn to "free ourselves" from these experiences simply in order to pay better attention to the other demands of life. For this task, various strategies for such "disengagement" with the body are learned or cultivated, including mental adjustments, resistance to reducing the self to the miseries of embodiment, and reconstructions of the self's identity so that what emerges is "a very different sense of myself, even as I have come to identify myself less with what is occurring in my body" (1996: 175). Wendell concludes (1996: 178):

> It is because they increase the freedom of consciousness that I am drawn to calling these strategic forms of transcendence. It is because we are led to adopt them by the body's pain, discomfort, or difficulty, and because they are ways of interpreting and dealing with bodily experience, that I call them transcendence of the body. I do not think we need to subscribe to some kind of mind-body dualism to recognize that there are degrees to which consciousness and the sense of self may be tied to bodily sensations and limitations, or to see the value of practices, available to some people in some circumstances, that loosen the connection.

Disability at the Intersection of Gender and Race in the Developing World

The value of Wendell's reflections is that she explodes any simplistic idealization of the notion of embodiment. At the same time, as we saw earlier among those working toward a sociology of impairment, attempts to "transcend" the body risk subordinating the bodily aspects of the disability experience to psychological, existential, or spiritual perspectives. This tendency is disconcerting especially when discussing the experiences of women in the developing world.[13]

We will discuss disability in the Two-Thirds World more extensively in the next part of this chapter. Here, however, I want to raise questions about when gender issues intersect with issues of race and ethnicity. If women with disabilities experience a "double handicap," then do women of color with disabilities experience a "triple handicap," and do such women in the developing world experience a "quadruple handicap" of sexism, racism, classism, and ableism? Such an extrapolation seems warranted given analysts who have described disabilities in developing countries as a "third world within the Third World" (Acton 1983: 84).

The fact is that disabled women have to strive not only against patriarchal and class prejudices but also against discrimination against disabilities. They are often the poorest of the poor and the most stigmatized, marginalized, and oppressed class of persons in developing nations. There is an overall lack of health care or rehabilitation services, lack of educational and vocational training, and lack of employment opportunities (see Economic and Social Commission for Asia and the Pacific 1995; Abu-Habib 1997). Whereas disabled men in developing countries can be married off to nondisabled women, disabled women in the Two-Thirds World have no such hopes and can only pray for a cure (see Vernon 1996; Hambwalula 1999). Even if they are married, disabled women in the developing world are twice as prone to separation, divorce, and domestic violence as nondisabled women (e.g., Turmusani 2001: 75). And tragically, single disabled women, especially the visually impaired or the mildly retarded, are vulnerable to being exploited by the prostitution industry.

To be sure, these generalizations need to be qualified as women with mild or invisible disabilities may still be able to work in the fields or in factories, and, perhaps more importantly, produce babies (who are then often cared for by grandparents or extended family members). Further, those with established disabilities may bring in disability pensions that sometimes are the only source of income for poorer families. Nonetheless, the prospects for disabled women in the developing world are on the whole bleak.

Factoring in issues of race serves to complicate matters further. Here I am referring less to overt acts of racism such as hate crimes (see Davis 2002: chap. 8), and more to the subtle but very real racism that is heightened in the experiences of people with disabilities. So even when education (for example) is available, nonwhite children may either be unfairly overrepresented or underrepresented in special education. On the one hand, unsurprisingly, "beliefs in the lower abilities and problem behaviours of black children should lead to their overreferral and placement in the subsystem devised for removing from education those who are regarded as inferior and troublesome" (Tomlinson 2004: 85). This may be part of the reason that the majority of the so-called situationally retarded population—those who are identified as retarded in some social systems but not in others—are children from non-Anglo backgrounds (see Mercer 1973: 91). On the other hand, those students of color with genuine learning disabilities or with borderline retardation may either be underrepresented if there are space or other constraints in educational systems or be segregated rather than integrated with other students (see Shapiro 1996: 110).

Against this background, the plight of the girl or woman of color with disability is even more problematic. As already noted, if disabled women have not been fully embraced by the feminist community and if disabled black males experience divided loyalties in their having to choose between the camps of race or disability "in an often desperate search for solutions to their difficulties" (Hill 1994b: 161; cf. Stuart 1993), then disabled women of color are even triply divided and marginalized by men (including men of color), women's movements, and disability organizations (Hill 1994a). In this context, disabled women of color have to deal with multiple levels of oppression: existentially with regard to self-identity; materially and financially with regard to resource inaccessibility; socially and politically with regard to isolation within and even from these various communities (cf. Stuart 1992). Ironically, the groups with whom women of color with disabilities seek solidarity are those that are either not eager to include women with disabilities (in the case of feminist or civil rights groups) or unable to empathize with people of color (in the case of predominantly white disability organizations).

In global context, then, women with disabilities confront a wide range of additional challenges. Hence there is a need for a much broader set of strategies of engagement that includes meeting and then looking beyond basic needs: challenging sexism within the disability movement; "gendering" the agenda of the disability movement; investing in research and communication; mainstreaming disability in the women's movement; supporting linkages between women with and without disabilities; facilitating gender training and capacity building; and empowering women with disabilities. Against this backdrop, the analysis of disability also needs to be much more interdisciplinary, even as the assessment of advocacy goals needs to be more sophisticated in terms of being able to engage these multiple realities and concerns.

When the issues are set in this wider framework, feminist scholars have begun to suggest that one way forward for disability studies is collaboration with postcolonial theory. When engaged with the concerns of the developing world, the postcolonial is both "after" the colonial (in the chronological sense) in terms of the post-World War II independence movement, even while "resisting" the colonial insofar as the legacy of colonialism (Eurocentrism, androcentrism, and modernist rationalism) still remains with us. What is attractive about postcolonial perspectives is their explicit attention to notions of hybridity that define identity not in essentialist terms, but as dynamic, interpersonal, and intersubjective processes negotiated out of the nexus of economic, political, racial/ethnic, and gendered interactions. The postcolonial is thereby an interstitial, liminal, and intersubjective space that accommodates and even celebrates the bodies and identities that have not fit into modernity's straitjacket. In the late modern context, because disability is fully identifiable neither on the terms of the medical establishment nor on the terms of social models and theories, it is a prime conversation partner for postcolonial theorizing. Ato Quayson suggests

(2003: 109), "[P]ostcolonial histories are the expressions of radical contingency, especially when these histories are 'littered with disembodied parts' as is the case in various African countries torn by present and past wars." In such a postcolonial and late modern world, civil reconstruction intersects with peace and justice concerns, globalizing economies, development strategies, and the variations of bodily impairment and disability.

But even more pertinent for us is that the postcolonial hybrid invites religion back into the conversation. As Sharon Betcher puts it (2001: 347): "Hybridity avoids the politics of apocalypse between the one and the 'other,' while creating a positive subjective location for cross-cultural, 'inalienably mixed' persons. . . . Repenting of religious holism, and therefore the idolatry of the normate, might allow the growth of a spirituality that respects finitude, the limits of bodies, and the heterogeneous communities of nature—a spirituality that tolerates uncertainty, indeterminacy, contingency, and ambiguity" (cf. Boyce and Weera 1999). Perhaps postcolonial theories of disability will open up a "third space" beyond ability and disability, a hybrid identity and location that is able to speak authoritatively between, around, and even beyond ableism and disablement (see Wilson and Lewiecki-Wilson 2002).

Disability, Development, and World Cultures

Before responding more intentionally to Betcher's invitation to religious studies to reengage the conversation, I want to focus more explicitly on disability in the world cultural context.[14] Our movement here will be from feminist and women's concerns in global context to a more general discussion of disability issues in the developing world. My goal is to fill in some of the details introduced in the preceding discussion in order to delineate more explicitly the global context for the discussion about disability in the world's religious traditions. In this section, then, we will discuss in order disability in general, and intellectual disability in particular, in the developing world before turning more specifically to a case study of the situation in India.[15]

Disability, Development, and Indigenous Cultures

Demographers estimate that upwards of 80 percent of people with disabilities worldwide live in developing countries (Fuller 2006:

386).[16] Disability workers in the global context are dealing with all of the issues already mentioned, albeit with the additional burdens of inadequate health care and medical supplies; dated technological supports; lack of educational, rehabilitational, and vocational services; inaccessible resources; and prejudicial social attitudes. In part because of underdevelopment, people in especially the Two-Thirds World are more vulnerable to disabling accidents and diseases, and to disabilities related to poverty, lack of nutrition, and environmental factors (Doyal 1983). In many cases, disability issues take a back seat to the quest for survival and meeting the basic needs of the household or community.

However, there are also some issues specifically related to the experience of disability in non-Western cultural contexts (see Holzer, Vreede, and Weigt 1999). In the first place, especially in underdeveloped areas, social relations are structured not by the market economy but by reciprocity and patron-client networks. In these basically premodern socioeconomic contexts, people with disabilities (except for the severely disabled who often do not survive the childhood years) generally fit a role somewhere in the social order. So rather than modernity bringing about technological advancements and the betterment of the situation of "the disabled," its individualism and capitalism (focus on profit and achievement) undercut the premodern social structure and undermine the sense of well-being based on family, clan, and communal relations (see pp. 96–97 above). Arguably, these rural environments are more inclusive and hospitable to people with disabilities before rather than after the onset of industrialization and modernization. One might say that there is a need for "integration" and "inclusion" in late modern societies precisely because modernity has ruptured social cohesiveness and segregated people with disabilities from their communities to begin with.

Also important and related to the preceding, indigenous societies less touched by modernity have retained social and environmental understandings of human identity, but these are slowly being replaced via the forces of globalization by individualistic or dualistic notions of the self as separated from others or from the natural world. Yet indigenous worldviews that are embedded in social practices have major implications not only for understandings about selfhood and community, but also for defining health, disease, and wholeness. Put bluntly, medical views of sickness and disability are interwoven with and oftentimes subordinated under social practices and cosmological assumptions about the way the world is and works. "Premodern" cosmologies, for example, might assume that disabilities are the result of parental or individual sins (from a previous life), astrological misfortune or other supernatural causes, or contamination through prolonged exposure of the pregnant mother to other disabled persons (Nicholls 1993; Saul and Phillips 1999). Often there persists in the background beliefs that disability is linked to witchcraft, the sorrow or anger of ancestors, broken religious taboos and laws related to pollution, or the will of God (Ingstad 1997: 85–97; note the anonymous author's self-understanding cited in the third introductory quotation to this chapter). This explains, at least in part, why immigrants from the developing world not only lose their social networks of support, but have a difficult time adjusting to the medical model of health care and disability that dominates the Euro-American West. One case in point was the epileptic Hmong girl in a northern California hospital system whose parents disagreed fiercely with the medical community about diagnosis (soul loss, possibly leading to vocational shamanism, versus physiological epilepsy) and treatment (folk remedies such as pig sacrifices versus Western medication) of their child. The reporter observed: "It was also true that if the Lees were still in Laos, Lia would probably have died before she was out of her infancy, from a prolonged bout of untreated status epilepticus. American medicine had both preserved her life and compromised it" (Fadiman 1997: 258).

Hence, in global context it is important to pay careful attention to the cultural, economic, and social backgrounds that inform views about disability. On the one hand, in rural and underdeveloped areas people with less severe disabilities may be quite "integrated" into their communities, having not yet been segregated by the forces of modernity. On the other hand, the more seriously disabled may be "hidden" away in the homes of parents or guardians. Even here, these cases may reveal, on closer examination, not neglect of such individuals but rather a carefully structured support system for them and their families. Inevitably, the hardships of the individual with disabilities are interconnected with the general

hardships that confront all household members because of challenging economic and social circumstances (see Ingstad 1995).

Things are just as complex in more urbanized areas. Here, the
complications are due not least to the fact that many countries have
modernized cities that practically sit adjacent to undeveloped vil-
lages without clean running water. As a result, there is a great deal
of unevenness in the urban South with regard to the diverse views,
services, and structures, even in single metropolitan areas, related
to disability. In a country like Malaysia, for example, one might find
in the urban centers both charity-care organizations and self-help
organizations (see Jayasooria 2000). The former would emphasize
residential care and sheltered workshops and be less engaged in
advocacy issues as an organization "for" people with disabilities,
while the latter would focus on community-based independent living and on providing grants and training opportunities to integrate people with disabilities into the broader economy and be
quite engaged in advocacy, often involving people with disabilities
themselves. Yet, the lines between such organizations are rarely
hard and fast, and they still serve or work with only a minority of
the disabled population.

The point to be made before moving on is that situating disability in global context requires careful consideration of cultural,
contextual, and developmental factors alongside analyses derived
from medical, sociopolitical, economic, and women's perspectives.
This is no less the case when we consider intellectual disability in
world context.

Intellectual Disability in Global Context

Much of the preceding general discussion about disability in world
context applies when considering the case of intellectual disability more specifically. Etiologies of intellectual disability continue
to include supernatural agents, witchcraft, punishment for parental sins or for the sins of a previous life, and even (as we saw in
chap. 2) frightening experiences during pregnancy (de Jongh 1996:
chap. 3).[17] For many in the developing world, "there is no distinct differentiation between religious, cosmic (fate) and magic
explanations" (Stahl 1997: 365). Further, studies confirm that mild
intellectual disability is less of a barrier to full participation in rural

communities when compared to more complex and technologically advanced urban regions in the Two-Thirds World (see Robinson 1978). Finally, even in the Euro-American West, non-Anglo cultural practices reveal, upon close examination, that different networks of support are operative around the families with intellectually disabled children. For example, single mothers raising intellectually disabled children, while stereotypically viewed negatively by whites, actually illuminate the vibrancy of the extended and church family in action in the African American and Latino American communities (Glidden, Rogers-Dulan, and Hill 1999: 282–83).

A number of issues, however, deserve more specific treatment when discussing intellectual disability in world context. The earliest research on intellectual disability in the non-Western world focused on identifying or labeling intellectual disability. In an essay published in 1970, Robert B. Edgerton observed that while few of the severely mentally disabled in non-Western contexts survived either birth or childhood, the mildly retarded were less stigmatized and generally not considered to be social problems. Yet it was precisely among this population that a variety of sociocultural factors were at work to "produce" the mentally retarded, such as social functionality or lack thereof (usually determined through caretakers, guardians, etc.), or incompetence in contracted relationships like marriage (those unable to contract or maintain marriages being more likely to be deemed and labeled as retarded). Edgerton concluded that "[m]ild mental retardation, in particular, is typically seen as being fundamentally social and cultural in every respect, and it is equally widely agreed that even severe and profound mental retardation cannot be understood, much less responded to effectively, without knowledge of the social and cultural system in which it occurs" (Edgerton 1970: 524).

Case studies have confirmed Edgerton's thesis at a number of levels. In his study of Inuit culture in northwest Greenland, Mark Nuttall (1998) documents that indigenous notions of intellectual competence have been challenged by the ideas and practices of encroaching (primarily Danish) settlers. "Outsider" perspectives on social and mental incompetence produced labels for the "retarded" that not only failed to take into account local definitions, explanations, and treatments, but also disrupted indigenous communal networks, and affected local models of personal and social identity. Hence, medical approaches to intellectual disability undermine both the social support systems already in place and the full humanity of people with intellectual disability in Inuit communities. As Nuttall notes (1998: 177):

> Being categorized as intellectually incompetent or as mentally ill by those in authority, and then being subjected to treatment or a special education outside the village, separates a person from a vital network of social, psychological and emotional support and places strain on indigenous models of personhood and humanity. . . . People who would ordinarily care for relatives who have been sent away from the village are themselves left feeling incompetent because their knowledge and abilities to care have been challenged and eroded.

This disconnect between medical accounts of intellectual disability and indigenous communal notions of social competence is seen also in cases where people are not labeled "retarded" until after their immigration to the West.[18] Even if normalization is an absolute concept, its application is, arguably, culturally relative: "Treat all people in the way that is customary to value people in the culture" (Piachaud 1994: 392).

The difficulty of applying this principle consistently across the world can be seen when we examine the case of a modernizing nation like China. In a fairly recent study, Frank Dikötter (1998) observes that the practices of sterilization, abortion, and eugenics in that country need to be interpreted against the backdrop of Chinese social and political history rather than according to Euro-American standards. In China's context, its historically eugenic practices are motivated less by ideas of hereditary causation and more by holistic notions of what it means to be human (which connect individual embodiment, social relations, environmental rootedness, and transgenerational relatives). Hence, "Eugenics was not so much a clear set of scientific principles as a modern way of talking about social problems in biologising terms" (1998: 4). Further, there exists a long tradition of political conservatism in China that even as recently as the late 1980s enacted laws prohibiting intellectually disabled people from having children. Yet such legislation has to be understood in the context of wider legal, economic, and political measures taken to control the population as a whole (1998: 172–73). Developments throughout the twentieth century, however, reveal that the Chinese understanding of intellectual disability has continued to shift under the impact of medical and scientific discoveries. Whereas earlier theories identified mental retardation as derived from such causal mechanisms as conception while under the influence of alcohol or cigarettes (1998: 45), these ideas are no longer very popular in the urban regions of China today. Still, China lags behind Anglo-American policies for welfare services and special education, although great strides have been made since the late 1980s (Altman and Li 1997; Kohrman 2005).

Finally, the issue of cultural deprivation needs to be lifted up in any discussion of intellectual disability in global context. There is widespread agreement that there was and remains a correlation between poverty and organic impairment, and that economic deprivation is liable to affect intellectual performance negatively.[19] Poverty remains, of course, one of the most ineradicable features of the global South. The risk factors related to the prevalence of intellectual disability are exacerbated by inadequate perinatal and neonatal care, nutritional deficiencies, infectious diseases, and environmental toxins or radiation (Durken 2002). For those who survive birth, impoverishment means that the intellectually disabled are less likely to reach adulthood, receive special schooling, and have access to adequate health care, vocational training programs, or other support services essential for adult life (McConkey 1996). The question of education and training is especially pressing, both because they are inaccessible even to people without disabilities and because many in the developing world assume that disabled children need care rather than education (Fraser 1988: 353). If the statistics are true that sociocultural and economic conditions account for up to 75 percent of the intellectually disabled population in the developing world (Bijou 1985: 53), then medical models of disability are all the more in need of critique from social, cultural, and economic approaches.

In sum, intellectual disability in world context invites multiple levels of analysis and response. At one level, service efforts should include the family, clan, and communal networks and resources available in local contexts (McConkey 2002). Yet, at another level, national policies need to be revised, and early intervention, accessible education, and employment support strategies informed by but not mimicking Western models also need to be implemented. Finally, our approaches to working with people with intellectual disabilities and their families will need to at least take into account if not combine with more traditional (indigenous and even religiously based) methods (Fraser 1988: 369). Such combinations are observed, for example, in developing nations like India.

Disability in India: A Case Study

As of the early 1980s, estimates put the number of intellectually disabled persons in India at more than 22 million (Prabhu 1983: 1).[20] In the Indian subcontinent, sociocultural deprivation appears to be one of the major culprits with regard to mild intellectual disability as it includes "many social evils like casteism, prejudice and discrimination, poverty, poor nutrition, inadequate health services, inferior education, and unemployment" (Sen and Sen 1984: 5). Aggravating factors on the Indian household scene include cramped living conditions caused by overcrowding of extended family, underachieving siblings and other related children, minimal mother-child relationship and interactions, parental behavior related to the low intellectual status, lack of adult aspirations for themselves and for their children, and a bare or unstimulating learning environment. All of these combine to depress rather than pique the curiosity of children during their formative years (Sen 1982: 55–62; Sen 1992: chap. 1). Many of these elements are outgrowths of the problem of caste, which affects intellectual disability not only in terms of the poverty and poor health it perpetuates but also in terms of the lack of material-ideological-cultural capital needed to stimulate cognition (Das, Jachuck, and Panda 1970). Further, even if people with intellectual disabilities find menial jobs, they are still stigmatized for their incompetence. Given that the empirical research seems to confirm the relationship between these "retarding" factors and the "plight" or condition of the intellectually disabled, especially in rural India, preventive strategies include the following large-scale initiatives: educating about consanguinity; helping ensure older women avoid late pregnancies; making accessible proper health care, nutrition, and immunization programs; avoiding or controlling obstetric complications;

meeting needs related to stimulus deprivation; enabling socioeconomic changes in families and communities; improving ecological environments; managing, training, and rehabilitating people with intellectual disabilities; and overturning the caste system (Sen 1988: 230–46).

Feminists have provided further critical analyses of disability in the Indian context. Anita Ghai notes (2002: 53) that "[i]n a culture where being a daughter is considered a curse, being a disabled daughter is a fate worse than death." Not surprisingly, prenatal screening has not only led to a declining birthrate for females but also stacked the odds against "imperfect" girls being carried to full term. Even if disabled girls survive childbirth and childhood, they are denied fulfilling their female roles and achieving their female identity since marriage and motherhood, much less employment, are not options for such "damaged" goods. Further, the stigma of disability attaches itself also to the mothers of disabled children who are divorced, abandoned, or even tortured for birthing such children (Ghai 2002: 62; 2003: 73–79). Ghai concludes: "I am absolutely convinced that disability in India is not a singular marker, as it is embedded within a matrix of poverty, caste politics, class struggles, types of impairments and above all patriarchy" (2003: 163).

This should caution us against merely transposing Western constructs of disability uncritically into the Indian context. Scholars like Ghai therefore advocate instead a postcolonial analysis of disability that takes into account the dominant cultural and religious narratives in Hindu India (Ghai 1999, 2001). To be sure, the meaning of disability in India is often understood in terms of "lack" or "flaw" as seen in the dethronement of King Dhritrashtra in the *Mahabharata* because of his visual impairment, or as associated with deceit, mischief, and evil as in the *Mahabharata* and *Ramayana* epics where "the central twist comes with the interventions of an orthopaedically impaired man and a dwarf woman" (Ghai 2001: 27). Further, there is the inviolable law of karma, which rigidly links disability to immorality or other misdeeds of past lives: "because of the particular effects of their past action, men who are despised by good people are born idiotic, mute, blind, deaf, and deformed" (*Manusmrti* 11:53, quoted in Leslie 1999: 35). Finally, there is also the Indian parallel to the Aristotelian idea about the inferiority of women. Manthara, a hunchbacked woman in the *Ramayana*, shoulders the blame for the upheaval of the kingdom since "her physical body betrays her guilt. For the physical body is not simply a reward or punishment for the accumulated effect of past merits and demerits; it precisely manifests the condition of the mind and nature within. The female body demonstrates that Manthara has attained a less advanced spiritual state than her male counterpart; the disabled body by definition contains a defective personality" (Leslie 1999: 35–36). Fundamentalist Christians might naively accept these connections between heathenism and disability given the prevalence of crippled and deformed beggars dotting Calcutta and other major urban areas in the Indian subcontinent (Miles 2002a: 23).

Yet, as with the biblical canon, there are also more positive themes regarding disability in the religious literature of India (Miles 1997, 1999c, 2002e). These include rituals and pedagogies of inclusion, informal and formal service traditions, "success stories" of disabled persons, and identification of some disabled individuals as children of God. Additionally, there were renowned scholars like Ashtavaraka, who had eight deformities, and poets like Surdas, who was blind. These were inspirations to the masses, strengthening them in adversity and enabling their resistance against oppression. Hence Indians can certainly "go west" and learn the "trade" of disability services, but when they return to India to implement these services, South Asian resources are needed in order to provide religious and cultural legitimation for these new sensibilities and practices. As M. Miles suggests (1999b: 251): "Unless they have integrated the conceptually foreign material with their own practice, concepts and culture, they are likely to find great difficulty either passing on a coherent message to the next generation of trainee professionals, or acting as competent guides or partners with disabled people or parents of disabled children."

Yet such integration serves not only Indians with disabilities but also other people with disabilities who are engaged with the religious traditions of India (see Nosek 1995). The application of yogic meditation in the lives of people with intellectual disability exemplifies the benefits derived from distinctively Indian and Hindu resources (Kent 1985). The argument is that yoga helps people with intellectual disabilities to coordinate the activities of their minds and bodies, reduce distracted states of mind, and achieve higher levels of daily activity (Vijay Human Services 1988: 4). Researchers suggest that "[w]ith longer practice of a few years, the spiritual leaning of the individuals take [sic] on a definitely deeper purpose and significance as the personality of the individual changes into a more self-confident and mature one. In short, Yoga is nothing more than a system of self culture which unfolds the best and highest potentiality of every practitioner, whether he be normal, sub-normal or abnormally gifted" (Poovadan 1975: 79). When yogic meditation does not displace but works alongside other medical, educational, econo-political, and sociocultural approaches, what emerges is a sophisticated set of practices that demonstrates the plausibility of religious perspectives on disability in a late modern world and provides a holistic mode of engaging the challenges of disability by addressing human minds and bodies within their wider environmental contexts.

Disability and the World Religions: A Brief Survey

One of the ideas that has emerged in this chapter thus far is that disability in world context is best understood and engaged when indigenous, cultural, and religious factors are taken into consideration. Since up to 70 percent of all people with disability worldwide live in regions where the Judeo-Christian worldview is only very marginally represented, if at all (Miles 2002b: 54), it is incumbent on any theology of disability to at least understand the basic ideas associated with disability in the world's religious traditions. Further, from a more strictly theological perspective, Christian theology in the twenty-first century should not be done in isolation from or neglect of other faiths (see Yong 2003a, 2005a: chap. 6). In the following, we sketch very briefly some traditional and more recent notions of disability in Judaism, Islam, and Buddhism. At the same time, readers should be warned of the impossibility of generalizing about any religion's views of disability as if such were homogeneous throughout that tradition (Miles 1999a: 50). Our goal is not comprehensiveness, but to get a very cursory sense of ideas and even resources from other world religious traditions for our project in part 3 of this book.

Judaism and Disability

Since we have already surveyed some of the Hebrew Bible's references to disability in chapter 2, our focus here will be on Jewish beliefs and practices regarding disability in general and intellectual disability in particular in the Christian era. We focus on the most comprehensive study to date, Tzvi C. Marx's *Disability in Jewish Law* (2002).

An ordained rabbi, Marx seeks to bring all sides of the Talmudic discussion to the table so as to develop a constructive halakic theology of ability. A number of points deserve mention. First, note Marx's claim that "the Jewish religion sees God as shaping an elect nation out of crippled and traumatized slaves" (2002: 15).[21] Second, while acknowledging that Maimonides and other Jewish scholars identified the image of God with the cognitive faculty and with speech, Isaiah 55:8—"For my thoughts are not your thoughts, nor are your ways my ways, says the LORD"—requires a more holistic and relational notion of the image of God that recognizes human beings called to be in God's presence as a relational other (2002: 23–24). Third, "The concept of interdependence means that every individual Jew acts as a guarantor for every other Jew's fulfillment of his covenantal obligations. . . . Bolstering the disabled individual's freedom to take responsibility is a way of giving him dignity in a culture where dignity is a function of this capacity" (2002: 43, 47). Fourth, acts of charity are an emulation of God that allow people to encounter and meet each other's needs. Precisely for that reason, "[t]he laws of charity suggest provisions to prevent the erosion of autonomy despite the dependence inherent in disability" (2002: 79).

Fifth, the liturgy functions variously to promote sensitivity to people with disabilities, as an occasion for thanksgiving, and to provide the opportunity for benedictions and blessings in response to the novelty and diversity of the creation of God (Marx 2002: 89–91). Now a distinction is certainly made between those with congenital disabilities (in which case, God is blessed as the creator of difference) and those whose disabilities emerged later in life (in which case, God is blessed as a righteous judge) (Astor 1985: 1). Yet (for example), the blind bless God for creating the luminaries of the heavens since even if they do not directly benefit from its lights, they benefit from others who are now able to see and also help them because of the light (Levin 1987: 126–27).

Sixth, Marx does tackle the question of whether or not people with disabilities can lead the religious liturgy. One of the criteria is that leadership possibilities for people with disabilities depends on how learned the congregation is, since their prevailing uninformed attitudes (prejudice) might hinder the participation of an individual with a disability when the law itself may allow it. Hence, there is always the need to educate the congregation (Marx 2002: 187–88). Yet there is also the aesthetic criterion: "There is a dimension of collective religious drama in which aesthetic considerations are weighty, transcending even the desideratum of maximizing the covenantal participation of the disabled by enabling them to take on the fullest possible halakically-sanctioned religious commitment" (2002: 174). Application of these various criteria has resulted, historically, in four interpretive stances of halakic law regarding the participation of people with disabilities: global exemption (which still does not place the disabled Jew outside the bounds of the covenant relationship); disqualification in specific cases; empowerment for select observances; and ambiguity in specific laws. The last category is growing given that the functional abilities of people with disabilities continue to increase with modern technology.

Marx does discuss the deaf-mute, the child who is not yet of the age of responsibility (usually six years old), and the mentally incompetent (*shoteh*), all of whom are treated together in the halakah (cf. Merrick, Gabbay, and Lifshitz 2001). I wish to pause for a moment on the question of whether or not such individuals are legally obligated to fulfill either religious or civil laws. The problem is that the lack of mental understanding (*da'at*) seems to exempt individuals from observing the law but that such exemption may relegate such a person to noncovenantal status in the case of religious obligations or may render him or her as socially or ritually invisible—"betwixt and between full personhood and nonpersonhood" (Abrams 1998: 128)—in the case of civil responsibilities. Insofar as a *shoteh* involves "a person who is profoundly mentally ill, for example, schizophrenic, or a person who is mentally disabled, for example, of extremely low intelligence" (Abrams 1998: 139), he or she was "repeatedly referred to as one who is free from the commandments and any punishment, whose purchasing is invalid and whose selling is invalid" (see Astor 1985: 61). Further, the *shoteh* could not recite the Torah; was cautioned against conducting ritual slaughtering as that demanded some technical competence; and could not own property, receive gifts or inheritances, be legal party to sales, or present legal testimony. Interestingly, the *shoteh* could marry even if such marriages could not be legalized by the rabbis (Astor 1985: 62–92).

The halakah also said that children with a mental age of at least six years (*da'at k'pe'utot*) were obligated to obey the law even if they did not understand it (Lifshitz and Glaubman 2002: 407). This interpretation motivated a rereading of the references to *shoteh* in the twelfth century through which widespread agreement was reached that the word was of functional rather than etiological import. This meant that each *shoteh* ought to be examined on a case-by-case basis so that his or her functionality could be determined (Lifshitz and Merrick 2001). People with intellectual disability may or may not be exempted from mitzvoth, depending on the severity of their disability; but exemption does not mean rejection from the community. Rather, the *shoteh* could be included in the community apart from keeping mitzvoth so long as they were accommodated to the level of their capacities.

Overall, Marx notes that halakic conservatism is important insofar as it cautions against rash transformation of Jewish culture. When care is taken to consult the tradition thoroughly, we can proceed inclusively to heed the spirit of the law so long as we are not violating the obvious letter of the law. But there is some elasticity within the halakah that reflects a dialectical tension between compassion and pragmatism, between ideal caring and realistic restraint. If being a Jew means not to suffer under the burden of the law, then "the obligation to observe the precepts is . . . an empowering privilege" (2002: 243). So while people with disabilities in general and the *shoteh* in particular are to be empowered to obey the precepts if possible, their dignity, ease, and comfort is to be respected.[22] In the end, the law is for the "healing of the world" (*tikun olam*—Deut 30:11-12), which begins for disabled people with overcoming stereotyped prejudices and promoting accessibility of services and resources (Marx 2002: 245–48).

Islam and Disability

Like Judaism, Islam also has an authoritative scriptural text (the Qur'an) and a weighty supportive tradition (the hadith, or sayings of Muhammad, and sharia, or code of Islamic law). Like in the Hebrew Bible, there are relatively few direct references in the Qur'an and Islamic sources to disabilities. But there exists some use of disabilities as metaphors for spiritual deficiencies, as well as other provisions to ensure "the disabled" are adequately protected and cared for (Miles 2002c). What may be distinctive to Muslim beliefs and practices, however, stems from the fact that, at least during the first millennium of the tradition, disability was caused primarily by wars (including religious wars) and the Islamic practice of corporal punishment for such violations as theft (cf. sura 5:38), marital infidelity, bearing false witness, drunkenness, and infliction of bodily injury (retaliation would be enacted for example, only if the perfect equality of an eye for eye could be achieved, and no satisfactory indemnification agreement could be worked out) (Haj 1970: chaps. 3–4). If the worst disability was understood to be disbelief in Allah,[23] it both justified religious wars against heretics on the one hand and the corporal punishment of deeds done against the will of Allah on the other. At the same time, given Allah's sovereign rule over the world, there is emphasis on the goodness of Allah's creation, recognition of Allah's wisdom in creating disabilities, confession of Allah's merciful kindness, and acknowledgment of Allah's admonishing the nondisabled to accommodate "the disabled" in their midst.

This range of understandings about disability can be seen in the different views regarding blindness in the Mamlūk period of medieval Islam (Malti-Douglas 1989). Various Arabic words for blindness denoted a physical defect, a congenital condition, blindness due to injury, or having one's sight being covered. As in the Western philosophical tradition, there was also the connection between blindness and women, the blind male considered in some circles to be inferior and of lower ontological rank. However, as women were often associated with physicality and sexuality, so also were blind males (there are very few accounts of blind females or disabled females in the literature) compensated with sexual virility. Further, there were debates about whether or not a blind person—such as the patriarch Joseph (cf. sura 12:84)—could still be a prophet or be used as a prophet. In any case, given the predominance of orality throughout the medieval Islamic period, the blind were often reciters of the Qur'an. Because the deaf were often mute, blind persons were "superior" to the deaf or other handicapped persons since the blind could still hear and recite the words of the Muslim holy book. Their services in these and other areas of Islamic life resulted in one massive chronicle of more than three hundred biographies of blind persons, mostly of more elite rank, by Mamlūk official Khalil ibn Aybak al-Safadi (d. 764/1362). Anecdotal evidence—for example, "Some said to Bashshār ibn Burd: 'God has never removed the two eyes of a believer without substituting some good for them. So with what did He compensate you?' So Bashshār replied: 'With not having to see disagreeable people like you'"; and in response to why he (presumably) as a blind person was carrying a lamp at night: "O busybody! I carry it with me for the blind at heart like you to be guided by it so they do not stumble upon me and make me fall and break my jaw" (Malti-Douglas 1989: 231)—suggests how the blind "reverses this relationship of normality/marginality and superiority/inferiority by casting the sighted person into the marginal, inferior category" (Malti-Douglas 1989: 232). The experience of blindness in medieval Islam turns out to be much richer and more complex than one would expect.

This variation of Islamic beliefs and practices regarding disability no doubt reflected the range of the Islamic theological framework. Within the canon of scriptural text, hadith, and legal code, disabilities served a wide range of functions: to expiate sins; to purify believers prior to the day of judgment; to illuminate Allah's love for the believer; to be a sign of faith, or to serve as a sign of righteousness; to be a means of punishment, or of multiplying rewards to believers who display contentment; and to enable the able-bodied to be thankful, and to appreciate Allah's power to determine the welfare of all people, including those with disabilities (see Al-Jibāli 1998: 102–6).[24] Some have therefore concluded that the Muslim stance toward disability is conflicted "because of the ambivalence of the Qur'an which sometimes emphasises the equal treatment of disabled people and at other times associated them with the wicked of the society" (Turmusani 2003: 58). Others

have argued that the contemporary (modern) notion of "disability" is not found in the Qur'an, and that most of the references to
disabling conditions (impairments) are viewed in morally neutral
terms, being neither blessed nor cursed, but with the full potential
for inclusion so long as the limitations of different abilities are kept
in mind (Bazna and Hatab 2005: 23–24).

With regard to people with intellectual disabilities, Arabic culture regarded them on the one hand "as those whose minds were
in heaven, and were considered special favourites in Paradise," and
on the other hand as "something shameful, an ordeal to be endured
by the family that has in its midst a disabled person" (Turmusani
2003: 49). There is also present an Augustinian-like emphasis on
disability as an expression of divine freedom to create diversity, so
also is disability not to be hidden; rather, "let others see him so
as to thank Allah for his favors and take lesson from His creating
people of varying levels of health and perfection" (Al-Jibālī 1998:
132). Further, the Qur'an specifically instructs that they be treated
equitably in legal transactions (2:282, 24:61), and that they be fed,
clothed, cared for, and spoken kindly to (4:5).[25] As in Jewish tradition, Islamic prescriptions for people with intellectual disabilities
focused on the legal and religious criteria for male ownership and
disposal of property (Miles 1992: 240–42). According to Islamic
jurisprudence, people with disabilities "are diagnosed as being such
by experts, and whenever a person is found to be disabled he is
not responsible for his speech and action. According to Islam, the
intellectually disabled are eligible for marriage and heritage, but
his behavior and decision-making is to be supervised by his guardian. The father of the disabled is his guardian and, if he has died,
the grandfather, the uncle or the older brother or the governor
(the state) must take upon themselves the responsibility" (Morad,
Nasri, and Merrick 2001: 69).

More important, there is a related category of persons in the
Qur'an, the *disadvantaged*, comprising the marginalized, the out-
cast, those in lower socioeconomic brackets, the abandoned, the
ignored, the discriminated against, the oppressed—all who do not
possess the valued traits of any culture or society (at whatever time
and place). These individuals are referred to much more often in
the Qur'an, and the call for action on their behalf is unmistakable.
Clearly, then, the Qur'an focuses "on people's attitudes as well as

actions towards the disadvantaged; promotes respect and esteem for the disadvantaged; expects personal responsibility and personal development from the disadvantaged; proclaims the right of the disadvantaged to full integration into society and full support; and affirms the responsibility and duty of society towards its disadvantaged members" (Bazna and Hatab 2005: 25).

Buddhism and Disability

Being unfamiliar with the vast scope of the Buddhist canon, my treatment of views of disability in the Buddhist tradition will be brief. On the one hand, Prince Gautama's confrontation with sickness, disease, and death led to his proclaiming the Four Noble Truths: there is *dukkha* (suffering); *dukkha* is caused by desire; desire and *dukkha* are impermanent and can be stopped; the way leading to the cessation of desire and *dukkha* is the Eightfold Path. Further, disabilities were surely associated with bad karma (in part the legacy of the religious traditions of the Indian subcontinent), even as people with disabilities were compensated for their trouble in certain respects or were thereby vocationally called in other respects (Matisoff 1978: 19–21). At the same time, later Buddhist traditions also developed from the basic framework of the Four Noble Truths an emphasis on the interdependence of all creatures and, concomitantly, an altruistic disposition toward and compassion for all sentient beings (Miles 1999a, 2002b).

It is the central idea of interdependence that has featured prominently in contemporary Buddhist views about disability. Interdependence means, at least in part, that birth and death are the two sides of the same coin and thereby dependent on one another. In this relational framework, "[i]mperfection is the essence of being organic and alive. Organic life is vulnerable; it inevitably ends in disintegration" (Tollifson 1997: 106). In reflecting on his friendship for over eleven years with Stephen, a man with intellectual disabilities, Peter Hawkins (2004) describes how their relationship grew from dualistically defined identities and evolved over time into what may be described as "interbeing." Stephen had become Hawkins's teacher, leading to Hawkins's insight (2004: 50) that "I am not a self that is separate from Stephen: who I am contains many elements that come about as a result of the relationship. He was not a self that was separate from me: who he was contained many elements that come about as a result of the relationship. I am who I am and he was who he was because of the relationship we had."

On the level of spiritual practices, as yogic meditation enables a degree of engagement with disability and disabling conditions not otherwise easy to come by, so also Buddhists advocate mindfulness practice for people with disabilities (Walker and Walker 1995). As Winfield Clark notes after thirty-five years as a paraplegic (due to an accident as a teenager) and over twenty years practicing Buddhist meditation, "[M]editation can help cut through some of the additional confusion created by having a body that is not 'normal'" (1995: 161).[26] Even if some people with intellectual disabilities are unable to cultivate yoga or mindfulness practice, the nondisabled who are able to do so will see the world in a more enlightened way and thereby relate to disabled people apart from the stigma and stereotypes that characterize conventional views of these phenomena. In any case, there are many threads in the Buddhist canon, including stories on specific disability themes that can and should be retrieved by those seeking a more comprehensive Buddhist perspective on disability.

In this and the previous two chapters, we have gained some critical perspective on disability in general and intellectual disability in particular as understanding of these experiences has evolved over the last two centuries. Whereas the earlier medical approaches to disability have remained with us, more recent social models have illuminated disability from cultural, economic, geographic, and political perspectives. What has emerged is the realization that disability can and should be assessed from a wide range of disciplinary, discursive, theoretical, and religious perspectives— even those of other faith traditions (Eiesland 1999). Scholars have therefore rightly begun to call for a multiple-model approach to disability. On their own, medical models tend to render patients as passive objects. Social models, however, may unwittingly adopt the values of capitalist society, including prioritization of work and an individualistic understanding of the notion of independence, and tend to assume that all persons with disabilities must have positive (modern) self-identities as disabled people (Marks 1999: esp. 87–89). Hence Jane Brett (2002) proposes an "alliance model" that includes both medical and social perspectives, even as Turnbull and Stowe (2001) advocate a five-pronged approach:

1. *Human capacity studies* focus on prevention, amelioration, privacy, individualized services, protection from harm, autonomy, empowerment and decision making, antidiscrimination, integration, productivity, and personal contribution
2. *Public studies* draw from the disciplines of law, political science, political economy, demographics, public administration, and social welfare
3. *Cultural studies* emphasize cultural responsiveness, classification, family integrity/unity, and family-centered approaches, drawing from cultural anthropology, sociology, literature, the performing arts, and history
4. *Philosophical/ethical studies* engage insights from theology and religion (I would not be hesitant to include spirituality) and finally
5. *Technology studies* are concerned with productivity and are informed by architecture theory, industrial engineering, ergonomics, and (I would add) telecommunications

Do not all of these perspectives need to be engaged in any contemporary effort to rethink disability and theology?

In this chapter, we have extended the cultural model of disability introduced in the previous chapter by engaging with feminist, indigenous/cultural, and world religious discourses on disability. Against this background, we have seen that the social model needs to be supplemented especially with perspectives that can register gender, race, age, and other cultural differences. Yet, even when this is done, we have seen that the plight of people with disabilities in general and people with intellectual disabilities in particular has been abysmal. On the one hand, feminist thought has only with great difficulty included disability perspectives, while on the other hand, multicultural and traditional religious perspectives have consistently perpetuated a bias against people with disabilities. We have also discovered that there are progressive movements across the world's religions attempting to retrieve and rehabilitate the best that these traditions have to offer in the service of combating the discrimination faced by people with disabilities.

I want to suggest that such explicitly theological models, acknowledged by Turnbull and Stowe but nevertheless relatively underdeveloped in comparison with other approaches, are precisely what is needed to empower the social liberation of people with disabilities. In continuing dialogue with the religious views of disability presented in the preceding pages, the constructive theological chapters in part 3 of this book will present an argument for how disability perspectives can be a catalyst for the renewal of Christian theology in the twenty-first century even as such a renewed theological vision can contribute to the formation of a more just, inclusive, and hospitable world for all people.

PART III

Reimagining and Renewing Theology in Late Modernity
Enabling a Disabled World

We are now poised to take up the central task of this volume: to reflect theologically on disability in general and intellectual disability in particular. Part 1 introduced our agenda as well as provided some biblical and historical background for a Christian theology of disability. Part 2 complicated that account by delineating how our contemporary experiences of intellectual disability have been shaped on the one hand by medicalized notions of disability that emerged in the nineteenth century, and have continued to evolve on the other hand by a range of social approaches to disability that have provided some critical perspectives on disability. Further, we have also seen how the economic, geographic, political, and cultural analyses of the social model need to be supplemented by feminist, indigenous, and world religious perspectives. Intellectual and physical disabilities in the twenty-first century are complex realities that often entail taken-for-granted assumptions about our late modern experience. Christian theology that does not interrogate these assumptions will be less capable of adequately engaging the phenomena of intellectual and physical disabilities. It will be even less capable of shaping appropriate Christian attitudes, postures, and responses to the experience of disability in our time.

My goal in the last four chapters of this book is to provide a theological account of disability in general and intellectual disability in particular.[1] I focus on seven of the traditional theological loci—creation; providence; the Fall; and theological anthropology, or what it means to be human (chap. 6); ecclesiology (the doctrine

of the church), including the sacraments and ministry (chap. 7);
soteriology (the doctrine of salvation), including the question of
healing (chap. 8); and eschatology (the doctrine of the last things),
including the doctrines of life after death and the resurrection
(chap. 9)—and argue that Christian theological reflection and
praxis in the twenty-first century can be invigorated and renewed
when the scriptural and dogmatic traditions of the church (most if
not all of which are silent about disability) are retrieved and rein-
terpreted in close dialogue with disability perspectives.

In turning to more strictly theological reflection, however, we
are not leaving behind the scientific, sociopolitical, and multireligious contexts engaged in part 2 of this book. Rather, we are taking
up the theological task as situated precisely where these domains
of our lives intersect. At the same time, readers should not expect
one-to-one correlations to be made between the discussions in the
previous part and those in the pages to come. At various places
more explicit scientific, social, political, or economic concerns
might be taken up. But more often, we proceed instead with the
awareness that part 2 has set the stage on which the whole of part
3 unfolds.

At the same time, the theological theme of pneumatology previously introduced (see pp. 11–12) will also inform the discussion
in a variety of ways. First, the pneumatological imagination continues to undergird our explorations insofar as it provides the epistemic "space" for us to entertain the possibility of doing theology
in dialogue with people with intellectual (and physical) disabilities.
Second, specific pneumatological motifs will assert themselves
more explicitly at various places, especially with regard to my own
constructive proposals. Finally, the pneumatological imagination
also invites us to think about a *performative* theology of disability
(see pp. 13–14). Hence, the following chapters are concerned as
much if not more with prescribing normative Christian practices
to be enacted as with describing theological ideas to be believed.
In that sense, all of the chapters in part 3 are soteriological, albeit
approached from various loci (e.g., the doctrines of providence,
the church, the *ordo salutis*, or life after death). I hope to show that
Christian beliefs arise out of our faithful reflection on the challenges of disability as we have experienced them, and yet always
return in the hermeneutical spiral to inform Christian practices in

late modernity. The question of how we should live is intimately connected with that of what we should believe. The phenomenon of disability engages these questions, and the results, I am convinced, are a renewed set of practices that is theologically informed and a renewal of the practice of theological reflection.

An important caveat before proceeding. The following discussions are not intended to be exhaustive regarding any of the theological loci, nor do they assume to take into account all disability perspectives. Much more can and should be said about each of these theological topics than is said here. What is presented, I suggest, are biblical texts and theological themes that emerge at the intersection of theology and disability studies and insights. Mine is only one proposal that, albeit systematic in certain respects, is meant as much to open up a conversation rather than to supply definitive pronouncements on the matters at hand.

VI

Reimagining the Doctrines of Creation, Providence and the *Imago Dei*
Rehabilitating Down Syndrome and Disability

Much of my life has been wasted and I am sometimes over-whelmed by the feeling that I have lived for nothing. This is the reason I want to tell my story. I want to leave something behind. I am neither angry nor bitter and I don't want to blame anyone for how my life has turned out. But no one should have to go through what I have been through. If my life can be a lesson in how not to treat anyone—disabled or non-disabled—I have accomplished something important.

—Thomas F. Allen, in Johnson and Traustadóttir 2005a: 201

Be glad and rejoice—for you have been chosen to share in the Passion of Christ who became the most disabled man when He hung on the Cross for love of us.

—Mother Teresa, quoted in Mehta 1983: xi

I do believe that at my birth
God ached with grief,
As this time Nature got it wrong,
Bungled His brief.

—Rosemary and Jenny Pratt, in Bowers 1985: 3

People with disabilities are like everybody else.

Each person is unique and important,

Whatever their culture, religion, abilities or disabilities.

Each one has been created by God and for God.

Each of us has a vulnerable heart

and yearns to love and be loved and valued.

Each one has a mission.

Each of us is born so that God's work may be accomplished in us.

—Vanier 2004: 172

After Mark's birth (on March 16), our mother's post-partum experience was understandably even more intense. At one point, she thought she heard the Lord saying that he was going to take Mark home, and she cried even harder, even though she had two other healthy boys. Then on April 5, Mom had a vision inspired by the Scripture "Out of the mouth of babes and sucklings hast thou ordained strength because of thine enemies, that thou mightest still the enemy and the avenger" (Ps 8:2, KJV). It dawned on her that the Lord gave his only Son, and with that, she agreed to give her life and Mark's back to the Lord, asking only for courage. That was her "breakthrough" from "my will be done" to the Lord's will being done. From Mom's perspective, Mark's life was and from then on would be a witness to God's larger plans for her, for him, for the family, and for others.

What, then, have been the treasures placed in Mom's heart as received from God through Mark's life over the years? First, Mom has come to see Mark as compassionate, lovable, and loving, and others who have come to know him have also recognized these qualities. Further, Mark is pure of heart, and his purity can and does inspire others to pursue after the purity and holiness of God. Finally, Mark is very sensitive to God. Not only does he know how to pray, he has also taught Mom how to pray without ceasing. Sometime a few years ago, Mark brought a Scripture verse to mother's attention—"But his word was in mine heart as a burning fire shut up in my bones" (Jer 20:9, KJV)—which became so powerful in terms of the empowerment Mom herself experienced in her body through reception of that word that she, in turn, shared it with the church congregation later. Mark is not just a person with Down Syndrome; rather, Mark is just another PK (pastor's kid) who is a full and participating member of his congregation.

Yet, Mark has also fallen short of the glory of God like everyone else. A case in point is his aforementioned stubbornness, which sometimes leads to extended periods of sulking and serious face-frowning—and on more rare occasions, foot-stomping and door-slamming—all of this registering his frustration when he feels he's being misunderstood. Because Mom is and has been the primary caregiver,[1] Mark often finds himself at odds with her when she denies certain of his requests or when she corrects him. Dad has often had to mediate between the two of them. He has taught Mark to pray through these periods of resentment, to get angry not at Mom but at the principalities and powers against which we are engaged, and to say to the adversary and accuser of all humanity, "Get thee behind me!" Mark will retreat to his room or to a restroom (when out and about in public), usually coming out after five to ten minutes (when in public) or even longer (when at home) saying, "I told him!" This leaves him smiling and feeling much better and, oftentimes, includes his saying "I'm sorry" to those with whom he felt contentious. In these and in many other ways, Mark is learning just like the rest of us about what it means to be conformed to the image of God in Christ.

The theological reflections that follow are motivated by questions that have emerged "on the ground" in our encounter with intellectual and physical disability and Down Syndrome. Our focus in this chapter ties together the doctrines of creation, providence, and theological anthropology (what it means to be human). We will be asking two specific sets of questions. First, how should traditional understandings of the doctrines of creation and providence be revised in light of our contemporary experiences of intellectual and physical disability? Second, how does our wrestling especially with intellectual disabilities such as Down Syndrome affect the historic Christian view of human beings as created in the image of God?

In the process of answering these sets of questions, we will sketch an outline of a Christology (the doctrine of the person and work of Christ) informed by disability perspectives and a theological anthropology informed by both Christology and pneumatology (the doctrine of the Holy Spirit). If in the Christian faith the person Jesus Christ is the most concrete revelation of God, then, we presume, the life, death, and resurrection of Jesus will provide important perspectives on the doctrines of creation and providence on the one hand, and on what it means to say that human beings are made in the image of God on the other. In that case, a Christology forged in dialogue with disability experiences and perspectives will be crucial to our task in this chapter. Further, if the Christian faith is distinctive precisely in its trinitarian understanding of God, then to be created in the image of God means to be created in the image of God as Father, Son, and Holy Spirit. In that case, the Christian pneumatological imagination ensures that the *imago Dei* is specified as the image of the triune God (the *imago trinitas*). We begin with the doctrines of creation and providence, proceed to Christology, and conclude with theological anthropology.

Creation and Providence

Traditional Christian teaching emphasizes God as the creator and sustainer of the world and all that is in it, and that sin entered the world through the human fall from grace into disobedience in the garden of Eden. How does our understanding of disability complicate this account? In this section, we look first at traditional doctrines of creation, providence, and the fall into sin, then interrogate these doctrines from disability perspectives, before attempting, finally, to sketch in response a theodicy—an explication of the problem of evil in light of the goodness and power of God.

Traditional Approaches to the Doctrines of Creation, Providence, and the Fall

The Christian doctrine of creation has come to include over the centuries the making of the visible and invisible world (original divine creation), the providence of God (ongoing creation or the preservation of the world), and the problem of evil (how can evil exist given an all-powerful, all-good, and all-loving Creator). With regard to original divine creation, there is a fair degree of dogmatic consensus across Roman Catholic, Orthodox, and Protestant lines on the following: that the world and all that is in it finds its origins and source in the creative will and work of the triune God; that the world as we know it is therefore contingent (as opposed to necessary) and dependent on God (as opposed to God being dependent on the world); and that God creates out of the divine wisdom, power, and love for purposes related to the glory of God that will be revealed fully only in the eschaton. Traditional Christian teaching has thereby perennially emphasized divine transcendence—theism as opposed to pantheism (God equated with the world) or panentheism (the world as included within the being of God), although this latter idea has gathered a stronger following more recently (e.g., Clayton and Peacocke 2004)—and the doctrine of creation *ex nihilo* over and against other ancient Near Eastern creation myths, Neoplatonic emanationism (creation as a necessary "overflow" of all things from God), or all forms of dualism (e.g., creation out of preexisting chaotic "matter").[2]

The world, as created, is contingent, limited, and finite (as opposed to the divine infinitude). Yet contingency, limitedness, and finitude are not essentially evil, even if the human experience of suffering (and evil) is sometimes derived from these realities. Rather, the theological tradition has always stressed the primeval goodness of the world that God made (Gen 1). More recent articulations of the Christian doctrine of creation have called attention to the integrity, plurality, and diversity of particular finite things (note that the creation narrative describes the origin of things by their being separated out of or distinguished from other things); the interconnectedness and interdependence of all things; and the dynamic, fluid, and yet purposeful character both of created particularities and of the world as a whole (see Migliore 2004: 103–6). These developments have led some theologians to explicate the doctrine of creation in trinitarian perspective, not only in terms of the world being created by the Father through the Word and Spirit (a motif articulated long ago by the patristic theologian Irenaeus), but also in terms of the Creation imaging the mutual indwelling, coinherence, or interrelationality (what the ancient Greek theologians called *perichoresis*) of the three divine persons (Moltmann 1993; Gunton 1993; Powell 2003). If in trinitarian theology the Father, Son, and Spirit are divine precisely insofar as they have their identity in subsistent (interpenetrating) relations with the other two persons, so also in a trinitarian theology of creation particular things are valued for what they are precisely because they are constituted by their unity in dynamic relationship with others (other things, creatures, human beings, and God).

This framework prevents an overly anthropocentric understanding of the created world, even as it enables proper emphasis on humankind within a more cosmocentric perspective. More importantly, this perspective allows us to register the modes of divine creation accomplished through the processes of differentiation. So in the creation narratives, we see the world emerging from out of primordial chaos through processes of division, distinction, and particularization, beginning with the separation of light from darkness and continuing in the separating out of species of plants and types of animals, each in its own or after its own kind (Gen 1:11, 12, 21, 24, 25; cf. Kass 1988; Hendry 1980: 169–70; Gunton 1993: 180–209). These primordial differentiations not only have ontological significance but also provide a creational framework to understand and value genetic variation, human embodiment, and intellectual range. Put in contemporary scientific terms, speciation differentiates *Homo sapiens* from other creatures and individuation differentiates human beings from one another, but neither of these processes denies the solidarity of human life with other creaturely forms of life (Jennings 2003: 98–102).

The Christian doctrine of creation also includes the doctrine of providence (Helm 1994). If God is the transcendent source of the world in the doctrine of creation, God is also immanently involved in the ongoing sustenance of the world in the doctrine of providence. But if the originally created world was recognized and declared by God to be good, then what happened during God's sustaining the world such that evil appeared? Is God not responsible for evil either in creating the world originally or in providing for it subsequently? This raises the problem of evil in its most challenging form: how can an omnibenevolent and omnipotent God allow the appearance and persistence of evil in a good Creation?[3] Whatever agreements regarding the doctrine of creation are to be found across the Christian community practically vanish when we take up the "unsolved problem" of the doctrine of providence (Link 2002).

The theological and dogmatic response to the problem of evil inevitably includes the doctrines of sin and the Fall. The central biblical texts for the Christian doctrine of original sin as it was developed by the patristic theologians were Genesis 3 and, especially, Romans 5. The Genesis narrative is well known and space constraints prohibit our recounting it in detail. Suffice it to say that the serpent tempts the woman by denying she will die if she eats of the fruit of the tree in the middle of the garden. Upon eating of the fruit, the man (*ha adam*) and the woman realize their nakedness and hide from God. God then curses the serpent and the ground of the earth, greatly increases the pangs of childbirth for the woman (does this mean that she would nevertheless have experienced minimal pain anyway?), announces her subjugation under her husband, and gives the man over to work the cursed ground. God then clothes the man and the woman, and, concerned that they now know good and evil and might "take also from the tree of life, and eat, and live forever" (Gen 3:22), drives them from the garden.

Instead of being developed by ancient Israel, the idea of a primeval fall can be said to be of specifically Pauline inspiration, although it did not solidify into the doctrine of original sin until the fifth century (see Wiley 2002: esp. chaps. 2–3). More specifically, early Christian interpreters developed the doctrine of the Fall from Paul's statement that "just as sin came into the world through one man, and death came through sin, and so death spread to all because all have sinned" (Rom 5:12; cf. 1 Cor 15:21-22). Building on this, theologians like Origen and Cyprian further reasoned from the psalmist's woe—"I was born guilty, a sinner when my mother conceived me" (51:5)—that Adam's sin was inherited by the rest of humankind through the act of sexual intercourse. From this emerged the logic of the Fall and redemption: if in the Fall human beings lost the primeval blessedness experienced in Eden, then in the salvation accomplished by Christ's recapitulating work human beings are restored to that originally perfect, innocent, and righteous relationship with God.

It was Saint Augustine who wove these threads together. The garden of Eden represents the paradisiacal blessedness lost by the fall into sin and death. Given the Latin Vulgate translation of the last clause of Romans 5:12 as "in whom all have sinned"—which could just as well be translated "because all have sinned," as has been done by Eastern theologians for centuries—Augustine concluded that all human beings are subject to death. More precisely, Adam's sin is transmitted through the act of sexual intercourse—the theory of traducianism further suggesting that the perverse nature of the soul is to be accounted for by its also passing on through the seed of the parents—and thoroughly infects the human will (here Augustine's target was Pelagius) resulting in human depravity. Only baptism can cleanse the stain of original sin (hence, for Augustine, the importance of baptizing infants, against the Donatists)[4] and restore the Edenic perfection and holiness to humankind. This Augustinian vision of paradisiacal perfection, the fall into original sin, and redemption and restoration to primeval Edenic life has since informed Christian theological reflection, at least in the Latin West.[5]

Creation, Providence, and the Fall: Disability Inquiries

It is this framework that has informed the bulk of theological reflection on disability. Put most succinctly, if God is the creator and sustainer of the world and all that is in it, then God is also responsible for disability. Theologians usually do not put it quite so blatantly, preferring instead to emphasize that while God does not directly cause disabilities God is in control of all things that happen, including disabilities, or that God only *allows* disabilities to happen.[6] Disability, after all, is the result of the temptation of Adam and Eve in the garden of Eden, their sinful act, and their subsequent fall from grace. Because of this "original sin," evil—including disease, disability, and ultimately, death—was released into the world and continues to operate. Since the originally good Creation is now fallen, corrupted by human sin, God allows but does not cause the suffering brought about by natural processes such as tsunamis, animal predation, abnormal chromosomal conditions, and accidents causing disabilities. Further, free fallen creatures are themselves responsible for moral evils of the sorts with which we humans are thoroughly familiar. Eschatologically, the Creation itself yearns with human beings for the final saving work of God when both moral and natural evils will be redeemed for the glory of God and ultimately overcome.

It is fair to say that our contemporary experiences of disability have reopened for consideration the details of this traditional doctrinal framework of creation, providence, and Fall. To begin, traditional theodicies (defenses of God in the face of the problem of evil) are much less plausible in the twenty-first century.[7] From a disability perspective, Jesus said only that the life of the man born blind would be lived for the glory of God, not that God somehow was the cause of the man's blindness.[8] Further, does not the traditional model perpetuate the link between sin and disability in a manner problematic for a theology of disability today? Finally, even if we could shift the responsibility of sin from the man and the woman to the serpent, this leaves unanswered the question of the source of the temptation: was this derived from the serpent, the devil himself, or even the primeval fall of angels, and what is the relationship of any or all of these to divine omnipotence and omnibenevolence?[9]

With regard to the doctrine of the Fall, does the expulsion from the Garden represent the fall from grace as understood by Christian theology? Put alternatively, are Adam and Eve historical beings, and is there a historical "fall" in this text?[10] The man and woman are not cursed, only the serpent and the ground. Does this explain in part why the doctrine of a fall did not emerge in the Hebrew Bible or later in the Jewish theological tradition? These are especially pressing questions given the emergence of modern paleoanthropology not only with regard to the fact that the Augustinian interpretation of a primeval paradise is being displaced by the idea of a progressive evolution of *Homo sapiens* from more primitive forms of life (see Hayes 1980: 72–73), but also with regard to theories of the appearance of hominids from multiple evolutionary lines rather than from a single human pair.[11] These questions extend to the doctrine of original sin in general and to the question of how to understand Paul's reference to Adam in Romans 5 in particular. While the Vulgate reading is grammatically possible, was it not driven by a theory of traducianism that is no longer plausible? If so, then death comes to all not because Adam's sinful nature was biologically transmitted to his descendents but, as modern translations have it, "because all have sinned." Further, if death came through sin, then what explains the cycle of death and birth that surely existed long before the appearance of human beings on earth? Finally, within an evolutionary framework, what accounts not only for the deaths of innumerable species but also for the incalculable genetic variations and mutations—most of which did not survive—prior to the arrival, much less the sin, of "Adam"?[12]

This final question is particularly relevant when considering genetic and chromosomal conditions such as Down Syndrome. Even if we have argued earlier that Down Syndrome is a peculiarly modern phenomenon in terms of our experience, it is also equally clear that trisomic mutations have been around for thousands and even millions of years, given their presence among gorillas and chimpanzees.[13] While chimpanzees normally have forty-eight (rather than forty-six) pairs of chromosomes, trisomy of their twenty-second chromosome not only results in forty-nine chromosomes but also produces parallel anatomical, phenotypic, neurological, and behavioral similarities to Down Syndrome. This is not to say that chimpanzees and other pongids (of the family of apes) also "suffer" from Down Syndrome; it only suggests that the kinds of genetic variations that have evolved the many species of both pongidae and hominidae (the family of human beings and their ancestors) have produced mutations like trisomy 21 (in human beings) and trisomy 22 (in chimpanzees) long before the appearance and "fall" of Adam and Eve from paradise.[14]

The same process of genetic variations over time that has produced the wide range of creatures within species (such as the incredible diversity of human beings) has also produced the many chromosomal patterns like that of Down Syndrome (cf. Iozzio 2005b). In fact, mutational configurations like trisomy 21 are, at one level, merely at the extremes of species variation. Put in biological terms, impairments "are central to evolutionary theory because they have been represented as either a failure of adaptation (an organismic regression to a prior primitive state) or as a site of potential species innovation" (Mitchell 2003: 692). More precisely, "genetic mutations (many of which are classified as today's congenital impairments) serve as catalysts for species differentiation over time," and during the evolutionary process, the social and environmental impacts on biological organisms also serve to transform impairment "from a presumed inferiority into unexpected adaptations within the origins of the species" (Mitchell 2003: 694–95). Conservative traditions are perfectly free to reject evolutionary science in their theological reflection,[15] but is it not disingenuous to accept the claims of the medical and technological sciences associated with Down Syndrome on the one hand and reject the converging results of the paleoanthropological, geological, astronomical, cosmological, and biological sciences on the other (cf. Falk 2004)?

What is needed is a reformulation of the doctrines of sin and the Fall that can provide a more plausible and coherent account for the experience of disability in our time. Allow me to suggest four constitutive elements for such an understanding of original sin. First, we might say that *ha adam* refers collectively to the "first self-aware hominids" (Collins 2003: 481) who as individuals and collectively suppressed the truth as they understood it and resisted rather than responded to God.[16] The sin leading to death in Romans 5:12

thus refers first to sin understood as willful acts of rebellion by self-aware free creatures, and then to the death that is the separation of sinful human beings from God rather than physical death.[17] This preserves both insights of the Genesis narrative and the Pauline interpretation, even as it is flexible enough to accommodate whatever scientific hypotheses might prevail. Second, the human rebellion against God manifests itself especially in violence committed against ourselves, our neighbors, and the natural world (see Suchocki 1994). This means we are less concerned with explaining how the primeval sin of *ha adam* resulted in disabilities than we are in explaining how disabilities are social manifestations of or occasions for human acts of violence and injustice (of discrimination, exclusion, and oppression). Third, the truth of original sin means that all human beings find themselves caught up through socialization in such a cycle of violence and injustice and each one of us perpetuates this reality to ourselves, one another, and our descendants even as we suffer from its effects. Since none are exempt from the universality of sin, the world does not divide itself up into the nondisabled (saint) and the disabled (sinner).[18] Finally, the truth of Romans 5 is not only the solidarity of all human beings with Adam in terms of our sinful acts that lead to death (5:12, 19a) but, more importantly, our solidarity with Christ in terms of his righteousness leading to eternal life (5:15-21).[19] This move accomplishes two things: it locates sin, death, and judgment in human dispositions, affections, and actions rather than in *ha adam's* singular headship or in human biology; and it accentuates Christ's redemption of all sinners, nondisabled and disabled alike.[20]

Providence and Evil: The "Four Fences" of Disability Theology

With this proposal on the table, a way back to a reconstructive theology of providence is opened. Here, however, we are confronted by a lack of theological consensus. In the Protestant traditions with which I am most familiar, there are historically two schools of thought, Calvinism and Arminianism, to which have been added recently process theology and Open Theism.[21] In brief, Calvinism, following the Augustinian tradition, emphasizes the sovereignty of God over all created things and events, defines creaturely freedom in compatibilist terms—the freedom to do what one wishes or desires that is compatible with divine sovereignty—and insists that God foreknows what God elects. Arminianism, for its part, reacted to Calvinism by highlighting God's interactivity with free creatures, defining creaturely freedom in libertarian terms—the freedom to do otherwise—and suggesting that God elects according to God's foreknowledge. Open Theism counters that if God already foreknows a future decision or event, then even God cannot change the future to make a significant difference (e.g., in response to prayer). Hence, both Calvinism and Arminianism are wrong to think that the future is already settled; rather, the future consists of possibilities and probabilities—some settled based on divine decision and action, others based on creaturely decisions and actions. And since God knows things as they are, God knows the future not as settled, but as open possibilities. Process theology goes further to suggest both that the dynamism characteristic of divine knowledge in Open Theism pertains also to the divine intentions—hence, God changes God's mind in response to creaturely decisions and actions—and that various levels of genuine freedom and spontaneity exist for all creatures and created things.

How does a theology of disability respond to these various theologies of providence? On the one hand, the criterion of faithfulness to the biblical and theological traditions has led some theologians with disabilities to affirm the Augustinian-Calvinist position. Harold Wilke, a theologian with a disability, reminds us (1982: 28), "Causation by God is again and again stated in the Bible. . . . Literally dozens of times the Bible reports that the disabling condition or situation is of God. You see God at work in this. God ordained the handicap."[22] The difficulty here is partly that less mature believers are inevitably traumatized from the sense of being victimized by God (Calder 2004). On the other hand, Open Theism and especially process theology might be in a better position to say that disabilities, especially congenital disabilities "caused" by genetic deviations, are random and fortuitous features of a world in which certain degrees of spontaneity and freedom exist (see Bonting 2005: chaps. 11–12). The difficulty now is how faith in divine providence can be secured, not only for our lives in the here and now but also with regard to the eschatological plan of God.

I suggest that a contemporary theology of disability should develop an understanding of divine providence along three lines.

To begin with, I am drawn to Deborah Creamer's (2004b: 130–33, 185–91; cf. 2005: 63–65) articulation of the concept of "limitness," which properly denotes the contingency and finitude intrinsic to creaturely existence without the negative connotations of the idea of "limitedness." When the limitations of human life are properly recognized, then our identities can more easily accommodate success and failure, prosperity and loss, and ability and disability. Theologically, when God is also understood as working with the limitations of the finite world God has created, we can more easily comprehend the scriptural references to divine perseverance, to divine strength, and to divine creativity. Finally, if sin is the exaggerating of our strengths and going beyond our finitude (limits), then God is "one who neither exaggerates nor denies limitation . . . and instead is represented as an authentic and fully grounded self" (Creamer 2004b: 274). The concept of "limitness" opens up theoretical space to rethink God's activity (as revealed in scripture), creaturely creativity (in terms of freedom exercised within constraints), and nature's courses and processes (in terms of the spontaneity and variation in the world).

My next line of approach, drawing from the "four fences of Chalcedon," suggests an analogous "four fences of a disability theology of providence." In the Chalcedonian definition regarding the person of Christ in 451 CE, the council recognized him as being "in two natures, without confusing the two natures, without transmuting one nature into the other, without dividing them into two separate categories, without contrasting them according to area or function" (Leith 1963: 36). These four "withouts" have served to demarcate the orthodox parameters of what may *not* be said about Christ: that the divine and human natures are not to be confused or thought to be changed (as did those who claimed Jesus was therefore neither divine nor human but some "third thing"), not to be divided (as did the more radical Monophysites), nor to be separated or hybridized (as did the more radical Nestorians). But since the creed does not proceed to affirm positively how the union of the two natures occurs, the mystery of the incarnation—Jesus as one person in two natures—is preserved.

Similarly, I want to suggest "four fences" demarcating what may *not* be said about the providence of God from a disability perspective; these are anticipated by the introductory quotations to this chapter. First, God's will is *not* arbitrary; hence, disabilities are neither merely accidents nor are they directly intended by God. On this issue, Thomas Allen is right to have said, "I don't want to blame anyone for how my life has turned out." Second, God's sovereignty and human freedom are *not* mutually exclusive. This means that insofar as there are things that we can do to minimize incidents of disability, we need to take responsibility for such actions. Here, Mother Teresa's response is apropos: while we might understand ourselves to have been called to participate in the passion of Christ, we nevertheless remain responsible not only for how we embrace that calling (i.e., with gladness and joy) but also for alleviating the suffering that comes with such participation (as did Mother Teresa herself). Third, God's will is *not* opposed to the laws of nature. On the contrary, the regularities and surprises of nature (which we should not think we will ever be able fully to explain) can be understood to be a gift of God precisely insofar as they make possible the ordering and diversity of human lives. As already noted, the regularized process of genetic variation and recombination makes possible creaturely diversity in general and human diversity in particular. From this perspective, Rosemary and Jenny Pratt suggestively note that disabilities are the product of nature, not of God. Fourth, God's will is not to produce two classes of human beings, whether the saved and the damned, or the healthy and the sick, or the whole and the disabled. This is not to deny that there are differences among people, but to say that God wishes all to be saved and whole.[23] Jean Vanier's insight is apropos: all people are valued of God.

Finally, my last response builds on the concept of "limitness" and the "four fences." I suggest that a disability theology of providence also serves to guide Christian discourse and praxis about disability. From the standpoint of pastoral care, this means that we should never tell a person with a disability that his or her disability is ordained by God. The "four fences" admonish us against imposing such an "explanation" on a disabled person. At the same time, people with disabilities may certainly adopt such a self-understanding (see Lovering 1985: 123). There is a huge difference between "confessing" such a view for someone and this person embracing such a self-understanding. On the one hand, if we are prepared to give thanks to God for being "normal" (for *not* being the result of genetic deviations), then we should also be prepared to give thanks to God for being "different" (for being the result of genetic deviations) (Creamer 2004b: 241).[24] On the other hand, even if we should thank God for all things (as commanded by scripture), we should also avoid speculating about how God causes all things providentially. The "four fences" invite us to move from the idea of divine omnipotence causing all events to the idea of divine omnicompassion redeeming all events (Cooper 1993: 63–67). With such a shift in thinking, we are obligated to embody God's compassion and invited to participate in God's redemptive work. Note that Jesus' words about the man born blind—"so that God's works might be revealed in him"—was followed immediately by, "We must work the works of him who sent me while it is day" (John 9:3-4). Hans Reinders thus rightly notes (2004: 432): "Saying that a disabled life is a blessing can be utterly false and deceitful, therefore, when not underwritten by acts of compassion." While God's creative sovereignty is shrouded in mystery, God's providential activity is ultimately redemptive, as clearly revealed in the life of Jesus Christ.

Disability, Christology, and the Image of God

The person of Jesus Christ provides additional theological resources for us to develop and articulate a theology of creation and providence in disability perspective. More specifically, the life, death, and resurrection of Jesus can help Christians rethink a central aspect of the doctrine of creation, namely, how to understand human creatureliness in theological perspective. In this section, we look at traditional construals of the doctrine of human creatureliness (theological anthropology), suggest in response how a disability perspective on the person of Christ helps us to reformulate our understanding of what it means to be human, and then focus on how the life and death of Christ illuminates the doctrine of divine providence as it relates to God's redeeming the world.

The Imago Dei: Traditional and Recent Models

There are two major issues related to the theological understanding of what it means to be human: the question of what constitutes the image of God (*imago Dei*), and the question of what defines human nature.[25] In this section, I lay out the major views on each issue, beginning with the latter question first, and identify some questions raised from a disability perspective.

What does human nature consist of? Perennially, the dominant positions were that human beings are constituted by spirit, soul, and body (the "trichotomist" view; cf. 1 Thess 5:23 and Heb 4:12), or by an immaterial spirit-soul or soul and a material body (the "dichotomist" view).[26] The dichotomist view has been more widespread historically and, under the influence of either Platonic or Berkeleyan idealism, it has produced various types of substance-dualistic construals of human beings as souls in or with bodies (Swinburne 1986; Cooper 2000; Moreland and Rae 2000). From a theological perspective, substance dualists argue, among other points, that only if human beings are seen as souls with bodies will it be possible for personal identity to persist in the "between" state prior to the resurrection. Even if we grant this point, the problems here are both the Cartesian one about how the material and immaterial realms relate to each other and the more recent neuroscientific evidence that correlates mental life with cognitive brain states. More holistic anthropologies that nevertheless distinguish between the soul and the body include neo-Thomist reinterpretations of the Aristotelian synthesis of human beings as creatures that include both essential form and quantitative shape; in this case, the soul is the form of the body (e.g., Machuga 2002). This formulation does connect the more holistic anthropology of the ancient Hebrews with contemporary scientific views of humanity (see Green 1998, 2004) and therefore seems to preserve better the intuitions of the biblical authors (especially in the Hebrew Bible) without the liabilities of substance dualism.

Yet, rather than retrieve and reinterpret Saint Thomas or even Aristotle, I prefer to explore the possibility of rethinking what it means to be human in dialogue with more recent views that suggest the soul as an emergent set of distinctive features and capabilities constituted by but irreducible to the sum of the body's biological parts.[27] Developed in part in dialogue with those working in the cognitive neurosciences, emergence is a theory of how mental (cognitional) properties—including morality, consciousness and self-consciousness, and aesthetic creativity—are dependent on but not fully explicable by physical (brain) properties. The classic example is Phineas Gage (1823–1860), the railroad worker who suffered a frontal brain injury and then experienced damage to the psychological, emotional, and social functions that were tied to the injured frontal lobes (Damasio 1994: chaps. 1–2). Over the last 150 years, cognitive science has confirmed states of consciousness as dependent on but irreducible to brain states, and thus developed the emergentist view of the human person.

Benefits of emergentist views include (a) the recognition that the human body and brain are essential features of human identity apart from which consciousness and self-consciousness are impossible, and (b) the provision of building blocks for a scientifically robust understanding of mental or downward causation (which most human beings take for granted but which yet remain rather inexplicable by science) without recourse to a body-soul dualism. Further, emergentism emphasizes the holistic character of human nature attested to in the Hebrew Bible but does so in terms of embodiment (without reduction to crass materialism), environmental and social situatededness (without insisting on either environmental or social determinism), and spiritual relationality (without insisting on a dualism between spirit and body, mind and brain). Finally, as I will show in the last chapter, I believe emergentism is compatible with Christian eschatology's emphasis on the resurrection of the body.

From a disability perspective, a number of points need to be emphasized. First, human embodiment cannot be relegated to secondary status in any theological anthropology. This is the case not only with regard to how physical and psychosomatic disabilities shape human identity and self-understanding (on which more momentarily), but also with regard to the fact that severe and even profound intellectual disability cannot be used as the sole measure of determining the personhood and intrinsic value of such individuals. In these latter cases, the human person must be understood to be at least embodied, even if one's spiritual capacities are less manifest phenomenologically. An emergentist anthropology is helpful in this regard precisely because it takes human embodiment constitutively. Second, emergentism's holistic account supports the arguments presented earlier (chaps. 3–4) regarding the need to understand physical and intellectual disability from multiple disciplinary perspectives: biological, social, political, economic, geographic, and so on. Again, human beings are constituted by these webs of significance even if irreducible to any one of them. This means, finally, that emergentism is at least suggestive regarding the transcendental value of each human life insofar as it sees the human person as including a reality that resists positivistic quantification. This is important because it is now possible to begin accounting for the human spirit, which manifests itself unmistakably in the experience of disability. As we saw earlier in Susan Wendell's feminist philosophy of disability (pp. 125–26), there is an aspect of human nature that enables us existentially to engage and even transcend our bodily experiences of disability even if such transcendence neither ignores nor wishes away the demands of the body.

We will expand on these ideas toward a theological anthropology later in this chapter. For now, we turn to discuss the three basic views of the image of God. Predominant is the substantive or structural view that understands the divine image as an inherent human capacity that reflects the character or attributes of God. Historically, a number of suggestions have been put forward regarding this feature being constituted by rationality or the capacity to reason; morality or the capacity to experience guilt, shame, and responsibility; spirituality or the capacity for religious experience; or the upright physical posture (from the Hebrew word for "likeness," *tselem*, in Gen 1:26). The intellect has persisted in the Christian tradition as the primary feature of the *imago Dei* due to the association between the Christian doctrine of Christ as the divine Logos or wisdom and the Aristotelian doctrine of human beings as rational or reasoning creatures. Hence, "man must be rational to have fellowship with God" (Gordon Clark, cited in Anderson 1982: 225). We have already seen, however, that this view has historically excluded not only the intellectually disabled but also the deaf-mute from being considered fully human (in chap. 2). In fact, not only is understanding the *imago Dei* in any of these terms problematic for those individuals who do not clearly exhibit them, but in effect the result is discriminatory and even oppressive for such people. This is not to deny that any or even all of these elements might contribute to our understanding of God (after all, the *imago Dei* reflects, at least in part, the character and reality of God—that is what it means). It is to say that the *imago Dei* is neither exhausted nor predominantly defined by any one of these features.[28]

The functional view holds that the *imago Dei* consists not in what human beings are but in what we do. Derived primarily from the biblical description in the creation narrative—"Then God said, 'Let us make humankind in our image, according to our likeness; and let them have dominion over the fish of the sea, and over the birds of the air, and over the cattle, and over all the wild animals of the earth, and over every creeping thing that creeps upon the earth'" (Gen 1:26)—it has emerged as the dominant view among Hebrew Bible scholars (Middleton 2005: chap. 2) who emphasize the image of God in terms of the human capacity to exercise dominion over the created order. Again, however, this view perpetuates a bias against people with disabilities who are oftentimes less physically and intellectually capable than others. Worse, it underlies the claim that "the mentally retarded are without the image of God [since] the *imago Dei* is basically centered on responsibility" (Towns and Groff 1972: 39). This was precisely the rationale presupposed in the euthanasia of "the disabled" in Nazi Germany, and which continues to inform our current practices of prenatal testing, selective abortions, and end-of-life caregiving. Again, this is not to say that the *imago Dei* excludes this capacity completely. But if we understand this gift (and responsibility) of God that empowers human dominion less as the power to rule *over* and more as the power to rule *with* others,[29] then that opens up space for us to see people with disabilities as manifesting the divine image precisely in their solidarity with others who are more actively engaged in exercising dominion in the world.

This interpretation of the functional view dovetails with the relational view that has emerged since the middle of the last century, especially in the work of neoorthodox theologians such as Karl Barth (1886–1968). Three aspects of Barth's theological anthropology are especially noteworthy for our purposes. First, for Barth, "real humanity" stands in relationship to God, self, and others (cf. Price 2002). Second, human relationality is most prominently featured in the biblical text in God's covenantal creation of *ha adam* "in our image" as male *and* female (Gen 1:26-27; cf. Krötke 2000: 168–69; Barth 1958: 288–90). Finally, Jesus Christ is *the* image of the invisible God and, as the consummate "man for others" (Barth 1960: 203–22), is also the prototypical image of what it means for human beings to be created in the image of God (Barth 1960: 222–84). In this view, the *imago Dei* consists neither in human structures nor in human functions but—and note that this is in line with the emergentist anthropology introduced above—in their relationship with God, their interrelationality with other persons, and their embodied interdependence with the world. This relational and Christological view seems to hold the most promise for a theological anthropology informed by disability perspectives. Yet, we still need to say much more about Christology in relationship to disability.

Jesus Christ as the Disabled God

At first blush one might ask, what does Jesus Christ have to do with disability? Any adequate response to this question cannot avoid engaging with Nancy Eiesland's model of Jesus Christ as the "disabled God" (1994). Although Eiesland writes as a trained sociologist (albeit with some theological background), her interests in this book are in developing a liberative theology of disability. Hence, Eiesland's project is both political and theological. She recognizes that apart from a revised theology of disability, reforms of ecclesial politics and practices will remain largely ineffective. An inclusive ecclesiology cannot be content to merely revise the traditional biblical theologies of disabilities since they are too deeply shaped by the motifs of bodily affliction, sin and punishment, and exclusion emergent from a plain-sense or ableist reading of scripture. So what we need is a new theological paradigm, one that locates disability not only in human bodies but also in the very life of God.

Eiesland's proposal derives from the truth "embodied in the image of Jesus Christ, the disabled God" (1994: 90). This image is informed along three lines of Christological reflection. First, the incarnation of the Son of God means that Jesus "had to become like his brothers and sisters in every respect" (Heb 2:17), without comeliness, despised and rejected, even to the point of an ignominious death on the cross. This Christologically defined *imago Dei* would thus be inclusive rather than exclusive of the human experience of disability. Second, and building on the first, Jesus' resurrected

body also bore the marks and scars of impairment left by the spear
in his side and by the nails in his hands and feet (Luke 24:39-40;
John 20:24-28). Recall that Jesus' revelation of his resurrection
body as including the marks of impairment was in response to
"doubting" Thomas's demand to "encounter the *authenticity* of the
risen Jesus" (Willis 2002: 224; italics mine). That resurrected bodies will "continue to bear the scars of human contingency" (Stuart
2000: 174) subverts the notion that the heavenly hope involves
the restoration of Edenic notions of human perfection. Finally,
the perennial Christian celebration of the life, death, and resurrection of Christ in the Eucharist also calls attention to the brokenness of the body of "the disabled God." Christ's broken body
not only unites the fragmented ecclesial body but also heals the
brokenness of our individual bodies precisely through including
each person around the Eucharistic fellowship regardless of his or
her in/ability.

The result is, contrary to the biomedical definition of disability, that people with disabilities also bear the image of God just as
Jesus represents the fullness of that image and its restoration to
the human race. Further, contrary to social constructions of disability in ancient Israel, people with disabilities can and should
be fully included in the redeemed community of God not only as
"weaker" members but also as full participants who minister out
of their "weaknesses," even as Jesus saves through the cross and
resurrection. Finally, and perhaps most importantly, Jesus Christ
as the "disabled God" has theological implications about divine
holiness as including rather than excluding impairing conditions.
People with physical and mental impairments are healed not only
after they are cured (as is suggested by the visions of the Hebrew
prophets and the gospel pericopes) but insofar as they are included
at the eschatological banquet just as they are (cf. Luke 14:15-24).

Of course, Eiesland's proposal builds on a long albeit minor
theological tradition of depicting or representing Christ as disabled. Medieval mystics such as Catherine of Siena understood the
wounds of Christ to be the site of healing for a broken world (Jeremiah 1995). Renaissance painter Andrea Mantegna produced the
Virgin and Child which, arguably (with the facial phenotype, wide
spacing between the first and second toes, size of child's fingers,

etc.), is a portrait of Christ "as a child with Down Syndrome" (Kidder and Skotko 2001: 144).[30] Dostoyevsky's *Idiot* (1955) features Prince Myshkin, a Christ figure who is epileptic. Each of these cases, of course, can be seen as extensions of the Isaianic "suffering servant" motif:

> he had no form or majesty that we should look at him,
>   nothing in his appearance that we should desire him.
> He was despised and rejected by others;
>   a man of suffering and acquainted with infirmity;
> and as one from whom others hide their faces
>   he was despised, and we held him of no account.
>
> (Isa 53:2b-3)[31]

At the same time, Eiesland's portrait of Christ as the disabled God has not gone unchallenged, even among theologians with disabilities. Graham Monteith (2005: 66–67) counterargues that God is not disabled, but that God suffers with "the disabled." Deborah Creamer (2004b: 260–61) suggests that while Eiesland's Christology may be helpful for some people, it does not account for those individuals who have a much more ambivalent and even negative view of their disabilities. More to the point, could the "disabled God" be a metaphor that distorts our view of God, and is largely ineffectual beyond showing that God is in solidarity with people with disabilities? With regard to intellectual disabilities, Christopher Hinkle (2003) questions the value of imagery about God as retarded. After all, God is intelligent and we, the image of God, are the most intelligent of God's creatures. So while Eiesland's theology of the disabled God is illuminating in various respects—particularly in highlighting God's embracing the full range of the human condition in the incarnation so as to insist on a truly liberative and inclusive community of faith—it is limited as an only or even dominant model for contemporary disability theology and Christology.

Redeeming the Imago Dei: *Theology of the Cross and Disability*

I suggest that one way forward that can include rather than abandon Eiesland's insights is to develop a liberation theology of the cross (*theologia crucis*).[32] Historically, a theology of the cross insists that God is paradoxically hidden but also revealed in the suffering, despair, and even death of Jesus on the cross. It is out of the darkness and the misery of the cross that God speaks and reveals God's redemptive plan for humankind. For this reason, Luther said that "[h]e deserves to be called a theologian . . . who comprehends the visible and manifest things of God seen through suffering and the cross."[33]

For our purposes, the theology of the cross provides a biblical framework for thinking about the connections between Christology, theology, and disability.[34] Now, on the one hand, we need to be careful about foisting an additional burden, that of the cross of Christ, onto the lives of people with disabilities. On the other hand, the experience of disability functions analogously to illuminate the redemptive power of the cross, not only because of the embodied suffering experienced by people with disabilities but also because of the social and interpersonal discrimination of "the disabled" (by the nondisabled), and because of the exclusionary political, economic, and ecclesial structures that marginalize them. In what follows, then, I explicate the potential of a theology of the cross for a liberation theology of disability in terms of the life, death, and resurrection of Christ.

A theology of the cross connects the life and death of Christ in a way that integrates the gospel accounts of Jesus' life and the epistolary reflections on the significance of his death. Because the Passion narratives dominate the gospel accounts while the other New Testament authors focus on the death of Christ, the life of Jesus may be uncritically dismissed as anticlimactic. Yet Jesus' life cannot be disconnected from his death, and a theology of the cross sees the entirety of the life of Christ as lived for others in anticipation of and shaped by the cross. As Paul puts it, Jesus accepting death on the cross was but an extension of the fact that he "emptied himself, taking the form of a slave, being born in human likeness" (Phil 2:7).[35] Hence, the broken body of Christ on the cross is foreshadowed by the humbleness of his beginnings in the manger, the breaking of bread and of the alabaster jar, his poverty and embrace of lepers and other marginalized people, among other aspects of the life of Jesus. At the same time, "[t]he nail-pierced hands of Jesus—the 'stigmata'—are the hands of one who cares for the stigmatized, who are in manifold ways pierced by the turned-aside eyes of fellow human beings" (Wilke 1981: 154). From a disability perspective, then, a theology of the cross insists that the life and death of Jesus serves as a redemptive model that values rather than marginalizes the brokenness characteristic of so much of human life.

A theology of the cross is also able to acknowledge that the significance of Jesus' life is focally illuminated in his death. More precisely, the cross reveals God's nonviolent response to sin in the world. Even before the foundation of the world, God determined to let sin run its course, even to the point of his beloved Son experiencing death on the cross. From a disability perspective, the cross reveals the emptied self of Jesus and the power of God. In fact, God's power "is made perfect in weakness" (2 Cor 12:9), and "God's foolishness [*tó moròn*] is wiser than human wisdom, and God's weakness is stronger than human strength" (1 Cor 1:25). Further, and more importantly, at the cross Jesus laid down his life as a sacrifice for sins (Heb 10:12). This sacrifice covers the sins of all people—both perpetrators and victims, oppressors and marginalized, nondisabled and disabled—as well as makes it possible for God to redeem the entire web of sin and its effects. To be sure, the cross signals in no uncertain terms God's wrathful judgment on sin, but it is also the basis upon which God announces forgiveness to all who are sinners. Finally, then, a theology of the cross invites us to extend the patristic insight "that which he has not assumed, he has not healed" (Gregory of Nazianzus 1954: 218) to the experience of disability. In this view, Jesus Christ who was "nailed to the cross, rejected by all, [and] expelled from the community, dies as the Handicapped One par excellence, having taken upon himself our handicap" (Marthe 1981: 86). Paraphrasing Augustine, "The deformity of Christ forms you. If he had not willed to be deformed, you would not have recovered the form you had lost. Therefore he was deformed when he hung on the cross. But his deformity is our comeliness. In this life, therefore, let us hold fast to the deformed Christ" (McDonnell 1992: 6).

In a sense, today we live in an extended "holy Saturday" (Lewis 2003; cf. Lewis 1982), between brokenness and wholeness, between creation and redemption. In this "between" period, Nancy Mairs insists that the cross is what signifies God in the world (Mairs 1993: 185). More eloquently, she writes:

> Perhaps because I have embraced a faith with crucifixion at its heart, I do not consider suffering an aberration or an outrage to be eliminated at any cost, even the cost of my life. It strikes me as an element intrinsic to the human condition. I don't like it. I'm not asked to like it. I must simply endure in order to learn from it. Those who leap forward to offer me aid in ending it, though they may do so out of the greatest compassion, seek to deny me the fullness of experience I believe I am meant to have. (Mairs 2002: 160)

But this embrace of suffering is never alone. Rather, the footsteps of the cross are trod by the body of Christ, and the resurrection means that he is able to be present with us, especially in the Eucharist. In this way, a theology of the cross bridges the life, death, and resurrection of Jesus and the life of the ecclesial body of Christ. From a disability perspective, "the broken body on earth is to be found not only in the Eucharist . . . , but also in the church, which is the broken body of Christ, and in the broken body of suffering humanity. . . . [Thus] brokenness lies at the heart of the paschal mystery and . . . the church is united through brokenness" (Hull 2003: 21).

To be sure, emphasis on the crucified life of Christ reflects more (Roman) Catholic sensitivities (Mairs is Roman Catholic). At the same time, it resonates with the (Lutheran) Protestant theology of the cross even as it cannot be disconnected from resurrection. In fact, the good news is that a theology of the cross necessarily connects Jesus's humiliation and his exaltation. Death is a prerequisite for resurrection (John 12:24), and Jesus' self-emptying precedes God's lifting him up and giving him a name above every other name (Phil 2:9-11). While we will comment more specifically about eschatological resurrection later, it is important to note here the possibility of living the resurrected life now, even in the midst of death and dying that is characteristic of life under the conditions of creaturely limitations and finitude.

It is on this basis that I suggest how a kenotic theology of the cross also helps us to reframe the doctrines of creation and providence in terms of a theology of redemption.[36] Here, the kenosis revealed in the life and death of Christ provides us with an analogical view of the kenosis of God in creation. A world that is contingent, that includes spontaneity, and that features free creatures is possible precisely because God "withdraws" himself in order to create "space" for others (the world and its various creatures). In such a world, genetic mutations have evolved creatures and whole species that have perished because of inability to adapt to their environment, have resulted mostly in spontaneous abortions, and have produced congenital disabilities (e.g., Down Syndrome); this same world has also allowed accidents to happen (e.g., head injuries), and disabilities caused by the irresponsibility of free creatures (e.g., fetal alcohol syndrome). But such a world of contingency, spontaneity, and possibility also has produced our amazingly vast and complex universe, innumerable plant and animal life-forms, and the remarkable creatures we call *Homo sapiens*.

At the same time, divine kenosis is not only God's mode of creation, but also the chosen mode of redemption. God's redemptive work as revealed in the cross and resurrection also illuminates divine nonviolent and nonintrusive action that effectively, even miraculously, brings life out of death, novelty out of impossibility, and beauty out of suffering and hardship. Divine providence, in this respect, works inconspicuously (as it did in the cross), preserving all that God sees as good, transforming what is fallen and in need of restoration, and bringing forth new life and, ultimately, a whole new world. Herein, a theology of the cross helps us to reinterpret the doctrines of creation and providence for a contemporary theology of disability.

Reimagining Theological Anthropology: Enabling Humanity

But if a theology of the cross illuminates the doctrines of creation and providence, Christ as the self-emptying man for others illuminates, as we had suggested earlier, the doctrine of theological anthropology. It is now time for us to back up this claim by sketching the contours of a disability-informed theological anthropology.[37] My thesis is that the *imago Dei* is less about some constitutive element of the human person and more about God's revelation in Christ and in the faces of our neighbors; yet the life of Jesus provides a normative account for what it means to be human, and the Holy Spirit creatively enables and empowers our full humanity in relationship to ourselves, others, and God, even in the most ambiguous of situations. In what follows, I will argue this trinitarian anthropological thesis within an emergentist framework—of human beings in the image of the triune God (as *imago trinitas*) as embodied or material, as interdependent or interrelational, and as transcending or spiritual—in dialogue with disability perspectives.[38]

Theological Anthropology and the Embodiment of Disability

After a long history of marginalizing the body, Christian theologians are finally beginning to see the importance of articulating a theology of embodiment.[39] Similarly, after an equally lengthy history of Christian exhortation to "the disabled" that they will be rewarded in the afterlife, the time is long overdue for a disability theology of embodiment. I suggest the following two trajectories to open the conversation.

To begin, a disability theology of embodiment is much better able to appreciate, account for, and nurture created particularity, uniqueness, and difference. By now we recognize that we need a theology of creation and a correlating theological anthropology that accentuates difference. The creation narrative suggests that the wind or breath (*ruach*) of God hovered over the waters precisely in order to nurture and even birth the many things of the world. In fact, God revels in plurality and difference, allowing the earth to bring forth its varied vegetation and the waters to teem with living creatures, creating multitudes of creatures to populate the earth and sky, and commanding that animals and humans be fruitful and multiply (Gen 1). On the one hand, a theology of embodiment calls for an acknowledgment of the close quantitative (biological) ties between human beings and the animal world (van Huyssteen 2004: 201; cf. MacIntyre 1999). On the other hand, the emergence of the human spirit marks a qualitative difference between pongidae and hominidae—a difference that truly makes a difference.

From a disability perspective, then, a theology of the body that emphasizes plurality and difference would see the Holy Spirit (the *ruach* of God) "not as the power to rescue and repair according to some presupposed 'original state' or ideal form, but as the energy for 'unleashing multiple forms of corporeal flourishing'" (Betcher

2004: 82).[40] In this case, the *imago Dei* can never be a single attribute, but requires multiple lenses to identify, behold, and appreciate (Deland 1999).[41] Without minimizing what the "Elephant Man" endured (see above p. 83), Joseph Merrick's life nevertheless is a stubborn reminder to the church that the image of God "is never fully graspable, knowable, possessible" (Graham and Oehlschlaeger 1992: 99). Such a theological posture would resist the "attempt by doctors and those of a medical disposition to suggest that God has it within his power to homogenize humanity by miraculously eradicating genetic diversity" (Monteith 2005: 146; cf. Scully 2002). People with disabilities are, in this theological construct, accepted, included, and valued members of the human family regardless of how they measure up to our economic, social, and political conventions.

The other trajectory for a disability theology of embodiment emerges from the recognition that it foregrounds the lived experiences of people with disability. Whether this derives from the fact that "disabled bodies are also sites of pain" (Stuart 2000: 166) is important, but not the main issue. The main issues are theological—hence the import of the doctrine of the resurrection of the body (see chap. 9)—and phenomenological, especially in being able to take into account the existentiality of disability. Only a theology of embodiment can begin to overcome Cartesian dualism and account holistically for the human experience as including other bodies, the environment, and technological enhancements or even substitutes for our bodily parts. So if for a visually impaired pianist the piano "is a *part of my body* that cannot be separated from me" (Iwakuma 2002: 78; italics in original), and if the cane is the "arm" of a blind person, then is not the wheelchair also a bodily extension of its user (cf. Dorn 1998: 190–99)?[42] Hence there is a recognition of the diversity of forms of human embodiment, even while there is an acknowledgment of the limitations—sometimes severe and profound—that attend with different levels of intensity along that spectrum.

Framed in this way, a theology of the body lifts up, values, and nurtures the full range of human embodiment. The intellectually disabled are no less fully human precisely because of their embodiment, even if they are severely or profoundly retarded.[43] Further, they are no less sexual beings who find fulfillment in sexual relationships even if they, along with many who are physically disabled, do require various kinds of supports in this arena.[44] Last, but certainly not least, the bodies of people with disabilities are to be valued and cared for. This includes the proper nutrition, rest, exercise, and even leisure. Against the capitalistic assumption that only those who are economically productive are entitled to leisure and play, a theology of human embodiment insists that leisure and play time are fundamental aspects of human identity, even for people with disabilities. In this case, entering into the world of leisure, play, and even competition with people with disabilities can help us to redeem the time in ways that undermine behaviors and practices that are driven by greed and self-seeking (see Carroll 1981).

But someone might object that to expend all of this energy on physical (or genetic) difference and disabled bodies is to neglect human souls. While I will address this issue at greater length later, a preliminary response harks back to the emergentist view proposed earlier in this chapter. Recall that an emergentist anthropology insists human souls are new levels of experience constituted by but irreducible to their bodily parts. I now want to expand this point in two directions. First, I suggest that it is precisely the emergence of the human spirit—in part explicated by the biblical author who wrote, "the LORD God formed man from the dust of the ground, and breathed into his nostrils the breath of life; and the man became a living being" (Gen 2:7)—which accounts for human consciousness and, for most although not all, self-awareness as embodied creatures. This is why human beings are never merely either (knowing) subjects or (material) objects, but are rather simultaneously subjective objects (bodies who know themselves as such) and objective subjects (thinkers or feelers who are nevertheless constituted by their bodies). Human persons are souls or spiritual beings in at least this sense.

Second, the meeting of human persons occurs in a relational (emergent) "space" that is mediated through our embodiment. This is the brilliant insight of French phenomenologist Emmanuel Levinas, who insisted that the other is revealed to me through his or her face, and that this revelation obligates me to the other, judges me as failing to meet the needs of the other, and binds me inextricably to him or her.[45] This means not only that the face of the other beckons me toward obligation but also that the face-to-face encounter also serves to reveal my self and my limitations. Thus, there is no meeting of human beings—disabled or otherwise—as whole persons apart from our embodiment. Similarly, there is no meeting of human souls (or spirits) apart from this encounter of living (enspirited, even ensouled) bodies.[46] This moves us from a pneumatological theology of embodiment toward a pneumato-theological anthropology of interrelationality.

Toward an Anthropology of Interrelationality

The notion of interdependence and interrelationality is the second key insight that a disability perspective contributes to a Christian theological anthropology (see section "Feminism and Disability" in chap. 5; cf. Schwöbel 1991; Black 1998). From an emergentist perspective, human relationality is simply a further level of reality that is constituted by interacting embodied human persons but not reducible to the sum of any number of individuals. Theologically speaking, however, the biblical witness also presents the Holy Spirit as the bond of human relationship (see Yong 2002: 28–34). Although this is especially clear with regard to members of the body of Christ (to which we return in the next chapter), I suggest that it is also possible to think about human relationality in general in pneumatological terms since the spheres of our interpersonal and intersubjective engagements are emergent at least in part because of God's giving us the breath of life. Note that I distinguish between interpersonal relations that may involve non-self-conscious persons—for example, those who have profound intellectual disabilities—from *intersubjective* relations that involve self-consciously engaged persons, although I insist that both levels of emergent relations are nevertheless grounded by human embodiment. To develop this idea, I want to first discuss human interrelationality descriptively before suggesting some more normative reflections.

I suggest that an anthropology of interrelationality is able to account for the interpersonal encounters and intersubjectivity most palpably experienced in and between relationships involving people with disabilities. This is clearly seen in the caregiver relationship, especially when involving individuals needing 100 percent care. In these cases, is not the dignity of the person with disability "attached" to the dignity of his or her parent (usually mother) or caregiver, such that we feel good when we see nondisabled caregivers take great pride in managing the appearances of those they are caring for? Hence, we rightly conclude that human worth inheres in the disabled body "not because she is a being with the capacity for rational practical reasoning, but *because she is a being who has become who she is through the loving care of a mothering person*—a person who herself embodies intrinsic worth" (Kittay 2003: 114, italics in original; cf. Bogdan and Taylor 1992: 287).

Further, there is the fact that the more severely or profoundly disabled express and manifest their self-identity precisely in and through their relationships of interdependence with others. If human lives find meaning in relationships, then such meaning might be expressed in certain cases only through such relationships (see Ferguson 2003). We can briefly assess these interdependencies by taking first the case of the severely physically disabled. In reflecting on her collaboration with Diane DeVries, a congenital amputee without arms and legs, over a span of twenty-plus years, Gelya Frank notes the convergence of their lives and their interdependence: Frank needed DeVries to complete her ethnographic fieldwork, to attain professional recognition, and to publish her work in a secular university tenure system (here Frank was especially vulnerable since she pledged never to publish anything about DeVries without her approval), while DeVries needed Frank for various social, material, and financial matters, to the point of even manipulating Frank in various respects as well as moving in with her for a short period of time (Frank 2000: chap. 7). At one point, Frank recalls DeVries introducing her as "my biographer" (116), communicating a sense of DeVries's "ownership" of the relationship. There is also a poignant scene (105–6) of Frank and DeVries praying together (the latter at one point a "born again" Christian and the former a Jewish child of Holocaust survivors), displaying the kind of interreligious hospitality that can occur when people meet at the intersections of "disability." But not only were their lives inextricably intertwined as two individuals, Frank wonders with the publication of her biographical ethnography whom DeVries really belongs to. Does she belong to herself, to Frank as her biographer, to us as readers of the biography? Frank reproduces an insightful student's reflection/response to her guest lecture with DeVries at the University of Southern California graduate course in 1979: "She [DeVries] is one of us, yet not one of us; is she above, below us, inside us—she has no place, she must be hidden for we cannot place her and categorize her. . . . It is I who am crippled not she—she can tolerate me but I can't tolerate her. . . . Why is she evil then—because she points to my inadequacy" (164).

This kind of symbiotic confluence also occurs when the relationship involves people with communicative disabilities. The cooperation between Ruth Sienkiewicz-Mercer and Steven B. Kaplan (1989) exemplifies the interdependence that emerges in these cases. Ruth was born with cerebral palsy in 1950, diagnosed at the age of twelve as an "imbecile," and hospitalized for sixteen years in part because of her practical immobility. Yet she learned how to communicate facially through gestures, sounds, eye, and lip movements; managed to enroll in school in 1969; and began "writing" her life story in 1976. Kaplan met her and they began collaborating in 1979. After working together for more than 2,000 hours over the next six years, they published *I Raise My Eyes to Say Yes* (1989). While the words are Kaplan's, nothing was published that was not approved by Ruth. Kaplan writes in the preface (1989: xv), "Whatever talents I brought to the party, ultimately I was a receptive subject. Ruth's eyes and mind utilized me—my mind, my eyes, my voice, my endless questions, and my writing faculties—as her word processor." In this sense, *I Raise My Eyes to Say Yes* is the product of a profound interpersonal and intersubjective relationship. This is the case also with many of the writings of people with intellectual disability (e.g., Chamberlain 1976; Atkinson 1997: 130–35).

From a theological perspective, I suggest a pneumatological framework helps us understand the emergent possibilities and actuality of such interpersonal and intersubjective relationships. The Spirit who has been poured out on all flesh is no respecter of persons (Acts 2:17, 10:34). People with and without disabilities can be caught up in the Spirit's blowing across the world, and in the process, their lives converge even as what emerges are new lives enriched one by the other. But in this case, an anthropology of interrelationality cannot remain merely descriptive, but must also speak prescriptively—normatively—in its theological voice.

One way for us to think about the normative implications of an anthropology of interrelationality is in terms of the notion of friendship.[47] Friendships are emergent realities constituted by but irreducible to two (or more) individual persons. A disability perspective exposes how modernity's notions of freedom, autonomy, and expertise undermine the kind of social flourishing that comes with mutuality, reciprocity, and interrelationality (see Shuman 1995). For its part, theology invites us to follow the leads of God, who called Abraham friend (Jas 2:23), and Jesus, who called his disciples friends (John 15:14). We can say that one of the gifts of God is the gift of friends. To be sure, people with disabilities gain from the friends they are gifted with, but the nondisabled are also graced through their disabled friends (witness the mutuality of Frank and DeVries). Grace is mediated, albeit in different ways. But the power of friendship is precisely that self-sacrificial mutuality emerges apart from what friends think they may gain from their relationships. Hence, the mutuality, reciprocity, and intersubjectivity of such friendships are not to be evaluated by tit-for-tat measurements, and genuine interpersonal relations are possible even with people with severe and profound intellectual disabilities. As Stanley Hauerwas says, "Friends need no justification. Friendship is a gift and, like most significant gifts, it is surrounded by mystery" (in Swinton 2004: 23). From the perspective of a theology of the cross, friendship is that mystery wherein we experience no greater love than the willingness to lay own our lives for others (John 15:13).

Hence, to befriend and to embrace friendship is to participate in the life of God as revealed in the life of Jesus. Friendship embodies and makes present in this world the peace of God (see Swinton 2000a: chaps. 6, 11; cf. Swinton 2000b). Friendship manifests commitment and mutual human valuation. A theological anthropology shaped by disability commitments would therefore emphasize friendship as a normative mode of human relations so that the transformative work of the Holy Spirit can shape, usually unobtrusively, those relationships of mutuality for the glory of God. When friendship flourishes—God's friendship with us and God's gift of friendship to us and for us—the us/them or nondisabled/disabled dichotomies are overcome (see Veatch 1986: 199–202).[48] Just importantly, friendship thrives from, inspires us to nurture, and invites us to practice the virtue of hospitality. As we shall see in the next chapter, hospitality cuts both ways, between and beyond the us versus them, so that all are transformed by the working of the Spirit of God.

Disability, the Human Spirit, and the Imago Dei

In theological perspective, friendship not only becomes a central feature of human relations, but also serves as a medium that makes present God's unconditional and saving embrace of all people. I suggest that this means how we treat others, even strangers, as friends is central to the gospels' account of how God's saving grace is made available to the world (cf. McFarland 1998: chap. 5). As Sharon Betcher notes (2000: 93), when she says as a person with a disability "Excuse me, I need your help"—"In that moment the frozen wall between us topples; in your converted countenance, I discern that, as if in the twinkling of an eye, you have been changed. For the 45 seconds I needed you, you did not feel extraneous to the world. Sometimes I will ask for help just to save you, the non-disabled, from superficiality and irrelevance—just to save us from your own worst fear." In that moment, God's saving grace is made available through "the stranger" or those on the margins, and we can receive this grace or not depending on how we respond. This is the criterion dividing the sheep and the goats at the judgment: "just as you did it to one of the least of these who are members of my family, you did it to me" (Matt 25:40).[49] Hence, the question concerns not the dependence of the disabled on the nondisabled but the other way around: the nondisabled are dependent on the disabled, whom God has chosen to be a means of saving grace.[50]

And why should we not expect God to be present in our embodied and face-to-face encounters with others? I have suggested that God's gift of the breath of life to the dust of the ground that constituted *ha adam* invites us to understand the human constitution in emergentist terms. In this framework, human souls are emergent from and constituted by human bodies and brains without being reducible to the sum of these biological parts. Similarly, human communities are emergent from and constituted by human persons without being reducible to the sum of these individuals. Finally, I am suggesting, the relationship between God and human beings is a further but definitive emergent level of reality that involves and is fundamentally constituted by our embodiment and our interactions with others and the world, but is irreducible to the sum of all of these parts as well.

Let me flesh out briefly how this multileveled emergentist anthropology engages divine transcendence in dialogue with disability perspectives. To begin, I suggest that we read the biblical references to the transcendental aspects of the human person in emergentist terms. Murdoch Dahl suggests (1962: 71–72) that "[t]he Hebrew mind never produces anything quite like an abstraction; 'soul' and 'heart' and 'flesh' each mean the totality of man considered from different aspects." Of course, there are abstractions (like Locke's) and there are abstractions (like Dahl's). I take Dahl's point to be that, theologically speaking, the Hebrew soul or heart captures the totality of the human person as he or she stands in relationship to God. From this, it is important to insist that such totality cannot be explicated merely in terms of the sum of its parts. Put this way, emergentist theory goes some way toward explaining how it is that people with intellectual disabilities encounter and relate to God. On the one hand, for people with various levels of developmental and learning disabilities, their cognitive capacities will be less heightened but their "spiritual antennae" will nevertheless be emergent in some respect. In these cases, as many professionals in the health care field have suggested, "spiritual awareness, or more precisely an awareness of God, is only marginally related to intelligence, if at all" (Webb-Mitchell 1993: 94).

So while the "spiritual antennae" of people who are profoundly disabled will lack a developed cognitive component, since the human soul is not reducible to cognition, other aspects of their embodiment will be activated by the relationships that sustain them. As John Swinton notes (1997: 24–25), in this relational framework, "[W]e can see that for the profoundly handicapped individual, awareness of the transcendent love of God is mediated through, and experienced in, temporal love, offered in loving relationships. It is therefore in the quality of our relationships, as opposed to the quantity of the intellect, that the image is restored." In an emergentist perspective, experiential faith is not inferior to cognitively engaged forms of faith precisely because we exist in relationship with God as whole beings. Put in theological terms, we encounter God in faith through various levels of consciousness and self-consciousness; in hope through various levels of longing and desire; and in love through various levels of affective, emotional, interpersonal, and intersubjective relations.[51]

Such a view also accounts for how human beings can remain in relationship with God even after having lost their cognitive capacities. Theologian Kathryn Greene-McCreight writes (2006: esp. chaps. 7–8) of her thirteen-year-long battle with severe manic depression and suggests that the soul as the center of each person's feeling, memory, and personality, and as the seat of each human being's capacity to be in relation to God, is unaffected when our emotions, memories, and personalities disintegrate because of mental illness. More important, the soul remains in relationship with God even when our brains deteriorate and our minds are "lost." In an emergentist perspective, the sum of the whole (the soul) after years of conscious (cognitive) relationship with God does not just disappear when the brain dysfunctions and the mind drifts (as happens with, e.g., Alzheimer's disease). Rather, the whole is indelibly shaped by the various parts of its experience and therefore other dimensions of the whole (e.g., the affections) remain informed and engaged by those experiences even after they cease in intensity. Hence, Greene-McCreight can experience and then recover from mental illness but yet still sense (at least affectively, no doubt) that she was in relationship with God all during that time. I suggest people with Alzheimer's or those in comas who may never regain their cognitive capacities nevertheless remain engaged in relationship with God (if they were believers before) even during these periods of degeneration and dying. For these reasons (among others), we must be vigilant and theologically responsible in our ethical posture toward end-of-life situations.

I want to be sure to remind the reader that my emergentist account is as much theological as it is (neuro)scientific. This is because of the robust pneumatological thread that winds its way through the construct. Not only does the breath of God give life to *ha adam*, it also informs our consciousness (traditionally understood in terms of the human conscience), our interpersonal and intersubjective relationship with others (traditionally understood in terms of the Holy Spirit as the communion of Christian fellowship; 2 Cor 13:13), and our relationship with God (traditionally understood in terms of the Spirit's drawing us into fellowship with God). In all of these ways, I suggest that the Holy Spirit is at work in all human lives to shape us in the image of God in Christ.

I have attempted especially in this last section but also throughout this chapter as a whole to suggest that Christian theological anthropology in the twenty-first century can and should be reimagined in dialogue with both disability and pneumatological perspectives. My thesis has been that the Holy Spirit creatively enables and empowers our full humanity in relationship to our embodied selves, to others, and to God, even in the most ambiguous and challenging of situations. In this sense, what it means to be created in the image of God has been initially glimpsed in the life of Jesus Christ but remains to be unveiled definitively only as the eschatological revelation of God is unfolded by the power of the Holy Spirit. As Ian McFarland puts it (2001: 13), a trinitarian theology of human nature cannot be comprehended in essentialist and ontological categories but is "an eschatological reality defined by the emerging pattern of relationships between those summoned by God in Christ." Therefore, self-consciousness is neither a necessary nor a sufficient criterion for the image of God; rather, on an emergentist-theological account, it is relationship with God that counts, especially that which we now anticipate as promised in the eschaton.[52] Human nature is in the making, performed by God in and through us as we are enabled by the power of the Holy Spirit. In this Christian self-understanding, the social space or "place" where this occurs most intentionally is the church. To the doctrine of the church, then, we turn in the next chapter.

VII

Renewing Ecclesiology
Down Syndrome, Disability, and the Community of Those Being Redeemed

There is no way that I could save myself for my husband. So I don't feel bad, but, like, if I went to the pastor or some of the families of the church and told them, they would look down on me so fast that it wouldn't be funny. If I came in that church pregnant they wouldn't throw me out, but they wouldn't be as warm and as friendly as they are right now. They would be very disappointed, let's put it that way. They think that I am the best girl, the sweetest and kindest and all that kind of stuff. I am sweet, but I have my ways of doing it. The family that I am going to live with knows I've fooled around. I let her know because I didn't want somebody else to tell her.

—Pattie Burt, in Bogdan and Taylor 1994: 196

I want to eat Jesus bread. . . . I can't wait until I can eat Jesus bread and drink Jesus juice. People who love Jesus are the ones who eat Jesus bread. . . . Jesus' skin and meat turned into bread and Jesus' blood and guts turned into juice—that's Jesus' bread and Jesus' juice, and I want to eat it and drink with all the other Christians at church 'cause I love him so.

—Judy, in Hoogewind 1998: 94

At the consecration of the bread something happened inside me. It's hard to explain. I was holding the bread in my right hand and I said the words, "This is my body. . . ." Right then

I was holding Vincent in my left, and it seemed that Jesus was telling me, "This is my body . . . ." It made a perfect circle, the same reality, the same Presence. Vincent's body, so broken and poor, was also the broken body of Jesus. I held both in my hands, and I knew both of them were sacred.

—Buser 1996: 80–81

The Eucharist,
and the washing of the feet of wounded people,
the broken body of Christ,
are in some ways
the same reality:
one giving meaning to the other,
one flowing from the other.

—Vanier 1988: 133

Mark loves to attend "ICF" (International Christian Fellowship, the church my father now pastors in Stockton). He loves seeing his friends, hugging them, and greeting new people. He loves the singing, sometimes to the point of dancing (or at least moving his flat feet and body to the beat of his own drum). Sometimes he's more active—clapping, lifting up his hands, waving, applauding; other times he's more subdued, closing his eyes and remaining "in the presence of the Lord." For new folk, the sight of a young man with Down Syndrome, the sound of his loud singing or exclaiming "Amen!" "Yes Lord!" and "Hallelujah!" or even the occasion when he brings forth words of exhortation from scripture (the Pentecostal tradition calls this prophesying) during the appropriate moments of the worship service—all of this may be jarring at first. But Mark knows that he is in the presence of God, and that worshipping God is more important than what others might think of him.

During the sermon, Mark listens and/or reads his Bible. After the sermon, during the altar time (ICF still features a regular altar call in the tradition of classical Pentecostal revivalism), Mark may be one of those who will come up to different individuals, both known and unknown to him, and lay his hands gently on them (usually their shoulders, sometimes their foreheads) and pray for them. If he prays aloud, those he is praying for may not quite comprehend the content of his prayers. But Mark steadfastly rebukes the devil and blesses the people of God in Jesus' name. Mark also seems to know when his mother's enthusiastic testimonies and words of exhortation have gone on too long (he might try to get her attention to conclude), and he often attempts to help younger children calm down during worship so that they would not hinder the flow of the service.

Otherwise, when home and not reading the Bible or watching videos (usually with a Christian message), Mark will more often than not be found listening to his worship tapes or CDs (he has never gotten into the habit of watching cable TV), sometimes for hours on end. On various occasions, he will lift up his hands in praise right there in his own bedroom. During family prayer times, he will usually add his own prayers at some point. Mark believes God answers prayer, especially prayers for healing. When I asked Mark what he usually prays for, he answered, "For people to get healed," for "salvation," and for "one nation under God with liberty and justice for all."

We turn in this chapter from the doctrines of creation, providence, Christology, and theological anthropology to the doctrine of the church. At one level, because this entire project is also, at least in part, a performative theology (see pp. 13–14), the overall question we are asking and seeking to answer is how then we should live. In that case, this chapter's response concerns the nature of the new community of God shaped by the life of Christ and formed by the Spirit of Jesus. At another level, insofar as this project can also be said to be driven by the quest to understand God's redemptive work in a world of many disabilities, the overall question we are asking and seeking to answer is ultimately soteriological. In that case, this chapter's response fleshes out the communal and ecclesial dimensions of God's saving work and bridges the reflections on theological anthropology in the previous chapter to the reflections on soteriology proper in the next. But inasmuch as this volume is finally a late modern reconstruction of the systematic theological loci in dialogue with disability perspectives, then this chapter focuses on ecclesiology and seeks to present a vision of the church that is not just relevant to but also constituted by the experiences of disability.

The argument of this chapter therefore unfolds in three parts. The first section presents an understanding of the church reformed and renewed by disability perspectives, while the next two expand on the practices and ministries of such a church for the twenty-first century. Throughout, our thoughts are informed, again, by disability interrogations on the one hand, and the pneumatological imagination on the other. If for theological anthropology pneumatological insights provide a framework to understand human beings as emergent self-conscious (spiritual) creatures in relationship with others and with God, for ecclesiology the doctrine of the Spirit helps us understand how the membership of all people—the strong and weak, the nondisabled and disabled—constitute the fellowship, communion, and ministry of the body of Christ. In other words, the church is the despised and marginalized of the world made strong not out of their own resources but by the power of the Spirit of God (Zech 4:6).

Toward an Ecclesiology of Inclusion

We begin our ecclesiological inquiry by outlining the contours of traditional ecclesiologies and noting more recent developments. Against this background, we focus on a case study of the L'Arche community established by Jean Vanier in order to gain some empirical traction for the more abstract reflections that follow about the doctrine of the church in disability perspective. The vision of the church to be developed in this section is that of the body of Christ as an inclusive and accessible fellowship of difference indwelt by the Holy Spirit.

Traditional and Recent Ecclesiologies

Traditional discussions of the doctrine of the church have focused on four or five questions of perennial dispute.[1] First, what is the nature of the church? The classical answer has been in terms of the four marks or notes of the church as one, holy, united, and apostolic. Second, what is the proper governing structure of the church? This has been an especially pressing question since the Protestant Reformation called into question the episcopal framework in favor of presbyterian or congregational forms of church government. Third, what is the nature of the sacraments of the church? Again, Protestantism has broadened the possibility of conceiving the sacraments from being media of divine grace to being symbols of human discipleship, with various ways to articulate these differences in between. Finally, what about the ordained ministry of the church—should it include women (and now, gays and lesbians)? Of course, neither these questions nor the proposed answers exhaust traditional ecclesiologies, but they have driven the ecclesiological conversation for the past few centuries, and some matters—for example, the ordination of gays and lesbians—show no signs of being resolved anytime soon. In any case, while an ecclesiology informed by disability perspectives will not need to be framed by the classical ecclesiological disputes and categories, it should nevertheless also have something to contribute to these debates, at least in the interests of renewing the practices of the church in the twenty-first century.

Nevertheless, there have also been some recent developments in ecclesiology that deserve mention in relationship to our project. Let me briefly mention here four trajectories: the church as charismatic fellowship, the church in the global South, the Emerging Church, and the postliberal church.

The Church as Charismatic Fellowship

Central to what I have called pneumatological ecclesiology is the idea of the church as a charismatic fellowship of the Spirit (see Yong 2005a: chaps. 3–4; cf. also Van Gelder 2000; Kärkkäinen 2002: pt. 2; Vondey 2004). Complementing more traditional understandings of the church as the body of Christ, pneumatological ecclesiologies emphasize the unity, holiness, and apostolicity of the church in terms of the Spirit's eschatological presence and activity that both marks the church as and transforms the church into the image of Christ. Further, the mission of the church is empowered by the Spirit, and the Spirit's empowerment comes on all equally, whether male or female, old or young, free or slave (cf. Acts 2:17-18; Gal 3:28), with the latter of each pair historically excluded or marginalized not only from positions of leadership and service but also from the community of faith. Finally, expanding on this point, the governance of the church is essentially pneumatic and charismatic rather than hierarchical: the church is led by the Spirit who is poured out on all flesh, even if the Spirit-filled and Spirit-led people of God are anointed to offices of service and need to discern the work of the Spirit in the midst of the church. So the point of pneumatological ecclesiologies is not to undermine the structures of the church, but to ensure that the church does not degenerate into a mere institution devoid of the Spirit's energetic endowments. In the process, might a reconsideration of the church as a charismatic fellowship of the Spirit turn out to be more inclusive for people with disabilities?

The Church in the Global South[2]

Insofar as the shape of Christianity in the twenty-first century is dominated by the shift from the Euro-American West to Latin America, Africa, and Asia, to that same extent thinking about the church is beginning to reflect perspectives derived from outside the Latin and Anglo-American orbit. Central to the ecclesiologies of the global South are the decentralization of the church and its ministries, especially in terms of empowering the laity; the emergence of women and youth, away from a patriarchally organized institution; and the focus on engaging issues related to poverty and social liberation, which are not clearly reflected in the earlier ecclesiological debates. While some of these features dovetail with the central elements of pneumatological ecclesiology, they are also important for this project precisely because of the urgency of disability issues in the global South (see again the middle section of chap. 5 on "Disability and World Cultures").

The Emerging Church

Not to be confused with the emergentist anthropology developed in the previous chapter, the Emerging Church is a distinctively twenty-first-century Anglo-American version of what is forming in the global South (McLaren 2000; Kimball 2003; Gibbs and Bolger 2005). Reflecting the demise of denominationalism, the church is now better considered in terms of networks, communities, and in theological terms, the wider kingdom of God. In a postmodern and even post-Christian context, the focus is on retrieving and embodying—rather than merely proclaiming—premodern beliefs in ways that build relationships with others. Shared practices are central to the Emerging Church mentality, whether that be in terms of participatory liturgies, multisensory and multimedia worship and teaching experiences, use of the creative and expressive arts, and hospitality and generosity shown to strangers and "outsiders." In this framework, there is less of a concern for drawing or maintaining hard-and-fast lines, whether institutionally (between church and world) or interpersonally (between believer and nonbeliever), and more of a concern for cultural relevance and engagement. Whereas the emphasis on welcoming strangers is focused primarily on those in other religious traditions, this Emerging Church conviction is nevertheless invaluable, as we shall see, for an ecclesiology sensitive to disability concerns.

Postliberal Ecclesiologies

The movement called postliberalism is characterized by its central conviction that theological liberalism is bankrupt precisely because it has capitulated to the norms of modernity—namely, Enlightenment rationalism, scientism, positivism, and secularism—and privatized the sphere of religion (see Hütter 2000; Goh 2000; Lindbeck 2002). Against the Enlightenment confidence in a universal reason, postliberal thinkers counter that all thinking, including modern rationality, is contextually situated and informed by distinctive traditions, texts, and practices. Postliberal ecclesiologies emphasize that the Christian tradition, the biblical narratives, and the church's practices shape a distinctively Christian way of life and thought. With the collapse of modernity's pretenses, the church can once again engage the public square on its own terms rather than on the terms of an allegedly neutral playing field.

Stanley Hauerwas has been one of the architects of the postliberal ecclesiology.[3] The significance of Hauerwas's ecclesiological vision is that it was shaped by his service during the 1970s–1980s on the Board of the Council for the Retarded of St. Joseph County, Indiana. Arguably, Hauerwas's ethical, theological, and ecclesiological project as a whole cannot be comprehended apart from his work with the mentally retarded early on in his career.[4] Emphases on virtuous practices, nonviolence, and communally shaped character are part of his insistence that the church should embody the kind of compassionate, peaceable, and hospitable posture exemplified in the life of Jesus, and that only such an orientation to the world in our time is capable of welcoming and embracing the oppressed, marginalized, and rejected, including people with disabilities. For Hauerwas, then, the church is measured not by the norms of modernity but by how well it embodies the life of Christ, how extensively it welcomes and is constituted by the weak, and how prophetically it holds up the mirror of the gospel to an unbelieving world.

L'Arche: Christian Community in Disability Perspective

In my community, we welcome Antonio, a man of twenty-six. His body was small and broken. He could neither walk, nor talk, nor eat alone. Physically, he was weak and constantly needed to be given oxygen. He did not live for long but, while he was, Antonio was a ray of sunshine. When we approached him and called him by name, his eyes shone with trust and his face burst into a smile. He was really beautiful. His littleness, his trust and his beauty touched people's hearts; people wanted to be with him. Poor and weak people can disturb us, but they can also awaken our hearts. Obviously, Antonio was demanding; he was so poor. He needed constant and competent support day and night. He needed to be washed and fed and to have people close to him. But at the same time, he awoke the hearts of assistants; he transformed them and helped them to discover a new dimension of humanity. He introduced them to a world, not of competition and action, but of contemplation, presence and tenderness. Antonio did not demand money, knowledge, power or position; he demanded communication and tenderness. Perhaps he revealed a face of God, a God who does not govern all our problems by force and extraordinary power, but a God who longs for our hearts, who calls us to communion. (Vanier 1997a: 223)

There are many people like Antonio in the L'Arche (The Ark) community. In fact, L'Arche communities are residential homes constituted by the severely and profoundly disabled, called core members, and their assistants. Its first home—established in 1964, at the beginning of the deinstitutionalization movement, at Trosly-Breuil, a village in northern France—consisted of two French Catholics, Jean Vanier (1928–) and Fr. Père Thomas Philippe (1905–1993), and two men with intellectual disabilities, Philippe Seux (1941–) and Raphaël Simi (1928–2003). Vanier had just completed his doctoral dissertation at L'Institut Catholique in Paris on the philosophy of happiness—in which he argued for the interconnectedness of justice, friendship, and spiritual contemplation (Vanier 1965)—and he was inspired by Philippe to put his ideas into practice. Since this "irreversible decision," as Vanier puts it, the vision of L'Arche has multiplied such that there are today more than 120 L'Arche communities on six continents and in thirty countries.[5]

I suggest that L'Arche embodies and manifests the values and perspectives articulated by the more recent ecclesiologies surveyed above. Long before the Emerging Church, L'Arche communities were already bringing strangers together and providing a hospitable environment wherein friendships between people with disabilities and their assistants could flourish. As if growing in tandem with the churches of the global South and as if announcing its own version of the postliberal vision, L'Arche has been a countercultural, egalitarian, and democratic community where strength has been manifest in weakness; where self-sacrificial love has resisted modernity's emphases on convenience, comfort, consumption, competition, and efficiency; and where the miraculous has been understood in terms of the ordinary and simple events of daily life: rising, dressing, working, eating, doing chores, sharing stories, helping, praying together, sleeping, and dreaming. And from a pneumatological perspective, L'Arche is animated by a deeply trinitarian vision: "[T]he Spirit's dwelling within the human person in the secret recesses of the heart, moving us to participate in Christ's mysteries and in the activity of the Beatitudes, is in itself a most ineffable mystery and gives the dimension of mystery to the human person" (Downey 1986: 104). Put alternatively, L'Arche can also be said to embody as a community the theology of the cross: "So many thousands of suffering people, with crippled bodies or crippled minds or crippled hearts, and yet the whole experience was one of joyful celebration. It was an overwhelming sign, a living proof that Christ is risen" (Fr. Bill Clarke, in Clarke 1973: 145). In a sense, L'Arche manifests the power of the Spirit, who brought forth life out of the death of Christ on the cross.

Yet L'Arche's vision of community can be understood to be but an extension of Vanier's theological anthropology.[6] While I have used the notions of embodiment, relationality, and transcendence in the tridimensional anthropology proffered earlier (see part three of chap. 6), these elements are also present in Vanier's thinking about what it means to be human, albeit under different categories. With regard to embodiment, for example, Vanier has given extended consideration to human sexual identity, especially given the arrangements of community life. So in his book, *Man and Woman He Made Them* (1985), Vanier wrestles deeply with our humanity, probing especially into the question of what it means to consider the intellectually disabled as embodied and holistic creatures. He notes (1985: 6–7) that in L'Arche, "freedom in sexual relations was not allowed, but we acknowledged the possibility that some people might be guided toward a greater autonomy and, eventually, towards human love in the bonds of marriage." Yet the communal practice of celibacy also mediates the mystery of love and of being in love with Jesus.

This mystery of love is central to the communal vision of L'Arche, which seeks to overcome the barriers between people through building relationships and friendships of mutuality, and through the practices of welcoming the stranger and the needy. For Vanier, the human journey proceeds from loneliness and rejection (due to fear) to belonging, from exclusion to inclusion, from brokenness to community, from oppression to liberation, through paths of healing, forgiveness, and freedom. Ultimately the friendship of Christ empowered by the Holy Spirit results in human reconciliation and communion. What does reconciliation mean but the redemption of both victims and oppressors, of the disabled and the nondisabled (cf. Vanier 1998a: 155–61), and what does "communion" mean but being with and walking alongside others, and being taught and healed by others (Vanier 1992: 16–18)? Hence, the heart becomes the most important symbol of L'Arche's communal and relational anthropology as it is in the heart-to-heart (Levinas would say, face-to-face) relationship that people discover not only themselves but also God.[7]

Human relationality mediates the redemptive power and presence of God (transcendence, as Wendell and I call it). Hence, at the center of L'Arche is the presence of the triune God. Jesus is perceived not only as embodied in the Eucharist but also in the broken bodies that constitute the L'Arche community. What is unique about L'Arche is that its Jesus piety and welcome of the stranger ("the disabled") is empowered by the wind of the Holy Spirit that is believed to blow even amid the lives of people of other faiths.[8] Early on in the evolution of L'Arche, its expansion to India in the early 1970s invited the experiment of Asha Niketan (Home of Hope), a multicultural, multireligious, and multiclass/caste residence in Bangalore (see Spink 1991: chap. 6). By 1987 the practices of this L'Arche community included a combination of the "sacrament"/celebration of footwashing (during which Christians renew their baptismal vows) and Hindu texts. Here Vanier also drew on the witness of Gandhi, especially the latter's opting to stay with untouchables in any city he visited, and to name them instead *harijans*, or "children of God" (Vanier 1998b: 84).

What emerged was the interfaith version of L'Arche, wherein its leadership and members aspired to "walk humbly with different traditions, not create its own church with its own rules, worship and liturgy. It means we must move slowly with different persons who come from different theological differences and disciplines, especially the ones around inter-communion. It means also that we share their deep thirst for unity and the recognition of all that unites us as followers of Jesus" (Vanier 1995: 79).[9] Of course, there are challenges such as how to honor differences, negotiate tensions between being a faith community and a center for professional help, and remain prophetic by paying close attention to "the disabled" while deepening the spiritual life of both core members and their assistants. Yet, at the same time, L'Arche communities work intentionally toward ensuring that all residents are enabled and empowered to "drink from the spring flowing in their own faith and tradition. They need to find support and nourishment in God's word, and in the writings and lives of the prophets and saints of each tradition. We must not set these differences up against each other, but try to find what unites us more deeply in our common love for God and those who are weak" (Vanier 1995: 106–7). In L'Arche, then, there is a common search for the mystery of God focused on the one hand on the person of Jesus but also released on the other hand to include other faith traditions by the Holy Spirit.[10]

The Fellowship of the Spirit: Elements of an Inclusive Ecclesiology

In what follows, I want to bring together the latest developments in Christian ecclesiology with the concrete vision of Christian community present in L'Arche. The result is a pneumatological ecclesiology of inclusion: the church considered as a charismatic and inclusive fellowship of the Spirit.[11] I need to be clear, however, that the inclusiveness we are talking about here is not the ideological posture already interrogated in our previous discussions of educating and integrating people with intellectual disabilities (e.g. as seen previously, pp. 68–71). Such inclusive ideologies, William Abraham (2005) reminds us, easily degenerate into idolatry when applied indiscriminately in the church. Rather, the kind of inclusiveness advocated here involves reversing the marginalization of people with disabilities to the periphery of the church and restructuring the church as a community of hospitality (see below, pp. 222–24).[12] In what follows, I consider three levels of such an inclusive ecclesiological vision.

At the biblical-theological level, an inclusive pneumatological ecclesiology builds on the pneumato-theological anthropology previously sketched (see pp. 184–87) and emphasizes not only the Holy Spirit's being poured out on all flesh (Acts 2:17) but also the Spirit as baptizing many members into one body of Christ (1 Cor 12:12-26). Whereas in the Lukan corpus the Spirit comes in power through Jesus and the church "to proclaim release to the captives and recovery of sight to the blind, to let the oppressed go free, [and] to proclaim the year of the Lord's favor" (Luke 4:18-19), in the Pauline framework, all members are equally included and valued. In fact, quoting Paul:

> [T]he members of the body that seem to be weaker are indispensable, and those members of the body that we think less honorable we clothe with greater honor, and our less respectable members are treated with greater respect; whereas our more respectable members do not need this. But God has so arranged the body, giving the greater honor to the inferior member, that there may be no dissension within the body, but the members may have the same care for one another. If one member suffers, all suffer together with it; if one member is honored, all rejoice together with it. (1 Cor. 12:22-26)[13]

Combined, then, a biblically informed and inclusive pneumatological ecclesiology emphasizes both that the church is liberated from whatever disabling barriers might exclude certain of her members from full access and participation and that the "weaker" members are accorded more honor by God and therefore are more central to the identity of the body of Christ.[14] A pneumatological approach is also fitting from a disability perspective since the Holy Spirit, who has traditionally been marginalized—known as the shy or hidden member of the Trinity (see Hordern and Bruner

1984)—is actually the one who acts as the champion and advocate of all people, especially the poor, the "weak," and the oppressed, and who initiates them into the body of Christ (see Block 2000: 138–41). The result is or should be a kind of hospitality in which us/them barriers are overcome. In this perspective, there is a mutuality and reciprocity that characterizes the relationship between the "weak" and the "strong" such that all suffer and rejoice with the challenges and victories of each other.

At the practical level, the church as the fellowship of the Spirit is charismatically empowered by the Spirit to witness to and participate in God's bringing about justice. God's work of justice not only vindicates the oppressed but also brings life out of death. It was at the cross that sin was judged but it was also from the cross that Christ was raised to life by the power of the Holy Spirit for our justification (Rom 1:4, 4:25) precisely so that the Spirit of Christ could be released to redeem the injustices of this world, liberate the oppressed, and reconcile oppressed and oppressor. From a disability perspective, the justification of God translates into both inclusion and accessibility. While the emphasis in the literature has been predominantly on physical and sensory accessibility (e.g., Benton 1995; National Organization on Disability 1996; Kutz-Mellem 1998; Penton 2001), the increasing availability of multimedia technologies means that the hospitality of the Emerging Church can and must be extended to people with disabilities. But going beyond physical and multisensory accessibility, the church must also be concerned with the fair and just integration of all its members (McNair and Smith 2000; Shogren and Rye 2005). This means that honor needs to be given where honor is due, and therefore that people with disabilities cannot be treated as if they were nondisabled. Hence, justice requires the church to walk a fine line. As Stanley Hauerwas puts it (1986: 185), "Retarded people cannot justly be treated 'just like everyone else,' as they often do require 'special education' which allows them to develop skills to interact in society in culturally normative ways. At the same time, to the extent they are singled out for 'special' treatment, we reinforce the unjust characterization of what it means to be retarded. . . . Rather, the true moral question is what kind of community ought we to be so that we can welcome and care for the other in our midst without that 'otherness' being used to justify discrimination?"

Last but not least, for our discussion, is the ecumenical and global level. When set against the background of the practices of the Emerging Church and in the context of the churches of the global South, the biblical metaphor of the Spirit's having been poured out on all flesh suggests that the experience of disability opens up further space for the kind of interfaith ecumenism that we have already seen embodied in the L'Arche community (cf. Yong 2005a: chaps. 4, 6). This means not only that the gift of the Spirit enables shared experiences, mutual witness, and deepened friendship but that such are potentially intensified in and through the presence of disability.[15] We have already seen how disability provided a bridge for the Christian Diane DeVries and the (cultural) Jew Gelya Frank to meet (p. 185). Another account is provided by Chris Maxwell, who was struck suddenly with encephalitis (an acute inflammatory brain disease caused by viral infection) and epilepsy resulting in permanent brain damage. However, this experience brought him into close relationship with a Jewish doctor, even to the point of making it possible for a conservative Protestant to enter into mutual prayer with a person from another faith (see Maxwell 2005: 109). The point is that in a postmodern, postdenominational, and even post-Christian context, the experience of disability cuts across even the staunchest of divides that separate human beings, making it possible for people to meet, to make friends, and to participate in and work together with God's bringing about peace, justice, and wholeness in a broken world. For this reason, the church considered as an inclusive fellowship of the Spirit cannot but be manifest in communities like L'Arche that embody the charismatic gifts of the Spirit in the world.

The Practices of an Inclusive Church

We now move from abstract and communal considerations to theological reflection on the concrete practices of an inclusive church when formulated in disability perspective. We will discuss, in order, the practices related to Christian initiation, the sacraments, and discipleship. We assume throughout this discussion the conviction about the church as the charismatic fellowship of the Spirit, even as we focus more exclusively on the challenges related to intellectual disability.

Initiation and Catechism

Historically, the process of Christian initiation has included catechism, baptism, and first communion (see McDonnell and Montague 1994). We will focus here predominantly on catechism, and turn to the sacraments of baptism and Communion in the next section.

Informed by certain readings of the New Testament that link salvation to baptism and forgiveness (e.g., Acts 2:38; John 3:5; Titus 3:5), the liturgical and episcopal traditions have long understood baptism as connected to the forgiveness of sins and the cleansing of the soul from original sin. In these churches, infants and children have been baptized regardless of the level of their intellectual capacities. In the last generation, however, there has emerged the conviction that even the baptism of intellectually disabled infants and children needs to be followed by catechism and confirmation. This has been related in part to the conviction that providing sacramental access to children with intellectual disabilities includes them in the work of the body of Christ, while also accomplishing the essential task of (re)affirming and embracing their families (Harrington 1982: 43).

On the Protestant side, however, things are a bit more convoluted. Most challenging for our purposes is the assumption in the Free Church (Believer's Church) tradition regarding the essential role of belief, understanding, and confession for Christian conversion. Insofar as "faith comes from what is heard, and what is heard comes through the word of Christ" (Rom 10:17), the deaf and the intellectually disabled generally have been thought of as incapable of receiving the gospel in some circles (Petersen 1960: 117). For Believer's Churches, further, the ordinance (rather than sacrament) of the Lord's Supper is also then limited only to confessing believers. We have cases, then, in which children and adults with intellectual disabilities are excluded from the Lord's Table in their conservative Protestant churches but sometimes participate in the Mass at the Roman Catholic midweek special program for people with intellectual disabilities (see Taylor 1985). These developments among others in conservative Protestantism have spurred rethinking even in these churches about practices regarding inclusion of people with intellectual disabilities. There is the growing realization that "admission—inclusion—will be somewhat hollow unless the people feel it is right. It is their acceptance that ensures the handicapped member truly belongs. The whole church needs to be big enough to carry the weaker member not so much by proxy faith as in corporate faith. Then the sacraments can above all be the way in which severely handicapped people know that they truly belong to the body of Christ" (Bowers 1988: 76).[16]

But if so, then the question becomes one of how properly to initiate people with intellectual disabilities. This is especially problematic in Protestantism with its conviction that salvation is effectively mediated through "knowledge" (of theological or doctrinal content) and that the catechetical process should be focused on cognitively imparting such knowledge to those seeking Christian initiation. However, we have now insisted that this Platonic and Cartesian anthropology is faulty precisely because of its subordination of the body (see pp. 181–83). In fact, "[i]t is often wrongly presumed that religion requires abstract knowledge, or formal operational reasoning. Actually, the practice of religion is very concrete. If one is open to the witness of those with mental retardation who have faith according to their capacity, it is easy to see how concrete faith is. The individual who has authentic mental retardation cannot manage formal operational thought processes and yet believes" (Harrington 1992: 34). Insofar as the Hebrew *yada* refers more to the knowledge of the heart than of the head, Protestants can now learn from Catholic and Orthodox traditions, especially with regard to how human knowing of God is mediated through formation, imitation, affectivity, intuition, imagination, interiorization, and symbolic engagement.[17] Thus, rather than propositions constituting the best form of catechesis, perhaps images, metaphors, paradoxes, humor, ritual, and stories mediated by a diversity of approaches—such as music, artistic media, and modeling—may be better (see pp. 69–71). These are certainly the more effective models of working with those with intellectual, learning, and developmental disabilities.

At the same time, catechesis for Christian initiation should not neglect the content of the gospel in the cases of moderate or mild intellectual disability. While implementing a distinctive pedagogy, such catechumens are not to be pitied, underestimated, or assumed to be "holy innocents" in any naive sense (Bissonnier 1979: 13).

Rather, they are to be basically oriented to the Christian faith in sessions involving parents or guardians. Such teaching should involve leading people with intellectual disabilities to a realization of what the sacramental signs are and how they function; an awareness of the various symbols deployed in the Christian rites; and an understanding of what is involved in confirmation and the life of Christian discipleship. In all of this, the catechist should also assume that at least an implicit awareness of morality, sin, and guilt is present, and that people with intellectual disabilities can experience the pardon and mercy of God (see Bissonnier 1962: 81–83). Catechism is thus an extended process, with each unit of instruction being carefully tailored to the catechumen, according to his/her specific situation and ability (Harding 1989). But what happens is a "'tuning together' the members of the Body of Christ in accordance with the way in which the Church 'chants' or expresses itself . . . , allow[ing] the child [or adult person] with disabilities a chance to work out his or her individual response to God and to comprehend in a profound way God's saving work in Christ" (Loaring 2000: 44). From a pneumatological perspective, it should be said that the Holy Spirit "lives in each person, no matter the extent of their disability. And so there is one at work in the heart of the person before I as a catechist ever arrive on the scene. My work is to be in touch with the Holy Spirit within myself and thus be sensitive to work on the level at which catechesis achieves its purpose" (Harrington 1994: 122–23).

Baptism and Eucharist

Upon assurance that the catechumen and his or her family are ready for the final step of Christian initiation, plans should be made to proceed with the sacrament (ordinance, for the Free Church tradition) of baptism. But baptism is not just an act of immersion or sprinkling but an entire ceremony that should be focused on showering the catechumen with the love of God so that he or she "feels noticed, affirmed, included, valued, and cherished" (Harrington 1994: 121). This happens through sounds, touches, environmental (social and architectural) ambiance, the catechist's relationship to the catechumen, the process of interactions (of discipling and disciplining), and the embrace of the entire community. So while we often said in the past "that such persons needed only the sacrament of Baptism in order to go to heaven . . . , today we see how persons—even those with severe disabilities—are transformed by belonging to a loving community of faith. We observe how the sacramental event gives people a history, a larger family, a feeling of belonging, and a future" (Bernardin 1985: 3). Baptism thereby enacts (or, in Free Churches, reenacts and symbolizes) the passing away of the old and the emergence of the person made new by the Spirit of God.

In liturgical and episcopal traditions, baptism gives the initiate full access to and reception of all the sacraments (Huels 1994; cf. Kern 1985: 91–110). Most important here is the fellowship around the Eucharistic Table (the Lord's Supper in the Free Church tradition). Now for those who have been baptized as infants, there is the question of how to recognize that they are ready for confirmation and first Eucharist. Joseph Bernardin suggests (1985: 5) that the catechist can only discern the readiness of the catechumen "if he or she has taken time to build an authentic relationship with the person." But, further,

> By what signs can a developmentally delayed person indicate readiness for the Eucharist? They are *desire*, *relationships* with people who share faith and prayer, and a *sense of the sacred* as manifest in behavior. Often these people cannot use words which express their understanding of the difference between ordinary bread and the Bread of God, but they can show that they recognize the difference by their manner, the expression in their eyes, their gestures, or the quality of their silence. God's desire to be in communion with the person can be presumed; the person's desire for communion must be awakened and sustained. (Bernardin 1985: 9; italics in original)

These signs are basically interrelationally, interpersonally, and intersubjectively discerned. They also reflect the recent shift in Roman Catholic theology of the Eucharist away from the scholastic understanding of the sacraments (with its emphasis on the substantive presence of Christ defined in Aristotelian metaphysical terms) toward a more personalistic and relational framework in which the sacraments are symbolically communicated, affectively engaged, and interrelationally experienced (see McKenna 1975;

Francis 1994). Partaking of the Eucharist then activates or intensifies the dispositions, affections, and sensibilities displayed by the catechumen so that faith is nurtured through interpersonal experiences rather than via knowing doctrines.

Inclusion around the Table of the Lord together with the community of faith opens up the new believer to the presence Jesus promised where two or three are gathered together or where bread is broken in his name. Hence, the Eucharist becomes the communicative medium through which the members of the body are connected in fellowship with one another and with God.[18] But this relational approach to the sacraments is also robustly pneumatological: "Its principle [sic] objective is to establish a relationship between the person and Christ" (Clifford 1984: 10), and this happens only by the power of the Spirit of Jesus. It is the Holy Spirit, the "bond of peace" (Eph 4:3) and the love of God poured out into human hearts (Rom 5:5), who is the communion that binds us to the grace of Christ and the love of God (2 Cor 13:13).

In this way, the Eucharist becomes a trinitarian experience through which all members of the body—the "weaker" as well as the "stronger"—encounter God in Christ by the Holy Spirit. From the one side, we might say that people with intellectual disabilities in particular are more attuned to the sacramentality of the eucharistic elements at an intuitive and material level related to their affective and embodied rather than merely cognitivist approach to the sacrament. This is captured in Judy's testimony (see introductory quotation) about ingesting the body and blood of Christ at his Table. From the other side, partaking of the Eucharist, or Lord's Supper, with people with physical and intellectual disabilities also serves to heighten congregational sensitivity as a whole to the presence of Christ by the Spirit in and through the sacramental event, as the (introductory) quotations of both Christella Buser and Jean Vanier confirm.

These "sacramental" mediations of the presence of Christ by the Spirit may also occur in the rite of footwashing (see Thomas 1991; Macchia 1997). In L'Arche, a form of this ritual is enacted in the daily caring for bodies, especially in their washing and cleaning (Allchin 1997). Jean Vanier notes (1998b: 37) that "[o]ne of the most meaningful moments of the day in La Forestière is bath time, a time of relationship, when by the way we touch and bathe each person we can help each one become aware of his or her own beauty and value." On the other side, equally powerful moments occur when core members who are sufficiently mobile wash the feet of assistants and through this act demonstrate the mutuality and hospitality of the fellowship of the Spirit (Vanier 1998b: 8–12). For non-Christian members who cannot or do not participate in the sacraments, the practice of body- or footwashing becomes the means through which lives are nevertheless touched by the gospel of Christ (Vanier 1983: 58).

But baptism and the Eucharist are not only for the benefit of catechumens or their families. Rather, in and through baptism of people with intellectual disabilities and their fellowship and presence at the Supper the love of God touches also the entire congregation (Webb-Mitchell 1996: chap. 2). This is because it is the work of the Holy Spirit not only to birth new members into the body of Christ but also to transform the body of Christ through the addition of new members. What results with Christian initiation is a new fellowship that now includes "us" and "them." This act of naming and baptizing is, after all, never performed individually but is always communally enacted. In this way, Christian baptism identifies the church as distinct and set apart from the world.

Liturgy and Discipleship

Christian initiation, however, is but the beginning of the lifelong task of following after Jesus. This holds as well for people with intellectual disabilities. Catechism then needs to be succeeded by discipleship. This happens both within and outside the liturgy.

Christian liturgy provides a context for a wide range of activities, including the worship of God, instruction in the faith, fellowship, and evangelism. From a disability perspective, however, I want to emphasize how the liturgy is a vehicle for individual and congregational transformation. Insofar as the liturgical practices of the church have historically formed its participants in exclusionary and oppressive ways—with people with disabilities experiencing that oppression through internalizing their marginalization both in the world and in the church—to that same degree an inclusive and accessible liturgy serves to liberate the people of God from their sinful ways (see Willis 2001). More precisely, the liturgy is the means through which the Holy Spirit sanctifies the body of Christ in the image of the resurrected one "until all of us come to the unity of the faith and of the knowledge of the Son of God, to maturity, to the measure of the full stature of Christ" (Eph 4:13; cf. Bissonnier 1979). How, then, does this happen?

To begin with, Christian worship should both involve and engage all congregants. For people with intellectual disabilities, we have to find creative ways to meet them personally, emotionally, and even physically (Trembley and Trembley 1996: 10–15). As Brent Webb-Mitchell writes (1996: 11), "If people with mental retardation find the church's rituals meaningless, perhaps the church should change the liturgy rather than make those with disabilities sit silently through it, or worse yet, have them leave."

Music is an especially powerful mode of engagement (Alvin 1976). In the liturgy, music also holds our attention, engages our emotions and affections, evokes our imagination, empowers creative expression, and encourages our affective engagement. More importantly, music contributes to our social adjustment and integration and is a means for developing our personalities, nurturing our self-identities, and maturing our emotions. "Music offers the possibility of communicating through the ears, eyes, skin and muscles. It is through this sensory-emotional approach that we are likely to offer the stimulation and nutrition which are necessary for growth and development" (Ward 1979: 37).[19] Because music is crosscultural and nonverbal, it bridges mind and body, influences both musical and nonmusical behavior, and facilitates learning and acquisition of skills even for nonverbal persons.

This is not to deemphasize the homily and the preaching of the Word, since the Holy Spirit can work through the sermon beyond what is propositionally understood by children (see Bacon 1993: 70–72). At the same time, the medium of story and myth should be lifted up and their retellings accomplished through symbolic enactments that engage individuals not only cognitively but also affectively and imaginatively (Hunt 1978: chap. 7). Teaching and instruction in the faith, similarly, should involve cooperative learning activities, service learning projects, teaming and peer tutoring, and differentiated instruction. Focus should be on strengths and needs of all learners (disciples), recognizing the mutuality of responsibility and the interconnectedness of each member of the class (see Anderson 2006).

Finally, the pedagogy of Christian discipleship should be fully engaging for all congregants. For the more severely and profoundly disabled, the spoken word is less important, and singing, music, drama, play, gestures, pictures, personal contact and participation, and the stimulation of the other four senses (e.g., through candles, lights, sounds) will be more engaging (Vogelzang 2001). Making available the full range of the creative arts—dance, clay activities, finger painting, tissue paper art, building from rocks and other natural materials, drawing, dramatic activities, music and sound production—will engage a much wider swath of the congregation, including people with disabilities (Sherrill 1979; cf. Webb-Mitchell 1993: chap. 15). But more important, the nurturing of creative expression in whatever form is central to the shaping of human identity, and this is no less so for people with intellectual disabilities. At the same time, the process of interpersonal interaction opened up by these disparate pedagogies not only heals and renews individual lives but also transforms the wider community of faith (see Webb-Mitchell 1996: chap. 13).[20]

In a sense, Christian discipleship is the same for all, regardless of dis/ability. In the case of people with intellectual disabilities, all I am suggesting is that we be more intentional about their discipleship. If following Jesus is but a matter of imitating him and those who follow him, then that applies also to people with intellectual disabilities. In that case, discipleship is about providing models for imitation (Loaring 2000: chap. 4), and such imitation comes through participation in the liturgies and activities of the church, especially listening and responding to lectionary readings and enactments of biblical stories. All of these forms of imitation and learning require community rather than just texts so that all members can learn how to "receive" the word of God and then live that out through the dance, singing, eating, or other forms of bodily expressions in and then "outside" the liturgical context. Within the life of the community of faith, full deployment of these practices will result in the edification of the whole body of Christ through the fellowship of the Spirit. In the process, we should not be surprised if the people with disabilities are taking in a lot more of "church" than what is apparent on the surface. "The way that we care for one another, confront painful truths about our life together, the songs we sing, prayers we pray, pictures we draw, and the rituals we observe and participate in are all-powerful and potent rather than meek and ineffectual practices" (Webb-Mitchell 1993: 146).

In the end, of course, Christian discipleship has as one of its goals to "challenge people to realize their full human potential in loving God, self and humankind" (Keck 1980: 11–12). But this is another way of saying that we work out our salvation as individuals in a community of faith even as it is God who is at work in us to save us (Phil 2:12-13). God's work, of course, is the justifying, regenerating, and sanctifying work of the Spirit that individually forms the servants of God and communally transforms the people of God. And all of this happens for the disabled and nondisabled alike through the practices we call church.[21]

Ministry, Disability, and Hospitality: Enabling the Church

In this final section we turn to the question of Christian ministry. My focus will be on the possibilities of Christian ministry by people with disabilities in general and people with intellectual disabilities more particularly. In the process, I will suggest how our considerations might even shed some light on the other disputed questions. We begin by explicating how traditional notions of ministries have often been directed at people with disabilities, proceed to develop the thesis that the charisms of the Spirit are available to all people regardless of dis/ability, and conclude with a renewed understanding of Christian ministry framed in terms of hospitality.

Ministry and Disability: Traditional and Pneumatological Approaches

Approaches to Christian ministry published during the last generation have usually emphasized ministry *to* people with disabilities and their families.[22] From a sociological perspective, of course, this is understandable given the deinstitutionalization movement since the 1960s (see pp. 55–77 above), which relocated many people with disabilities into their communities and thus brought them at some point into contact with their neighborhood churches. Many of these approaches to ministry were actually quite helpful, especially those being written from perspectives informed by people with disabilities themselves (e.g., Cox-Gedmark 1980) or derived out of personal experiences of disability (e.g., Colston 1978). Emphases were inevitably found on major themes such as encountering disability (including the tension between grieving and hoping, acceptance and resistance), motivating the will to live amid the will to wholeness, reexamining sexuality, supporting parents and families, promoting relationships, and sustaining material support systems. Pastoral insights were shed on these matters, as well as on more traditional theological concerns such as theodicy-related matters (why does God allow such "bad" things to happen to us?), spiritual support, and the process of death and dying (see van Dongen-Garrad 1983). Collaborations between pastoral care and professional workers also produced first-rate volumes that covered issues across the spectrum of the disability experience (e.g., Hollins and Grimer 1988). Last but not least is the genre of "how-to manuals." These have discussed recruiting and training leaders and ministers to "the disabled," developing curricular ideas, and providing lesson plans (e.g., Clark 2000).

Slowly, however, there has been the gradual realization that people with disabilities, even those with intellectual disabilities, should not just be the objects of Christian ministry. Rather, the church needs to begin discerning where, when, and how people with disabilities can be engaged in the doing of Christian ministry. After all, people with disabilities are not only passive subjects but also active agents who can make a difference (see discussion above, pp. 7–8). The learning process associated with this increased awareness can be seen in successive editions of *All God's Children* by Joni Eareckson Tada and Gene Newman. The subtitle of the first edition, *A Handbook to Help Christ's Church Minister to Persons with Disabilities* (1981), was shortened in the second edition to *Ministry to the Disabled* (1987). The most significant change, however, occurred in the third edition, subtitled *Ministry with Disabled Persons* (1993). But the content of the 1993 version is hardly revised from the 1987 volume. The notion of partnership between abled and disabled is not present even in the book subtitled *Ministry with Disabled Persons*. In fact, the back flap of this third revised edition still uses the language about ministering "to" the disabled. In short, even by 1993, Tada and Newman's title has become more inclusive, but that effected change neither in the rhetoric nor content of their book.

Even today, much of conservative Protestantism—within which Tada and Newman are ecclesially located—continues to operate in terms of ministering *to* people with disabilities. Perhaps this is part of the legacy of the Levitical prohibition against including people with disabilities in the ministry of the priesthood (see pp. 22–23). Yet only those who adhere to a fundamentalistic and literalistic hermeneutic appeal to these Levitical texts to justify the exclusion of people with disabilities from contemporary ministry. But the question is whether or not we have made sufficient gains on this issue that people with disabilities are actually seen as ministers rather than remaining as objects of pity, charity, and ministry. On this matter, things are still not so encouraging. For example, a recent book by prominent evangelical theologian R. T. Kendall (2004) perpetuates the notion that people with disabilities are inevitably objects of Christian ministry. Kendall does admonish against patronizing people with disabilities, and they are encouraged to accept themselves (rather than wallow in self-pity or in complaining to God), and others are also urged to accept them. But disabilities remain lessons used by God to teach us (the nondisabled) to empathize with others less fortunate, and Kendall says nothing about a political or social justice engagement with regard to the issue of disability.

My goal here is not to suggest that the church needs to stop ministering to people with disabilities. All people need ministry, not only those with disabilities. However, an inclusive and charismatic ecclesiology cannot be content to divide the fellowship of the Spirit into two groups: the (nondisabled) agents of ministry on the one side, and the (disabled) recipients of ministry on the other. Rather, Tada and Newman's intuition that people with disabilities are able to minister alongside the nondisabled needs to be pursued and developed so that they can be included rather than remaining excluded from participating in the redeeming work of God.

In contrast to these more traditional notions of Christian ministry vis-à-vis people with disabilities, a view of the church as charismatic fellowship emphasizes that *all* members of the body of Christ are empowered by the Holy Spirit to witness to and accomplish the works of God in the world (cf. Acts 1:8). A disability perspective, in addition, focuses on how the Spirit is the author of life out of death, of resurrection out of crucifixion, and of power out of weakness. More to the point, not only does the Spirit lift up and honor the "weaker" members of the body (1 Cor 12:22-24; see pp. 204–6) but the Spirit also demonstrates the wisdom of God in choosing to use foolishness (*morían*) and weakness to shame the wise and the strong (1 Cor 1:20–2:4). In fact, Jesus said to an insulted, persecuted, and strenuously tested Paul: "My grace is sufficient for you, for power is made perfect in weakness" (2 Cor 12:9).

It is out of "weakness," then, that the power of the Holy Spirit is released, and the grace of God is made most evident. Disabilities qualify rather than disqualify people for Christian ministry. For this reason, the creed of the Association of Physically Challenged Ministers of the United Methodist Church reads: "In the name of Christ we are hosts and agents of hospitality. We are the church. We claim our place with others in reconstructing the table of Christ so that all may approach it together as brothers and sisters in Christ, one Body, united and whole" (Betenbaugh and Procter-Smith 1998: 302). After all, are not pastoral counselors with disabilities, for example, better able to empathize with their parishioners' challenges and hardships than those without disabilities (cf. Hunt 1986: chap. 4)? Are not people with disabilities most aware of the vulnerability that attends to all human lives and perhaps therefore most sensitive to the possibility of finding the strength of God offered through others?

Intellectual Disability and the Charisms of Ministry

But what about people with intellectual disabilities in particular? How is it possible for them to be ministers of God's saving and revelatory grace to a hurting world? I suggest that it is especially the severely and profoundly disabled, in part because of their not resisting the Spirit, who are most able to be iconic charisms of God's presence and activity in the world.[23] Allow me to expand on how people with intellectual disabilities embody through the gift of the Spirit the charisms of teaching, healing, and prophecy.

To be sure, people with intellectual disabilities do not generally teach and prophesy like most others who do so. But as with all of the spiritual gifts, the responsibility resides with the congregation to discern and carefully weigh the various manifestations purported to be of the Spirit (1 Cor 14:29). Hence, the question is not whether God can use people with intellectual disabilities, but whether the rest of us are sufficiently able to discern what God is saying and doing through their lives. For those with eyes to see and ears to hear, the charisms of the Spirit will surely be manifest through the witness of the intellectually disabled. After all, "[d]evelopmentally disabled persons, who have been baptized and have agreed to belong to the community of faith through catechesis and liturgy, are not passive members of the Church. They are full members who belong and contribute according to their capacity. A child who is profoundly disabled and cannot speak or move can still contribute to those around him or her by a loving presence" (Bernardin 1985: 7).[24] For those who are sensitive enough to the Spirit's working, then, "the most severely handicapped are the teachers of those less handicapped" (Downey 1986: 93).

Henri Nouwen, the spiritual theologian, writes precisely about encountering God through the lives of core members of the L'Arche community in which he lived and worked. It was Adam Arnett (1961–1996), a severely disabled young man (crippled, mute, and epileptic) assigned to Nouwen's care, who opened up windows into new perspectives on the Apostle's Creed (Nouwen 1997). Before meeting Adam, Nouwen had wondered "when and how I will learn to fully live the Incarnation. I suppose that only the handicapped people themselves will be able to show me the way. I must trust that God will send me the teachers I need" (1990: 151). This realization prepared him to learn about the life, death, and resurrection of Christ through Adam. Adam's early years of being hidden away (institutionalized) are suggestive about the silence of Jesus' early years, even as Adam's final years of extended sickness (including double pneumonia in the fall of 1994) illumine from another vantage point the Passion of Christ, and Adam's life-story preserved in Nouwen's book testifies to the hope of resurrection and ongoing life in Christ. More importantly, Adam's life brought the good news of Jesus into his world simply by being there as a silent witness. "Jesus didn't accomplish much during his lifetime. He died as a failure. Adam didn't accomplish much either. He died as poor as he was born. Still, both Jesus and Adam are God's beloved sons—

Jesus by nature, Adam by 'adoption'—and they lived their sonship among us as the only thing that they had to offer. That was their assigned mission" (Nouwen 1997: 37). For Nouwen, then, "Adam is my friend, my teacher, my spiritual director, my counselor, my minister" (1997: 53).[25]

But Adam was also a conduit for God's gift of healing dispensed by the Holy Spirit. In reflecting on the daily care—washing, dressing, feeding, and so on—that intertwined his life with Adam's, Nouwen writes: "Adam was a true teacher and a true healer. Most of his healing was inner healing that announced peace, courage, joy, and freedom to those who often were hardly able to acknowledge their wounds. Adam, by his eyes and by his presence, said to us, 'Don't be afraid. You don't have to run away from your pain. Look at me, be close to me, and you will discover that you are God's beloved child, just as I am'" (1997: 64–65). During Nouwen's own period of emotional breakdown, Adam cared for him: "As I lived through this emotional ordeal I realized that I was becoming like Adam. He had nothing to be proud of. Neither had I. He was completely empty. So was I. He needed full-time attention. So did I. I found myself resisting this 'becoming like Adam.' I did not want to be dependent and weak. I did not want to be so needy. Somewhere though I recognized that Adam's way, the way of radical vulnerability, was also the way of Jesus" (1997: 79). For Nouwen, then, Adam's life manifested and embodied the resurrection power of Jesus: "I am a witness of Adam's truth. I know that I couldn't have told Adam's story if I hadn't first known Jesus' story. . . . Adam had lived the story of Jesus that I have been telling every day to anyone who wanted to hear it" (1997: 127–28).

Living with people like Adam since 1964 also convinced Jean Vanier that "people with handicaps are prophetic" (Vanier 1995: 114). Wolf Wolfensberger goes further (in Gaventa and Coulter 2001b: 16–30) to enumerate ten signs of the intellectually disabled as being thrust by God into a prophetic role in our time. He points out that people with intellectual disabilities today are:

- much more public and visible
- more internationally renowned
- sharing their lives and living with nondisabled people

- a humanizing influence on others by their presence and actions
- conduits of the manifest presence of God
- speaking in tongues, not only in prayerful "non-languages" but also in prophetically recognizable "languages"
- demanding that their societies pay more attention to the poor, the oppressed, and the marginalized
- parodying the arid intellectualism that overestimates itself, as well as announcing as bankrupt the intellectual and technological achievements of modernity
- embodying the "dance of spiritual joy", and
- witnessing to the truth through their persecution, even to the point of martyrdom (especially in the high numbers of selective abortions).

While Wolfensberger's language may itself be criticized as overreaching in various respects, he rightly calls attention to the prophetic quality of the lives of people with intellectual disabilities for those who have eyes to see, ears to hear, and hearts ready to be transformed.

Implicit in Wolfensberger's analysis, however, is a prophetic dimension to the lives of people with intellectual disabilities that needs to be specifically thematized. This has to do with Paul's claim that God confounds the wisdom of the world with what the world considers as foolishness. Rather than assuming that people with intellectual disabilities are the foolish, my claim is that their lives embody the wisdom of God in ways that interrogate, critique, and undermine the status quo. To see how this is the case, note what Michael Oliver, an advocate of the social model of disability (see the discussion in chap. 4), says about how wheelchair users call into question the very "normalcy" of walking. Oliver argues that even the very activity of "walking" expresses ideological, cultural, and social conventions. More precisely, "rehabilitation is the exercise of power by one group over another and further, that exercise of power is shaped by ideology. . . . [W]alking is rule-following behaviour; not-walking is rule-ignoring, rule-flouting or even rule-threatening behaviour. . . . Not-walking or rejecting nearly-walking as a personal choice is something different however; it threatens the power of professionals, it exposes the ideology of normality and it challenges the whole rehab enterprise" (Oliver 1996b: 104).

While perhaps an extreme set of claims from one perspective, I suggest that when combined with Wolfensberger's suggestion (above), the lives of people with intellectual disability prophetically call into question our taken-for-granted assumptions about how we organize and structure the conventions of "normalcy" in exclusive ways.[26] My claim is that an inclusive and charismatic ecclesiology informed specifically by the experiences of intellectual disability overturns our assumptions about strength and weakness, about power and incapacity. Further, such an embodied ecclesiology calls attention to how "weak" and strong are truly interdependent in ways we have not begun to realize. Understood in this way, the church recognizes the presence and contributions of the "weak" as central to her identity: the church would no longer be the church apart from those seen as the "weak" of the world.

Disability, Hospitality, and the Renewal of the Church

In the closing pages of this chapter on ecclesiology, I want to suggest that disability perspectives invite us to reconsider the charismatic ministry of the church in the twenty-first century in terms of the charism and virtue of hospitality.[27] Not only is the theme of hospitality interwoven throughout the Bible—for example, from Abraham's hosting of the three strangers (Gen 18) to the injunction "Do not neglect to show hospitality to strangers" (Heb 13:2a)[28]— but hospitality can also be recognized as a charism of the Holy Spirit, who invites, lures, embraces, and nurtures human life in the discipleship of Jesus. The blending together of these themes— hospitality, disability, and discipleship—can be seen in the parable of the great dinner (Luke 14:15-24). From a disability perspective, Jesus' parable about the great dinner reveals that the stranger, the marginalized, and the excluded—as metaphorically signaled in the poor, the crippled, the blind, and the lame of the parable—are invited guests of the dinner just as the nondisabled are.[29]

Brent Webb-Mitchell (1993: chap. 6; 1994: chap. 4) suggests that other lessons from this parable include understanding what happens at such meals as experiencing the common grace given to all by God, fellowshipping around a common table, embracing a common reliance on God, and sharing a common life together as equals in the eyes of God. I would point out that this parable is sandwiched between two other parables: one treating the theme of hospitality and humility (Luke 14:7-14), both the hospitality of hosts encouraged to invite the poor, the crippled, the lame, and the blind, and the humility of guests in their response to and behavior at the dinners to which they are invited; and the other treating of Christian discipleship (Luke 14:25-33), especially in its focus on counting the cost of following Jesus. Together, the trio of parables suggest that the Holy Spirit is the Spirit of hospitality who embraces, includes, and empowers the poor, the crippled, the lame, and the blind at the center of the Christian life of discipleship.

The fact of the matter, however, is that the lives of people with disabilities remind us that we are all "outsiders" to others in different respects. This means that even the people of God have perennially been hosts who have entertained strangers, as well as strangers who have been welcomed as guests. The Spirit of hospitality renews the church precisely by embodying the wideness of God's generosity, compassion, mercy, and kindness so as to embrace in solidarity the strangers who are poor, crippled, lame, and blind (see Merrick 1993). When rightly led by the Spirit, the entire congregation is transformed into a nurturing caregiver (Preheim-Bartel and Neufeldt 1986: chap. 3; Allen and Allen 1979: chap. 8), even as individuals within such congregations become "Christian poets" who participate in the redemptive work of God (Keck 1996: 196–201).

What does this mean practically for the church understood as the fellowship of the Spirit? First of all, the church's ministry of hospitality means that rather than discarding or rejecting disabled babies, we would be shaped into the kind of people who welcome such children into the world, and who work together to support one another in raising such children as unto the Lord (Beise 2005). After all, as Stanley Hauerwas rightly insists (1998: 151), the existence of people with disabilities requires no more or less justification than the existence of nondisabled people. Hence, the point is not that when confronted with certain prenatal testing results we would somehow have to make the "right" decision and choose to keep rather than abort our children. Rather, the point is that when certain habits, virtues, and practices are cultivated, they shape and form the dispositions, commitments, and values of communities and individuals in those communities.[30] A truly "Christoform" community lives out of the death of Christ and embodies the theology of the cross by the resurrection power of the Spirit.[31] Such a fellowship of the Spirit fears neither death nor hardship, much less disability, and is therefore poised to be the kind of hospitable community that can welcome and embrace even those diagnosed with little potential for life as most of us know it. All of this happens, of course, only through the sanctifying work of the Holy Spirit, who imparts Christ's righteousness so that the charity that welcomes, includes, and embraces may abound (Cochran 2005).

After birth (or adoption, or initiation), then, the Spirit of hospitality further transforms the communion of saints in and through their practices of caregiving. This is because the process of inclusion affects both the individual and the community. Brett Webb-Mitchell talks about this in terms of "crafting Christians into the gestures of the body of Christ." He writes (1998: 273), "Gestures involve a people's thinking or feeling or their being engaged by the Spirit of God; but they are enacted through the body, following the intent of mind and spirit." It is especially the severely or profoundly disabled who elicit and solicit new gestures amid the community of faith. In fact, if Christian learning combines both knowledge (what to do) and action (gestures—when and how to do them), then Christian discipleship requires mentors. In that case, people with disabilities become the mentors who are inspired by the Spirit to reshape the gestures of the body of Christ.

This means, then, that people with disabilities are not only the guests who are recipients of the hospitality of others. Rather, they are constitutive members of the body of Christ who are also charismatically empowered through the fellowship of the Spirit to be hosts who extend hospitality to others and mediate the hospitality of God.[32] Ian Cohen (1997) suggests that inasmuch as people with disabilities are the strangers whom both Israel and the church are called to receive, to that extent they are also the priests who mediate the relationship of the church with God. Paradoxically, then, in extending hospitality to people with disabilities the church participates in and receives the hospitality of God. Put another way, if in fact Christian ministry is not only *to* but also *with* people with disabilities, then the nondisabled can learn through the perspective of those labeled disabled such that there is a reversal of roles: able-bodied persons are now guests, and "the disabled" are hosts (cf. Webb-Mitchell 1994: 152). Herein is made manifest the mutuality and reciprocity of the work of the Spirit of hospitality whereby strangers are transformed into friends (Swinton 2001, 2004a).

I have suggested in this chapter that in the postmodern, post-denominational, and even post-Christian world of the twenty-first century, the church is fully the charismatic fellowship of the Spirit only insofar as she is an inclusive community of hospitality wherein the disabled and the nondisabled together welcome, befriend, and embrace the stranger, the marginalized, and the disenfranchised. This is the work of the Spirit: to renew the church, to transform lives, and to reconcile people to each other and to God. I have argued that such renewal, transformation, and reconciliation is mediated by and occurs in and through the Spirit's presence and activity in the church's practices, sacraments, and liturgy. More precisely, the inclusive hospitality of the Spirit liberally dispenses the charisms of ministry to all people—the "weak" and the "strong" alike—so that the "disabled" and nondisabled are equally instruments of God's reconciling and transforming power. Hence discussion of the church as the charismatic fellowship of hospitality leads us to the doctrine of salvation, to which we now turn.

VIII

Rethinking Soteriology
On Saving Down Syndrome and Disability

They, the people of Fort Worth, sent me here to die, yet I don't hate them. But do or should I love them? I knelt and asked God to show me in my heart, the correct attitude. Should I love my oppressors and adversaries?

—McCune 1973: 84

You want to know 'bout love? . . . Love is when you care for somebody, and you be willing to go out of your way and do anything for that person, and to take care of that person, and if they have problems, that you can help them out any way you know how. If they sick, that you can bring 'em medicine, or give 'em a helping hand. That's what love is.

—Jesse, in Simon 2002: 116

We don't need to be cured in order to live. What we need to do is make our needs known. The parents must accept the disability, not fight against it, and open up the right paths for the child so that it arrives at the point where the disability presents the least hindrance. If the child can develop her or his own way of living, the society will learn to understand it and provide the necessary tools.

—German Perez Cruz, in Holzer 1999: 270

Mine . . . and yours . . . and every neighbor. That's what we
are here for, to take care of each other. If God did it, then no
one would ever have to learn about kindness. . . . He did his
job. . . . He gave me lots of people who were supposed to take
care of me. . . . I believe in God and people who believe in God
know that there is only an "us." Man made a "them" by putting labels on people and locking them away. I am "us" now
because I am free. They are still "them" because they are not.
Our job is to make "them" "us" and we will in time.

—Noreen, in Hingsburger 1992: 134, 142–43

*In what ways has God used Mark's life to touch other lives over the years?
My mother can spend an entire day (if you had the time) testifying of God's
graciousness through Mark. In 1982, shortly after his heart surgery, my
parents took Mark to Malaysia. He was getting around a bit by then, and
his life story provided numerous opportunities for Mom to share about God's
goodness in their lives. Many conversations were initiated simply because of
her open display of and publicly demonstrated love for her (handicapped) son
in church. Later, on another trip to Malaysia in the early 1990s, Mark told
his misbehaving cousins, "Children, obey your parents in the Lord," and
then "rebuked" his aunt (who had raised her voice), "No yell, no scream,
no shout!"*

*Over the years, there have also been (innumerable) occasions with doc-
tors, nurses, and other patients (and especially their parents) when opportunities have been presented to Mom to bear witness to the Lord's working
in and through Mark's life. She will be the first to give glory to God for
positive reports from Mark's doctors, even as she will be the first to begin
praying when not-so-positive news is received. She tells of when Mark was
in his late teens and one of his teachers at the University of the Pacific (in
Stockton) mentioned that Mark had been a blessing in her life, reminding
her of the Lord's desire to be in relationship with us.*

*Then there was the occasion, in 1994, while at home, when Mark was
filled with the Holy Spirit and spoke in tongues for forty minutes. Mom
admitted to doing just a bit of "coaching" at the beginning, but after his
"breakthrough," Mark spoke on his own accord.*

*Finally, Mom recalled once when Mark came alongside her during an
ICF worship service to lift up his mother's hand. At first, she was embar-
rassed since she thought that she would lift up her hands at her own instiga-
tion. However, after the service, another woman came and told Mom that
she wished she was as free as Mark to worship God. Mom can tell of other*

*occasions during worship when God has used Mark's example to liberate
others from their anxieties, fears, and despair.*

*In each of these ways and more, Mom believes Mark's life has been
a conduit for the grace of God to be manifest to others. What else is this
than the saving work of God expressed in the life of an individual who is
otherwise dismissed and marginalized according to the norms of this world?
When I asked Mark what it meant to him that Jesus was his savior, he
answered, "He is my best friend."*

Our discussion in this chapter focuses on soteriology, the doctrine
of salvation. At one level, all that has been said in part 3 of this
book has not only involved implications for soteriological reflection but has also been implicitly soteriological. So an understanding of an emergentist theological anthropology as embodied and
relational already suggests that the formal doctrine of salvation
must pay attention if not specifically thematize bodily wholeness
and interpersonal reconciliation, and the view of the church as a
charismatic fellowship of the Spirit further suggests that soteriological formulation includes a communal dimension. At another
level, however, we might also say that the movement of the last
three chapters has been from humanity understood in creational
terms (theological anthropology) to humanity understood in communal terms (ecclesiology) to humanity understood in theological
terms (soteriology), and that in each of the theological loci there
are embodied/individual and relational/social dimensions. In that
case, the doctrine of salvation articulated here is informed by both
the theological anthropology and the ecclesiology of the preceding chapters and makes explicit the multiple dimensions of what it
means to say that human beings are caught up in the saving work
of God. But insofar as we reserve for chapter 9 the discussion of
the eschatological dimension of salvation, our focus here will be on
soteriology understood in terms of experiencing the redemptive
power of the Spirit of God in the here and now of this world.

The thesis to be argued in what follows is that salvation is the
transformative work of the Spirit of God that converts human
hearts from lives of sin, estrangement, and inauthenticity to lives
of peace, wholeness, and reconciliation between human beings and
God. Disability perspectives punctuate this discussion by interrogating and then reshaping the soteriological hypothesis at three

levels: first at the level of traditional soteriological articulation, then at the level of the Christian doctrine of the healing of the body (and mind), and finally at the level of the social model that emphasizes the marginalization, oppression, and injustice perpetuated by ableism against people with disabilities. As we proceed through this inquiry, we shall see that salvation is both the work of God and of human endeavor, involving the body and the soul, encompassing the individual and society. In this scheme of things, again the lines between disabled and nondisabled are blurred, not because we are ignoring the particularity of the phenomenology and experience of disability but because the wholeness of the "disabled" is intimately tied with the wholeness of the nondisabled and vice versa in God's salvific plan.

Rethinking the *Ordo Salutis*

We begin with traditional soteriology as seen in the classical Protestant articulation of the "order of salvation" (*ordo salutis*).[1] This provides a backdrop against which to examine how the experience of disability both confirms and calls into question the traditional formulation. A reconsideration of the classical *ordo salutis* in disability perspective, we shall see, will be not only dynamic (thematized in terms of the *way* of salvation, or *via salutis*) but also multidimensional.

Salvation in Classical Protestant Theology

While the New Testament nowhere provides an exhaustive *ordo salutis*, Saint Paul's thoughts in the eighth chapter of Romans comes closest to providing such a summary: "For those whom he foreknew he also predestined to be conformed to the image of his Son, in order that he might be the firstborn within a large family. And those whom he predestined he also called; and those whom he called he also justified; and those whom he justified he also glorified" (Rom 8:29-30). This text suggests that salvation proceeds from God's foreknowledge to predestination to calling to justification and to glorification. Two further perspectives can be elaborated from this account.

From God's point of view, as it were, salvation can be said to be initiated through the mysterious capacity of divine foreknowledge, predestination, and calling or election. From this perspective,

salvation is wholly a work of God, since justification and glorification can also be said to be God's undertaking that human beings
experience (passively). Further, other New Testament terms such
as conversion, adoption, regeneration, and even sanctification
imply that these are accomplished by God and experienced by
human beings as events that happen to them. The Westminster
Confession therefore summarizes the *ordo salutis* as beginning with
God's eternal decree of creation, fall, and election (Hendry 1962).
These divine decrees are then unfolded historically in God's effec-
tual calling of the elect; God's justifying, forgiving, and adopting
(regenerating) them; God's enabling their repentance, sanctification, and perseverance in faith; and God's providing assurance of
saving faith in this life and glorifying grace in the life to come. Put
in this way, salvation is wholly a gift of God that unmeritorious
human beings receive with gratitude and respond to through acts
of worship.

From the point of view of human experience, however, things
are a bit more complicated. In the Protestant framework, while
justification and glorification are undoubtedly associated with
the workings of God, conversion and sanctification almost always
involve either human response to or cooperation with God. If salvation is by grace through faith and "not the result of works, so
that no one may boast" (Eph 2:9), so also "faith by itself, if it has
no works, is dead . . . [and] a person is justified by works and not
by faith alone" (Jas 2:17, 24). Further, while Calvinist theologians
will not usually separate God's foreknowledge and God's predestination (they are considered to be the knowing and willing aspects
of God's one and undivided nature), Arminian thinkers read Paul
as basing God's predestination on God's foreknowledge of free
human actions (Rom 8:29). So if the Holy Spirit calls, humans
believe and respond; if the Spirit convicts, humans repent and confess; if the Spirit regenerates and makes holy, humans cease from
sin and persevere in holiness. Arminians thereby agree with the
more synergistic perspectives of Orthodox theology: salvation is
initiated by God but involves and solicits human choice, decision,
and action.[2] This does not mean human beings do not thank and
worship God for salvation, but rather that thanksgiving and worship are among many other human responses to and responsibilities before God.

This is not to say, of course, that Arminian theology reflects more human perspectives while Calvinist theology presents more divine points of view. From a broadly Reformed point of view that can claim a degree of consensus even across Calvinist and Arminian lines, classical Protestant soteriology also distinguishes between objective and subjective aspects of salvation. The former involve divine election, justification, reconciliation (union with Christ), adoption, and glorification, while the latter include calling, conviction, conversion, regeneration, and sanctification.

From a performative perspective (see pp. 13–14), however, I suggest that both Calvinists and Arminians (and anyone else, for that matter) are mistaken if they believe we are able, even with the revelation of the Scriptures, to explicate definitively the mystery of salvation from God's point of view. Rather, since "[a]ll scripture is inspired by God and is useful for teaching, for reproof, for correction, and for training in righteousness, so that everyone who belongs to God may be proficient, equipped for every good work" (2 Tim 3:16), a performative soteriology is focused on unfolding how our soteriological beliefs provide a definitive grammar that guides Christian practice. In this case, soteriology is not merely a descriptive explanation of what happens but a prescriptive rule of faith and conduct that is normative for the Christian experience of God's saving grace.

Within such a performative framework, then, the perennial questions about the mystery of salvation regarding infants, the unevangelized, and the intellectually disabled are not merely abstract speculations but are directly pertinent to Christian discipleship and mission.[3] With regard to infants, for example, Protestants who reject the Catholic doctrine of baptismal regeneration debate over whether infants are saved because they are part of the elect or because they have not reached the age of accountability when they became guilty for their sins. With regard to the unevangelized, the debate rages over whether they are lost because they are not elect or because they have rejected the light available to them. With regard to people with intellectual disabilities, especially those severely and profoundly retarded, how does God's saving grace intersect with their inability to respond, at least in any discernible manner, to the call of the gospel?

Complicating Salvation: Intellectual Disability and Down Syndrome

Let us further inquire into the complications regarding classical Protestant soteriology from perspectives illuminated by the experience of intellectual disability.[4] From a conservative Protestant point of view, "[p]ersons who are profoundly retarded and have extremely low levels of comprehension are safe within God's saving grace. While the fact of salvation is a mystery in itself, what we do know about God is sufficient to know that His love encompasses those of a 'childlike' nature" (Nabi 1985: 103). While this posture also accounts for the salvation of infants, it is inconsistently applied with regard to adults who are unevangelized. The usual answer that is given is that those who reach an age of accountability (which God recognizes) will then be guilty of their sins as their conscience pricks them, so that adults who die apart from believing in and confessing Jesus Christ as Lord and Savior, even if unevangelized, will be subject to the judgment to come (Heb 9:27). Part of the problem with this response is that nowhere does the Bible, which is the final theological and doctrinal authority for conservative Protestants, clearly introduce this idea regarding an age of accountability. In other words, if infants and the intellectually disabled will be judged graciously by God given their "low levels of comprehension," then will not God also judge the unevangelized graciously according to their various levels of comprehension? The reluctance of most conservative Protestants to make this further move can be understood, at least from a sociological perspective, as related to the fact that infants and intellectually disabled are members of their own families, friends, and churches, whereas the unevangelized are usually also strangers, ethnic and racial others from distant lands, or people in other religious traditions.

Alternatively, other conservative Protestants discuss the salvation of the intellectually disabled in this way: "Eighty-nine percent of the retarded population is in the Educable category. Many of these people have reached an age of accountability" (Tada and Newman 1987: 17). Even if we granted the notion of the age of accountability, there are three sets of further questions that arise. First, what is the age of accountability, and how is that determined? Is the age of accountability that of educability, as implied in the quotation? If so, is not that also rather problematic as educability is a fluid process by any standards of measurement?[5] Second, what about the other 11 percent who are not educable? Are they lost or saved because of their lack of educability? Third, is the criterion for believing and confessing indispensable for salvation?

It is this last assumption that may be the most problematic theologically, as our experience with people with intellectual disability is slowly revealing. When it is written, for example, that "[t]hose who believe in him are not condemned; but those who do not believe are condemned already, because they have not believed in the name of the only Son of God" (John 3:18), it is fair to ask whether or not those who are condemned for not believing are the unevangelized or those who have heard and understood the gospel but nevertheless have rejected it. The usual response is that the condemned are the unevangelized if referring to adults but not if referring to infants or the intellectually disabled, since the former are capable of believing and confessing while the latter groups of persons are not. Beyond the fact that this distinction seems rather arbitrary, what about the fact that in the Johannine gospel, faith or belief is not only a cognitive act of assent to propositions but also a personal posture of trust and commitment to act out that trust (Moloney 1993: 198)? Further, there are numerous other scriptural criteria regarding salvation: e.g., doing the will of the Father (Matt 7:21); feeding the hungry, clothing the naked, caring for the sick, and visiting those in prison (Matt 25:31-46); doing good versus evil (John 5:29).

The point is not to insist on a salvation of works rather than one of grace through faith. In fact, even shifting to a works-salvation is problematic since the severely and profoundly disabled are as incapable of works as they are of believing in and confessing Christ. At this level, as the introductory quotations of both Jesse and Noreen imply, people with intellectual disabilities are not motivated to earn their salvation by loving or caring for others, but their love and care for others seemingly bubbles forth from a profound sense of interrelationality. But, then, for the moderately and mildly disabled, the problem arises on the other side: that of a "behavior mod God" who rewards them for good behavior and punishes them for bad behavior (see Webb-Mitchell 1993: chap. 22). To shift from faith to works in the case of people with intellectual disabilities would be counterproductive to nurturing faith and the reception of God's grace.[6]

What about the possibility of postmortem evangelization with regard to people with intellectual disabilities? Wolf Wolfensberger speculates (in Gaventa and Coulter 2001b: 77) that "when a human soul departs the body without having had the opportunity to exercise intellect and will to decide for or against God, God will do what He apparently did with the other spirits, viz., the angels: upon departure from the fallen body and its shackles, God offers the now unimpeded soul a sufficient glimpse of His identity to enable it to make a fundamental choice." While an admittedly exploratory idea, the only developed tradition of thought regarding postmortem salvation is the Roman Catholic doctrine of purgatory, and that is only weakly attested to in scripture. Further, Wolfensberger's hypothesis seems to involve a number of problematic metaphysical assumptions such as anthropomorphic view of spiritual beings (angels and evil spirits), a static notion of eternity, and a dualistic (body-soul) anthropology. While we will discuss the eschatological existence of human beings in the next chapter, suffice it to say at this moment that the idea of a postmortem evangelism of people with intellectual disabilities such as what Wolfensberger proposes, while appealing in some respects, is unnecessary at one level and raises more theological and philosophical questions than it answers to be of much assistance.

Where, then, are we with regard to soteriology in general and to the question of the salvation of people with intellectual disability in particular? One response is a humble agnosticism, certainly appropriate when prioritizing salvation as God's initiative and therefore as belonging to God to pronounce. Another response might be to distinguish between *pistis* (faith) and *gnosis* (knowledge) and say that human beings are always in a *pistis* relationship with God, even if some might not be able to articulate that in terms of *gnosis* (Trembley and Trembley 1999: 76–80). Since genuine pistis can never be fully displayed through gnosis, we should engage people with intellectual disabilities on the level of *pistis* rather than of *gnosis*. The problem here is both that faith seems stripped of almost all content and that there is an implicit universalism that undercuts libertarian human freedom.

Reordering Salvation: Disability, the Spirit, and the Via Salutis

I suggest instead that we rethink the ordo salutis in dialogue with
the emergentist anthropology and the pneumatological ecclesiology previously developed. The strength of the classical Protestant
ordo salutis is its recognition of the dynamic nature of salvation as
including both objective and subjective elements within a developmental framework. The weaknesses of the *ordo salutis* are its rigid
framing of the sequence of salvation and the underdevelopment
of the ideas of human beings as embodied and social creatures. I
propose therefore to reformulate the *ordo salutis* in two pneumatological directions: one that takes into account the Spirit's transforming work in the many spheres of human life, and the other
that understands conversion as a fluid set of experiences reflecting
the dynamic movements of the Spirit.[7] With regard to the former
trajectory, because human beings are embodied, economic, political, social, temporal, and environmental creatures, the saving work
of the Spirit involves the forgiveness of sins, healing of the body,
reconciliation of enemies, liberation of the poor and oppressed, the
establishment of a new community of peace and justice, and the
new creation of the cosmos. With regard to the latter trajectory,
because human beings are temporal creatures, the saving work of
the Spirit involves the calling, conversion, and transformation—
oftentimes through crisis experiences—of our minds (the intellect),
wills (morality), habits (affections), relationships (the interpersonal
sphere), and hearts (symbolizing our standing as whole creatures
before God). In other words, human salvation is a complex reality that extends across the many dimensions (synchronic) and processes (diachronic) that constitute human lives. We may be more
or less converted and transformed at one level than at another at
any point of our lives, even as conversion and transformation in
any sphere impacts the other spheres of life, and even as conversion in any sphere can be neglected or intensified from moment to
moment. The result, I suggest, is a pneumatological way of salvation—a *via salutis*—that emphasizes the synergism of the saving
work initiated by the Holy Spirit and the multifaceted possibilities
of human decision and responsibility across space and time.

What does this mean with regard to the salvation of people
with intellectual disabilities? In 1965 Harold Stubblefield asked

whether or not such people had religious consciousness and therefore also religious responsibility. He pointed out the Hutterites
said yes to the former but not to the latter, while the Lutherans
said yes to both. Stubblefield concluded, then, that this question
is better answered *a posteriori* than *a priori*. After all, people with
intellectual disabilities (much like people without intellectual disabilities, I would add) vary across a wide range in their capacities to theologize and move beyond anthropomorphisms. Hence
there could be no categorical answer to this question; rather, each
person should be evaluated (and, might we hypothesize, will be
so evaluated by God) on a case-by-case basis (Stubblefield 1965:
58–63). Forty years later, the empirical evidence has further complicated our understanding of how individuals are socially, culturally, and relationally shaped even as we determine to some degree
how these influences are integrated into our lives (Elliott 2003).
We can now say that each person with intellectual disability stands
in a unique relationship of moral and spiritual responsibility before
God (Hegeman 1984: chap. 10), one dependent on the degree to
which the various intellectual, moral, or social dimensions of life
are emergent in that life.

But this response leads theologians like John Swinton (1997)
to turn the question around. Rather than asking whether people
with intellectual disability are religiously conscious or responsible,
he inquires into how they become religiously engaged. If human
beings are multidimensional, dynamic, and relational through and
through (see discussion on pp. 184–87), then with regard to people with intellectual disabilities, relational criteria come into play
that are not exhaustively determined or constricted to the intellect
(even if such criteria do not have to be independent of the intellect
for those who are intellectually capable). There can be a genuine
affective apprehension of and even conversion to God for those
with profound cognitive disabilities whereby their existence in loving relationships mediates real saving experiences of God (Swinton
1997: 24–25).

Let me explicate Swinton's hypothesis with regard to the doctrine of conversion. If people with intellectual disabilities need
to be converted, how does such conversion occur? Through the
conversion experiences of nondisabled people to them, I reply. As
Frances Young puts it (1990: 177, 183), we need "a re-orientation

which can face and accommodate the challenge that the handicapped present . . . to our ideology of what is human. . . . It is not the handicapped who need community care. It's US. To learn from the handicapped requires a new heart and a new spirit within us, but if we are prepared to learn, it will produce the new heart and new spirit and we will be immensely enriched—indeed, it will be our salvation. We shall discover what it really means to be human." As importantly, I suggest, our conversion facilitates their own, so that what emerges is a new community consisting of us and them, beyond us versus them.

The conversion of people with intellectual disability would then be bound up in their relationships among themselves, with others, and with God. So, at the affective level, they could experience a kind of moral conversion that sets them in right relationship to others, even if at the cognitive level they might not be able to understand what it means to stand justified before God in Christ. Further, there may also be other relational signs that genuine conversion is taking place such as when people with intellectual disabilities exercise charity to strangers, lovingkindness to their perceived enemies, or forgiveness to those who they believe have wronged them.[8] And insofar as much more will be demanded of the nondisabled because they have received more (Luke 12:48), their conversion will involve their righting the practices and structures that perpetuate injustice against the "weak" in their midst. In this perspective, conversion understood as justification involves not only our turning to and standing rightly before God in the life, death, and resurrection of Jesus Christ but also our reconciliation with one another (hence the importance of forgiving the sins of others; cf. John 20:23) and our creation of just structures that organize the various spheres of our relationships with one another.

We will further explicate the details of this soteriological vision in the last part of this chapter. Meanwhile, to summarize the discussion so far, I am suggesting that a pneumatological approach to soteriology results in a *via salutis* that preserves the dynamism inherent in the classical *ordo salutis* but expands on the traditional formulation to include the many dimensions that constitute human experience. In this framework, the Spirit of God meets us individually wherever we are, through whatever interpersonal, social, and especially ecclesial relations that sustain and structure the webbed fabric of our lives. Yet, because human beings are free creatures with the capacity to respond to and work with the Spirit of God, Christian mission remains essential. With regard to people with disabilities, mission and evangelism should be multifaceted. But rather than drawing up educational IEPs (individualized educational plans; see p. 68), Christian mission involves spiritual IEPs that attempt to discern what the Spirit is already doing in the lives of people with disabilities. The goal of Christian mission, as with Christian discipleship, is the formation of each person more fully into the image of Jesus Christ by the power of the Spirit.

Salvation as Healing

Having mapped the pneumatological *via salutis*, however, we must now focus on the question regarding the relationship between salvation and the healing of the body. Not only does the New Testament word *soteria* mean "health" or "wholeness," as we have already seen, the ministry of Jesus included healing and the anticipation of the prophets was that human bodies would be made whole in the coming reign of God (see pp. 24–27). Further, if our emergentist anthropology also assumes the constitutive fundamentality of embodiment (pp. 181–83), then no explication of the doctrine of salvation articulated in dialogue with the experience of disability can avoid dealing with questions related to healing. In the following discussion, then, we look at traditional theologies of healing, interrogate them from disability perspectives, and sketch an alternative theology of healing that includes but does not conflate healing and curing.

Traditional Theologies of Healing

The New Testament's witness to God's healing power has shaped the history of Christianity up to the present day (Kelsey 1976; Kydd 1998; Porterfield 2005). Those recognized as saints were often conduits of healing to the lives and bodies of the faithful (see pp. 31–33). In revival movements that have come and gone over the centuries, healing has always played a central role.

One of the more recent revival movements that began at the turn of the twentieth century and continues to spread especially in the global South is modern Pentecostalism (see Yong 2005a: chap. 1). The early modern Pentecostals embraced a fourfold gospel of

Jesus as Savior, baptizer in the Holy Spirit, healer, and coming
King (Dayton 1987: 21–23). They were convinced that the message of the gospel included the healing of the body according to
the New Testament proclamation that "[h]e himself bore our sins
in his body on the cross, so that, free from sins, we might live for
righteousness; by his wounds you have been healed" (1 Pet 2:23;
cf. McCrossan 1982). Further, the Pentecostal focus on the power
of the Holy Spirit brought with it also an emphasis on the spiritual
gifts, including the charism of healing (1 Cor 12:4-7). Given the
assumption that all members of the body of Christ are empowered
by the Spirit in some way, all might also be conduits of the Spirit's
healing gifts. So, "Are any among you sick? They should call for
the elders of the church and have them pray over them, anointing
them with oil in the name of the Lord. The prayer of faith will
save the sick, and the Lord will raise them up; and anyone who has
committed sins will be forgiven. Therefore confess your sins to one
another, and pray for one another, so that you may be healed" (Jas
5:14-16). Not surprisingly, one of the reasons people continue to
be drawn to Pentecostal Christianity is that they (or people they
know, whether friends or loved ones) have been touched by God
through a healing experience (see Hardesty 2003; Harrell 1975;
Ervin 2002).

A more recent variant of Pentecostalism is the charismatic
renewal movement that began in the mainline Protestant churches
in the late 1950s and early 1960s and then spread to the Roman
Catholic Church in the late 1960s. Again, healing played a central role in these charismatic renewal streams. At the same time,
however, a subtle shift took place with regard to healing practices.
Whereas Pentecostalism emphasized the healing of the body, the
charismatic renewal expanded the healing work of God to deal
with the wide range of psychosomatic illnesses and sicknesses more
prevalent in the Anglo-American West. Fr. Francis MacNutt,
O.P., one of the first Catholics involved in the renewal, identified
four basic types of sicknesses requiring four approaches to prayer
and healing (1974: chap. 11): physical sicknesses from disease or
accidents requiring physical healing; emotional illnesses from
hurts in our past requiring inner healing or healing of memories;
sickness of our spirit resulting from sin requiring repentance; and
sickness or illness resulting from demonic oppression requiring

deliverance through exorcism. This kind of multilevel approach to healing has become fairly standard in circles influenced by Pentecostalism and the charismatic renewal (e.g., Wimber and Springer 1987; Wagner 1988).

One of the positive developments in the theology of healing that has emerged is a retrieval of the biblical understanding of healing as wholeness (Ram 1995). Building on MacNutt's analysis, there is now greater awareness of the interrelatedness of at least the first two types of sicknesses he describes. Further, there is also greater sensitivity to the interpersonal dimension of wellness, health, and wholeness: estranged relationships often result in physical or psychosomatic illnesses. Finally, there is also more sensitivity to local or contextual explanations and practices in etiologies of sickness and illness. Particularly when dealing with indigenous populations in the global South, more attention is paid both to environmentally related prescriptions (e.g., herbal medicine) and to supernaturalistic understandings, especially those related to demonic beings (see pp. 26 and 132). Whatever one may think about the causal connections between sickness and sin or demonic forces, an emergentist perspective (pp. 170–72) would explicate all sickness and illness in relational terms so that they are finally constituted by but yet irreducible to the body. In this case, a holistic view of health and healing cannot disregard human embodiment, although, as I will clarify shortly, we need to distinguish between healing the body and curing the body.

It is also fair to say, however, that beliefs and practices related to alternative medicine and demonic interventions have never disappeared even in the Euro-American West, and they may even be a growing phenomena at this time. In fact, in certain streams of the Pentecostal and charismatic renewal movements, these are the dominant etiologies for the persistence of sickness, illness, and even disability. People are not healed (or cured) because of demonic interference, sin in their lives, or a lack of faith in God's power to heal (unbelief being understood as another form of sin). In these cases, healing can only come through exorcism (which is also one of the charisms of the Spirit identified by Paul; 1 Cor 12:4-7), repentance from sin, or repentance from unbelief. Needless to say, these assumptions have been extremely problematic when applied uncritically to people with disabilities.

Interrupting the Healing Service: Disability Interrogations

Unfortunately, the Pentecostal and charismatic renewal movements have resulted in just as many if not more disappointments
and negative experiences than healings for people with disabilities.
The complaints about Pentecostal-charismatic healing practices
are legion in the disability literature. Many who experience the
onset of disability later in life are initially drawn to Pentecostal-
charismatic healing revivals, have been laid hands on and prayed
for, but leave disillusioned if not crushed that God has not healed
them. Robert Lovering, a paraplegic as a result of polio, thus
insists (1985: 135) that "to be taught and believe that God—yours
or mine—selectively reaches down and restores some disabled persons to wholeness is a cruel and damaging hoax." Others like Harold Wilke go further to suggest that when charismatic groups say,
"If your faith were only strong enough, you could see," the blind
person could retort, "If *your* faith were strong enough, *you* could
cure *me!*" (Wilke 1984: 130; italics in original).

People with disabilities have also discerned that physical healing may not be God's will, especially in the short run. In hindsight,
Mary Semple sees her brain tumors as vessels from God that saved
her from an abusive marriage (Newell and Semple 2002: 108).
Further, in reflecting on her experiences with churches, Semple
talked about people who "don't go to church, don't profess to be
Christian, yet offer me more comfort than those who do. They
openly acknowledge my obvious deformities without fear. They
see beyond themselves to me. For those moments, they put their
feet into my shoes and glimpse my pain. They ease my burden in
this way. They validate my presence and my worth. Thank you"
(109). This assessment emerged, undoubtedly, out of her experiences with charismatics and their practice of cursing sicknesses "at
their roots," to which Semple wondered how her tumors could
have been cursed without the curse also affecting her. Semple's
question may also be pertinent to people whose disabilities are
congenital and identity forming, like those with a trisomy of the
twenty-first chromosome. In these cases as well, can the trisomic
variation be cursed without affecting the person?

In the final analysis, the more that people identify with their
disabilities, the less likely will they be drawn to ministries of healing,

whether of the Pentecostal-charismatic or the generically Christian sort. In the words of a parathlete and disability activist: "Just turn on the TV some night and watch those guys, preaching and telling all the people in wheelchairs to come forward and be healed. You think that helps gain people's respect for what we can do?" (Todd, in Eiesland and Saliers 1998: 221). But this is not only a matter of what people with disability can do; it is more importantly a question about who they are as people. As Susan Gabel (1999: 46) notes, "The claim 'I am disabled' is, in essence, a statement of resistance to those who would label or construct me in the image they have created of me. This is its discursive importance. It is my contention of my being." From this perspective, it is not people with disabilities who need healing, but people without disabilities who need to be transformed.

Returning to a theological framework, then, Robert Molsberry, a United Church of Christ pastor who was left a paraplegic as a result of a hit-and-run accident, resists the idea that God overrides the laws of nature in any arbitrary fashion. For those who say to people with disabilities, "God will perform a miracle in your life," Molberry's response (2004: 69) is that "God already had performed that miracle. I'm alive! . . . The problem with seeing salvation for the disabled only in terms of a medical cure for their condition is that this model identifies people with disabilities as imperfect people. I don't feel I'm less than a person in this disabled body. Putting life on hold until a cure is found reduces us to medical patients, not full persons with business to take care of, families to love, and adventures to live." Put alternatively, theologian Timothy Gorringe suggests (2002: 49) that "handicap constitutes a critique of idolatry of the young, fit, healthy body." In this framework, to pursue healing as if this were God's only response to disability would then be idolatry.

Not all people with disabilities have the same attitude toward healing, however. People with congenital disabilities obviously have adapted to their conditions so that their response is much different from that of those who confront disability later in life. Yet, even those who have long ago adapted to their disabilities admit that this did not come easily, nor has life been just rosy since their adjustment. So Hugh Gallagher, a quadriplegic from polio from age nineteen, provides an honest and poignant account about how accessibility helps but does not completely remove the challenge of living with a disability, either at the personal-existential level or at the social-interactional level. He confesses that after many years, "I bombed out of Super Cripdom. My body collapsed physically, and I plunged headlong into a deep and chronic clinical depression, which took me years to climb out of" (Gallagher 1998: 246). So, even after forty years as a person with disability and thirty years participating in the disability movement, being disabled is not OK with Gallagher. He concludes, "I *live* in my ghost. . . . Disability and denial are inseparable. . . . In my lifelong struggle with disability I lose. And yet, most paradoxically, somehow, the ghost inside the reality, the self, prevails" (Gallagher 1998: 5; italics in original). In cases like Gallagher's and others, the phenomenology and lived existential experience of disability should not be disregarded.

But there are also disabling conditions that are genuinely related to disease such as tuberculosis (in undeveloped countries) and cancer. If we now have vaccines that have virtually eliminated tuberculosis, why should cancer patients also not hope for cures for their conditions (Sontag 1977)? And for disabling diseases for which we do not yet have cures, is not prayer appropriate and the hope in divine healing valid? So after years of struggling with multiple sclerosis, Nancy Mairs (see pp. 178–79) insists that she "hates" and "loathes" not herself but her disease (Mairs 1986: 12, 16, 17); in fact, "if a cure were found, would I take it? In a minute. I may be a cripple, but I'm only occasionally a loony and never a saint. Anyway, in my brand of theology God doesn't give bonus points for a limp" (1986: 20).[9] Similarly, biblical scholar Carole Fontaine suggests in light of her bout with chronic illness that we can and should embrace the image of "Jesus as healer," especially when the focus is on what he does not do in comparison to what happens in our health care systems; rather Jesus is "a decidedly un-capitalistic, selfless health care provider. . . . When human doctors fail, a miracle-working rabbi is a blessing indeed" (Fontaine 1996: 297). From a theological perspective, then, is not healing still an important element of the gospel in the twenty-first century?

To be sure, disability advocates may say these are socially conditioned responses of the psychologically and religiously immature. Even Mairs is ambivalent: "I'd take a cure; I just don't need one" (1986: 20). So if we take a people-first approach, on the one side are proposals to move away from talking about healing disability, while on the other side are those insisting that healing is what they need. Whither a theology of disability?

Curing and Healing: Renewing Theology of Disability

I suggest that one way forward out of this dilemma is to distinguish between disability on the one hand and illness, sickness, or disease on the other. Following Anita Silvers (1999: 187–88), I propose that the latter can be improved while the former cannot. Illnesses, sicknesses, and diseases are traceable to specific physiological sites, even if their effects are globally diffused through the entire body. Disabilities, however, are often localized impairments. Further, disability delimits specific areas of functioning while illnesses result in whole-body debilitation. Finally, we might expect sick or ill persons to be unable to perform *all* normal tasks, whereas people with disabilities could be limited in the performance of *some* normal tasks but could also engage other tasks quite well.

Building on this distinction, theologian Jennie Block suggests (2000: 103–4) that we need a new hermeneutic for the biblical passages that distinguish between illness and disability, and hence also distinguish between curing (physical) and healing (holistic). People with illnesses or sicknesses need to be cured in order to be whole, whereas people with disabilities, like Mairs, may take a cure but do not need it in order to be whole. In some cases, the gospel emphasis is on curing, but in all cases people are made whole. Hence Norman Habel asks (1981: 12–13), rhetorically, "Do the gospels assume that Jesus came to remove impairments rather than enable people to overcome them?" If so, "Can Jesus' relation to disabilities in life be meaningful if he is continually portrayed as a 'miracle worker'?"

Another way to parse the difference between curing and healing is to suggest that while the former focuses on the bodily sphere, the latter includes a social dimension of reconciliation, inclusion, and solidarity (Black 1996: chap. 8; Senior 1995: 12–13; German Perez Cruz, in introductory quotation to this chapter). People with Down Syndrome who do not have significant physical disabilities, for example, do not need to be cured; like all other people, however, they do need to be loved. To be sure, in some cases, curing precedes healing, such as when lepers are cleansed (or

when demoniacs are delivered) precisely in order to facilitate restoration to their communities. Yet, in the parable of the great dinner, the crippled, blind, and lame are invited and included just as
they are. Our focus, then, should be on how Jesus' ministry makes
people whole. As theologian Graham Monteith notes (2005: 138),
"The concentration on the single symptom reduces the eventual
religious significance of the incident and takes away the holistic
understanding which is central to the social model of disability."

Contemporary religionists who have come to grips with the
limitness (see above, p. 167) or finitude of human existence and
capability realize that while we remain a long way from finding
cures for everything, there are a wide range of religious resources
that have yet to be tapped that can facilitate the healing of human
hearts and communities. Even scholars in the Pentecostal and charismatic renewal movements have begun to explore how religious
commitments empower human beings to live as whole creatures
with one another even if they do not experience the cures that they
believe God can bring about (Kärkkäinen 2002: chap. 12; Mittelstadt 2004; Warrington 2005). Less and less, then, is the idea of
healing tied exclusively to the idea of curing.

Having established this line of thought, however, we should
not forget that salvation may include cures even if it is not limited
to curing. But while the church should not neglect this aspect of her
ministry, its approach should recognize the mystery of God's freedom in interacting with each human situation. Roy McCloughry
and Wayne Morris (2002: 112–14) are helpful in suggesting the
following approaches to the ministry of healing:

- The sick and disabled must be treated with respect and
  integrity.
- Do not link sickness and disability with sin, lack of faith, or
  the demonic.
- Clear biblical and theological explanations should be provided about the symbolic media (anointing oil, laying on of
  hands, etc.) involved in the Christian practice of healing.
- No pressure should be applied to the sick or disabled, and
  all should be taught to recognize that curing is not the
  measure of their success or failure as individuals or of the
  ministry of the church.

- Do not assume that persons coming forward for prayer want to have their visible impairments or disabilities prayed for.
- Release the sick and disabled to pray for others.
- All prayer for the sick or disabled should be followed up with referrals to professional or social services as appropriate since the church does not own the copyright on healing.
- Make explicit the connections between physical healing and social justice.
- Get medical confirmation when possible.
- Each person should be encouraged to narrate his/her own story (testify) according to his/her own experience.

In all of this, the church needs to be open to criticisms from within and without the congregation about its healing ministries and practices.

When healing is reconfigured in relational terms as including but not reducible to curing (Lay 1998: pt. 5), then the way is open to include even people with intellectual disabilities in our rites of healing. In their discussion of "How to Celebrate the Healing Stories," Gijs Okhuijsen and Cees van Opzeeland suggest (1992: 46) people with intellectual disabilities can "recognize how some of Jesus' healing power for the sick of his day is still working, right now, in the care and help given them by therapists and group leaders. With this perspective, there is cause to celebrate small miracles. This way, helpers and residents alike get the opportunity to present to God all that is on their minds, the struggle to keep up the fight, the moments of discouragement and failure." The story of the paralytic let down through the roof, for example, can be focused on the helpers and the technological aids—with the lowering device analogous to contemporary canes, crutches, walkers, and various types of wheelchairs, along with the manufacturers and workers who mass-produce these accessories—while the Pentecost narrative can utilize breathing exercises to enable realization of the Spirit's gracious gift of the breath of life (Okhuijsen and van Opzeeland 1992: 48–51, 61–64). In relational perspective, healing takes place in community, sometimes including cures, but more often reconciling lives who were formerly strangers to one another.

Toward a Holistic Soteriology: Disability and Human Wholeness

In this chapter thus far we have suggested an expansion of the *ordo salutis* in the direction of a multidimensional *via salutis* and distinguished a theology of curing from a theology of healing with the latter including but not limited to the former. It is time to tie the threads together to develop a holistic theology of salvation in light of the experience of disability. The following extends the emergentist anthropology developed earlier—human beings as embodied, relational, and transcendental (see chap. 6)—by way of correlating the multidimensionality of what it means to be human with the multidisciplinary approaches to disability (see pp. 148–50) toward a pneumatological theology of salvation. And insofar as the theology of disability being developed in these pages is also a performative theology that is normative for human actions, to that extent the ideas in this section also culminate the argument of this book in terms of prescribing the redemptive practices of the body of Christ as empowered by the Holy Spirit.

Renewing the Body

A holistic theology of salvation must begin, following the emergentist anthropology, with human embodiment. We had previously argued that while human life is a gift of the breath of God that is irreducible to the body, yet life is never apart from the body. Salvation—health, wellness, and wholeness—must therefore at least begin with the body. We will develop this line of thought from biological and psychosomatic perspectives.

At the biological level, a holistic soteriology cannot ignore the salvation of the body. Part of the challenge today, of course, is that over the course of the last one hundred–plus years, the responsibility for healing seems to have shifted more and more from religious practitioners to medical professionals and researchers. The confluence of medical, technological, and economic discourses that emphasize rehabilitation, retraining, redeploying, reintegrating, repairing, and replacing all suggest that we now have increasing capacities to enable people with disabilities to resume their place in society (Stiker 1999: 124–28; cf. pp. 71 and 95–96). Like a messiah, modern biomedicine presents "endless rehabilitative technologies, which . . . promise to make us whole. That is to say, modernity's assumption of dominion over the earth, with technology being one of the tools thereof, also had its outcroppings for people with disabilities: prosthetics enjoined us to wholesomeness" (Betcher 2001: 345). This is the case in developed regions of the world to such an extent that "[i]nfirmities do not raise metaphysical problems so much as technical ones, to be taken in hand and administered by social workers, vocational trainers, and medical and legal specialists. The assumption is that we master all the outcomes; every condition can be treated and adjusted, though not all can be cured" (Whyte 1995: 270). Not surprisingly, biomedicine has a much greater cultural salience in the Euro-American context than elsewhere.

But from a theological perspective, what is the role of modern medicine? Is it the savior we sometimes assume it to be? The answer to this question cannot but be a resounding "No!" As we have already seen (pp. 51–54), medical models and the unique historical trajectory of medicalization have contributed to the exclusion of people with disabilities in general and people with intellectual disabilities more specifically from citizenship and civil rights (see Carey 2003). But the power and authority of modern medicine is also dangerous in its totalitarian posture (versus interdependence) and its promise to deliver more (salvifically speaking) than it can. From a Christian point of view, then, the goal cannot be to discard medicine, but to resist its seductions, to harness its power in redemptive ways, and to cultivate the virtues and practices that shape Christian life such as hospitality, patience, and the worship of God (Shuman and Volck 2006). The salvation of the body must finally rest on the power of God. Human bodies will eventually die and rot away in their graves, but the God of Jesus Christ is the God who raises the dead.

At the psychological level, a holistic soteriology cannot simply dismiss the phenomenological and existential experiences of disability. In his autobiographical ethnography of slowly losing his ability to walk (from 1971 to 1986) due to spinal cord disease, anthropologist Robert Murphy provides a poignant glimpse into the personal and psycho-existential dimensions of the disability experience. Murphy recounts (1987: esp. chap. 4) his struggles with lowered self-esteem related to constant thinking about himself in terms of physical deficits, sustained and strong undercurrents of anger, and the slow and agonizing embodiment and acquisition of a new and undesirable self-identity. From a psychological perspective, then, salvation includes the process of coming to grips with disability (valuing denial, but moving on), a course of rehabilitation as a lifelong process, and the gradual achievement of a sense of transcending both the experience of disability and the dichotomy of disability versus normalization (see Vash 1981: 131–34; cf. p. 126). In this process, of course, religious rituals mediate healing at least in the sense of enabling people with disabilities to adapt to and exist with their condition (see Csordas 1994: 71–72). From the perspective of spiritual formation, the goal is to gain, through the workings of the Holy Spirit, what Marva Dawn (2002) calls "joy in our weakness."

I suggest further that at the center of psychological well-being is the experience of love. If the human quality of life is intrinsically tied to the experience of friendships and meaningful relationships (see pp. 71 and 186–87), then to say that "[t]he worth of persons is in the love of others for them" (Pailin 1992: chap. 5) is to make a theological and soteriological claim above all else, regardless of what kind of disability is in question. Hence Pekka Louhiala also suggests (2004: 7) in her book on intellectual disability: "Loving . . . is a mental function, and most people with intellectual disability are as able to love as those of us with better intellectual capacity. In fact, they have also been characterized as 'congenitally unable to hate.'" To love is to allow the love of God that has been poured out in our hearts through the Holy Spirit to flow out into the lives of others. To be loved is to allow the love of God given by the Spirit to reach us through the lives of others. Love is the presence and activity of the Holy Spirit that heals and renews our hearts, and therefore also our minds and ourselves.

Reconciling Humanity

To talk about the healing power of love, of course, requires us to talk about relationships. At one level, salvation is about the healing of relationships, and a holistic approach to soteriology must develop interventions that nurture human relationships and community (see Downs 1996). I want to flesh out this hypothesis in terms of the objective and subjective dimensions of the *via salutis*.

From a disability perspective, the objective dimensions of salvation can be said to be the gracious relationships through which God sustains human life and nurtures human flourishing. This begins, of course, with the family relationship. The experiences of disability foreground more explicitly what is taken for granted in the parent-child relationship: the dependency of all human beings on others (see Rapp and Ginsburg 2004: esp. 181–85). All the more crucial, then, is it for the church to encourage, support, and nurture healthy and loving family relations. In the words of Esther, a severely disabled teenager, spoken at the service marking her family's temple's commitment to inclusion: "To parents that have kids with special needs: You need to learn to be patient because it's not your fault that your kid was born like this. If your child is having a hard time, you can give them a hug and say 'Everything's going to be okay,' and put your arms around them and be loving to them"; further, "When asked, at age twelve, what the meaning of life was, she answered without hesitation: 'to love people'" (Gottlieb 2002b: 20). Esther had been touched by God in and through her family and the lives of those in her Jewish community. She was now ready to be an instrument of God's saving work in the lives of others.

Of course, the gracious and saving work of God is present not only in Jewish temples or synagogues but also in congregations that are the body of Christ. If God's election, calling, and predestination is said to be preliminarily or preveniently manifest in the loving relationships of human families, then they are also actualized and embodied in the church as the fellowship of the Spirit. From the perspective of disability, then, the work of the church is to form the people of God into a welcoming and inclusive community of healing. With regard to infants and children with disabilities, Hans Reinders puts it (2000: 176) succinctly: "the future of disabled people in our society will in large part depend on whether or not there will be such people. . . . [T]he crucial question then becomes how liberal society can produce the kind of people who are willing to have themselves transformed by what their society portrays and evaluates as defective children."[10] After all, it is the church as the communion of the Spirit that is able to overcome the original sin of individualism, hedonism, and narcissism that we have all been socialized into. In this view, then, a theology and soteriology of disability prioritizes the corporate dimensions of the doctrines of election and predestination: God calls us through the grace extended in our families and communities of faith, and the saving work of God in our lives begins through these relationships.

Along the *via salutis*, however, there are also subjective experiences, encounters, and engagements with God's saving work. From a disability perspective, the subjective dimensions of salvation can be said to be those moments when human beings experience the sustaining and empowering work of God in palpable, affective, and at times, cognitively self-conscious ways. What we call conviction, for example, is our awareness that things are not right between ourselves and others; regeneration could be experienced in terms of the revitalization of lives, neighborhoods, and communities (see Perske 1980). In the end, the good news of salvation is, as David Pailin notes (1992: chap. 6), "that we belong." From a disability perspective, God declares God's acceptance of our lives through the welcome and embrace of others: "The idea of God may not make a lot of sense to some people, and for some it may make no sense at all, but the reality of loving care, reverence and respect from others can be known for it can be experienced" (Pailin 1992: 138).

Let me expand on this point through a discussion of the doctrine of justification. Without neglecting the objective dimension of this doctrine with regard to God's declaring sinners just on account of the sacrifice of Christ, the disability perspective illumines the subjective dimension of this doctrine with regard to the social constitution of human identity (see chap. 4). In their analysis of the rights of people with intellectual disability, Damon Young and Ruth Quibell (2000) argue that because the notion of rights emerged out of the history of Western atomistic individualism, the question of rights itself "stems from a view of humans as atomic individuals, rather than collaborative participants in a *culture*" (759; italics in original). The way forward is to understand the stories that shape our collaborative cultural project. In fact, our coming to know the (multidimensional) narratives of people with intellectual disabilities will lead to an adjustment of our cumulative social relations: "This understanding of peoples' stories is how *justice* is achieved. By sharing a story, we may '*do justice*' to one another. . . . [If] change is possible at all, it is not because of the might of 'rights,' but because people have the ability to understand stories larger, longer and ultimately different from their own" (Young and Quibell 2000: 760–61; italics mine).[11] In this framework, then, the justification of people with intellectual disabilities depends on their own self-advocacy and self-testimony (to the extent that is possible) as supported by the advocacy and testimony of many others (pp. 7–11). As Stanley Hauerwas aptly puts it, our attempts to defend the lives of those with disabilities by insisting on their personhood is backward since "we are trying to put forward 'person' as a regulative notion to direct our health care as substitute for what only a substantive community and story can do" (in Swinton 2004: 115). Rather than being found in or through our medical systems, personhood emerges in communities of care wherein human lives are rescued from marginality and justice emerges through the common narration of our stories together.

This relational account of justification in particular and of the various dimensions of the *via salutis* in general is both pneumatologically shaped and performatively normative. Interpersonal relationality and testimony, after all, is specifically the work of the Spirit, who comes in power so that the people of God can be "witnesses in Jerusalem, in all Judea and Samaria, and to the ends of the earth" (Acts 1:8). Further, the fellowship of the Spirit includes but goes beyond friendships to the point of empowering the laying down of life even on a cross, but does so precisely in order that life may flourish as nourished by the seeds of self-sacrificial love. In both of these senses, a holistic approach to soteriology is also performative in terms of prescribing practices of the church that are convicting, justifying, reconciling, and regenerating of human lives and communities.

Renewing the Late Modern World: Toward a Theo-Econo-Politics of Disability

Finally, a holistic soteriology goes beyond addressing individual and interpersonal concerns to addressing the structures that organize and shape human life. Insofar as the church is called to be a witness to the gospel and a leaven in the world, to that degree the church also participates in the saving work of the Spirit of God to redeem and renew the fallen powers at work in the various dimensions of human life. Yet again, a pneumatological theology of the cross (pp. 176–80) emphasizes that the redemption of the powers "is made perfect in weakness" (2 Cor 12:9),[12] and the church acts as a fallen power when it relies on her own strengths, rather than on God. Empowered by the Spirit, the church comes to embody what I call a theo-econo-politics of disability.

In such a theo-econo-political vision, people with disabilities are central to the church's mission to announce the kingdom of God and be a vehicle for its manifestation in the here and now. Such a vision for the coming kingdom is articulated in other words by Jewish philosopher Roger Gottlieb (2002a), as informed by his experience of caring for his severely disabled daughter, Esther. In Gottlieb's analysis, cancer, for example, is not only a biological or genetic matter, but it is also "a social product" (181) in the sense that over 80 percent of cancers in the world are caused by environmental pollution. Further, preventive research is minimal (98 percent of research goes into seeking cures) since cancer patients have become a lucrative market; hence, "public health and environmental policy are way down on the list of priorities" (185), even as we are still losing the war to cancer. Simultaneously, the same chemicals that alter cell structure to promote cancer can cause birth defects as well. For Gottlieb, then, religious resources need to be brought to bear not only to encourage individuals and foster community but also to transform the social and political structures that endanger human flourishing.

To be sure, such a theo-econo-political transformation will not happen overnight, and Stephen Pattison's (1994) analysis of the mental health care system provides additional perspective on why this is the case. He suggests that traditional pastoral care and chaplaincy training from predominantly humanistic psychological disciplines has not included the kind of critical theories of action or social analysis needed to engage with sociopolitical issues such as class, power, race, gender, justice, and inequality. So while "social and political factors impinge on what is called mental illness to a very significant extent" (84), most psychiatric and pastoral professionals focus usually on one-to-one relationships and look at mental illness in bio-psycho-physiological terms, to be treated with drugs, therapeutic interventions, or behavioral modification techniques. In Pattison's view, the psychiatric hospital is a microcosm of the larger capitalist order, created to control "an unwanted, powerless, economically unproductive, stigmatised group and it is funded accordingly" (148). Even with the new developments in "community care" and "community care ethics," the framework still operates within a medical rather than sociopolitical model, so that the prospects for the future of the care of the mentally ill are not much different from present operations. Insofar as chaplains are employed by psychiatric hospitals, they are supposed to "oil the psychiatric machine" rather than prophetically upset that status quo. In short, an entire mental health care industry structured around "caring for these individuals" does not invite focus on the wider social framework that contributes to precisely such problems (cf. Newell 2006: 273–75). Pattison concludes that pastoral care needs to be liberated from its "therapeutic captivity," and that we need to subvert this entire framework of "therapeutic individualism" (213–19). In this way, the church's work in the world can be extended to include sociopolitical analysis focused on the transformation of the structures that liberate the poor and the oppressed.

Still, even if a Christian theo-econo-politics of disability does not describe a present reality, it is nevertheless a kerygmatic pronouncement intended to inspire and be normative for Christian practices. Moreover, from a Christian theological perspective informed by the experience of disability, the doctrine of salvation is ultimately impotent apart from its capacity to address prophetically the social and political structures of this present world order. Hence, for example, the doctrine of justification cannot be limited only to the reconciliation of human relationships (see above, pp. 252–53) but must also at least announce if not empower the rectification of human injustices (Altmann 1992; Tamez 1993). In this framework, conversion, justification, and liberation are interconnected, even as self, neighbor (which in the global perspective also includes the stranger), and God are also interconnected.[13] Rather than remaining merely at the subjective level of individual testimonies, justification must also be understood in objective terms with concrete historical effects. And where people are subjected to violence and condemned to death as nonpersons by exclusive economic, political, and military systems, then the doctrine of justification becomes a liberative spiritual weapon that affirms the lives of the poor, the oppressed, and the excluded. In this view, justification is not only God's pronouncement of justice but also God's liberation from injustice that benefits all, judges and redeems the fallen powers, and enables the renewal of a just world.

Hence, a holistic soteriology of disability is not only theological but also economic and political. By economic, I mean that the salvation of all human beings, both disabled and nondisabled, must involve the redemption, healing, and transformation of our present fallen economy of laissez-faire capitalism (pp. 96–99). The problem with laissez-faire capitalism is that it is driven by profit and (to use a more hamartiological term) self-seeking. Normed by the "bottom line," economic ventures—whether related to architectural projects, telecommunication and technological developments, corporate structuring, vocational employment (see Anderson 2005; Goggin and Newell 2003)—have to appeal to the widest of the market while inviting minimal investments. This gives rise to practices that reinforce the social conventions of "normalcy" and "deviancy," and that are incapable of appreciating and valuing difference.

A disability perspective would emphasize instead "the promise of mutual relation as an empowering grace" that suspends the "laws of production and distribution so characteristic of the economy of exchange" and enacts an "economy of grace" where there are "no calculable 'reasons' that bid [us] to enter into contractual relation with it in order that [we] gain something in return. For it shows itself as a value precisely in its weakness, in its inability to offer 'anything' in return" (Reynolds 2005: 203). This new economy of grace is most palpably embodied in the L'Arche community where the mutuality and reciprocity between core members and assistants rejects the one-way flow of benefits characterizing medical and charitable paradigms (Cushing and Lewis 2002; cf. pp. 200–203 above). In this way, a theo-economics of disability serves as a prophetic sign of the Spirit for the transformation of the economics of the present order. Note, however, the difference between a redemption of the economic powers that be versus their rejection. Even people with disabilities realize that it is the capitalist economy of the West that is responsible "for the greatest amount of economic growth in human history" (Batavia 2001: 110). For this reason, my suggestion is that a theo-econo-politics of disability cannot dispense with capitalism altogether but must be discerning about its weaknesses even while redeeming its strengths so that its benefits can be distributed in the most inclusive manner possible this side of the eschaton.[14]

Of course, any redemption of our economics must also include a redemption of our fallen politics (pp. 91–95). Part of the problem with our political structures, as has already been noted, is that they are built on the foundation of modern individualism. So, for example, the Americans with Disabilities Act (ADA) may be unworkable because it is laden with special interests, calls for legal rather than interpersonal engagement, lacks enforcement capability, and cannot be fully implemented given the separation of church and state. In this framework, the ideology of the ADA is in many ways oppressive rather than liberative:

> People with disabilities, their families, and their friends truly believed the story they were being told and invited to live by the nation-state. They were told they could be independent individuals, free to make choices, to live wherever they wanted, to be masters of their destiny. They were told that science was their friend, protecting them and those like them, and that it was constantly looking for new ways to aid them. They were told they now had civil rights protected by law. By believing what they were told by the nation-state, however, they were actually being made more and more dependent on the state's largesse. Indeed, as they find themselves being made *truly* independent now—free from all the programs and monies of the state [due to budget cuts]—people with disabilities and their families are realizing too late exactly *how* dependent they have been. And they are discovering that, despite their hopes that they would still receive some help, the nation-state really wishes they weren't here. (Webb-Mitchell 1996: 133–34; italics in original)

What we need, then, is a theological politics of interdependence and interrelationality to sustain our political life together. In the words of Alasdair MacIntyre (1999: 130), we need a new narrative in which "it is taken for granted that disability and dependence on others are something that all of us experience at certain times in our lives and this to unpredictable degrees, and that consequently our interest in how the needs of the disabled are adequately voiced and met is not a special interest . . . , but rather the interest of the whole political society, an interest that is integral to their conception of their common good."[15] In this vision, it is neither the lordship of the market, nor of the U.S. Congress, nor of Caesar in his many guises, that will mediate salvation; rather, "Jesus is Lord" is the powerful confession of the powerless against the powerful (Green 1987) that holds the political lords of this world accountable to a transcendent authority. Only such a theologically informed politics, I suggest, will foster the kind of community, friendships, and solidarity that will be healing and saving for all people, including those with disabilities.

In this and the last chapter, I have suggested that it is only when the church works out of her weakness that the redemptive power of the Holy Spirit can be unleashed to accomplish the renewal and redemption of the present world order. This may indeed include cures for people with disabilities; but even without such and surely while awaiting such, the saving work of the Spirit brings about the healing of people's lives, the reconciling of human and communal relationships, and the transformation of the social, political, and economic structures that shape all of our interactions. Such is the salvation of people with and without disabilities alike, understood holistically. Simultaneously, this saving work of God also heralds and even ushers in the reign of God through the power of the Holy Spirit. To be sure, in the present time of "holy Saturday," we live betwixt and between the already and the not-yet. Yes, in the outpouring of the Holy Spirit the last days are already upon us in some way (Acts 2:17); but no, we still await with anticipation and longing for the Spirit to transform the face of the earth so that the renewed creation will finally bear the full and splendorous image of the Son of God. But does that mean, then, that in the coming eschatological kingdom we will no longer need the weakness of disabilities as the "glue" to the kingdom?

IX

Resurrecting Down Syndrome and Disability
Heaven and the Healing of the World

Our bodies are like cars. Some people go through life in a fine sedan, some in a sleek sports car. You have a luxury model. . . . But mine is an old clunker. Some people drive smoothly through life, while I go clattering down the road. But when we get to Heaven, my body will be just as good as anyone else's. In fact, I'll probably be a Cadillac then.

—Larry Patton, in Kastner 1989: 160

"Will I be retarded when I get to heaven?" The parents answered that she would not. There would be no sickness, no pain. Everyone would be perfect. To this she responded, "But, how will you know me then?"

—Anonymous, in Gaventa and Coulter 2003: 132

"Barbara, will there be Nintendo in heaven?" *I don't know, Mark, but whatever you need to be happy God will give you.* "But will there be Nintendo there?" *Mark, when you were a baby you needed a bottle. Do you want a bottle now?* "No." *So maybe when we get to heaven we won't want what we do now.* "But will there be Nintendo in heaven?" *If you need Nintendo in heaven to be happy, Yes, Mark, there will be Nintendo in heaven.*

—Shisler 1998: 43

[We] asked [Peter, a L'Arche member] what he did when he prayed. He replied: "I listen." Then the person asked what God says to him. Peter, a man with Down's Syndrome, looked up and said: "He just says, 'You are my beloved son.'"

Vanier 1992: 23

Mom has always believed that Mark will be healed, if not in this life, then in the life to come. Of this, she is convinced. Yet, like any loving parent, Mom wonders about Mark's future, especially since she and Dad are no longer as young as before. Mom is concerned about Mark's increased stubbornness, especially about how she reacts to him. Mark is and has always been quite friendly, even in public. What if people did not accept him, or if strangers took advantage of him? Yet, in all of this, Mom has learned to trust God that all things will work out for good. Through it all, God has given grace sufficient for each day to get through life's challenges. Mom realizes that it was good that God did not ask her ahead of time if he had permission to bring Mark into her life as she probably wouldn't have been able to handle it. But now, daily, she thanks the Lord for him.

What about Mark? What do you think heaven will be like, Mark? "Singing in the heavenly choir with the angels," "resurrection," "Easter," and "being with Him."

If one of the goals of this volume is to articulate a theology of disability that can inform the shape of Christian practices in a world of many disabilities, then it may seem that with the previous chapters on theological anthropology, ecclesiology, and soteriology, our task is finished. Further, why proceed to add a chapter on eschatology—the doctrine of the end—given the contentiousness of the issues at stake? Yet, not to speak to the topic of eschatology would leave this book incomplete for at least three reasons. First, the reimagining and renewing of theology in late modernity will be partial if one of the central loci of the Christian theological system as traditionally understood—its heavenly hope—is left untreated. Second, the Christian doctrine of salvation has perennially included, if not sometimes focused only on, the doctrines of heaven and eternal life, and to say nothing about eschatology now would render the soteriological vision of the last three chapters less than comprehensive. Finally, if in fact Christian beliefs also inform Christian practices (and vice versa), then to neglect eschatology is to commit the irresponsible act of leaving uncriticized the eschatological assumptions that shape Christian life in this world, often to the detriment of the lives of people with disabilities. In short, I will argue that this last chapter on eschatology is essential for the renewal of theology more so because of its implications for the present life than because it gives us license to speculate about the life to come.[1]

We begin by laying out traditional notions of eternal life and the doctrine of the resurrection and subject them to critical questioning from disability perspectives. The middle section will develop a dynamic eschatological vision from biblical, historical, and theological perspectives. We will conclude by speculating about everlasting life and the resurrection of the body in disability perspective. Now while discussion about bodily resurrection can neglect the communal dimension of human identity, we should be mindful throughout the following discussion of previously developed insights from emergentist and relational anthropology, pneumatological ecclesiology, and holistic soteriology as each of these perspectives will temper our rethinking eschatological ideas in dialogue with the disability experiences solely along individualistic lines. And, as before, we anticipate the dialogue will be mutually informative, resulting both in the renewal of theology and the redemption of disability.

Resurrection: Traditional Formulations and Disability Critiques

Our focus in this volume is on the edifying conversation between theology and disability. In part for this reason, our reflections will be limited to the doctrines of eternal life and the resurrection of the body, rather than focusing on the *parousia*, the millennium, the final judgment, hell, universalism, annihilationism, or other eschatological themes. This is not to say that these doctrines are irrelevant to the project of a disability-informed eschatology. But our energies will be consumed with articulating a positive vision of eternal life in disability perspective quite apart from having to resolve these other contested eschatological topics. We begin by presenting historical views on heaven and the resurrection. From there, we will proceed to identify traditional and more critical disability perspectives regarding the heavenly hope.

Heaven and the Resurrection: Historical Perspectives

The doctrine of the resurrection has been central to Christian faith since the earliest moments of its history. Grounded in the belief in the resurrection of Jesus himself (see 1 Cor 15:1-6), the idea of bodily life after death then fed Christian understandings of the doctrine of heaven as well (Rev 21–22).[2] How, then, did these doctrines develop? We will focus our overview on Christian ideas regarding the resurrection of the body, as that is the most pertinent eschatological motif for the dialogue between theology and disability.

After Saint Paul (to whom we will return below), a wide range of ideas regarding the resurrection body proliferated in the history of the Christian tradition (Bynum 1995). By the postapostolic period, there was already a growing conviction that the resurrected body would be free from its imperfections, and that even amputated limbs would be restored. Against the Gnostic spiritualization of the body, Tertullian argued (in Souter 1922: 153–54) that while we will not need the services of our bodies (e.g., limbs), they nevertheless will be resurrected and preserved for judgment. Tertullian's rejection of the Gnostic spiritualization of the body can also be seen as an extension of how the doctrine of the resurrection in the early church resisted the dominant intellectual idea of the immortality of the soul, which rendered embodiment as inferior (see Setzer 2004: chap. 3).

This emphasis on the import of the body even in the hereafter continued throughout the first Christian millennium, especially in the work of Augustine (354–430). While the early Augustine developed a rather ascetic model of heaven informed by his Manichaean leanings (and influenced by the desert saints), the later Augustine, working among urban Christians, revised this toward a more ecclesiastical, social, and embodied notion of the afterlife (Marrou 1966). Like Tertullian, the late Augustine emphasized that the bodies of the saints eat and drink (only for pleasure, not because of need), and that the resurrected body is aesthetically perfect (yet there will be no sexual temptation), except for the scars of the martyrs, which enhance their appeal. What about the *monstra* of which we have already seen Augustine comment (pp. 30–31)? In the eighty-seventh chapter of the *Enchiridion*, Augustine writes

(1994b: 265): "We are not justified in affirming even of monstrosities . . . that they shall not rise again, nor that they shall rise again in their deformity, and not rather with an amended and perfected body. . . . And so other births, which, because they have been either a superfluity or a defect, or because they are very much deformed, are called *monstrosities*, shall at the resurrection be restored to the normal shape of man."

In book 22 of the *City of God*, Augustine makes three further arguments. First, since Jesus died at the age of thirty and was resurrected in a form recognizable by his disciples, and since the scriptures declare that the goal of Christian discipleship is for every believer to attain "to maturity, to the measure of the full stature of Christ" (Eph 4:13b), Augustine concludes that "every man shall receive his own size which he had in youth, though he died an old man, or which he would have had, supposing he died before his prime" (*City of God* 22:15; 1994a: 495). Second, building on Luke 21:18—"But not a hair of your head will perish"—he argues that "whatever deformity was in it, and served to exhibit the penal condition in which we mortals are, the substance is entirely preserved, the deformity shall perish" (22:19; 497). Finally, Augustine concludes:

> [T]he body shall be of that size which it either had attained or should have attained in the flower of its youth, and shall enjoy the beauty that arises from preserving symmetry and proportion in all its members. . . . Or if it be contended that each will rise with the same stature as that of the body he died in, we shall not obstinately dispute this, provided only there be no deformity, no infirmity, no languor, no corruption,—nothing of any kind which would ill become that kingdom in which the children of the resurrection and of the promise shall be equal to the angels of God, if not in body and age, at least in happiness. (22:20; 499)

Clearly, then, Augustine was concerned with what we call the continuity of personal identity—that we rise with the "same body" (O'Collins 1994: 72–73)—for the resurrection.

Augustine's views on monstrosity and the fall from a perfect Edenic paradise (pp. 160–61) combined with his thinking about the resurrection, especially of the saints, carried the day for much of the next millennium. Thus, the medieval monastic manual *Elucidation* (ca. 1100) envisioned heaven and the new creation as the restoration of the paradise of Genesis 2–3 (McDannell and Lang 1988: 70–79). Otto, bishop of Freising (1114–1158), also followed Augustine's line of thinking: "We must not suppose that giants are brought back in such great stature, dwarfs in such extreme littleness, the lame or the weak in a state so feeble and afflicted, the Ethiopians in an affliction of color so disagreeable, the fat or the thin in their superabundance or their lack of flesh, to a life which ought to be free from every blemish and every spot" (Otto: 1928: 470). But the bishop of Freising went on to address further the question of who will be included in the resurrection. With reference to the Deuteronomic law that provides for restitution of a child killed during gestation in the womb, Otto answers, "[E]verything to which the description 'a rational and mortal animal' applies will rise either to life or to death" (470). To which he adds, "All the others, creatures that lack reason, however nearly they approach the human form (as for example apes), or by whatever form the ancient enemy mocks the human race (as for instance fauns), and all other creatures of this sort have, as is well known, no part in this resurrection" (471).[3]

Thomas Aquinas (1225–1274) also appealed to Augustine in his thinking about the resurrection of the body. In question 80 of his *Summa Theologica*, Aquinas argues (1941: 2:956–57) that all members of the body will rise again, albeit cleansed internally (in terms of the entrails of the body) and externally from all impurities (e.g., sweat, waste, urine), and amputated or lost limbs will be restored. But also important for our purposes, Aquinas emphasized human beings as rational intellects and hence defined full perfection and the beatific vision in these terms. Peter Byrne summarizes the implications of Aquinas's theological anthropology for his understanding of heaven:

> Inculcation of a range of intellectual, moral and theological virtues is necessary in order for the individual to acquire the ability to partake in that vision. So the path to blessedness is closed to those incapable of the necessary development. It must follow from an account of human teleology such as Aquinas provides that, to the extent that human beings are defective in the foundation of moral capacities, namely

intellect and will, then they are incapable of blessedness. They will be excluded from perfect relationship with God and thus salvation. So Aquinas' account is written as if there are no cognitively disabled people, or as if they do not matter. (P. Byrne 2000: 147)

If this were all that medieval theology had to say about heaven, of course, then it would be bleak indeed for people with severe and profound disabilities. However, in the mystical tradition with which theologians like Aquinas interfaced on other doctrinal and theological motifs, heaven was seen in the ecstatic terms of sexual union with God. The dominant imagery here was very sensual and even embodied in contrast with Aquinas's more intellectualist approach (McDannell and Lang 1988: 94–107).

In any case, by this time the hope of the early Christians had been developed into a full-fledged theology of the resurrected body. All throughout, the church combated popular fears regarding the decay and putrefying of the body with the conviction that the divine power sufficient to overcome death, dismemberment, and even mutilation could reunite the body wholly in the resurrection. As Caroline Bynum concludes (1995: 225), "By the early decades of the thirteenth century, only heretics thought the elect would leave the body behind in the ascent to salvation. Only heretics were willing to jettison the individuality the body might express—in even the fingernails and its boots."

Disabilities and the Heavenly Hope

By the early modern period, the doctrines of heaven and the resurrection were firmly lodged in the Christian consciousness in terms of the power of God to restore to Edenic perfection whatever plagued human embodiment in the present life. For John Wesley, the recognized founder of Methodism, this applied also to those "infirmities" that we today might call psychosomatic or biocognitive:

I mean hereby, not only those which are properly termed *bodily infirmities*, but all those inward or outward imperfections which are not of a moral nature. Such are the weakness or slowness of understanding, dullness or confused of apprehension, incoherence of thought, irregular quickness or heaviness of imagination . . . the want of a ready or retentive memory. Such, in another kind, are those which are commonly, in some measure, consequent upon these; namely, slowness of speech, impropriety of language, ungracefulness of pronunciation; to which one might add a thousand nameless defects, either in conversation or behavior. These are the infirmities which are found in the best of men, in a large or smaller proportion. *And from these none can hope to be perfectly freed, till the spirit returns to God that gave it.* (in Hunt 1978: 27–28; italics mine)

The assumptions of the theological tradition from Tertullian through Augustine and Aquinas are here made explicit with regard to people with disabilities. The heavenly hope that includes the resurrection of the body is the means through which God "will wipe every tear from their eyes. Death will be no more; mourning and crying and pain will be no more, for the first things have passed away" (Rev 21:4).

Christian theological thinking today—whether by Roman Catholics, Orthodox, pietists, evangelicals, Pentecostal-charismatics, or even by those from the various mainline Protestant traditions—remains dominated by this eschatological vision, and this is no less the case with regard to the experience of disability. This was certainly Larry Patton's hope with regard to comparing the "clunker" body of his earthly existence with the "Cadillac" body of his heavenly home (see introductory quotation to this chapter). The case of Oliver de Vinck, as told by his older brother Christopher (de Vinck 1988), is also exemplary. Oliver (1948–1980) was born blind, mute, crippled, and brain-damaged, and lived at home lying in bed all his life, growing to no more than the size of a ten-year-old. Christopher recollects:

Oliver was always a "hopeless" case, yet he was such a precious gift for our whole family. . . . This child has no *apparent* usefulness or meaning, and the "world" would reject him as an unproductive burden. But he was a holy innocent, a child of light. Looking at him, I saw the power of powerlessness. His total helplessness speaks to our deepest hearts, calls us not merely to pious emotions but to service. Through this child, I felt bound to Christ crucified—yes, and also to all those who suffer in the world. . . . I have made my peace with the coming of Oliver's death. I cannot see it as a tragedy. I know that the child who lived in apparent void and darkness *sees God, lives forever in health, beauty and light.* Here on earth, he was loved. His presence among us was a mysterious sign of that peace the world cannot give. (de Vinck 1988: 87–88; first italics in original, second italics mine)

My point is not to call attention to Christopher de Vinck's idealization of severe and profound disability in Roman Catholic terms of holy innocence, but to focus on his view of the heavenly hope as it related to his disabled brother. For many other Christian believers with disabilities, heaven symbolizes "a magnificent and much better place," freedom from their disabilities, and the full disclosure of the meaning of a tried and burdened life (see Canda 2001: 122, 126–27).

Even in more progressive Protestant circles, adherence to historic and orthodox forms of the Christian faith inevitably brings with it the embrace of a fairly traditional view of heaven in terms of the eschatological hope. For Episcopal theologian Samuel Wells, people with disabilities will be reintegrated into the new creation:

[T]he final unity of the severely mentally disabled and the "able-bodied" is an eschatological one, portrayed perhaps in the relation of the *gerim* to the Israelites in the Old Testament. The *gerim* were sojourners or resident aliens who could not be integrated into society. In other words the analogy for the mentally disabled is not the poor or marginalized, for there is no question of full integration. The analogy is of the sojourner, who always reminds the Israelite that once the Israelites were sojourners in Egypt. Part of the experience of the able-bodied is that, in the land of the mentally disabled, they too feel like resident aliens. And in the language of the New Testament, the whole people of God are *gerim*, longing for their homecoming in heaven. (Wells 2004: 184)

For Wells, then, the experience of disability reminds us of the fallenness of Creation, but also points toward the redemptive power of God. While we do not know how the *gerim* will be eschatologically united with the whole people of God—Wells does not suggest how the final reintegration is accomplished—nevertheless Christians proclaim by faith that this will happen. For mainstream Christian belief and piety, then, heaven represents the final overcoming and healing of disability, once and for all.

Disability and the Deconstruction of Heaven

Yet the heavenly hope is not articulated in the same way across the disability spectrum. Rather, disability perspectives exhibit much more ambiguity and range when it comes to the eschatological vision. In the following, I present four levels of responses.

At one level, there is the case of how to understand the eschatological lives and roles of the saints. Historian of American Catholicism Robert Orsi tells of his uncle Sal, who had cerebral palsy, and of Sal's relationship with the patron saint of people with disabilities, Margaret of Castello (see p. 32 above). Margaret was a limped, hunched, blind, and dwarfed woman who accomplished more than two hundred miracles and was beatified in 1609, even though her canonization has been stalled. Yet, Sal anticipates recognizing Margaret in heaven and saying, "I like it that there's somebody up there . . . like us" (Orsi 1997: 41). This suggests not only that Margaret will retain the features of her disability even in her resurrected body, but also that Sal anticipates that the vestiges of his disability will not completely disappear even in the eschaton. Extrapolated from the quotation of Peter, a L'Arche member with Down Syndrome, above (see introduction), the sense is that all will be OK in heaven not because bodily or cognitive parts have been "fixed," but because the people of God will be fully in the presence and love of God.

At a second level, then, this leads to the conviction of people with disabilities who reject the idea that their heavenly bodies will be restored to what the Christian tradition understands in terms of Edenic perfection. Sociologist and theologian Nancy Eiesland (see pp. 174–76), who grew up Pentecostal and with a form of degenerative bone disease, also tells of frequenting faith healers but not being cured. In response to the idea that she would be made whole in heaven, Eiesland says (2001–2002: 2), "[H]aving been disabled from birth, I came to believe that in heaven I would be absolutely unknown to myself and perhaps to God. My disability has taught me who I am and who God is." Similarly, feminist philosopher Susan Wendell insists:

> Yet I cannot wish that I had never contracted myalgic encephalo-
> myletis [a form of chronic fatigue immune dysfunction syndrome],

because it has made me a different person, a person I am glad to be, would not want to have missed being, and could not imagine relinquishing, even if I were "cured." . . . I would joyfully accept a cure, but I do not need one. If this attitude toward "cures" were taken for granted in my society, then the search for them would not be accompanied by insulting implications, as it often is now. (Wendell 1996: 84).[4]

Neither Eiesland's nor Wendell's responses should be read as a stubborn insistence on preferring disability to ability. Rather, both rightly call attention to how living with disabilities shapes our lives, relationships, and identities in substantive rather than incidental ways. As already discussed (pp. 181–84), an emergentist anthropology that foregrounds the bodily constitution of the human person cannot dismiss the phenomenological and existential experiences of disability as inconsequential.[5] To say that people with disabilities (such as Eiesland or Wendell) will no longer be disabled in heaven threatens the continuity between their present identities and that of their resurrected bodies.[6]

This question regarding personal identity is all the more pertinent in the case of people with intellectual disabilities in general and people with Down Syndrome in particular. In reflecting on the life of her severely disabled son, Arthur, theologian Frances Young queries (1990: 61–62):

> There is no "ideal Arthur" somehow trapped in this damaged physical casing. He is a psychosomatic whole. . . . What sense would it make to hope for "healing" in cases like this? Suppose that some faith-healer laid hands on Arthur tomorrow and all his damaged brain cells were miraculously healed, what then? Brains gradually develop over the years through learning. There are sixteen (now twenty-two) years of learning process that he has missed out on. In what sense could we expect normality, even if the physical problems were sorted out? The development of our selves as persons is bound up with this learning process. . . . I find it impossible to envisage what it would mean for him to be "healed" because what personality there is is so much part of him *as he is*, with all his limitations. "Healed" he would be a different person. (italics in original)

Not only does Young's view of the human being as a psychosomatic whole map well onto the emergentist anthropology developed in this book, but transposed into an eschatological perspective, her analysis also has implications for the traditional heavenly hope: if Arthur is an individual whose "whole personality is damaged and lacks potential for development," then "the easy option of thinking that a soul survives whatever the state of body or brain, and that all the wrongs of this world will be put right in the next, simply will not do" (Young 1990: 59–60). As has been pointedly asked: "Could someone imagine their daughter with Down's syndrome as being her true self in the new heaven and new earth without some manifestation of her condition?" (Samuel and Sugden 1998: 435; cf. anonymous quotation in the introduction to this chapter). Stanley Hauerwas forcefully puts it (1984: 69): unlike cancer or other diseases by which cells can be eliminated without eliminating the person, "To eliminate the disability [of retardation] means to eliminate the subject."[7] In short, if people with Down Syndrome are resurrected without it, in what sense can we say that it is they who are resurrected and embraced by their loved ones?[8]

Finally, however, we return to Eiesland to push the fourth and more deeply theological dimension of this question. Building on her earlier work on the "disabled God" (including my expansion in the direction of a disability theology of the cross—in chap. 6), Eiesland suggests (1994: 89) an eschatological image of disability that pertains not only to creatures but also to God:

> I had waited for a mighty revelation of God. But my epiphany bore lit-tle resemblance to the God I was expecting or the God of my dreams. I saw God in a sip-puff wheelchair, that is, the chair used mostly by quadriplegics enabling them to maneuver by blowing and sucking on a strawlike device. Not an omnipotent, self-sufficient God, but nei-ther a pitiable, suffering servant. In this moment, I beheld God as a survivor, unpitying and forthright. I recognized the incarnate Christ in the image of those judged "not feasible," "unemployable," with "questionable quality of life." Here was God for me.

We have already seen that not all people with disabilities agree with Eiesland's theological vision. However, my point is simply to show that disability perspectives raise probing questions about traditional eschatological articulations concerning the heavenly hope and the resurrection of the body. If they are to survive the interrogations informed by the experience of disability, our eschatological and theological visions may need reformulation.

Toward a Dynamic Eschatology

I suggest that part of the problem with traditional eschatological views is not so much the aspects related to heaven as a symbol of Christian hope as the more static conception of eternal life undergirding this hope. Hence, I propose a more dynamic eschatological vision that will preserve both the core biblical teachings related to the heavenly hope and the critical insights derived from the experience of disability. I will develop the central elements of this dynamic eschatology from out of a dialogue with the Pauline statements about the resurrected body and with Gregory of Nyssa's doctrine of everlasting progress (*epectasis*). Our goal is to clear out some theological space to think afresh about the resurrected body in relationship to intellectual and physical disability and how such ideas are important also for life in the here and now.

Rereading 1 Corinthians 15 in Disability Perspective

Any theology of the resurrection formulated in dialogue with disability perspectives will need to grapple with Paul's explicit teaching in the fifteenth chapter of the First Epistle to the Corinthians. In brief, the apostle's main point is that the doctrine of the resurrection is central to Christian belief and practice, and that the resurrection of Jesus not only supports the Christian hope of bodily resurrection but also guarantees that God has and will finally defeat death, our final enemy. Along the way, Paul turns to the questions regarding the how of the resurrection and the what of the resurrected body. The relevant passage for our purposes is as follows:

> There are both heavenly bodies and earthly bodies, but the glory of the heavenly is one thing, and that of the earthly is another. There is one glory of the sun, and another glory of the moon, and another glory of the stars; indeed, star differs from star in glory. So it is with the resurrection of the dead. What is sown is perishable, what is raised is imperishable. It is sown in dishonor, it is raised in glory. It is sown in weakness, it is raised in power. It is sown a physical body,

it is raised a spiritual body. If there is a physical body, there is also a spiritual body. Thus it is written, "The first man, Adam, became a living being"; the last Adam became a life-giving spirit. But it is not the spiritual that is first, but the physical, and then the spiritual. The first man was from the earth, a man of dust; the second man is from heaven. As was the man of dust, so are those who are of the dust; and as is the man of heaven, so are those who are of heaven. Just as we have borne the image of the man of dust, we will also bear the image of the man of heaven. (1 Cor 15:40-49)

At first glance, this passage seems to support the traditional beliefs of the church. If the resurrection body is imperishable, glorious, powerful, and spiritual, then all diseases, illnesses, sicknesses, and disabilities will be removed; deformities will be reshaped; and abnormalities will be corrected. The resurrected body will be free from its earthly imperfection, weakness, and brokenness. But if this is the case, is it possible to take into account critical disability perspectives (such as those already seen in this chapter) in our rethinking of eschatology? Three exegetical comments can be made in response.

First, whereas other apocalyptic texts emphasize the discontinuity between this life and the life to come as well as the vindication of the righteous (in the face of martyrdom) (Cavallin 1974: chap. 7), Paul's main concern is the spiritual elitism of the Corinthian church as manifest in their thinking themselves as charismatic (*pneumatikoi*), and their depreciating physicality and materiality (to the extent of being antinomian regarding prostitutes, eating meats offered to idols or in pagan temples, filing lawsuits against fellow believers, etc.). This led Paul (and the early Christians) to argue that "the spirit must submit to the [resurrected] body, not seek to be freed from it" (Setzer 2004: 150, 152). Hence, for Paul, resurrection is neither resuscitation (which preserves continuity) nor re-creation (which severs identity); rather, since "flesh and blood cannot inherit the kingdom of God" (1 Cor 15:50), Paul teaches a resurrection of the body that preserves but also transforms personal identity (Fee 1987: 776–77).

Second, what does it mean to say that the resurrection body is imperishable, glorious, and powerful (15:42-43)? Imperishability, according to the Aristotelian conceptions of the first century, simply refers to the heavenly "stuff" that, in contrast to early "stuff," is not subject to decay (Padgett 2002: 161). This therefore does not touch the question of disability. The gloriousness of the resurrected body is contrasted with the dishonorable character of the present body. This contrast is subject to aesthetic criteria unless other norms are invoked to define what dishonor and honor or glory mean. Within the larger context of this passage, the criterion of the resurrected body is the last Adam, or Jesus Christ, and in his case, we have already seen that the body of the resurrected Jesus retained the scars of his Passion in his hands and side (see pp. 175–6). Hence, an understanding of glory in this text is compatible with the idea that the resurrected body retains the marks of personal identity rather than removes them.

But there is still the question of the resurrected body's power, which is contrasted with weakness. Now we cannot connect Paul's use of "weakness" earlier in the letter with the experience of disability (see pp. 201–6) without also making that same connection here. Two lines of response, however, are possible. On the one hand, the context here may be with regard to the dead or buried body rather than to living "weak" bodies (Orr and Walther 1976: 347), and in this case, the power of the resurrected body is contrasted with the decayed bodies of the dead and buried. On the other hand, it could also be, according to first-century assumptions about the heavenly elements, that the power of the resurrected body "less describes its permanent heavenly state than the nature of its being raised" (Fee 1987: 785). The power here thus pertains to the Spirit's life-giving act rather than to some quality or attribute inherent in the resurrected body.

Third, the various contrasts should also be subordinated to the primary contrast that Paul makes in this passage regarding the physical body patterned after the first Adam, who "became a living being" (through his being animated by a soul), versus the spiritual body after the last Adam, who is a life-giving spirit (15:45) (Collins 1999: 569). In this case, the emphasis is—following a similar line of argument in Romans 5 (see p. 165 above)—on anticipating the resurrected body in the image of the last Adam rather than on restoring some kind of prefallen bodily form associated with the primeval Adam.[9] Hence, the Christian hope in God who raises the dead speaks to the eschatological transformation of the body

not necessarily in terms of becoming able-bodied (Samuel and
Sugden 1998: 433–34) but in terms of bearing the image of Jesus.
And while we do not yet fully know what that image will be in the
eschaton—"when he is revealed, we will be like him, for we will see
him as he is" (1 John 3:2b)—we know that this is not incompatible
with the resurrected body carrying the marks of our earthly lives,
and yet somehow transforming them. The resurrected body will
therefore be both continuous and discontinuous with our current
bodies, but the norm will be the resurrected Christ, not our conventions of able-bodiedness.

In sum, I believe that Paul's discussion of the resurrected body
is capable of engaging with critical insights derived from the experience of disability. However, we are still a long way from articulating a dynamic eschatological theology of the resurrection that
can accommodate disability perspectives. For our next steps toward
this end, a helpful ally is to be found, surprisingly, in the work of
the patristic theologian Gregory of Nyssa (d. ca. 385/386).

Gregory of Nyssa's Doctrine of Epectasis

Gregory's contribution to a dynamic eschatological vision lies at
two levels: that related to his doctrine of the resurrection body,
and that pertaining to his doctrine of everlasting progress ascend-
ing toward the divine being. We begin with the former.

In reflecting on the life of his sister, Macrina, Gregory suggests that she would bear the scars of a healed tumor in her resurrection body since her cadaver retained the scar visibly. This scar,
in life, death, and eternal life, is "a memorial of the divine intervention, the result and the occasion of perpetual turning toward
God through the action of grace" (cited in Bynum 1995: 86). To
be sure, in line with the broader Christian tradition, Gregory also
affirmed that the resurrection will not include the bodily impurities of the present life. But against Origen's anthropology involving preexisting souls, Gregory's more Aristotelian view of the soul
as the substantial form of the material body led him to believe that
the eschatological image of Christ and God required the resurrection of the body. "Because of the internal coherence of the human
person, the soul—which preserves most fully in itself the form
(εἶδος) that is the person's principle of continuity in change—'recognizes' that form as it is stamped on every particle of its body's

matter, even after death and decomposition" (Daley 1991: 87). Hence, Macrina's scars marked that body as uniquely hers, even in the afterlife.[10]

But if the soul is the principle of each person's continuity in change, then does that change terminate with the resurrection of the body? In response, Gregory develops the idea of the soul's perpetual journey—*epectasis*—in the afterlife that is driven by both philosophical-theological and exegetical considerations.[11] Building on the tradition stretching from Philo through the second-century Alexandrian theologians (see Ferguson 1973), Gregory's doctrine of *epectasis* is framed within a metaphysics of divine infinity that includes within it the Platonic theory of the soul's ascent to God. From a theological perspective, Gregory adds that the divine infinity includes the divine perfections that transform human creatures so that they are able to participate in the divine life (deification, or *theosis*). Given the soul's nature as potency, its participation in God expands its horizons as it is caught up in the dynamic movement of fulfillment and transformed by the power of the Spirit "from one degree of glory to another" (2 Cor 3:18). In this framework, salvation is conceived in dynamic terms: "For this is truly perfection: never to stop growing towards what is better and never placing any limit on perfection" (Gregory, in Callahan 1967: 122).[12] But Gregory is motivated not only by philosophical concerns. Rather, his thinking is permeated throughout by biblical considerations. Building on the Pauline claim "I do not consider that I have made it my own; but this one thing I do: forgetting what lies behind and straining forward to what lies ahead" (Phil 3:13), Gregory suggests it is the desire of the heart transformed by God that drives us deeper and deeper (or further and further) into the apophatic reality of God. For Gregory, this divine mystery is also imaged in terms that draw from the Canticles as the "darkness of the wedding chamber" (see Laird 2003).

Gregory's entire commentary on the Song of Solomon can be understood as an elaboration of his dynamic eschatological vision. The love of the lover that drives the pursuit of the Beloved is understood analogously as the love of the human soul in its pursuit of God. In his comments on Canticles 2:8-17—on the bride's movement toward the groom, drawn by him—Gregory says (1987: 119): "The bride at this point partakes in the good as much as she can. Then he starts again to draw her to participate in a higher beauty, as if she had never tasted it. Thus, as she progresses, her desire grows with each step. And, because there is always an unlimited good beyond what the bride has attained, she always seems to be just beginning her ascent."[13] In this perspective, "the desire of those who thus rise never rests in what they can already understand; but by an ever greater and greater desire, the soul keeps rising constantly to another which lies ahead, and thus it makes its way through ever higher regions towards the Transcendent" (Gregory 1987: 162). If the infinity of God cannot be exhausted, then the movement of the soul will never be completed either. Gregory makes this point in a passage (223–24) that needs to be reproduced in full:

> The soul that looks up towards God, and conceives that good desire for His eternal beauty, constantly experiences an ever new yearning for that which lies ahead, and her desire is never given its full satisfaction. Hence she never ceases to *stretch herself forth to those things that are before* [Phil 3:13], ever passing from her present stage to enter more deeply into the interior, into the stage which lies ahead. And so at each point she judges each great marvelous grace to be inferior to what is yet to come, because each newly won grace always seems to be more beautiful than those she has previously enjoyed. It was in this way that Paul died daily. . . . For each moment that he participated more deeply in life he died to all that was past, forgetting those graces which he had already attained. And so the bride that ever runs towards the Spouse will never find any rest in her progress towards perfection. She has gardens of pomegranates flow from her mouth; she prepares food for the Lord of creation, and entertains Him with her own fruit. She waters her gardens, and becomes herself a well of living water. She is shown to be radiant and immaculate on the testimony of the Word. But then she advances even farther, and perceives something even more marvelous. (italics in translation)

It should be clearly stated, however, that for Gregory, the soul's desire for goodness, truth, and beauty is unlimited not because of its own inherent capacities but in view of God's deifying grace.

In fact, Gregory's homilies on the Canticles are premised on the transcendence of the divine nature, which holds forth the hope of our eternal journey into the depths of God. More importantly, the imagery of the dove and the wind in the Song are suggestive for Gregory of the "wings" of the human spirit and the empowerment of the Holy Spirit in the soul's ceaseless flight toward the infinite gloriousness of God (Gregory 1987: 213).

The main concern that arises is whether or not Gregory's dynamic eschatology undercuts a sense of closure provided by more traditional conceptions of the heavenly hope. Are things too open-ended in the soul's *epectasis* as conceived by Gregory? Here, Gregory's apophaticism must be appreciated. In his *Life of Moses*, Gregory argues that

> that which is limited cannot by its nature be understood. And so every desire for the beautiful which draws us on in this ascent is intensified by the soul's very progress towards it. And this is the real meaning of seeing God: never to have this desire satisfied. But fixing our eyes on those things which help us to see, we must ever keep alive in us the desire to see more and more. And so no limit can be set to our progress towards God: first of all, because no limitation can be put upon the beautiful, and secondly because the increase in our desire for the beautiful cannot be stopped by any sense of satisfaction. (Gregory, in Musurillo 1961: 147–48).[14]

In a sense, what for human beings is closure in terms of satisfaction and perfection is for God a further invitation to creatures through deifying grace to "travel" the continually receding horizons of the eschatological *epectasis* into the divine life. So whereas bodily appetites admit of limits, spiritual aspirations can deepen forever without limit given the infinite divine "object" of the soul's desires (Ferguson 1973: 71–74).[15] The Song therefore serves for Gregory as a brilliant illustration of the *eros* of God that is unveiled through the soul's everlasting journey amidst the dialectic of mystery or hiddenness and revelation.[16]

In sum, for Gregory, the afterlife is an unending journey of the individual as he or she is transformed from perfection to perfection into the glorious knowledge, beauty, truth, and love of God. Assuming the Neoplatonic ideas of God understood as infinite and unlimited and the spiritual life as a purifying ascent (begun in the ascetic practices of this life) into the infinite depths of the divine being, eternal life involves our ever-intensifying participation in the life of God without ever losing our status as creatures. Further, there is perpetual growth in the knowledge of God without our ever becoming omniscient (an attribute of divinity alone). Finally, if human experience reveals the possibility of ever-deepening love tomorrow without deeming yesterday's love as inferior, so also will be the relationship of the soul in its eternal journey toward and with God.

Dynamic Eschatology: Pneumatological Perspectives

Both Paul and Gregory of Nyssa have helped us rethink the resurrection and the heavenly hope in a more dynamic framework. It is now time to pull these threads together into a more holistic eschatological fabric. What holds these various ideas together, I suggest, is pneumatology.

It is a rather obvious theological move to appeal to the doctrine of the Holy Spirit in the attempt to shift from a static to a dynamic view of eternity. Throughout the biblical text, the Spirit is understood as the elusive, shifting, and energetic wind (*ruach*, or *pneuma*) of God, whose ways we can neither fully discern nor anticipate (cf. John 3:8). Further, the scriptures testify to the Spirit as the conduit and conveyer of the new and unexpected works of God—for example, hovering or sweeping over the new creation, empowering the resurrection to new life, ushering in the forever-anticipated year of the LORD, and serving the invitations to the New Jerusalem. Together, these pneumatological characteristics suggest that life in the Spirit is forever the "arrival" of a new creation, the engaging of new and ever-receding horizons, and the surprising transformation from glory to glory into the new image of Jesus. In this life, Protestants and Catholics have called this the process of sanctification, while orthodox Christians have used the language of deification (*theosis*). I see no reason to think that the process of deification is limited to the work of God in the present life, especially when the infinite qualitative distinction between God and creatures is taken into account (as it is in Gregory's theology).

I suggest that a pneumatological perspective can provide support for our dynamic eschatology along at least two lines. First, pneumatology provides a theological link between the emergent anthropology of our present constitution and the resurrection life that is to come. If human personhood is an emergent entity dependent on the dust that is our bodies and brains but irreducible to that because of the gift of the breath of God, then heavenly life is also similarly dependent on the resurrection of our bodies (and brains) even if irreducible to that because of the life-giving spirit of the last Adam. In this case, human bodies that are the temple of the Holy Spirit in this life (1 Cor 3:19, 6:19-20) anticipate being hosts of the resurrecting power of the same Spirit in the life to come (see Brodeur 1996). The resurrection body is hence both continuous with and yet transformed—sanctified and even beatified (Sherry 1992: 165–69)—by the life-giving Spirit of God.

But more importantly, while the body is an indispensable "material" cause of human personhood, the soul is the emergent form of the body rather than being reducible to the body's processes. As an "almost infinitely complex *information-bearing pattern*" (Polkinghorne 2004: 161; italics in original), the soul is shaped dynamically by the body's social and environmental relations and interactions over time. In that case, the resurrection body expresses "our total personality, spiritually transformed. It would point not so much to our identity at one moment of life, namely the moment of our physical death, but to what we have become: including our physical/mental potentialities, our sociohistorical environment, our experiences, values, commitments, and decisions" (Cooper 1993: 69). And how is this possible? Through the resurrection power of the Holy Spirit, who redemptively transforms human lives by providing enlarged and meaningful personal narratives—through a new input of information, to use Polkinghorne's terms—but does so without erasing the continuity of personal identities between this life and the next (hence sins are forgiven rather than simply erased, or as I hope to show momentarily, disabilities are redeemed rather than expunged).

When set in Gregory's dynamic eschatological perspective, the redemptive transformation that occurs with the resurrection is only the beginning rather than the end of the soul's eschatological journey with and to God. As theologians John Polkinghorne and Michael Welker put it (2000: 13):

If it is intrinsic for human beings to be embodied in some form (so that resurrection, rather than spiritual survival, is the Christian hope), then it may be that they are intrinsically temporal beings. If that is so, the life of the new creation will have its own new time and its own new, salvific process. Judgment will then involve a coming to terms with the reality of ourselves, and a purgation of what we are in order to become what God wills to be. Fulfillment will not happen in a timeless moment of illumination but through an everlasting exploration of the riches of the divine nature, an experience that may be characterized as our entering into "eschatological joy."

In this view, the Spirit who begins a good work in us in this life continues that work in life everlasting. Eternal life with its static implications now becomes everlasting life with its more dynamic and fluid shape.

I need to clarify, however, that this eschatological vision does not mean that there will be hierarchies in "heaven." Here Gregory's Neoplatonic metaphysics of ascent is misleading because it implies that those higher up are closer to God than those lower down. But what if we worked with a participatory metaphysics of true infinity wherein the actual infinite contains all within "itself" even as it is impossible for us to "reach" that infinitude by mere counting? In this metaphysical framework, no matter how high up the "ladder" one "climbs," there remains an equal distance between all rungs on the "ladder" and the infinite gloriousness of the divine "essence." In the words of Maria Egg-Benes, "Measured then against the Absolute Perfection, the difference between me and a Mongoloid is really so small that it is hardly noticeable" (quoted in Sen and Goel 1984: [1] page unnumbered).[17] Nevertheless, two caveats are important. First, that all rungs of the "ladder" are equally distant from the unlimited nature of the divine does not mean that all persons are indistinct and that individual differences are effaced in the afterlife. Rather, individual characteristics are preserved precisely as each person perpetually engages others and the divine life in varying degrees of depth, intensity, and intimacy at each level (see Shults 2003: 186–88). Second, the *epectasis* is not self-defeating and hence completely unlike Sisyphus (who was condemned to endlessly pushing a boulder up to the summit only for it to tumble back down and have to begin again) because, paradoxically, individuals at each rung of the "ladder" participate in the glory of God to the full extent of their capacity as creatures at that level, even as the divine gift of their self-transcending nature also ensures that their desires for God will always respond to the divine lure, which in turn deepens their experience of God at the next level. In short, differences are preserved in the eschatological long run even as there is no "room" in the eschatological "body politic" of God for hierarchical relationships of oppression.

On Salvation as Eternal Transformation: Everlasting Life beyond Dis/ability

But what are the implications of dynamic eschatology for theology and disability? In her reading of Gregory's commentary on the Song of Solomon, theologian Sarah Coakley (2002) notes that even in the eschaton, unexpected gender reversals occur such as when at one moment Christ courts the neophyte as "Sophia," a female figure, but later embraces the adept as a bridegroom. In this way, Coakley suggests, Gregory's eschatology illumines how gender will be transformed—so that in Christ "there is no longer male and female" (Gal 3:28)—albeit not eliminated. Similarly, I suggest, Gregory's dynamic eschatology illumines how disability will be transformed even if its particular scars and marks will be redeemed, not eliminated. In this view, the body itself finds its rest in the unending process of being transformed by the glory of God in ways that overturn the binary dichotomies not only of male/female but also of disabled/nondisabled. It is now time to specify what a pneumatological and dynamic eschatology might mean for overcoming the "us" versus "them" in the human experience of dis/ability. I will present some suggestions with regard first to the individual resurrection of the body and then to the social reconciliation and healing that combines to constitute the Christian eschatological hope. This chapter concludes by taking up the question of why speculative eschatology is important for Christian theology in late modernity.

"But We Will All Be Changed": Transforming Down Syndrome, Redeeming Dis/ability

A pneumatological and dynamic eschatology does not neglect but rather begins with the redemption of human bodies (Rom 8:23-25).

While this eschatological hope is anticipated by all human beings, not just people with disabilities, the combination of Eiesland's theology of the resurrection body and Gregory's theology of *epectasis* suggests that the Spirit's redemption of the human body retains some continuity with the present life even amid its transformation. Is it possible to conceive that the glory and power of the resurrection body will derive not from some able-bodied ideal of perfection but from its being the site of the gracious activity of God's Spirit? In this case, might not the unending journey of the resurrection body also be from glory to glory and from perfection to perfection?

Set in this dynamic pneumatological perspective, might we be permitted the following speculations? Deceased infants—whether healthy, microencephalitic, or otherwise disabled, whether dead from natural or other causes—would have a glorious and powerful resurrection body not measured by Arnold Schwarzenegger or Miss U.S.A. in their prime but by their nestedness in the communion of saints and by the redemptive caregiving in the eschatological community. Hence there is continuity and discontinuity with the resurrection body: on the one hand, infants are recognizably infants in the eschaton, although, on the other hand, their bodies are no longer subject to decay even as we are unable fully to anticipate the mysterious transformation of the resurrection body. But the work of the eschatological Spirit also means that infants do not stay infants eternally, but are unendingly transformed along with other members of the eschatological community in and toward the triune God.[18]

I further speculate that people with intellectual or developmental disabilities, such as, those with Down Syndrome or triplicate chromosome 21—will also retain their phenotypical features in their resurrection bodies.[19] There will be sufficient continuity to ensure recognizability as well as self-identity. Thus, the redemption of those with Down Syndrome, for example, would consist not in some magical fix of the twenty-first chromosome but in the recognition of their central roles both in the communion of saints and in the divine scheme of things.[20] Henri Nouwen suggests, in reflecting on the life of Philippe, another L'Arche core member whom he (Nouwen) was responsible to assist:

Philippe's body is a body destined to a new life, a resurrected life. In his new body he will carry the signs of his suffering, just as Jesus carried the wounds of the crucifixion into his glory. And yet he will no longer be suffering, but will join the saints around the altar of the lamb. Still, the celebration of the resurrection of the body is also the celebration of the daily care given to the bodies of these handicapped men and women. Washing and feeding, pushing wheelchairs, carrying, kissing, and caressing—these are all ways in which these broken bodies are made ready for the moment of a new life. Not only their wounds but also the care given them will remain visible in the resurrection. . . . [Philippe] will rise from the grave with a new body and will show gloriously the pain he suffered and the love he received. It will not be just a body. It will be *his* body, a new body, a body that can be touched but is no longer subject to torture and destruction. His passion will be over. What a faith! What a hope! What a love! The body is not a prison to escape from, but a temple in which God already dwells, and in which God's glory will be manifested on the day of the resurrection. (Nouwen 1990: 162–63)

Of course, the ongoing work of the eschatological Spirit means that people with Down Syndrome will also continually increase in goodness, knowledge, and love, vis-à-vis both the communion of saints and the triune God, all of which will have implications for their bodily and our corporate transformation as well.

Similar speculations would apply for all persons—from the young to the elderly—along with their differing bodily afflictions and conditions, whether that be the wide range of intellectual or developmental disabilities, Alzheimer's, chronic illness, polio, multiple sclerosis, Lou Gehrig's disease, congenital amputees, and so on. Precisely because the meanings of our lives are constituted by but irreducible to our bodies, so also will the resurrected body be the site through which the meaning of our narratives are transformed (and that, eternally). Hence, philosopher Jerry Walls suggests that while the Christian tradition is right to insist that our resurrected bodies will be healed,

[t]his is not to deny that such defects will continue as a part of human identity in heaven. Those who negotiated this life with the additional struggles of mental or physical deformities will retain the memories

of doing so as well as the positive character traits they formed as a result. Indeed, such struggles may have been means of grace that taught lessons of humility and dependence upon God. This is as true for those who have cared for such persons as it is for the persons themselves. The extra sacrifices of kindness and patience given on behalf of handicapped persons also shape the identity of those who offer them in faith and love and will remain a part of their history. (Walls 2002: 112)

But on the other side, this admission should also not then reduce the experience of disability to an instrumental status, whether for the sanctification of the person with disability or for the opportunity granted to nondisabled people to exercise charity. Rather, a dynamic theology of the resurrection insists on what Barbara Patterson calls an "inclusive embodied" notion of eschatological redemption whereby "all redeemed bodies participating in this restoration are good, and all redeemed bodies retain their particularity and diversity" (1998: 127). This diversity is precisely what was heralded as the goodness of God's creation even as it participates in the gloriousness of the eschatological redemption. In this way, the continuity between this life and the next is preserved, even as the disabilities of the human bodily experience are redeemed.

It is this redemption of disability that must be accentuated if the doctrine of Christian hope is to be reimagined and renewed for the twenty-first century. Even if there will be continuities between our present embodiment and the resurrected body, there will also be unfathomable discontinuities when we are transformed in the eschaton. If the continuities enable both self- and other-identification, the discontinuities reflect our hope in the redeeming grace and transforming power of God. To be sure, as previously noted, people with disabilities have their place at the eschatological banquet (Luke 14:12-23), and there are other strands in the Hebrew prophets that indicate eunuchs will be accepted in the Day of YHWH (Isa 56:3-5), as will be the blind, lame, and others with physical impairments (Jer 31:8; Mic 4:6; Zeph 3:19; cf. also Melcher 2004). This is not to imply, however, that people with disabilities will stay merely blind, lame, and crippled in the eschatological long run. Eschatological salvation means not only that there will be no more oppression, marginalization, or discrimination because of physical or mental impairments but also that there will be unexpected transformations—both suddenly and eternally—now inconceivable to us.

"Death Has Been Swallowed Up in Victory": Reconciliation and the Healing of Disability

Beyond the redemption of embodied disabilities, however, I suggest that a pneumatological and dynamic eschatology also features a robust theology of social reconciliation. If disability is never only a matter of individual embodiment but is always also an economic, political, and social experience (see chap. 4), then the heavenly hope must redeem not only individual bodies but also heal and reconcile human relationships. Further, salvation is, finally, an overcoming of the death that isolates people from healing relationships. In that case, the ultimate reconciliation involves the flourishing of love between God's creatures and between creatures and their Creator.

Hence, a pneumatological perspective broadens the more individualistic reading of Gregory's *epectasis* eschatology to include the more corporate conceptions of his theological anthropology (see Greer 2001: 98–102). The experience of salvation culminates in the communion of the redeemed, the "fellowship of the Spirit," and the reconciliation of all Creation to God. In this eschatological community, there will be a healing of broken relationships, a vindication of the oppressed, the exacting of justice on oppressors, the forgiveness of sin, and the reconciliation of all persons, including victims and victimizers (Volf 2000). In this scenario, of course, people with disabilities are often the oppressed, but sometimes they are also the victimizers of others. That all of these can be accomplished together is impossible in human perspective, but points to the unfathomable miracle of the gospel.

When set in the more dynamic pneumatological framework, I suggest that this eschatological reconciliation is better conceived as an ongoing work of the Spirit that continually forms the new "body politic" of individuals and communities who continuously realize and actualize the healing and saving grace of God in eternity. In this way, the healing of the world will involve the many dimensions of our lives. Our embodiment; our affections;

our moral selves; our interpersonal relationships with family and friends; our biological, political and structural relationships with preceding and succeeding generations; our interconnectedness with all others whose lives we have impacted and vice-versa; and our relationship with the triune God, in whom we all live, move, and have our being (Acts 17:28)—each of these domains will be transformed over the eschatological long run. The heavenly vision is hopeful precisely because finally God is the ultimate and eschatological caregiver who oversees the mutuality and reciprocity of forgiveness, caring, and reconciliation within the redeemed communion of saints (Keck 1996: chap. 5).

This final reconciliation that includes the mending of our own lives is possible, I suggest, because of God's redemption of the interpersonal, social, and environmental structures of Creation itself (see Knitter 2004: 68–69). Perhaps this explains the presence of the "leaves of healing" for individuals and for the nations that we find in the eschatological presence of God (Ezek 47:12; Rev 22:2; cf. Avalos 1995: 369–71). Insofar as the wholeness of individual lives is bound up with the lives of many others, the healing of the one in the eschaton has to be the healing of the many and vice versa. As Jürgen Moltmann puts it (2000: 252):

> God's judgment means the final putting to rights of the injustice that has been done and suffered, and the final raising up of those who are bowed down. So I conceive of that "intermediate state" as a wide space for living, in which the life that was spoiled and cut short here can develop freely. I imagine it as the time of a new life, in which God's history with a human being can come to its flowering and consummation. I imagine that we then come close to that well of life from which we could already here and now draw the power to live and the affirmation of life, so that the handicapped and the broken can live the life that was meant for them, for which they were born, and which was taken from them.

(Now, as an aside, Moltmann's comments are set within the context of a discussion of what he calls "the spoiled and curtailed life." Since Moltmann rejects the doctrines of soul sleep, reincarnation, and purgatory, he appeals to the theological tradition's speculations about an intermediate state between death and resurrection in order to speak about how spoiled or curtailed lives are healed and broken communities are made whole.[21] Yet he does recognize that his theory of the intermediate state parallels the Catholic doctrine of purgatory, which states, "All who die in God's grace and friendship, but still imperfectly purified, are indeed assured of their eternal salvation; but after death they undergo purification, so as to achieve the holiness necessary to enter the joy of heaven" [*Catechism of the Catholic Church* 1995: 291]. From a Protestant theological point of view, I also cannot go all the way with the Roman Catholic understanding of purgatory, but I do appreciate its logic insofar as it dovetails with my retrieval and expansion of Gregory's theology of *epectasis*. Defined first at the Council of Lyons II in 1274 and then reaffirmed and clarified at Florence [1439], Trent [1563], and Vatican II,[22] the doctrine of purgatory is scripturally based especially on Paul's statements regarding the judgment that burns up whatever is without quality—wood, hay, or straw—even while the individual is saved, "but only as through fire" [1 Cor 3:15b]. But purgatory is not hell; rather, historically, emphasis has been placed on the soul as embracing the purging "fires" that alone will purify it so that it can be fully wrapped up in the presence of divine love. In this case, there is a paradoxical joy in suffering and suffering in joy throughout the purgatorial experience [see Catherine of Genoa 1979]. Hence, the Catholic doctrine of purgatory features a dynamic eschatological scenario that goes off on a tangent from but nevertheless complements the vision of Gregory of Nyssa. Further, the theology of purgatory opens up a third eschatological category that goes beyond "saved" and "damned," even as the dynamic eschatology I am proposing cuts through the binary oppositions of "nondisabled" and "disabled." Finally, the purpose of the doctrine of purgatory is to comfort the saints, especially with regard to those who have gone on before them; similarly, I suggest, a dynamic eschatology is better suited to comfort those who remain behind insofar as it better preserves the personal identities of those who have gone on before even as it reinforces the Christian hope about the transformation of the whole communion of saints. The main differences between the Catholic doctrine of purgatory and what I am proposing are that the penitential nature of the purgatorial process is lacking in my account—a point Moltmann also makes in distinguishing his theory from the Catholic teaching—and that the social dimension of my dynamic eschatology is less prominent in the Catholic doctrine.)

The result is a redemptive space wherein interpersonal healing and reconciliation is facilitated and wherein there is finally no more "disability" (at least none definable in social terms). In the new created order, every life, "impaired" in its own way, will grow in goodness, knowledge, and love. Death is overcome once and for all as each person will experience the paradox of full salvation with the communion of saints in the presence of God on the one hand, but yet be "on the way" in realizing and actualizing the many dimensions of God's transforming power on the other. In this way a pneumatologically and dynamically conceived eschatology emphasizes the wholeness of the redeemed community (rather than the mere healing of our bodies), both the continuity and the discontinuity of our resurrected bodies (enabling recognition of self- and other-identity, but resisting our images of how things should or must be according to either ableist or normate assumptions), and the everlasting (rather than an eternal once-and-for-all) transformation of our lives in the eschatological long run.

"I Am Making All Things New": Renewing the Cosmos

I want to begin this last leg of our journey with the Rabbi Nahman of Bratslav's (1772–1810) "Tale of the Seven Beggars."[23] The seven beggars each have disabilities: blind, deaf, stutterer, twisted neck, hunchback, no hands, and no feet. While at one level these disabilities represent the exilic and broken character of human life, at another level they carry in their disabilities the perfection of the world to come and point ahead to the mending of the present world (*tikun olam*; see p. 143). What is wrong is not so much the beggars but the present world that is incapable of being hospitable to them. So the blind beggar is prevented from seeing this world not because he is unable to see but because he is unwilling to see (why look either at this world's exilic condition or at its illusory perfection?), desiring only to see the eschatological world. The stutterer cannot speak "normal" words both because this world is not normal (it is broken) and because the eschatological world is not present to be spoken of clearly now; to be sure, the stuttering beggar can still utter theologically complex riddles and divine praises without impediment, but he cannot otherwise talk and live "normally" in this exilic state. And the hunchback is hunched precisely because he carried the weight of the world on his shoulders, and so on. Hence,

> The deformity of each beggar is the result of being confined to the natural world which each has already transcended by means of perfecting a particular virtue. Thus, from the perspective of the imperfect world, perfection appears deformed. The zaddik [Nahman the narrator of the tale] is always a deformed creature as he refuses to submit to nature. More precisely, he is deformed because he carried the burden of transforming the children [of this world] to see the world "otherwise." (Magid 2002: 355)

So while exile is the domain of sadness, yearning, longing, and hoping, it also serves as the key to experiencing redemption, because the exilic experience is the experience of instability that opens up one of two possibilities: that of skepticism, hopelessness, and resignation, or that of prayer and redemption. For Nahman, prayer is the witnessing activity that both suspends rationalism and protests against autonomous reason, and so potentially changes exilic nature and redeems the world. More importantly, it is prayer that miraculously renews the Creation, and this is the exilic vocation of the beggars, of the *zaddik*, of Israel, which prays and therefore brings about the not-yet even in the now. To be sure, Rabbi Nahman's hopes are that the Messiah will return to restore the world to its preexilic condition, but the delayed arrival of the final beggar (who never makes an appearance in the tale) suggests that the mending of the world may be endlessly deferred.

What Nahman understands as the movement from nature to exile to redemption, Christian theology schematizes as creation-fall-redemption. But Nahman's seven beggars also teach us that the eschatological healing of disability and the renewal of the cosmos not only belong to the far-off future, but have already begun in the here and now. More to the point, it is the task of the people of God to pray for and embody the reconciling, healing, and mending power of God in the present world (see also Marx 2002: 245–58). Similarly, from the Christian point of view, both the individual dimension of the resurrected body and the social dimension of the reconciliation of the communion of saints are essential aspects of the renewal of the entire cosmos announced in the life, ministry, and resurrection of Jesus and confirmed in the Spirit given for the last days (Acts 2:17). So since the coming kingdom of God is already present, albeit not fully manifest, the renewing work of the Spirit is in motion amid the groanings of the created order. This means that the doctrine of the resurrection is not only a speculative idea concerning the life to come but also a concrete set of mandates regarding the Christian way of life in the here and now (see Janssen 2000: 73–78). More precisely, the doctrines of the resurrection and the heavenly hope are important because they are part of the Christian grammar that governs Christian practices. Eschatological images are powerful because they shape our sensibilities, orient our affections, and inspire our actions.[24]

If we do not interrogate our traditional ideas about disability vis-à-vis the heavenly hope, we will lack the necessary theological and theoretical resources to challenge the status quo. For example, a recent book by renowned evangelical pastor-theologian John Ortberg has the catchy title *Everybody's Normal till You Get to Know Them* (2003). Of course, this is true, and Ortberg has an insightful chapter on breaking down the barriers toward a more inclusive church, which discusses how Jesus embraced the outcasts of his society. However, in his final chapter, Ortberg talks about heaven in terms of "normal at last." Here, he emphasizes community, acceptance, and the embrace of God's presence, but somehow the idea that "everybody's normal till you get to know them" does not apply in the heavenly state. In this case, then, the particularity, difference, and diversity so important for this life disappear in the resurrection. But if Ortberg goes down this eschatological road, how then can particularity and difference really matter on this side of the eschaton? The result is that Ortberg's eschatology undermines his ecclesiology, and the church is left with a less robust theological rationale for embracing diversity in its constitutive practices before the sounding of the final trumpet.

By contrast, a disability perspective embraces a much more complex eschatological vision that in turn jars us from the dogmatic and practical slumbers of our present existence. So, for example, Sharon Betcher's "confession" requires the articulation and implementation of an ethics of alterity that can work with the differences characteristic of life as we know it: "[P]ersons with disabilities constitute the refusal of not only the American ideal, but Christian eschatological idealism: We refuse to be resolved, saved, made whole, thereby 'invalidating' eschatological idealism and hopefully some of the aggressive pity, preferring our histories of flesh, even as functionally enabled by technology" (Betcher 2004: 99). In this viewpoint, the goal can no longer simply be the elimination of disability; rather, the healing of the world will require all people to work together in order that the divine purposes can be accomplished.

How, then, can or should the work of the renewal of the cosmos be practically engaged? What would it mean for us to embrace differences rather than discriminate and exclude on that basis? The Christian heavenly hope is possibly the most extensive vision of inclusion in our theological repertoire. The question is whether we will truly open up the doors to God's embracing and empowering difference, rather than attempt to retain control over who is in or out according to our conventions regarding the present scheme of things. If in the new creation there will be neither disability nor nondisability, then can we now in this life participate in the Spirit's work of healing the entire body politic, the people of God, so as to facilitate the new normative order of God revealed in Jesus Christ (see Nelson 1990)?

Can we imagine the Deaf anticipating "when we get to heaven, the signing will be tremendous!"?[25] If so, then we can also imagine a present world order in which the signing is equally tremendous, and we will commit ourselves to work toward such a world wherein Deaf people can flourish in all of the ways that God has intended. The same goes for the experiences of those across the disability spectrum. In each case, our eschatological images will dictate how we organize, structure, and arrange our present life in this world. Thus Christian beliefs and practices are intertwined, and Christian theology and doctrines are not only descriptive but normative, not only speculative but performative, not only eschatological but transformative of and redemptive for the present world order.

In the last four chapters I have suggested a reimagining, revisioning, and renewal of a few of the major theological loci. I have argued against the traditional idea of people with disabilities as abnormal or less than fully human, against the conventional notion of the church as exclusive of "disabled people," against the stereotypical equation of the curing of disabled bodies with the salvation of God, and against the eschatological definition of heaven as exclusive of people with disabilities. Yet my objectives have not been solely negative in focusing on clearing away these misunderstandings. Rather, my goal throughout has been to articulate a more inclusive view of what it means to be human, a more hospitable image of the church, a more holistic understanding of divine salvation, and a more expansive image of God's eschatological hospitality—all driven by the conviction that Christian beliefs matter for Christian practices. This work of redeeming disability and renewing humanity and the church is barely begun. Come, Lord Jesus, and pour out your Holy Spirit afresh, that we may be empowered to accomplish your will to renew the whole of Creation.

Epilogue

In reflecting on life with his disabled child, famous Japanese novelist Kenzaburo Oe noted (1996: 44–45), "Essentially, in writing a novel about a handicapped child one is building a model of what it means to be handicapped, making it as complete and comprehensive as possible yet also concrete and personal." In one sense, I have attempted to do something similar except that I have deployed the genre of systematic theology rather than the novel (see also Oe 1995, 2002). To be more precise, I have attempted to make sense of the life of my brother within its wider ecclesial, social, political, economic, cosmic, and finally, theological contexts.

In the process of this project, I have learned a great deal. Disability advocate and theorist Tanya Titchkosky writes (2003: 28–29), "Disability, *as teacher* . . , is only possible if we suspend, even momentarily, the need to fix disabled persons or fix up society's treatment of us" (italics in original). Her claim rings true to my own experience. From a more ecclesiological and theological perspective, Stanley Hauerwas puts the same point slightly differently: "Christians thus learn that people with mental handicaps are not among us because we need someone to be the object of charity, but because without these brothers and sisters in Christ we call 'retarded', we cannot know what it means rightly to worship God. . . . For their great strength is their refusal to be victimized by the temptations to become a victim. Through their willingness to be present in church, they provide the church with the time to be church" (Hauerwas 1995b: 60). Both Titchkosky and Hauerwas challenge us to engage disability not only from a posture of charity but from one of mutuality. Disability is not just a problem with which we have to do (although it certainly is that, in various respects), but it is also an aspect of human life through which all of us, including us more or less (temporarily) able-bodied and able-minded ones, can be enriched, if we were only willing to do such.

So what next? To be sure, there are the interpersonal postures, attitudes, and languages that we need to cultivate in our relationships and approach toward one another so that people like Mark will be free to be himself, and so that all of us will be less shackled by the social conventions that we have inherited. But there are also the practical tasks of training seminarians, church workers, and the laity, and of transforming church practices so that people with disabilities will be included as full participants in the body of Christ. Last but by no means least, we need to connect with social workers, educators, service providers, medical professionals, and lawmakers in order to change our economic, political, legal, and social structures so as to produce a more just society with less discrimination against people with disabilities than currently exists (see Landes 1997). And we should not underestimate the importance of religious and theological perspectives for all of these tasks. Matthew the evangelist records Jesus as saying, "The harvest is plentiful, but the laborers are few; therefore ask the Lord of the harvest to send out laborers into his harvest" (Matt 9:37-38). How can the nondisabled among us live in solidarity with people with disabilities so as to build a more just and humane world?

But what next theologically? In the preceding pages I have attempted to say something about the doctrines of creation, the Fall, original sin, providence, the *imago Dei*, Christology, pneumatology, theological anthropology, ecclesiology, sacraments, ministry, the *ordo salutis*, healing (and curing), resurrection, and the heavenly hope from disability perspectives. Some of these doctrines have been the subject of more focused treatment, while others have been more diffused and interwoven throughout the last four chapters. Whole books still need to be written on each locus as we have only begun to scratch the surface of what insights the experience of disability can contribute. Further, there are other theological topics that we have not broached (except tangentially), including the doctrines of God proper, revelation, and theology of nature. Finally, there is the area of practical theology, including ethics and pastoral care. We have made some comment on these topics, but they deserve fuller treatment in light of the kind of systematic rethinking of the theological loci that we have attempted here.

Yet the most important question is for those of us who are nondisabled and who have the power to do something about making the world more hospitable to those with disabilities. If you have stayed with me through this very long book, I now ask: will you repent of your complicity in discriminating against people with disabilities? And following from that, what will you do with the gifts God has given you to renew the world? Insofar as this book assumes the unity of belief and practice and understands theological doctrines to be emergent from and yet informative for Christian performance, to that degree the end of this book is an invitation to serious Christian discipleship. Christian commitment may require revision of many of our theological understandings, but for Christian thought and practice to be inclusive, especially of people with disabilities, we must take up the task of reimagining theology and renewing the church in late modernity.

Notes

Preface

1 Philosopher Peter Byrne (2000: chap. 2) prefers the language of "cognitive disability" since "intellectual disability" does not quite fit those with conditions like autism who nevertheless have high IQs. However, the dominant term in the wider medical and social science literature remains intellectual disability (e.g., Harris 2006), so I stay with it.

Part I

Chapter 1: Introduction

1 "The retarded" will always appear in quote marks in this book, either because the words are being quoted or in order to alert us against objectifying some people and reducing them to this one feature of their identity.

2 Hence, "the retarded" could not "know" anything; or even if they did, theirs was a "rejected knowledge" that did not count. This was the plight, of course, not only of the "retarded," but of all people with disabilities (see Newell 2006).

3 Buck's daughter, Carol Grace, was born with phenylketonuria, an inherited genetic enzyme disorder that causes severe mental retardation when left untreated. Buck later became a remarkable writer and novelist, whose life story, with and apart from Carol, is told by Conn 1996 (see also Raessler 1994). For other parental accounts of wrestling with institutionalization, see Worswick 1978 and Kupfer 1982.

4   The first generation of such parental narratives include Rogers 1953; de Vries-Kryut 1971; Greenfeld 1972, 1978; and Monty 1981. A second generation of parental autobiographies (with biographies of their children) has increased in sophistication: e.g., Jablow 1982; Bérubé 1996; Bakely 1997, 2002; Stallings and Cook 1997; Beck 1999; Kaufman 1999; Bolduc 1999; Sullivan 2004. There have also been sibling accounts, such as Lee 1961; Cairo and Cairo 1985; de Vinck 1988; Simon 2002; and David B. 2005, an innovative and moving narrative utilizing the genre of the comic-cartoon. We will return to some of these accounts later.

5   See Dybwad 1990, Tamler 1993, and Jones and Barnes 1987. Of course, parental narratives cannot be said to be authoritative without qualification, since inevitably the story is told from their perspective rather than from that of their children (see Couser 1998). Still, any telling of the story is better than none at all, and from a theological point of view, in the end only God's account can correct the distortions in all human perspectives.

6   See Langness and Levine 1986; Atkinson, Jackson, and Walmsley 1997; and Atkinson et al. 2000. Life history research collaboration has also been adapted by advocacy and self-advocacy groups for their purposes; see Goodley 2000 and Goodley and Van Hove 2005.

7   Disability autobiographies of note include Gibbs 1981; Zola 1981; Murphy 1987; Callahan 1989; Sienkiewicz-Mercer and Kaplan 1989; Webb 1994; Spufford 1996; Grandin 1996; Clare 1999; Schneider 1999.

8   Publications of persons with Down Syndrome include Paul Scott's diaries (Seagoe 1964), Nigel Hunt's memoir (Hunt 1967), David Dawson's handwritten notes (Edwards and Dawson 1983), Gretchen Josephson's poems (Lubchenco and Crocker 1997), and Roland Johnson's autobiographical recollections (1999). There is also the transcribed interview with Al Lansing, an adult with intellectual disability (Easterday 1980).

9   Another actor with Down Syndrome is Chris Burke, who was the main star of ABC's Life Goes On, a family drama series that aired from 1989 to 1993, besides playing supporting roles in a number of other shows and movies; see Burke and McDaniel 1991.

10   Here, following Paul Ricoeur's saying that "the symbol gives rise to thought" (1969: 347–57).

11   Rosie Castañeda and Madeline L. Peters define *ableism* as "the discrimination against and the exclusion of individuals with physical and mental disabilities from full participation and opportunity within

society's systems and activities" (in Adams et al. 2000: 320). Ableism is manifest in the belief of the majority of nondisabled people in their superiority, and it privileges the nondisabled (Johnson 2006: 105). Society is culpable in discrimination against those with disabilities as ableism operates individually, culturally, and institutionally. See also Hales 1996 and Moore, Beazley, and Maelzer 1998: chap. 6.

12 Block identifies herself as a "secondary consumer": one who is not herself disabled but has a disabled family member, and has worked extensively with persons with disability (as a professional service provider for more than eighteen years). Her book *Copious Hosting* is one of the best books available on the church and disability. For another viewpoint about the challenges involved in writing "about" or "for" especially those with intellectual disabilities, see Hauerwas's reflections "On the Ethics of Writing about the Ethics of the Care of the Mentally Handicapped" (1998: 144–47).

13 Another theologian who has made the connection between the Holy Spirit, Christian doctrine, and the practices of the church is Reinhard Hütter 2000: esp. pt. 3. We meet at this juncture, although my own approach is from a Pentecostal perspective in contrast to Hütter's formerly Lutheran, now Roman Catholic background.

14 Others who are making the argument that theological doctrines are emergent from and normative measures of church practices include Lindbeck 1984; Cunningham 1998; Buckley and Yeago 2001; and Volf and Bass 2002.

Chapter 2: The Blind, the Deaf, and the Lame

1 Throughout this chapter I will put the noun "disability" in quotation marks to remind the reader that the phenomena of blindness, deafness, lameness, and so forth, in the biblical narrative are not identical to that found in our modern experience. More explicit argument for this distinction will be advanced in chapters 3 and 4.

2 There is one text that has been cited as indicative of intellectual disability: Paul's exhortation to "comfort the feebleminded" (1 Thess 5:14; see Barr 1904: 25); however, *oligopsuchous* is better rendered "timid" or "fainthearted" rather than "feebleminded." All biblical quotations in this chapter and its notes are from the King James Version unless otherwise noted, since it is the KJV that has been most popular and influential in the English-speaking world from its inception through the nineteenth century (the period covered here).

3 An older catalogue is Preuss' from the perspective of Talmudic medicine (Rosner 1978), while a more recent overview is Holden's survey

of bodily deformities in the Old Testament, Apocrypha, pseudepig-rapha, and Midrashim (1991).

4   One author goes so far as to say, from this verse, that "God claims to have created the mentally retarded" (Krentel 1986: 51). This gets us into the difficult area of theodicy, to which we will return in chapter 6.

5   Note the "disability" metaphors such as "lame" and "blind" func-tioned not only with regard to the priesthood but also, at different times in Israel's early history, with regard to common worshippers (Olyan 1998) and even the kingship (see Ceresko 2001).

6   An interesting prohibition since, as noted by Siegel (2001: 34), the Deaf are unable to hear curses directed at them. Still, on this point, Melcher (1998: 69) is correct to read Leviticus 19:14 as opposing the use of Leviticus 21:16-23 in an exclusionary sense for our time.

7   Plus, a holy God who alone can provide the perfect priesthood leads to a Christ who is able to serve as the high priest precisely because he is "holy, harmless, undefiled, [and] separate from sinners" (Heb 7:26). It is assumptions about such an "unblemished" Christ that have perpetuated the Levitical ban against persons with "disabilities" throughout the history of Christianity.

8   I need to be clear here that I am not endorsing this as the proper understanding of the covenantal curses but simply highlighting the received ableist reading of this text. My thanks to Kerry Wynn for helping me to rephrase some of the language in this paragraph.

9   With regard to the theological question, Amanda Tan (1994: 101) suggests that John 9:3 could be read as saying that either the blind-ness was purposefully caused by God so that God's glory could be manifest through it or that divine glory could nevertheless be revealed through God's healing of the man's blindness. I would favor the lat-ter reading. With regard to the ethical question, I would agree with Ernest Ezeogu, (2003: 10) who urges us to read the verse in light of what Jesus says in 9:4—"I must work the works of him that sent me, while it is day: the night cometh, when no man can work"—so that we would see blindness as Jesus did: "not as an occasion for curious speculation [e.g., about etiology or theodicy] but as a challenge for practical engagement."

10   Some commentators (L. Morris 1995: 272; Beasley-Murray 1999: 74) agree that in this case, this man's "disability" was related to his sin (especially in contrast to the congenitally blind man of John 9; see Schneiders 2002: 200), although a third (Keener 2003: 644–45) says that the Gospel author also implied that unlike the man born blind who became a disciple of Jesus (John 9:38), this paralytic seemed

to have rejected and/or betrayed Jesus instead (5:15). Another passage that seems to connect sin and "disability" is the healing of the man lowered through the roof (Mark 2:2-12). However, Kerry Wynn (1999) convincingly argues in this case that the act of healing is separated from the act of forgiveness of sins, and that the faith of the man and his assistants results in his forgiveness (2:5, 9) rather than in his healing.

11 The phenomenological similarities between the experiences of this boy with a "dumb and deaf spirit" and severely or profoundly retarded children undergoing epileptic seizures have been noted by some interpreters (e.g., Moede 1988: 43–44). For some historical perspective on religious and theological interpretations of what we now call epilepsy, see Temkin 1971: 91–92, 138–61.

12 Hence, a no-win situation when interpreting this passage: either we say that John is not concerned about the physical blindness of the man but about the spiritual blindness of the Pharisees, in which case we fuel the charges of anti-Semitism that John has been accused of; or we say that this passage is focused on the problem of physical blindness, which fosters the anti-disability attitudes we mentioned above. In either case, as Koosed and Schumm (2005) note, "Blind disciples would have been an affront to Jesus' power."

13 The problem is that the line between metaphor and reality is less easily demarcated than many biblical scholars and theologians realize (see Dolmage 2005). This is precisely why we need a new theology of disability for late modernity—the task of this book.

14 On the difficulty in simplistically equating premodern and modern notions of the term disability, see Bredberg 1999. The most complete history to date is Stiker 1999. Briefer overviews include Hegeman 1984: chap. 11; Webb-Mitchell 1994: chap. 3; and Covey 1998: chap. 7.

15 In the following, I rely primarily on Garland 1995 and Rose 2003.

16 During the medieval period, Genesis 30:37-42 was understood to be suggestive of how the imagination of mothers can affect the formation of infants (see Wilson 1993: 27–28). This theory of "maternal impressions" survived in the West through the nineteenth century, as seen in the chapter by that title in the 1889 Keating's *Cyclopedia of the Diseases of Children* (see Warkany 1977: 10).

17 The evidence suggests that Greek attitudes toward their imperfect young were far more diverse than the alleged standard practices of infanticide/exposure suggested by nineteenth-century scholars (see Rose 2003: chap. 2). Infanticide lay in the provenance of the state (the council of wise men) and occurred only when deformed infants

were thought to be omens of impending harm. On the practice of infanticide in ancient China, see Waltner 1995.

18 This identification of the female with deformity continued in the West through the early modern period; see Deutsch and Nussbaum 2000.

19 The standard history of mental retardation (Scheerenberger 1983) says practically nothing about the first millennium (cf. Judge 1987: chap. 1).

20 Even if Nicholas was a historical figure, tradition tells us that Saint Nicholas was the "protector of *innocentes*," an ambiguous Latin term. In the Nicholas legend, *innocentes* could refer to the condemned citizens of Myra, both men and young boys, or to the prisoners of Myra (see Jones 1978: 41–42).

21 For information on this point in particular, and on Augustine's views regarding what we now call intellectual disability in general, I am grateful to Professor Tim Stainton for his willingness to share the draft version of his unpublished manuscript with me.

22 Miles refers to Luther's 1519 lectures on Galatians (1964: 2484–49), in which Luther was citing Jerome's commentary.

23 *De generatione stultorum* was written about 1530, but not published until 1567. I put "foolishness" in quote marks since C. F. Goodey (2004: 290–95) cautions that Paracelsus's *stultorum* does not map conveniently with our contemporary notions of intellectual disability. Page references to this work in the following quotations are from the translation by Cranefield and Federn (1967).

24 Fools are thereby comparable in these instances to prophets whose ecstatic experiences of God lead them "out of themselves" so that the unsullied "inner man" could be free to mediate the holiness of God (Cranefield and Federn 1967: 69–73). Here, Paracelsus anticipates the later idea of "holy innocents," except that for Paracelsus, the fool is "actively holy" (1967: 73).

25 Cranefield and Federn suggest that the Vulcani can be understood as a premodern metaphor for "the multitude of developmental processes" at work in the "formation" of the "trisomy of the 21 chromosome," but they also remind us that in Paracelsus's worldview, the Vulcani were more apt to be identified with the angels of Genesis 1:26 (1967: 167–68).

26 As we shall see, Zacchias's classification anticipated the early twentieth-century nomenclature of moron, imbecile, and idiot.

27 The following overview of Locke's discussion of the "idiots" relies heavily on Goodey 1994. My citations and quotations from Locke's *Essay* are from Nidditch's edition (Locke 1975).

28 Similarly, for Kant, "the dumb could never attain the faculty of Reason itself, but only, at best, a mere 'analogy of Reason'" (Rée 1999: 93, a translation from Kant's *Anthropologie* [1798], in *Gesammelte Schriften* [Berlin, 1917], 8:155).

29 In his *Essays on the Law of Nature* (ca. 1660), Locke wrote (1965: 203): "There is no reason that we should deal with the case of children and idiots. For although the law is binding on all those to whom it is given, it does not, however, bind those to whom it is not given, and it is not given to those who are unable to understand it."

30 As another example, Burt was able to distinguish between the beliefs and practices of the Pentecostal church she attended after deinstitutionalization from the services held at the residential facility she used to live in. Further, she was able to provide an apology for why she did not (even could not) meet the norms for sexual behavior expected by the church parishioners, but was also able to see their side of things (see Burt's discussion of these issues in Bogdan and Taylor 1994: 183–97). These reveal that "retarded" as she was thought to be, Burt did not just believe all that she heard in church.

31 A strategy similar to Wynn's of rereading from disability studies perspectives the Mephibosheth story against the backdrop of developments in the Davidic monarchy has recently been offered by Jeremy Schipper 2006.

32 Disabled characters in fairy tales are not always good, but span a wide moral range (see Franks 1996).

33 This is the predominant strategy of both the Disability Studies Group of the American Academy of Religion and the Disability Studies and Healthcare in the Bible and Near East group of the Society of Biblical Literature; for an overview of the latter's research trajectory, see Raphael 2004. A book that appeared too recently to be taken into substantive account in this volume, but which exhibits a similar strategy of reading the biblical text in a redemptive manner from a disability perspective is Parsons 2006.

Part II

Chapter 3

1 Even in Aquinas, there are no less than twenty different terms describing and calling attention to the wide range of "fools" known to the medieval mind, many overlapping with, but none matching exactly, modern notions of congenital intellectual disability; see Lauand 2001.

2   As the following discussion shows, each of these terms are socially weighted, with distinctive disciplinary connotations. For example, while most individuals with Down Syndrome (a medical diagnosis) have some kind of learning disability (a category from the field of special education), most people with learning disabilities do not have Down Syndrome. The discussion in this and the next chapter is designed precisely to identify how these different vocabularies clarify and yet also oftentimes confuse the issues.

3   The various histories of intellectual disability that include discussion of Down Syndrome are Kanner 1964; Rosen, Clark, and Kivitz 1976; Scheerenberger 1983; Tyor and Bell 1984; Ferguson 1994; Trent 1994; Noll 1995; Jackson 2000; and Trent and Noll 2004. For a short sketch, see Stroman 1989: chap. 4. See also my comments in chap. 2, the section "'Disability' in the History of Christianity," pp. 27–38.

4   De Paul insisted that the mentally ill and mentally retarded were persons, not witches; Pinel transformed asylums from being prisons to being sites of "moral" management and formation; Esquirol divided mental retardation into two levels: imbecile (higher) and idiot (each with degrees of variance also); and Itard's claim to fame was his working with a feral child known as "the wild boy of Aveyron." For discussions of the contributions of these individuals and others, see Scheerenberger 1983: 44–55, 74–78.

5   As we shall see later (pp. 82–84), the "strange other" and the "foreigner" have always been too easily conflated.

6   One study that has explored the explicit connections between feeble-mindedness and prostitution during this time is that by Paula Bartley (2000: pt. 3). For a mid-twentieth-century report on the "social problem of mental deficiency," see O'Connor and Tizard 1956.

7   From the standpoint of the medical institution, morons could do manual labor, were educable, and could learn through punishment; imbeciles could do only simple menial work, were trainable (through rote lessons), and could only be pitied and locked away; and idiots could not even maintain themselves, were too severely or profoundly retarded to learn, and probably were also sufficiently physically disabled so as not to be capable of breaking rules or laws. See Noll 1995: 2–3, for how these categories played out in institutions in the southern United States during the first quarter of the twentieth century.

8   From the beginning, even penologists questioned how it could be known definitively that mental deficiency was inherited, since the inheritance of criminality was yet to be proven (Tyor and Bell 1984: 120). These cautions went largely unheeded given the wider social concerns.

9   The argument did not mention that Buck's child originated, in all probability, from her rape by the nephew of her adoptive mother. (I say "in all probability" since this piece of information came from the "Buck v. Bell" entry in the *Wikipedia*, http://en.wikipedia.org/wiki/ Buck_v._Bell, the reliability of which is not assured. I was unable to corroborate this claim in other sources on Buck's life that I had access to.) Accessed March 18, 2007.

10   Carrie's sister, Doris Buck Figgins, was sterilized in 1928, discharged two years later, married and lived a relatively normal life, trying to get pregnant, and found out in 1979 that she was barren because of her sterilization: "I'm not mad, just broken hearted is all. I just wanted babies bad. . . . I don't know why they done it to me. I tried to live a good life" (in Noll 1995: 73).

11   Hoche and Binding's first argument continues to be widely assumed, especially as public sentiments remain largely with parents who kill their severely disabled children in order to alleviate their suffering. Two of the more famous cases to date are discussed by Brockley 2001 and Enns 1999. There is also the case involving a mildly retarded older sibling who euthanized his more severely retarded younger brother (see Bogdan 1992). Again, the public expressed similar sympathies regarding this "mercy killing."

12   Sharon Snyder and David Mitchell have recently produced a book-length argument (2006) that the practices of scientific research and experimentation that "produced" the eugenics movement—in order to "fix" disability—during the first quarter of the twentieth century continue to shape the oppression of people with disabilities today.

13   Reflecting on the challenges of independent living for her mildly retarded daughter—including car repossession, bad credit, a broken marriage, and so on—Sandra Kaufman points out (1999: 226) the fact that "our children have real deficits sometimes gets lost in today's emphasis on their civil rights." For more on the challenges of deinstitutionalization, this time from the perspective of one working with the mentally ill, see Johnson 1990.

14   Friendship, the most important ingredient, is still an elusive goal given the high turnover rate of social service workers, professional caregivers, and residential supervisors. But even if the turnover rate were not an issue, it is nevertheless still the case that professional caregivers and support workers "hardly ever think of their 'clients' as friends. They may be very fond of them, they may even say they love them, but only reluctantly is such affection interpreted as friendship" (Reinders 2005b: 54).

15   Johnson and Traustadóttir (2005a: 35) tell of Thomas F. Allen, whose IQ ranged over 30 points over forty years, and Richardson and Koller (1996: 121) indicate more recently that shifts have exceeded 40 points in a few cases. Janet Carr (1995: 167) also notes that the IQ range of "the retarded" (10–70) is actually greater than that of "normal" persons (70–130).

16   This was even higher for Jews (83 percent), Hungarians (80 percent), Italians (79 percent), and Russians (87 percent) (Smith 1985: 127). Is there any correlation between these numbers and the fact that it was eastern and southern Europeans who were most heavily restricted by the Immigration Act of 1924?

17   Mentally retarded individuals were also gainfully employed in support of the effort during World War II (Evans 1984: 184).

18   For a history of the AAMR/AAMD, see Sloan and Stevens 1976.

19   Scientific research on Down Syndrome in particular and intellectual disability in general has literally exploded in the last thirty years. Studies in the vanguard of such research include Dobbing 1984; Gustavson 1987; Pueschel and Rynders 1982; Pueschel and Pueschel 1992; Epstein and Patterson 1990; Lott and McCoy 1992; Hogenboom 2001; Lubec 2003; and Malard 2004.

20   It is estimated that up to 25 percent of all miscarriages are caused by trisomic conceptuses (Hassold, Sherman, and Hunt 1995: 1).

21   In 1953, 53 percent of infants with Down Syndrome died in their first year; more recently, the survival rate is upwards of 92 percent (Rogers and Coleman 1992: 22).

22   Although we should be careful to draw too simplistic a causal line between trisomy 21 and intellectual disability since how the disability manifests, its degree of severity, and even the shape of the phenotype are arguably influenced also by environmental conditions (see Sober 2000).

23   I have not been able to identify the percentage of intellectually disabled with Down Syndrome. However, as of the mid-1990s, it was estimated that there were 15 persons with intellectual disability of any kind (from those with developmental delays to the profoundly retarded) for every 1,000 persons in the United States, a total population of approximately 3,887,158 plus or minus 1.9 percent or 75,440 (Larson et al. 2000: 7). Not surprisingly, Accardo and Capute (1998) have called attention to the fragmentation of scientific research on intellectual disability into diverse and specific syndromes.

24   See Marino and Pueschel 1996; Smith and Warren 1985; Warburg 2002: 101–4; Warkany, Lemire, and Cohen 1981: 41–47; Roizen

2001; Patti and Tsiouris 2003; Sillanpää 1996: 420–22; Malard 2004; Kannann 1987; and Lancioni, O'Reilly, and Basili 1999.

25 For discussions of the special issues present in the lives of persons with severe and profound mental retardation, see Cleland 1979; Greer, Anderson, and Odle 1982; Murphy and Wilson 1985; and Meyer, Peck, and Brown 1990.

26 The most comprehensive study of the daily transactions between "nondirective" counselors, doctors, and parents-to-be who have to make tragic decisions is by Bosk 1992. Martha and John Beck, who were both completing Harvard Ph.D.s when their baby was diagnosed as having Down Syndrome, tell of the pressure of Harvard life in which John's dissertation adviser expected him to have the baby aborted for his career's sake, even as the professor himself had his wife's baby aborted (who was not even "abnormal") at a crucial state in his Ph.D. program; worse, this prejudice against "deformed babies" was widespread even among the Harvard medical community (see Beck 1999: 205–23). A concurring perspective from a physician is Ralston 2000.

27 See also George Neumayr's article, "The Abortion Debate that Wasn't," *Seattle Post-Intelligencer*, July 17 2005 (http://seattlepi.nw source.com/opinion/232776_focus17.html), which notes that an even higher percentage of fetuses with cystic fibrosis and other disabilities are being aborted per Kaiser Permanente's admission that 95 percent of its patients in Northern California choose abortion after they find out through prenatal screening that their fetus will have such diseases. Thanks to my colleague Mark Mostert for pointing me to this news article.

28 On this point, see Hauerwas 1984: 93–101; Hauerwas 1986: 159–81; Reinders 2000: chap. 10; and Michalko 2002: chap. 3. For an autobiographical account confirming this very point, see Webb 1994.

29 More to the point, "the genotype does not accurately predict phenotype" (Ross 2003: 81).

30 See President's Commission 1983: chap. 6; Weir 1984; Sparks 1985; and Kennedy 1988. In brief, part of the result of the Baby Doe case was the Child Abuse Amendments Act in 1984 (PL 98-457), which required states to establish reporting procedures regarding medical neglect, declared that withholding life support from disabled infants was medical neglect (unless the child would die anyway), and allowed states to develop procedures to prevent medical neglect of severely disabled infants.

31 For discussion of disability perspectives that argue against the abortion of fetuses with Down Syndrome, see Bérubé 1996: chap. 2; Saxton 1997, 2000; Buchanan et al. 2000: chap. 7; Asch, Gostin, and Johnson 2003; and Wasserman, Bickenbach and Wachbroit 2005.

32 The whole notion of "quality of life" is problematic not only on its own terms but also when applied to assessing cases involving persons with intellectual disabilities; see, e.g., Goode and Hogg 1994; Hensel 2001; and Schalock 2004.

33 For extensive discussion of Down Syndrome across the life span, see Cicchetti and Beeghly 1990; Rowitz 1992; Zigler and Bennett-Gates 1999; and Cuskelly, Jobling, and Buckley 2002.

34 Physician Allen Crocker also noted (1998: 302–3) that the children who were operated on "did not look like they had Down Syndrome in the conventional sense of the word, but they assuredly did not look normal either."

35 For overviews of the movement toward integration and inclusion, see Pasanella and Volkmor 1981; Tomlinson 1982; Barton 1988; Fulcher 1989; Skrtic 1995; Vlachou 1997; Dmitriev 1997; and Armstrong and Barton 1999.

36 Some suggest that full inclusion has done more harm than good for some intellectually disabled students who also have behavioral problems. "Because many school districts believe that compliance with P.L. 94-142 means that they must mainstream their retarded students, these districts may be unwittingly shaping their retarded students' future delinquent behavior" (Greene 1991: 131).

37 Further, at the philosophical level there is the objection that mainstreaming deaf children into regular classrooms is actually a form of exclusion and discrimination rather than of inclusion (see Lane 1997: 164). Of course, raising the question about deaf children introduces the convoluted debate about whether or not deafness can or should be classified as a disability. Meanwhile, the question of whether or not the ideology of inclusion is discriminatory is not easily dismissed; see Mostert 1991; Mostert 1999–2000; and Jaeger and Bowman 2002.

38 From the perspective of parents of children with developmental and learning disabilities, many have opted for special schools even in the era of inclusion because the physical environment is more accessible; the curriculum is more sensitive to the needs of their children; the staff–student ratios are lower; and integration is targeted, albeit circumstantially (see Jenkinson 1997: chap. 6).

39 Research on language development among individuals with Down Syndrome has been spearheaded by Belgian psychologist and lin-

guist Jean Rondal (see Rondal 1994; Rondal and Edwards 1997; and Rondal and Buckley 2003). Other studies include Jones and Cregan 1986, Chapman 1997, and Chapman 2003. For more on the tendency of people with intellectual disability to reify nouns rather than work with abstract ideas and symbolic concepts, see Kumin 1994: chaps. 5–6.

40 On other neuroscientific studies of Down Syndrome, see Becker et al. 1991; Wishart 1995; Mattheis 1995; Shaywitz and Shaywitz 1996; Hand, Clinton, and Hiemenz 1999; and Rondal 2004: 72–74.

41 Biographies of savants include Chand 1997 (about Radhika's artistic talents); Monty 1981 (about Leslie Lemke's piano playing); and Cameron 1998 (on Hikari Oe as composer).

42 It is in this connection that Howe (1989: 88–90) introduces Howard Gardner's theory of multiple and independent, even if not entirely noninterdependent, intelligences (see Gardner 1993, 1999): linguistic, logical-mathematical, spatial, musical, bodily-kinesthetic, interpersonal, and intrapersonal. If I were writing a book on educating people with intellectual disability, I would begin with Lynda Crane's insistence (2002: 26) that Gardner's theoretical categories are useful "because they suggest the need to look at each person's strengths and weaknesses."

43 Now available are various telecommunication devices, accessible computer hardware (e.g., keyboards and screens), and a wide range of adaptive technologies (e.g., screen readers, voice recognition systems, hearing assistance devices); see Meyers 1988; Nagler and Nagler 1999: pt. 4; Fleischer and Zames 2001: chap. 9; and Mates 2000.

44 Elizabeth Stuart (2000: 166) asks whether the labeling of toilets "men," "women," and "disabled" communicates something else other than to offer directions. Informative and insightful discussions of sexuality and disability in general include Greengross 1976; Duffy 1979; Vash 1981: chaps. 4–5; Zola 1981: chap. 11; Nagler 1990: pt. 5; Humphries and Gordon 1992: chap. 6; Shakespeare, Gillespie-Sells, and Davies 1996; and Nemeth 2000.

45 Up to 30 percent of boys and 70–80 percent of girls have been abused; see Gething 1997: 207; cf. Elkins 1995: 263; Stromsness 1993; and Tse 1993.

46 There is little research about homosexuality among persons with intellectual disabilities. Schwier and Hingsburger (2000: 123) suggest that homosexuality may have been more of an issue in institutional contexts when the sexes are generally separated, resulting

in greater confusion about sexual identity. Yet others suggest that if census statistics are correct, then up to 10 percent of the 7.5 million intellectually disabled Americans, or 750,000 of them, are gay, lesbian, bisexual, or transgender (Allen 2003: 10).

47 Of children born to women with Down Syndrome, 35–50 percent have trisomy 21. Although hard data is still forthcoming, there is only one documented instance of a male with Down Syndrome fathering a child (Massimini 2000: 99).

48 With regard to "support services" like physician-assisted suicide, the disability movement may give the impression that they are divided when in fact they really are not. Organizations such as Not Yet Dead argue that assisted suicide is "the ultimate act of oppression" (Longmore 2003: 197) when not accompanied or preceded by guarantees of the right to self-determination, independent living, equal access, and so on, and that counseling for those requesting to die should be done by those knowledgeable about the oppressive sociopsychological conditions of disabled life. The founder of AUTONOMY, Inc., Andrew Batavia, argues that even persons with disabilities should have the right to end their lives with integrity, but also goes on to say, "[U]ntil society provides people with disabilities all the resources they need to live independent, dignified lives, we should not even be thinking about providing assistance in ending life" (2004:65). Batavia (a high-level quadriplegia) agrees it is precisely because we do not do the former that we have persisted in oppressing the disabled, leaving them to think they have no other options than to end their lives.

49 Elks summarizes (1993: 206):

> It seems very unlikely that the existence of tacit, if not outright approval for euthanasia, resistance towards sanitary reform, poor conditions in institutions, and high death rates of preventable infections in institutions were purely coincidental. Is it not a little too convenient that tuberculosis, to which the "feebleminded" were believed to be especially susceptible, just happened to flourish in the conditions found in large, overcrowded institutions and was the major cause of their deaths? Is it pure coincidence that eugenicists were aware that hostile environments had a long history of use in killing unwanted people?

50 To which, Noreen, an older woman who was mentally retarded, said in reflecting on institutional life: "That's kind of funny because most times families didn't come either. Our friends would be all alone at their own funerals. It really hurt, too, because often we were the only family we had. It was wrong not to go" (quoted in Hingsburger 1992: 73).

Chapter 4: Deconstructing and Reconstructing Disability

1   While Mark's teacher, who enjoys working with him, told me at one point that in her twenty-two years of working with developmentally disabled adults, Mark is the most stubborn she has ever met (must be a Yong trait!), our mother's perspective is that this obduracy did not emerge in Mark until after he was encouraged by this same teacher to be an adult and to think more independently.

2   The social model of disability has been developed variously—e.g., Brechin, Liddiard, and Swain 1981; Shearer 1981; Oliver 1990; Barnes, Mercer, and Shakespeare 1999; and Smart 2001: pt. 2. For a multileveled and multidimensional theory of disability similar to the one being developed here, see DePoy and Gilson 2004.

3   Arguably, freaks were the prototypical "missing link" in the emerging evolutionary hypothesis of late-nineteenth-century Darwinian science; see Thomson 2003: 133–34, and Bogdan 1988: 134–42.

4   For discussions of the freak show, see Drimmer 1973; Fiedler 1978; Bogdan 1988; Thomson 1996; and Thomson 1997: pt. 2.

5   For discussions of disability culture, see Yates, Ortiz, and Anderson 1998; and Longmore 2003: chap. 11. For a bibliography, see Brown 2000.

6   For overviews of media representations of disability, see Gartner and Joe 1987; Barnes 1992; Hevey 1992; and Nelson 1994. On disability in theater and film, see Tomlinson 1984; Klobas 1988; Cumberbatch and Negrine 1992; Norden 1994; Smit and Enns 2001; and Fahy and King 2002.

7   But not all laws have been free from prejudice against people with disabilities. A 1911 Chicago city ordinance stated: "It is hereby prohibited for any person who is diseased, maimed, mutilated, or deformed in any way so as to be an unsightly or disgusting object to expose himself to public view" (Fries 1997: xi). Other more helpful laws regarding the physically and intellectually disabled prior to the civil rights movement include the Mental Deficiency Act in England (1913), and in the United States: PL 113, which made vocational rehabilitation available to the physically and mentally handicapped (1943); the National Mental Health Act (1946); the Vocational Rehabilitation Act (1954); and PL 88-164, the Mental Retardation Facilities and Community Mental Health Centers Construction Act (1963). For historical perspective, see Switzer 2003; and Clements and Read 2003.

8   On Roosevelt and his disability, see Goldberg 1981; Gallagher 1985; and Houck and Kiewe 2003. A short account is Milam 1984: chap. 8.

9   On the disability rights movement, see Driedger 1989; Shapiro 1994; Bryan 1996: chap. 2; Pelka 1997; D'Lil 2001; and Fleischer and Zames 2001.

10 On the reception of the ADA, see Stefan 2001; Engel and Munger 2003; O'Brien 2004; and Colker 2005. On the struggle for disability rights in general, see Johnson 2003.

11 If the U.S. Supreme Court continues to focus on the letter of the law rather than the intent of Congress in passing the law, the full implementation of the ADA may still be far ahead of us (O'Brien 2001: 211–16; Parmet 2003).

12 On the geography of disability, see Dorn 1998; Kitchin 1999; Gleeson 1999; Butler and Parr 1999; Steinfeld and Danford 1999; and Golledge 2004.

13 Frank Bowe (2000: chap. 2) has articulated seven principles of universal design: equitable use (useful for and accessible to people with diverse abilities); flexibility in use (accommodates a wide range of preferences and abilities); simply and intuitively used; informationally perceptible even to those with sensory impairments; a low tolerance for error (minimum hazards and adverse consequences for accidental or unintended actions); involving low physical effort (minimum fatigue production); and appropriate size for limited space (or for the size of the user's body). For more on the theory of universal design, see Steinfeld and Danford 1999: pt. 1.

14 The issues of disability, social welfare, and employment policies and legislation are complex. Standard introductions include Stone 1984; Coudroglou and Poole 1984; and Reno, Mashaw, and Gradison 1997.

15 How was incapacity for gainful employment measured? Here the economic system met with the medical system so that disability as a clinical concept validated certain categories of persons (the sick or impaired) as recipients of benefits (Stone 1984: chap. 3). Yet the question of how clinical medicine could translate into economic assessment was never clarified.

16 Talk of disability rights, however, is risky, especially when during periods of high unemployment rates the majority population feels an additional "squeeze" from disabled workers (Yelin 1997).

17 The issues about persons with disability in the workplace are discussed in Coudroglou and Poole 1984; Thornton and Maynard 1989; and French 1994.

18 Disability advocate Marta Russell (1998: chap. 14), for example, suggests that a truly free market must liberate people with disabilities into the workforce. This market reorganization should be prescribed

by the following: democratic control; corporate and governmental accountability; campaign finance reform; elimination of corporate subsidies (return corporate tax rates to the levels of the 1950s); electoral reform; deaccumulation of capital; decorporatization of the media; environmentally sustainable development; universal access; disability-sensitive universal health care; shrinking the income gap; fair taxation; full employment, with living wages; disability benefits; flexible work, schedules and environments; job sharing; retention and reconfiguration of social security; equal education rights; quality child care availability; occupational safety; balanced budget; and global vision and sustainability. Sounds good. The question is how do we accomplish all this? I will return in chapter 8 to discuss some of these issues in more of a theological context.

19 A prime example is theoretical physicist Stephen Hawking, who has lived with the incapacitating effects of amyotrophic lateral sclerosis, or Lou Gehrig's disease, since the mid-1960s. For details of Hawking's life with disability, see Bowe 1981: chap. 5; O'Brien 1997; and Cropper 2001: chap. 29.

20 For the emerging shape of disability studies in academia, see Mitchell and Snyder 1997; Linton 1998; Linton, Mello, and O'Neill 2000; Mitchell and Snyder 2000; and Snyder, Brueggemann, and Thomson 2002.

21 For our purposes, "social construct" assumes the preceding discussion about how human lives are socially, culturally, politically, geographically, and economically construed. So whenever the language of "social construct" appears in what follows, the reader should be aware that we are engaging not only the social dimension of that claim, but also its more robust version that includes these other domains.

22 A description of the institutional development of the mental retardation industry is provided in Cocks et al. 1996; for an overview of the economics of mental retardation, see Conley 1973.

23 Looking back, "moron," "imbecile," and "idiot" came into wider public prominence in the context of nineteenth-century educational optimism and expanding industrial economy. By contrast, "feebleminded" was set in the medical narrative of the early twentieth century, "mentally defective" was a psychological category, and "mentally deficient" a social category. More recently, "mentally retarded" is set within a parental framework, even as "learning disability" and "developmental disability" are comparative markers in the field of early childhood education. Today, the more scientific categories are "cognitive disability" or "intellectual disability." For discussion, see Devlieger 2003.

24 For the wide range of issues that emerge when the lives of people with intellectual disabilities intersect with the criminal justice system, see the entire issue of the *Journal of Intellectual Disability Research* 46(4), suppl. 1 (2002), which is devoted to this topic.

25 Another study of aboriginal cultures resulted in similar findings (Hayes 1996). The complicating issue here is whether or not aboriginal peoples have greater difficulty comprehending nonaboriginal laws to begin with. Further, there are socioeconomic and cultural factors such as poor health, high mortality rates, and morbidity issues that probably play a role in affecting how people with intellectual disabilities perform within the framework of a foreign criminal justice system.

26 The discussion about the inequities that people with intellectual disabilities are subjected to in the process of interrogation are drawn from Sigelman et al. 1981; Perske 1991: chap. 3; Perske and Dicks 1995: 80–84; Byrnes 1999: 316–17; and Luckasson 2001.

27 Hollins, Clare, and Murphy (1996a, 1996b) have thus produced an important resource to help people with intellectual disabilities understand their interactions with the justice system. I wonder, however, if these materials are readily accessible to such individuals who find themselves in these circumstances.

28 Similar criticisms have also been launched against the Paralympics; see Goggin and Newell 2000.

Chapter 5: Disability in Context

1 This theme of disabled or wounded healer is also developed by Henri Nouwen 1972, Frank Moore 1990, and Vicki Noble 1993. For more on disability in the Native American context, see Joe 1988.

2 Aristotle's view that "the female is a misbegotten male" was perpetuated by no less a medieval philosopher and theologian than Aquinas (see *Summa Theologica*, 1 pt., question 92, art. 1, reply 1). However, Aquinas limited this defectiveness of the female to its particular nature, and suggested that with regard to its universal nature "woman is not misbegotten, but is included in nature's intention as ordered to the work of generation" (1941: I.489).

3 On women and disability, see Campling 1981; Browne, Connors, and Stern 1985; Saxton and Howe 1987; Fine and Asch 1988; Stewart, Percival, and Epperly 1992; Rousso 1993; Holcomb and Willmuth 1993; J. Morris 1995; Keith 1994, 1996; Walsh and Heller 2002; and Banks and Kaschak 2003.

4   For an intensely personal discussion of the challenges confronting women with disabilities who desire and then proceed to bear children, see Finger 1990. For other issues related to disability and parenting, see Wates and Jade 1999.

5   As one wife put it: "[W]hat solves the problem of sex and sexuality for disabled people is often quite inadequate for the partners of disabled people" (M. Cohen 1996: 119).

6   In this and the next subsection, I use "feminist with disabilities" as a shorthand to refer inclusively to feminists who are themselves disabled, feminists who are caregivers of other persons with disabilities, and feminists whose thinking is informed by disability perspectives. "Feminists with disabilities" is just much less cumbersome. Other feminist discussions of disability that we will not engage include Morris 1996; Thomas 1999; Fawcett 2000; and Keith 2001.

7   This is also the case in the arena of feminist theology— e.g., Elshout 1999.

8   Diane Herndl's study notes (1993: 220) that "it is because women have had more cause to be uneasy in our culture than men that illness is figured as feminine."

9   Madonne Miner (1997) points out that men come to recognize the embodied character of their identities *after* experiencing disability, while women are much more perceptive about the material and gendered aspects of their identities both before and after the onset of disability.

10 A specifically disabled feminist ethic of care needs to call attention to "the gendered division of caring" whereby "women are being recruited to perform increasing amounts of caring work for people with disabilities, without being paid for it. This suggests a conflict between the disability reform and women's concerns and the danger of exploiting women in the efforts to liberate people with disabilities. . . . Policy makers and service providers need to become aware of the stereotypical and gendered assumptions underlying most disability policies and practices" (Traustadóttir 1999: 202).

11 Wendell's position is parallel to Barbara Fawcett's (2000), which sees disability as dynamic, fluid, and contested (and contestable), always calling forth new strategies and responses depending on the situation at hand.

12 I would add that the impact of this claim derives more from the fact that Wendell is a disabled person rather than that she is a feminist, since all other critical theories—whether feminist, race, ethnicity, or gender—"pose a less radical challenge [than critical disability theory]

to the material, if not necessarily the normative, conditions of contemporary North American society" (Devlin and Pothier 2006: 20).

13   For introductory texts on women and disabilities in global context, see Driedger and Gray 1992; Driedger, Feika, and Batres 1996; Lewis and Sygall 1997; and Hans and Patri 2003.

14   I will not discuss disability in Europe in part because I have already touched on various aspects of disability in Britain, and in part because much of the European continental scene mirrors developments in the Anglo-American world. However, there are some peculiarities related to Scandinavia and eastern Europe that may be of interest; see Daunt 1991; van Oorschot and Hvinden 2001; Clements and Read 2003; and Lawson and Gooding 2004.

15   On the growing literature on disability in global context, see Werner 1987; Coleridge 1993; Peters 1993; Üstün et al. 2001; Priestley 2001; and Stone 2005.

16   At one point, it was estimated that approximately 10 percent of the world's population was disabled (see, e.g., O'Toole and McConkey 1995: 3, and Khan and Durkin 1995: 1), in which case over 500 million of 600 million disabled persons would have been found in the developing world. More recently, however, such estimates have been revised downward to include only moderately and severely disabled people (since mild impairments are not only difficult to detect, but may not be disabling or may be only temporarily disabling), and to take into account that disabling environmental factors such as malnutrition are no longer as widespread. Yet development also enables the emergence of an older population, which in turn brings about other kinds of disabilities. So in developing regions, estimates of 4.8 percent (approximately 234 million) in 2000 are projected to rise to 8.5 percent (approximately 525 million) in 2035 (Helander 1999: chap. 2).

17   In rural Bangladesh, up to 85 percent of persons still hold to the notion that intellectual disability is a curse from God, and an additional 10 percent believe it to be related to the sins of ancestors (see Zaman et al. 1990: 146).

18   O'Connor, Fisher, and Robinson (2000) tell of Teresa, a non-English-speaking Puerto Rican who moved to the United States with her husband and two children, and was thereafter identified as mildly retarded. This was incomprehensible to her since she was basically able to keep up with the daily affairs of her family, and get involved in biweekly meetings at her local Catholic parish. So now Teresa has workers from three different agencies who provide support, but the

challenge is that her idea of what her needs are differs from those of the service providers.

19 Bob Hurley went so far as to say that there was a "misplacement of the poor in institutions for the mentally retarded" (1969: 48–52). Edgerton himself wrote (1979: 49): "[A] child born and raised in an urban ghetto or an impoverished rural environment is fifteen times more likely to be labeled mentally retarded than a child of the same age from suburbia."

20 For introductory discussions of disability in India, see Mehta 1983. For research on intellectual disability in India, see Sen 1982 and Sen 1992.

21 God's selection of the stutterer Moses is repeatedly appealed to; see Marx 2002: 52; Levy 1995: 168; and Schwartz and Kaplan 2004: 172–76.

22 In this way, the halachic authors signified their concerns for meeting the needs of people with disabilities, over and against the *Aggadic* quest for etiological understanding (with its focus on the question of origins) and the prophetic anticipation of eschatological healing (focused on the extinction of disability); on this point, see Blau 1916: 43–49.

23 "And whoever turns away from My reminder, his shall be a straightened life, and We will raise him on the day of resurrection, blind" (sura 20.124); "And whomsoever Allah guides, he is the follower of the right way, and whomsoever He causes to err, you shall not find for him guardians besides Him; and We will gather them together on the day of resurrection on their faces, blind and dumb and deaf; their abode is hell" (17.97). See also suras 7:179 and 22:46.

24 We have no space to survey all of the many Qur'anic references to the blind: 2.15, 2.18, 2.171, 3.49, 5.11, 5.71, 6.50, 6.104, 7.064, 10.43, 11.24, 13.16, 13.19, 17.72, 17.97, 20.124, 20.125, 22.46, 24.61, 25.73, 27.66, 27.81, 28.66, 30.53, 35.19, 40.58, 43.40, 47.23, 48.17, and 80.2.

25 Arguably, the sura "Surely the vilest of animals, in Allah's sight, are the deaf, the dumb, who do not understand" (8:22) refers figuratively to the lack of understanding in the deaf and dumb rather than to people with intellectual disabilities.

26 Similarly, Lorenzo Milam, disabled since 1952 after a bout with polio, writes in his book *CripZen* (1993: 174): "Buddhists tell us that the body's pain, the body's pleasure—as well as book-learning, passion, hope, and hopelessness—may be illusional. You and I might be in an especially good position to study this."

Part 3

1 This task is barely begun. Two insightful and succinct essays are those by Betenbaugh 2000 and Joeckel 2006. A book-length collection of essays focused on theology and Alzheimer's disease has been compiled by McKim 1997. I will refer to and interact with others' efforts in the pages to follow.

Chapter 6: Reimagining the Doctrines

1 The careful reader will notice that these biographical vignettes of Mark have been told primarily from mother's point of view. This is not only because she has been the primary caregiver for Mark, but also because she is the more talkative one compared with our father. This was one point, however, when Dad chimed in on the conversation about Mark's life.

2 More recently, however, scholars have retrieved the argument for creation out of a primeval chaos; see Levenson 1988; Löning and Zenger 2000: 11–17; and Keller 2003. A recent defense of the traditional doctrine of creation *ex nihilo* is Craig and Copan 2004. While one might argue that the doctrine of creation out of chaos is more conducive for a theology of disability, my own formulation does not depend on having to decide between the two.

3 A now classic text on the problem of evil is Gilkey 1959, while a status *quaestiones* of the discussion is Whitney 1989.

4 Until the "invention" of limbo in the thirteenth century, the majority of theologians agreed with Augustine that unbaptized infants were doomed to hell, even if their punishments were less severe than those of other sinners (see Rondet 1972: chap. 15). In Protestant terms, this perdition awaited also the fate of the unevangelized, including people with intellectual disabilities who are unable to believe and confess Christ.

5 Its influence can be seen a millennium later in Milton's classic *Paradise Lost* (see Fiore 1981).

6 Evangelicals will tend to emphasize God's *allowing* disabilities to happen (see Treloar 1998: 102–7), while Reformed thinkers will go so far as to talk about God being in control over and revealing God's glory through all things, disabilities included (see Kim 2001: chap. 7).

7 On the many questions that the traditional responses continue to give rise to, see Tilley 1991; Pinnock 2002; and Boyd 2003. It might also be said that theodicy issues have effectively hindered the emergence of a constructive theology of disability (see Joeckel 2006: 334–35).

8   And, as Kerry Wynn (2007) argues, the glory of God was displayed in the life of the man born blind not so much through his healing but—in contrast to the other man who was also healed at the pool of Siloam (John 5)—through his response to his healing and witness to Jesus.

9   The final chapter of Leonard Kriegel's *Falling into Life* (1991: 175–95) raises the theodicy issue in disability perspective in ways that remain, for him, conclusive about remaining an unbelieving Jew. At the same time, Kriegel, crippled (his self-identification) by polio since the age of eleven, also writes (1991: 151): "The believer who falls seriously ill finds God's presence in the pain to which he must bear witness; the nonbeliever, on the other hand, insists that God's absence is confirmation enough that suffering is a simple accident. But both believer and nonbeliever discover that illness makes the idea of God curiously personal."

10 More and more biblical scholars are seeing the early chapters of Genesis as an alternative to other creation myths of the ancient Near East rather than as a historical account, so long as we understand "myth" to mean an explanatory story rather than a fanciful tale. Patricia Williams (2001: 38) cites James Barr and Claus Westermann, among other biblical scholars, who question that this narrative presents a doctrine of a fall, and puts forward her own variation of the doctrine of original sin that does not assume Adam and Eve to be historical persons. For an older argument against the idea of a literal, historical fall, see Tennant 1968.

11 Two generations ago Pope Pius XII condemned the theory of polygenism as incompatible with the doctrine of original sin in his encyclical *Humani Generis*, 37 (Pius XII 1950: 22). Augustine Kasujja notes (1986: 177–80) that even if the theory of monogenism has by and large been discredited by the scientific community, a convincing and coherent polygenetic hypothesis has yet to emerge. Hence evangelical biblical scholars and theologians continue to affirm the traditional view of Adam as a historical person from whom the rest of humankind descended (e.g., Grenz 1994: 190–95; Blocher 1999: 39–42). All the more reason to develop a theory of sin and the Fall that might be plausible regardless of what the empirical evidence eventually decides.

12 These and many other questions evolutionary science raises for the traditional doctrine of original sin are identified by Dubarle 1967: 230–37; Trooster 1968; Korsmeyer 1998; and Corey 2000.

13 For the syndrome phenotype during the early or middle Neolithic period (6500–4000 B.C.E.), see Diamandopoulos, Rakatsanis, and

Diamantopoulos 1997. On trisomic mutations of gorillas and chimpanzees, see Bérubé 1996: 24–25; McClure, Belden, and Pieper 1969; and Polani and Adinolfi 1980: 223, and the literature cited there.

14 The "fall" from paradise therefore "explains" the origin of evil in the world, including, arguably, congenital impairments. In fact, a number of other cultural cosmologies—e.g., the Japanese *Nihongi*, the Hindu myth of Prajapati, the Samoan myth of Nareau, and the southern African story of the Great Mother Goddess of creation—involve "disabilities," revealing the "very early human desire to explain congenital impairment" (Selim 2006: 1: 319).

15 Even conservative evangelical theology is increasingly engaging the issues at the interface of the religion and science dialogue, even to the extent of accepting the theory of evolution at some level. On these developments, see Yong 2007a and the essays in Miller 2003: esp. pt. 2.

16 From a more textual point of view, *ha adam* could also be understood to refer to what Dexter Callender Jr. (2000) calls "the primal human" who is seen as the intermediary between God and God's people—from Israel's point of view, the representative king, priest, and prophet. For ancient Israel, *ha adam* as the primal human falls out of proper relationship with God, others, and the world because of exercising wrong decisions related to knowing good and evil (Callender 2000: 66–70).

17 That death in Romans 5:12 refers to spiritual separation from God is pointed out by Joseph Fitzmyer (1993: 412), in connection with 5:21, which mentions "eternal life through Jesus Christ." This makes eminent sense since it is implausible to think otherwise that Adam was a historical but immortal being destined to live forever apart from his disobedience, a point that even conservative scholars will grant (e.g., Bray 2000: 6).

18 The empirical evidence for the universality of sin and solidarity of sinful humanity is undeniable. This is vividly illustrated in Michael Dorris's description (1989: 264) of his son, Adam, who suffers from fetal alcohol syndrome:

> My son will forever travel through a moonless night with only the roar of wind for company. Don't talk to him of mountains, of tropical beaches. Don't ask him to swoon at sunrises or marvel at the filter of light through leaves. He's never had time for such things, and he does not believe in them. He may pass by them close enough to touch on either side, but his hands are stretched forward, grasping for balance instead of pleasure. He doesn't

wonder where he came from, where he's going. He doesn't ask who is he, or why. Questions are such a luxury, the province of those at a distance from the periodic shock of rain. Gravity presses Adam so hard against reality that he doesn't feel the points at which he touches it. A drowning man is not separated from the lust for air by a bridge of thought—he is one with it—and my son, conceived and grown in an ethanol bath, lives each day in the act of drowning. For him there is no shore.

19 All the major commentators on this passage emphasize this point; for a succinct statement, see Stuhlmacher 1994: 82–88.

20 James D. G. Dunn reminds us that the point is not that Paul has to be right about Adam as a single individual but only that he was drawing on a common understanding of Adam available to his first-century readers and listeners. So Dunn concludes (1988: 289) that "an act in mythic history [Adam] can be paralleled to an act in living history [Christ] without the point of comparison being lost." In my view, Adam is understood historically, albeit in corporate—the first self-aware hominids— rather than individual terms, but the comparison of Christ's superlative act still holds.

21 For an overview of these theologies, see Tiessen 2000 and Robinson 2003. I discuss these views especially with regard to the doctrine of God's foreknowledge in Yong 2003b: 143–51.

22 Roy McCloughry and Wayne Morris agree that "[n]one of us is a surprise to God, or an accident or an embarrassment," but also note: "It is interesting that many non-disabled people are prepared to question God's power when a person is born or later becomes disabled but are less inclined to do so when the problem that causes nearly all disabled people to suffer—socio-economic, political and environmental exclusion—is discussed" (2002: 34, 32).

23 What this means for understanding the doctrine of healing will be discussed below in chapter 8.

24 A disability perspective would insist that Luther's catechism that said, "I believe that God has made me as I am," should apply also to all people. Perhaps the image of God is most clearly exhibited in human lowliness rather than in the success stories of the human race (see Newbigin 1981: 35–36).

25 Interestingly, the definitive history of the doctrine of the *imago Dei* or human nature has yet to be written, although most texts in systematic theology that discuss theological anthropology do survey both issues. My account relies on Anderson 1982: 215–26; Erickson 1984: vol. 2, chaps. 23–24; and Grenz 1994: chap. 6. As will be evident from

my sources, I will approach the discussion of the *imago Dei* from a Christian point of view, albeit in full recognition of the fact that the origins of the idea are to be found in the Hebrew Bible and that the Christian development of this concept, especially in the trinitarian direction that I will be advocating here, will be resisted by Jewish theologians. On this issue, I can only remind my Christian colleagues that Christian ideas are no less susceptible to retrieval, revision, and extension by theologians in other religious traditions (e.g., Islam).

26 Since this is a work of Christian theology, I do not introduce monistic theories of human nature in the traditions of Stoicism, Skinnerian behaviorism, or Marxist materialism.

27 One simple example of emergence is water from carbon and oxide, neither of which on its own has the capacities that H^2O does. To be sure, there are different emergentist anthropologies currently being explored by Christian philosophers, including theological versions such as Murphy's nonreductive physicalism (1997: chap. 10), more helpful in its robust defense of human morality as an emergent reality, but less helpful with regard to the baggage carried by physicalist models of the human person; Hasker's emergent dualism (1999), valuable for its strong link between the emergent soul and its bodily substratum, but perhaps problematic in insisting on the language of dualism rather than monism in describing the body-soul relationship; Corcoran's materialist view (2006), which insists that human persons are constituted by but not identical with their bodies, even if the materialist label may be a stumbling block; and Clayton's emergentism (2005), which is firmly rooted in evolutionary biological considerations. All these positions hold in common the idea that human minds (or souls) are dependent on the material body in some respect without lapsing into a purely naturalistic or materialistic ontology of human persons. For further discussion, see also Green and Palmer 2004; and Yong 2005c: 96–100, 2005d: 147–52.

28 As Eva Kittay, a feminist philosopher and mother of a severely disabled daughter, Sesha, puts it in conversation with her son, Leo (Sesha's brother): if our anthropologies—whether philosophical *or* theological, I would add—cannot include Sesha, "they are at best incomplete, at worst faulty. And that is not because Sesha is so different from us, or even because she is so much like us, but that at the very core, we are so much like her. We understand so much more about who we are and what moves us, when we see what moves Sesha" (Kittay and Kittay 2000: 172).

29 This point is argued by Middleton (2005: chap. 7, esp. 297) both exegetically (he notes God's primordial generosity in Genesis 1 is

such that God is a giving and gifting God who shares power non-violently with creation and its creatures, including humans) and ethically (to guard against the violent, abusive, and oppressive use of uninhibited power).

30 This painting (see the front cover) is discussed further by Stratford (1982, 1996: 7–9). David Hingsburger (1992: 49) recounts a conversation he had with a candidate for the priesthood: "I know the first time I saw a black representation of the Christ, I felt a charge through my whole spirit. It was like I was acknowledged, all of me, my blackness included. So it was important for me to know how these disabled people would respond to that question. I wondered if I could get them to see Jesus in a wheelchair or having a thick tongue and a broad neck. Wouldn't that be exciting?"

31 Others who have connected the threads between the suffering servant motif, Christology, and disability include Wilke 1980: 22–25; Greeley 1989; Govig 1989: 39; and Mitchell-Innes 1995: 3.

32 For the origins of the theology of the cross in the thinking of Luther, see McGrath 1985. See Hall 2003 and Thornton 2002 for systematic and pastoral-practical explications, respectively. Already a modern classic is Moltmann 1974, whose *theologia crucis* was formed out of his experience as a POW in World War II.

33 This is Thesis 20 of Luther's Heidelberg Disputation in May 1518; see Lull 1989: 31.

34 Others working on a theology of disability who have been drawn to a theology of the cross include Moede (1982), Schurter (2003), and Fast (2004). Feminist theologians have also retrieved the motif of the theology of the cross to engage with the question of human suffering—e.g., Solberg (1997) and Thompson (2004).

35 Paul's "kenosis hymn" (Phil 2:5-12) is central to my articulation of a disability theology of the cross; see Sanders 1971: chap. 3, and Martin 1967.

36 The following ideas are not new—see, e.g., Moltmann 1993, Polkinghorne 2001, and Power 2005: chap. 8—although I am the first, to my knowledge, to develop them vis-à-vis a theology of disability.

37 As Robert Perske notes (in Gaventa and Coulter 2003: 119–20), "It is more comfortable for a pastor [or anyone] to talk about a mentally retarded child's situation in psychological, medical, and social terminology. But, when he dares to draw theological understanding from this gutsy human situation some of his theological beliefs will be shaken." In the following, I hope to make good on the earlier promise to provide a theological anthropology in disability perspective.

38 I take the language of *imago trinitas* from Medley 2002, although the details are my own. For other trinitarian anthropologies, see Downey 2000; Grenz 2001; and McFarland 2005. One more subtly trinitarian but more overtly triadic anthropology—human beings in nature, society, and history—is Pannenberg 1985. My own work is indirectly informed by rather than directly indebted to these others.

39 Unsurprisingly, women have led the way—e.g., Moltmann-Wendel 1995, Prokes 1996, and Isherwood and Stuart 1998. But see also the work of Vagaggini 1969 and Gorringe 2002: esp. chap. 5.

40 From a Daoist perspective, the *Zhuangzu* mentions quite a diverse number of persons with deformities and suggests that the "effortlessness" of the Way molds human beings each one individually in his or her wider context so that there is a kind of naturalness to all individuals that is nevertheless not necessarily reified once-and-for-all in that "shape." M. Miles suggests (2002d: 97), "Here is a 'social model' more holistic than merely seeing disability created by environmental and attitudinal obstacles and pressures. It extends to the continuous interface of deforming and enabling aspects of each society upon each individual; yet it also reflects the possibility for the individual's response to have a powerful effect on society."

41 Edmund Santurri proposes a "thick description" of the *imago Dei* that includes "a variety of disparate properties and relations—again, human visage and general physical comportment, but also distinctively human gestures and emotional capacities (e.g., to laugh and cry), infant-parent relational attributes, moral capacities, and rational endowments—in short, all those properties and connections we tend to associate with the human way of life" (1992: 119).

42 This explains in part why "newly disabled individuals are ashamed of their aids *because they have started embodying objects as a part of themselves*," versus congenitally disabled persons who find wheelchairs and so forth liberating (Iwakuma 2002: 79). So also is it understandable that wheelchair-basketball players are quite fussy about the look, structure, and operational options of their chairs since their chairs are an extension of themselves. For a moving account of a love-hate relationship with the wheelchair—"salvation" in some respects, but "damnation" in others—see Kreigel 1998: chap. 2.

43 On the one hand, this is echoed by Siegfried Pueschel, M.D., who said after the birth of his son, Christian, "Chris taught me that an IQ score is a demeaning measure of human potential and human qualities" (2002: 154). On the other hand, of course, IQ scores are sometimes the sole factor that preserves the right to education for some disabled children.

44 The church has been especially neglectful in this area, even with regard to the nondisabled. But see an emerging literature: Colston 1978: chap. 5; Cox-Gedmark 1980: chap. 5; Raine 1982; and Vrede-veld 2001. For Jewish insights into this question, see Narot 1973.

45 I discuss these aspects of Levinas's views at greater length in Yong 2002: 188–92. I have since found Hans Reinders (2000: chap. 9) making an argument similar to Levinas's, within the framework of questions related to intellectual disability, that "moral responsibility is grounded in the fact that the life of the 'other' is given to us, which requires that we respond appropriately" (124).

46 Even in the Internet age, the meeting of minds is mediated through bodies extended by computer technologies (see p. 71).

47 The following is meant only as a modest contribution from disability perspectives to the theology of friendship; see Southard 1989; Rouner 1994; and Adeney 1995: chap. 3.

48 And this can happen also—even if it requires much more intentional engagement on the part of caregivers in their positions of authority and power—in the relationship between the professional caregiver and the "client," as William Gaventa (1993) reminds us. This is because, as Gaventa has noted in personal communication, the caregiver who befriends his or her "clients" says not "what's good for us is good for us and what's good for them is good for them," but "what's good for them is good for us." What emerges, then—consistent with our emergentist anthropology—is the realization that "something in the friendship is greater than the sum of its parts" (Gaventa 1993: 52). Gaventa's disability theology of friendship is rooted in careful dialogue with the classical and biblical traditions.

49 I am aware that some commentators understand the stranger et al. in this passage to refer to believing disciples—members of Jesus' family in general and (missionary) bearers of the gospel in particular, who in the early Christian period were often incarcerated for preaching the gospel, hence they were found in prison—and that the sheep and the goats are judged based on how they treated the followers of Christ. However, even for those who think that the "least of these" refer to believers, the fact is that the sheep and the goats are at least not making the connection between these believers and Christ who inhabits their lives: "both the just and the unjust did not know they were encountering Christ in 'the least'" (Gray 1989: 354). There is also another tradition of interpretation that emphasizes that this scene appears to be of the final judgment—it includes "all the nations" (Matt 25:32)—and that most of the "world" will never have had the opportunity to interact with Christian disciples. Finally, the intert-

estamental literature suggests the possibility of understanding these as the generally needy of the human family (see Davies and Allison 1997: 418–29; Tisera 1993: chap. 10; and Boers 1971: chap. 3). In the end, even if the "least of these" refers to believers, they would also include the marginalized, oppressed, and disabled, and my point would still hold.

50 Jürgen Trogisch, who works with severely retarded children, puts it this way (1982: 44): "In reality it's us, the non-disabled, who are in need of rehabilitation because we haven't learned to live with people like them."

51 Might this also explain, at least in part, our experience of people with Down Syndrome as more empathetic than most others? "This aptitude to act out of empathy rather than self-interest may not be a strictly biological trait, but it is mysteriously associated with having an extra twenty-first chromosome. As it happens, because our society considers keen competitiveness more valuable than empathetic helpfulness, people with Down Syndrome are considered 'deficient' because of their 'inability' to keep their eyes on the prize" (Wong 2002: 102).

52 I thank Hans Reinders (personal communication) for helping me to see this point more clearly.

Chapter 7: Renewing Ecclesiology

1 These issues are discussed at length in Erickson 1984: vol. 3, pt. 11; Grenz 1994: pt. 5; and Migliore 2004: chaps. 11–12. For an overview of various ecclesiological models, see Dulles 1974.

2 Roman Catholic theologians who have lived and worked in the global South have led the way in reflecting afresh on the meaning of the church in a post–Vatican II context; see, e.g., Bühlmann 1976; Burrows 1980; Boff 1986; and Richard 1987.

3 Although Hauerwas does not identify his vision of the church using the postliberal nomenclature, he has dialogued and collaborated with postliberal theologians from the beginning. Hauerwas himself has published only essays and sermons, so an overview of his doctrine of the church is not easily found in one place (but see esp. Hauerwas 1981, 1983, 1995a). See also Thomson 2003 for as systematic an overview of Hauerwas's ecclesiology as one is likely to find.

4 This was mentioned in a session on Hauerwas's theology of disability at the 2005 annual meeting of the American Academy of Religion by Samuel Wells, who wrote a dissertation on Hauerwas's theology. I could not, however, find this statement in Wells's book (2004). For

Hauerwas's thinking about intellectual disability, see also Hauerwas 1982, 1984, 1986, and 1995b; and Swinton 2004b.

5   See Spink 1991 for Vanier's biography. A growing secondary literature on L'Arche includes Clarke 1973; Clark 1974; Downey 1986; Mosteller 1988; Acheson 1989; Buser 1996; and Young 1997.

6   Vanier has written over twenty books thus far. The most pertinent to his theological anthropology and vision of community are Vanier 1985, 1988, 1992, 1997a, and 1998a.

7   As Vanier puts it (1997b: 12), "People with mental retardation do not find pleasure in ideas about God; their joy is in living with Jesus, feeling he is close, knowing him as friend. Their hearts are searching for love and for presence. That explains why they are open in a special way to Jesus, the Word made flesh, who is present among us, who came to reveal his friendship with each one of us." Michael Downey thus writes (1986: 70) of Vanier's anthropology of the heart: "Deep communion with God does not take place at the level of reason or intellect. Rather, as the tradition of the mystics reminds us, union with God occurs at the fundamental base and core of existence: the heart."

8   Thus the import of the third part of chapter 5 on disability in world religious context. We need to envision a Christian theology of disability at least in part in dialogue with the theologies of people in other faiths. For more on this pneumatological approach to theology of religions, see Khodr 1972; Dupuis 1977; and Yong 2003a.

9   From this, the L'Arche Charter was revised in May 1993 to read: "Communities are either of one faith or inter-religious. Those which are Christian are either of one church or inter-denominational. Each community maintains links with the appropriate religious authorities and its members are integrated with local churches and other places of worship" (Vanier 1995: 119).

10 Many residential homes for people with intellectual disabilities in the Euro-American West acknowledge what has been called "resident agenda," which means that staff members attempt to meet the spiritual and religious needs of their residents even if they do not share the same faith. Hence the possibility for interreligious encounter and experiences where staff are exposed to, even invited to participate in, the practices and worship experiences of people of other faiths.

11 The idea of an inclusive church is central to many ecclesiologies shaped by disability perspectives: e.g., Paton 1976: 61–62; Potter 1993; Browne 1997; Pierson 1998; Claydon 2004; and Fritzson and Kabue 2004; cf. also the Pastoral Statement of U.S. Catholic Bishops

on People with Disabilities, November 16, 1978, http://www.ncpd. org/pastoral_statement_1978.htm.

12 Most important for framing a theology and ecclesiology of inclusion is the biblical narrative; see, e.g., Simmons 1996; Law 2000; Clarke 2002; and Spina 2005.

13 In the context of L'Arche, all core members are weak at least in terms of their intellectual disabilities, if not also with regard to their physical condition. Of course, not all people with disabilities are weak in these senses. For this reason, unless quoting other sources, I will use the language of "weakness" (1 Cor 12:22) in quote marks in the remainder of this book to remind us that while there are some persons with disabilities who are genuinely weak in the plain senses of that term, there are other persons with disabilities who are not weak and (more importantly) do not consider themselves in terms of weakness, but are presumed to be such simply because of their impairments.

14 While it is true that "[a] society is always only as strong as its weakest member" (Moltmann 1998: 121), more strongly put, people with disabilities are not the burden but the "glue" of the Christian community (Thornburgh 1992: 5).

15 An intra-Christian ecumenical encounter mediated by disability is told by the mother of Jan de Vries, who was born with Down Syndrome in 1970 (de Vries-Kryut 1971). The decision was made not to institutionalize but to bring up Jan at home. However, starting in 1947, Jan's Dutch Reformed parents enrolled him in St. Ursula's and Jan was taught by Roman Catholic sisters because they would accept and work with his strengths and weaknesses. Jan's life served as an ecumenical bridge between Calvinists and Catholics, a major accomplishment indeed, given Protestant-Catholic relations in the 1950s.

16 This is also a challenge for other faith traditions, as seen in the life of Henry Edson, who felt that he really didn't become a man until his fiftieth birthday when he celebrated his Bar Mitzvah (Schwier 1990: 130–36).

17 These modes of engagement are discussed and defended in Hunt 1978: chap. 7; Plumlee 1981; Loaring 2000, chap. 3; and Carmeli and Carmeli 2001.

18 In fact, for the severely and profoundly disabled who can neither communicate nor feed themselves, mealtimes occupy a major portion of the daily activities and are paradoxically life-sustaining and arduously complicated simultaneously (cf. Perske et al. 1986). In these cases, then, the L'Arche community treats the entire meal with its creative interactions between assistants and core members as occasions to celebrate the life-affirming presence of God.

19 This is also the reason why music therapy has enjoyed varying degrees of success with people with disabilities. It involves "the use of music as a therapeutic tool for the restoration, maintenance, and improvement of psychological, mental, and physiological health and for the habilitation, rehabilitation, and maintenance of behavioral, developmental, physical, and social skills—all within the context of a client-therapist relationship"; in the end, "[m]usic therapy is normalizing, it is socializing, it is humanizing" (Boxill 1985: 5, 12).

20 In this regard, Younghak Hyun's essay (1985) on the crippled beggars' dance illuminates how this ritual serves as an assertion of the humanity of the poor and the oppressed (the *minjung*) in the Korean context. Hyun's suggestion "Maybe this is a revelation that compels us to recognize and respect the humanity of the underdogs instead of treating them as lower beings than the topdogs or the ordinary people" (35) applies also to the creative expressions of all who have been marginalized in whatever context.

21 An excellent overview of religious ministries and services with people with intellectual disabilities is provided by Gaventa 1986.

22 This has been and remains the tendency, especially when dealing with the intellectually disabled; see Kemp 1958; Rolfsrud 1961; Bogardus 1969; Monroe 1972; Welborn and Williams 1973; Paterson 1975; Ohsberg 1982; Estes 1984; Nabi 1985, 1988; and Bittner 1994. For an overview of the literature through the early 1980s, see Oosterveen and Cook 1983.

23 In what follows, I expand on Jürgen Moltmann's insights about "the charisma of the handicapped life" (1992: 192–93). (Thanks to my student Benjamin Robinson for reminding me of this passage.) On the one hand, I want to be cognizant of Sharon Betcher's blistering critique (2001: 346) of Moltmann's idea, which she believes both objectifies the person with disability as a "charism" of the Spirit and ignores the social justice dimensions of disability. Betcher's concerns certainly need to be heeded, and in chapter 8 I hope to provide a theological account of social justice vis-à-vis disability perspectives. On the other hand, I also want to argue here (with Moltmann) that all members of the fellowship of the Spirit are potentially vehicles for the charisms, and that this should not be exclusive of the most severely and profoundly disabled in our midst.

24 It is in this sense that I understand William Gaventa and Roger Peters (2001) to talk about how the intellectually disabled can be our spiritual guides, functioning perhaps like the desert fathers who led in solitude (communicating through means other than language) and through lives of prayer. Similarly, Kato Shōshun (1998) writes about

"dullard" Zen masters who demonstrate their enlightenment and lead by example and silence, rather than through verbal instruction.

25 See also the testimony of J. B. and Emily Murray about their son John, especially after he passed through to an agonizing death at the age of six: "[F]rom time to time we see glimpses in their being [little John's siblings] of the sacramental significance that was daily present in his, and we are grateful" (Murray and Murray 1975: 232).

26 The parents of children with intellectual disabilities are often the most sensitive to the ways in which the lives of their children resist and interrogate the oppressive structures of "normalcy." On this point, see Brent Webb-Mitchell's discussion of "the prophetic voice of parents with disabled children" (1993: chap. 5).

27 I develop some biblical aspects of this vision of hospitality in Yong 2007b. The only other persons I am aware of who have made the connection between hospitality and disability are Mary O'Connell (1988) and Ryan Parrey (2005); however, O'Connell's work is more practice-oriented while Parrey's is philosophical rather than theological. For other theologies of hospitality, see Keifert 1992; Pohl 1999; Richard 2000; and B. Byrne 2000. A relatively recent book that already has just about attained the status of a classic is Miroslav Volf's *Exclusion and Embrace: A Theological Exploration of Identity, Otherness, and Reconciliation* (1996). Although the exclusion Volf addresses is manifest in the violence of ethnic wars, his insights regarding embrace, otherness, and reconciliation are just as applicable to the exclusionary violence suffered by people with disabilities.

28 The rest of Hebrews 13:2 reads: "for by doing that some have entertained angels without knowing it." In the Orthodox tradition, John Chryssavgis (2002: 7) tells of Abba Agathon, who cared for man with cerebral palsy and served him as requested. At the end of the story, "[t]he disabled man said: 'Agathon, you are filled with divine blessings, in heaven and on earth.' Raising his eyes, Agathon saw no one at all; it was an angel of the Lord" (cf. Wilke 1980: chap. 1).

29 William Swartley (1997: 187) goes further to say of this parable that "[i]f one does not come to the feast that *now* already had been prepared in Jesus' offer, one will not be eligible to eat the bread of the coming messianic feast" (italics in original).

30 Apart from these virtues, as Alasdair MacIntyre notes (2000: 81–86), even legislation like the Americans with Disabilities Act would be beside the point.

31 The idea of "Christoform service in and to suffering" is presented by Joel Shuman (1999: 97–103) in the context of discussing how the sacraments shape the capacity of the church to care for members of Christ's body who are sick and/or dying.

32 I argue this point about the reversals of guests and hosts in Yong 2008: chap. 4.

Chapter 8: Rethinking Soteriology

1   For overviews of Protestant soteriology see Erickson 1984: vol. 3, pt. 10 (a Reformed perspective); Grenz 1994: chaps. 15–16 (an Arminian-Pietist-Baptist perspective); and Collins 1997 (a Wesleyan perspective).
2   Contemporary Arminianism is defended in Pinnock 1988 and Walls and Dongell 2004. I will return in the final chapter to say more about Orthodox perspectives on soteriology.
3   On the question of the salvation of infants, see Firey 1902; Kuiper 1942; and Geisler 2004: 433–54; on the salvation of the unevangelized, see Crockett and Sigountos 1991; Okholm and Phillips 1995; and Fackre, Nash, and Sanders 1995.
4   In this following discussion, I will use the terminology of "intellectual disability" to refer especially to the severely and profoundly retarded who demonstrate low levels of cognitive capacity.
5   Some rightly argue that "even as children of normal intelligence receive recognition as responsible persons by degrees only and not in totality, so also the mentally retarded should be treated similarly with regard to religious responsibility" (Towns and Groff 1972: 40).
6   Further, I wonder about Tzvi Marx's distinction between the redemption from Egypt and the covenant at Sinai:

> The God of Exodus welcomed the disabled in a way that the God of Sinai could not. . . . While the same God is the ground of the redemptive and covenantal experiences, the role into which man is cast is not the same in both contexts. To merit redemption, it is sufficient to have suffered. Suffering is not a stigma, but a badge of entitlement. The blind, the lame, the deaf, the mute, and the mentally disabled are exemplary instruments for the redemption by divine grace, hesed, underlying the Exodus event. The Sinai covenant, by contrast, is most appropriate to whole-bodied people. That which is irrelevant in meriting redemption—a reasonable degree of competence and understanding—is indispensable for assuming the yoke of covenant. (Marx: 2002: 244–45)

In a sense, this is a Jewish version of what in Christian thought often goes by the label of dispensational theology, a tradition with which I have decreasing affinity. Perhaps Reformed theologians might be able to map Marx's account into their own covenantal understanding of the God-world relationship, but as a Wesleyan-Pentecostal theologian, I will merely mention these possibilities and leave it to others to develop them as they may be so inspired.

7   I develop these ideas in Yong 2005a: chap. 2, in dialogue with the Wesleyan theology of salvation (e.g., Gause 1980 and Collins 1997) and Donald Gelpi's (1998) theology of conversion.

8   Forgiveness is not just a vertical affair with God but a horizontal interpersonal and intersubjective matter: "If you forgive the sins of any, they are forgiven them; if you retain the sins of any, they are retained" (John 20:23). In the case of Billy McCune—labeled retarded (a high-grade moron) in 1944 (with two periods of institutionalization for feeblemindedness); enrolled in the navy (released for ineptitude); sentenced to die for rape (of a thrice-married woman, which relationship McCune insisted was mutual), which sentence was later commuted to life imprisonment (see Lyon 1971)—salvation involved, as the opening quotation in this chapter denotes, a sense of being able to forgive those who he felt were his oppressors and adversaries. To be sure, there is the open question of due process in his case. But McCune can only be responsible for his forgiving (to the extent that he understood what the issues were, his own culpability, and the notion of forgiveness itself), not for what the criminal justice system may nor may not enact on his behalf (see also discussion on pp. 111–13 above.

9   Leonard Kriegel is another self-confessed cripple (from a polio virus at the age of eleven)—preferring that moniker over "handicapped" or "disabled"—who acknowledged, "Ask me to give up the most visible symbols of being a cripple—in my case, the braces and crutches on which I walk—and I will jump at the chance" (1991: 62–63). When compared with his autobiography written at the age of twenty-seven (Kriegel 1964), the anger felt at what polio had taken from him is now better managed, but no less palpable.

10 Specifically with regard to the medical treatment of handicapped newborns, I agree with David Smith, who writes: "[L]oyalty is what the people of God owe defective babies. We owe them respect and hope, care and comfort for their body, fair play and due process. Sometimes this will mean we have to kiss them goodbye—but never without having made them welcome, never without a hug, and never without regret" (1987: 515).

11 See also Frank 1995 and Couser 1997, both of which discuss the importance of especially autobiographical storytelling—testimonies—for the forming of personal identities and the making of meaning. My focus on people with intellectual disabilities with limited

capacities to tell their own stories leads me to emphasize the many biographical perspectives that must be combined to provide a sense of the complexity of such persons' lives.

12 The proposed translation is by R. C. H. Lenski, as cited in Dawn 2001: 37. From this, Dawn goes on to suggest that the church lives in her weaknesses by embodying the apostles' practices (fellowship, breaking of bread, prayers, economic redistribution, and worship), and through donning the armor of God (Eph 6): truth, justice, peace, salvation as liberation, and the word and prayer.

13 In a relational framework, the justification of any one is inextricably tied to the justification of others. As Jürgen Moltmann puts it (1983: 143–45), the liberation of the person with disability is also at the same time a liberation of the nondisabled.

14 As a theologian rather than an economist, I do not have any concrete economic proposals. I am drawn to Kathryn Tanner's *Economy of Grace* (2005), especially in her theological emphasis on redeeming rather than abolishing capitalism through shifting from a win/loss competitiveness to win/win noncompetitiveness in order to work toward market equilibrium of supply and demand that would result in the benefit of all. Yet her proposals have come under severe critique by economists for rehashing older Keynesian models that are no longer viable (Claar 2006). We need more theologians working together with economists on these kinds of matters.

15 In an insightful study of disability in Australia, Gerard Goggin and Christopher Newell (2005) provide a suggestive sketch of various spheres that would be impacted by a new political order inclusive of people with disabilities: health and welfare, sport, biotechnology, and citizenship. A theo-econo-politics would indeed involve the transformation of the present order as we know it.

Chapter 9: Resurrecting Down Syndrome and Disability

1 At the same time, inevitably this chapter on eschatology and bodily resurrection will be speculative, much more so than previous chapters. Hence there will also be longer quotations here than elsewhere in this volume, just so that readers get a better feel that the ideas suggested are emergent from the wider conversation rather than reflecting only my own idiosyncrasies.

2 For a comprehensive discussion, see Simon 1958. A history of Christian ideas about heaven is McDannell and Lang 1988. An overview of the recent discussion related to the resurrection is O'Collins 1978.

3   Otto does, however, say that "all defects will be taken from bodies, but the natural state of the bodies will be preserved. Now the female sex is not a defect but a natural state" (1928: 469–70).

4   Simi Linton, who sustained a spinal cord injury in an auto accident in her late teens, writes that after some thirty years she had "made a commitment— to live this life the way it was. . . . I suppose then I wasn't rejecting 'cure,' I was choosing not to participate in the quest for one" (2006: 69).

5   So, for example, Donald Kirtley's research (1975: esp. chaps. 6, 8) on blindness suggests that while it may not alter an individual's over-all personality structure, it significantly affects his or her mode of cognitive functioning and complicates his or her social relationships. In other words, blindness matters, and its experiences shape us into people we would not otherwise be apart from it.

6   Of course, things are never that simple. While most wheelchair users, for example, are grateful for the increased mobility afforded by their chairs, one study documented that over 66 percent either hated the wheelchair or were ambiguous (even resentful) about it (see O'Connor and Meakes 2001: 301).

7   Similarly, Tim Stainton (2003) argues that unlike physical disabilities or weak-identity characteristics (such as the "fourth child"), intellec-tual disability as an "identity-constituting characteristic" raises the question of prenatal testing to a whole new level since such "spoiled identities" now pertain not to an accidental feature of the fetus or to generic fetuses but intrinsically to the identity that gives those fetuses moral status (rather than, as it is assumed, renders these fetuses morally inferior). Stainton distinguishes his argument from a pro-life perspective in that his concern is not to oppose abortion in general but to argue both against the choice of terminating pregnan-cies "based on the specific identity characteristics of the fetus which are identity constituting" (2003: 537) and against testing for intellec-tual disability at all since the primary motivation for such testing is to eliminate such pregnancies. While I am sympathetic to Stainton's argument, my aim here is not to endorse his policies against prenatal testing but to call attention to how intellectual disability is a strong identity characteristic that cannot be eliminated without eliminating the person.

8   Building on Hauerwas's line of thinking, John Swinton also rejects the idea of "healing Down Syndrome" since this assumes a kind of "normality" and theory of identity that cheapens the identities of people with trisomy 21 (2001: 40, 47–48). Going further, philoso-pher Peter Byrne insists that traditional soteriology is "dangerously

delusive: namely that by some magic wave of the divine wand *this person* who is autistic or Down's or whatever can be transformed and their disability washed away" (2000: 153, italics in original).

9 From a critical disability perspective, the problem is not with the first Adam as such, but with assumptions about "his" being a perfect, complete, and finished product. Modern evolutionary biology and paleontology have thoroughly undermined such an understanding of the primordial *ha adam* (see pp. 163–64), and this process has returned us to the views of early patristic thinkers such as Irenaeus and Theophilus of Antioch who saw Eden as representing humanity at its infancy stage (see Delumeau 1995: 230–33; Towner 1984: 79–82). So rather than the heavenly body being understood as a restoration of an original ideal, the new creation is directed forward to a yet-to-be-disclosed eschatological consummation (DeVries 1994).

10 Gregory's view on this point would also be adopted by the theological tradition. By the time of the Scholastics, it had become standard: "Although all defects were repaired in rising (even the defect of babyhood or senility), the virtuous would not all shine with the same glory. Never losing its sex or size of the scars of its suffering, the body that returned was a conveyor of status and experience" (Bynum 1995: 136–37).

11 The doctrine of *epectasis* appears throughout Gregory's works, especially in his commentary on the Canticles (1987). For a succinct statement, however, see Gregory's ascetical manual "On Perfection" (in Callahan 1967). A cursory overview is provided by Jean Daniélou (in Musurillo 1961: 56–71).

12 Recall earlier that I introduced Deborah Creamer's notion of limitness as applicable also to God (p. 167). The difference is that Creamer suggests divine limitness vis-à-vis the Creation and creaturely freedom, whereas Gregory's focus is on divine infinity and unlimitedness vis-à-vis God's own being.

13 On Song of Solomon 2:13b—"Arise, my love, my fair one, and come away"—Gregory writes: "For one who has been called to rise in this way can always rise further, and one who runs to the Lord will always have wide open spaces before him. And so we must constantly rise and never cease drawing closer. As often as the bridegroom says 'Arise' and 'Come,' he gives the power to ascend to what is better" (1987: 119).

14 Gregory's eschatological aesthetics anticipates that of Jonathan Edwards much later. Edwards, the Puritan theologian, not only privileged beauty over the other transcendental concepts but also explicitly depicted spiritual formation in aesthetic terms. In his "Miscellany" on

"Happiness," Edwards spoke of an "eternal progress" in the discovery of beauty and happiness: "[H]ow happy is that love in which there is an eternal progress in all these things, wherein new beauties are continually discovered, and more and more loveliness, and in which we shall forever increase in beauty ourselves. When we shall be made capable of finding out, and giving, and shall receive more and more endearing expressions of love forever, our union will become more close and communion more intimate" (Edwards, in Townsend 1972: 195). I am grateful to F. LeRon Shults for pointing me in the direction of Edwards's *Miscellanies*.

15 Frances Young suggests (1990: 221–22) that while Gregory's vision might seem oppressive in terms of never arriving, yet

> each crest is a kind of perfection, a kind of wholeness, and the next target is only presented when you are in danger of falling back. This concept of perfection is dynamic, relational, has an inbuilt reciprocity involving receiving and achieving, and it is communal because there is a diversity of routes, a richness of different perspectives, and endless potential for creativity. The proper analogy for wholeness is not individual: it is the lover and beloved, of endless discovery and rediscovery of joy in one another. The Song of Songs . . . for people like Origen and Gregory . . . expressed the love-songs of Christ and his bride the Church, the love-songs of God and the soul he woos.

16 David Tracy (2005) hence calls for theologies of infinity (wherein novelty, surprise, inexhaustibility, and diversity are central features) to replace theologies of totality (in which closure is provided by the conventions that suit our purposes).

17 Warren Brown puts it this way: "We're all in some ways autistic in the sense that God is extending to us asymmetrically a relatedness that we only barely reciprocate. So, in that sense—in any absolute sense—our differences in abilities or capacities are not nearly as critical as the fact that God is extending to us and relating" (quoted in Holeman 2004: 211).

18 Interestingly, liberal Protestant theology in the late nineteenth century also thought about heaven in terms of "eternal motion and progress." In this view, children who died would continue to be taught by their parents (recall the emphasis on education, as in the theology of Horace Bushnell), and they would grow both "physically and spiritually" (McDannell and Lang 1988: 268, 286). There would be rest in terms of freedom from strain and fatigue, and so on, but there would be plenty of activity too: "Work was worship and celestial progress

was God's eternal gift" (287). The difference, however, is Gregory's steadfast *theological* rather than anthropological focus: dynamic eschatology is about the soul's journey to God rather than merely about the soul.

19 An unknown sixteenth-century Flemish artist had just such an intuition in his portrayal of an angel with the phenotypical features of Down Syndrome (see Levitas and Reid 2003; cf. http://www.metmuseum.org/Works_Of_Art/viewOne.asp?dep=11&viewMode=1&item=1982.60.22); in this case, the claim that Down Syndrome is identifiable in the resurrected body is but an extension of the Matthean idea that humans "neither marry nor are given in marriage, but are like angels in heaven" (Matt 22:30).

20 Put less speculatively, Roy McCloughry and Wayne Morris suggest (2002: 73), "Perhaps she will exhibit the characteristics of Down's syndrome but, like the scars of Jesus, these will have a different significance in heaven. Perhaps not. . . . Presumably also, the heavenly city will be a fully accessible environment."

21 I am unsure what to think about the traditional doctrine of the "intermediate state" given my commitments to an emergentist anthropology. If human beings are constituted by (even if irreducible to) their bodies, then there can be no proper human "existence" after death and prior to the resurrection of those bodies. However, the biblical data can be read in a way that does not necessarily demand a dualistic construal of the relationship between the human soul and body. Even the appearance of Samuel to the medium of Endor can be understood as made possible by a resuscitation theory (see Arnold 2004). Clearly, while much more work needs to be done in this area, at the very least it can be said that an emergentist anthropology takes the resurrection of the body as constitutive of human personhood and identity in the afterlife much more seriously than any dualistic view can.

22 For an overview, see Sachs 1993 and Armstrong 2003: chap. 7. Historical perspectives are provided by Schouppe 1973 and Le Goff 1984. Note also that Anglicans such as C. S. Lewis (1964: 107–11) have been open to the doctrine of purgatory.

23 Nahman was a great grandson of Rabbi Israel ben Eliezer, more famously known as Baal Shem Tov (Master of the Good Name), the recognized "founder" of the eighteenth-century Jewish Hasidic movement in what is now Ukraine. Nahman published two volumes of Torah discourses/homilies and, posthumously, thirteen tales, *Sippurei Ma`asiyot*, which conclude with the story we are focusing on here. Shaul Magid (2002), on whose essay I depend in what follows, argues that this last tale is the culmination of Nahman's theology and

anthropology of exile and redemption and represents his last will and testament.

24 Richard Fenn (1995) documents the impact of eschatological ideas on how we organize our lives in his study of the transformation of the idea of purgatory in the early modern period. Whereas the traditional doctrine emphasized the purging of human souls after death, Protestant Puritanism focused instead on the need for disciplined suffering in order to redeem, make up for, and buy back lost time in the present life. Repentance, penance, and purgation now should occur on a daily basis, instead of happening to us later on. In this way, rather than rejecting purgatory, the English Protestants redefined it, and did so in ways that made a very palpable difference for Christian practices in the present age.

25 By extension, of course, can we imagine with Mark (see introductory quotation to this chapter) that there will be Nintendo in heaven? This is not an idle question of speculative theology. Rather, as Robert Cummings Neville (1996: ix, 270–71) shows in his discussion, inspired by C. S. Lewis, about whether or not there will be cigars in heaven, the power of Christian symbols are such that properly understood "in broken innocence" they mediate creation's finiteness to divine infinitude (or immanence to transcendence, or the historical present to the eschatological future). The more powerful the symbol, the more it speaks to us about both existential salvation and eschatological plenitude.

Abbreviations

AJMR	*American Journal on Mental Retardation*
DHS	*Disability, Handicap and Society*
DS	*Disability and Society*
DSQ	*Disability Studies Quarterly*
ETDD	*Education and Training in Developmental Disabilities*
ETMR	*Education and Training in Mental Retardation*
ETMRDD	*Education and Training in Mental Retardation and Developmental Disabilities*
Impact	*Impact*: Published by the Institute on Community Integration (UCEDD), available at http://ici.umn.edu/products/newsletters.html
IRRMR	*International Review of Research in Mental Retardation*
JARID	*Journal of Applied Research in Intellectual Disabilities*
JDPS	*Journal of Disability Policy Studies*
JIDD	*Journal of Intellectual and Developmental Disability*
JIDR	*Journal of Intellectual Disability Research*
JRDH	*Journal of Religion, Disability & Health*

JRH   *Journal of Religion and Health*

MR   *Mental Retardation*

MRDD   *Mental Retardation and Developmental Disabilities*

MRDDDB   *Mental Retardation/Developmental Disability Data Brief*

MRDDRR   *Mental Retardation and Developmental Disabilities Research Reviews*

RE   *Rehabilitation Education*

References

Abraham, William J. 2005. "Inclusivism, Idolatry, and the Survival of the (Fittest) Faithful." In Mark Husbands and Daniel J. Treier, eds., *The Community of the Word: Toward an Evangelical Ecclesiology*, 131–45. Downers Grove: InterVarsity.

Abrams, Judith Z. 1998. *Judaism and Disability: Portrayals in Ancient Texts from the Tanach through the Bavli*. Washington, D.C.: Gallaudet University Press.

Abu-Habib, Lina. 1997. *Gender and Disability: Women's Experiences in the Middle East*. London: Oxfam.

Accardo, Pasquale J., and Arnold J. Capute. 1998. "Mental Retardations." *MRDDRR* 4:2–5.

Acheson, Jean. 1989. *Portraits of Healing, Prayers of Wholeness*. Notre Dame, Ind.: Ave Maria Press.

Acton, Norman. 1983. "World Disability: The Need for a New Approach." In Oliver Shirley, ed., *A Cry for Health: Poverty and Disability in the Third World*, 79–85. Frome, U.K.: Third World Group for Disabled People and Appropriate Health Resources and Technologies Action Group.

Adams, Maurianne, Warren J. Blumenfeld, Rosie Castañeda, Heather W. Hackman, Madeline L. Peters, and Ximena Zúñiga, eds. 2000. *Readings for Diversity and Social Justice*. New York: Routledge.

Adeney, Bernard T. 1995. *Strange Virtues: Ethics in a Multicultural World*. Downers Grove: InterVarsity.

Albrecht, Gary L. 1992. *The Disability Business: Rehabilitation in America*. Sage Library of Social Research 190. Newbury Park, Calif.: Sage.

341

Alexander, Duane. 1998. "Prevention of Mental Retardation: Four Decades of Research." *MRDDRR* 4:50–58.

Al-Jibālī, Muhammad. 1998. *Sickness: Regulations and Exhortations.* Arlington, Tex.: Al-Kitab and as-Sunnah Publishing.

Allchin, A. M. 1997. "The Sacraments in L'Arche." In Frances M. Young, ed., *Encounter with Mystery: Reflections on L'Arche and Living with Disability,* 101–18. London: Darton, Longman and Todd.

Allen, David F., and Victoria S. Allen. 1979. *Ethical Issues in Mental Retardation.* Nashville: Abingdon.

Allen, John D. 2003. *Gay, Lesbian, Bisexual, and Transgender People with Developmental Disabilities and Mental Retardation: Stories of the Rainbow Support Group.* New York: Harrington Park Press.

Altman, Reuben, and Yung-Chang Li. 1997. "Comparison of Special Education Legislative Mandates in the United States, China, and Taiwan." *ETMRDD* 32(2): 154–62.

Altmann, Walter. 1992. *Luther and Liberation: A Latin American Perspective.* Trans. Mary M. Solberg. Minneapolis: Fortress.

Alvin, Juliette. 1976. *Music for the Handicapped Child.* 2nd ed. London: Oxford University Press.

American Association on Mental Retardation (AAMR). 1992. *Mental Retardation: Definition, Classification, and Systems of Supports.* 9th ed. Washington, D.C.: AAMR.

Anderson, Carolyn Anne. 2005. "Real and Ideal Spaces of Disability in American Stadiums and Arenas." In Shelley Tremain, ed., *Foucault and the Government of Disability,* 245–60. Ann Arbor: University of Michigan Press.

Anderson, David W. 2006. "Inclusion and Interdependence: Students with Special Needs in the Regular Classroom." *Journal of Education and Christian Belief* 10(1): 43–69.

Anderson, Ray S. 1982. *On Being Human: Essays in Theological Anthropology.* Grand Rapids: Eerdmans.

Angrosino, Michael V. 1998. "Mental Disability in the United States: An Interactionist Perspective." In Richard Jenkins, ed., *Questions of Competence: Culture, Classification, and Intellectual Disability,* 25–53. Cambridge: Cambridge University Press.

Aquinas, Thomas. 1941. *The Summa Theologica.* 2 vols. Rev. Daniel J. Sullivan. Chicago: Encyclopaedia Britannica, Inc.

Aristotle. 1943. *Generation of Animals.* Trans. A. Peck. Cambridge: Harvard University Press.

Arnold, Bill T. 2004. "Soul-Searching Questions about 1 Samuel 28: Samuel's Appearance at Endor and Christian Anthropology." In Joel B. Green, ed., *What about the Soul? Neuroscience and Christian Anthropology*, 75–83. Nashville: Abingdon.

Armstrong, David. 2003. *A Biblical Defense of Catholicism*. Manchester, N.H.: Sophia Institute.

Armstrong, Felicity, and Len Barton, eds. 1999. *Disability, Human Rights, and Education: Cross-cultural Perspectives*. Buckingham, U.K.: Open University Press.

Asch, Adrienne. 1989. "Reproductive Technology and Disability." In Sherrill Cohen and Nadine Taub, eds., *Reproductive Laws for the 1990s*, 69–117. Clifton, N.J.: Human Press.

———. 2003. "Disability Equality and Prenatal Testing: Contradictory or Compatible?" *Florida State University Law Review* 30:315–42.

Asch, Adrienne, and Michelle Fine. 1988. "Shared Dreams: A Left Perspective on Disability Rights and Reproductive Rights." In Michelle Fine and Adrienne Asch, eds., *Women with Disabilities: Essays in Psychology, Culture, and Politics*, 297–305. Philadelphia: Temple University Press.

Asch, Adrienne, Lawrence O. Gostin, and Diann M. Johnson. 2003. "Respecting Persons with Disabilities and Preventing Disability: Is There a Conflict?" In Stanley S. Herr, Lawrence O. Gostin, and Harold Hongju Koh, eds., *The Human Rights of Persons with Intellectual Disabilities: Different but Equal*, 319–46. Oxford: Oxford University Press.

Asch, Adrienne, and David Wasserman. 2005. "Where Is the Sin in Synecdoche." In David Wasserman, Jerome Bickenbach, and Robert Wachbroit, eds., *Quality of Life and Human Difference: Genetic Testing, Health Care, and Disability*, 172–216. Cambridge: Cambridge University Press.

Astor, Carl. 1985. *Who Makes People Different: Jewish Perspectives on the Disabled*. Ed. Stephen Garfinkel. New York: United Synagogue of America.

Atkinson, Dorothy. 1997. *An Auto/Biographical Approach to Learning Disability Research*. Aldershot, U.K.: Ashgate.

———. 2000. "Bringing Lives into Focus: The Disabled Person's Perspective." In David May, ed., *Transition and Change in the Lives of People with Intellectual Disabilities*, 157–75. Research Highlights in Social Work 38. London: Jessica Kingsley.

Atkinson, Dorothy, Mark Jackson, Lindsay Brigham, Sheena Rolph, and Jan Walmsley, eds. 2000. *Crossing Boundaries: Change and Continuity in the History of Learning Disability.* Kidderminster: British Institute of Learning Disabilities.

Atkinson, Dorothy, Mark Jackson, and Jan Walmsley, eds. 1997. *Forgotten Lives: Exploring the History of Learning Disability.* Kidderminster: British Institute of Learning Disabilities.

Augustine. 1994a. *The City of God.* Ed. Marcus Dods. American Edition of the Nicene and Post-Nicene Fathers, first series, vol. 2. Peabody, Mass.: Hendrickson.

———. 1994b. *The Enchiridion.* Ed. Philip Schaff. American Edition of the Nicene and Post-Nicene Fathers, first series, vol. 3. Peabody, Mass.: Hendrickson.

———. 1994c. *Anti-Pelagian Works.* Ed. Peter Holmes and Robert Ernest Wallis. American Edition of the Nicene and Post-Nicene Fathers, first series, vol. 5. Peabody, Mass.: Hendrickson.

Avalos, Hector. 1995. *Illness and Health Care in the Ancient Near East: The Role of the Temple in Greece, Mesopotamia, and Israel.* Harvard Semitic Monographs 54. Atlanta: Scholars Press.

B., David. 2005. *Epileptic.* New York: Pantheon Books.

Bacon, Richard. 1993. *Revealed to Babes: Children in the Worship of God.* Audubon, N.J.: Old Paths Publications.

Bakely, Donald C. 1997. *Bethy and the Mouse: A Father Remembers His Children with Disabilities.* Cambridge, Mass.: Brookline Books. Repr. from Newton, Kans.: Faith and Life Press, 1985.

———. 2002. *Down Syndrome, One Family's Journey: Beth Exceeds Expectations.* Cambridge, Mass.: Brookline Books.

Banks, Martha E., and Ellen Kaschak, eds. 2003. *Women with Visible and Invisible Disabilities: Multiple Intersections, Multiple Issues, Multiple Therapies.* New York: Haworth.

Barnartt, Sharon, and Richard Scotch. 2001. *Disability Protests: Contentious Politics, 1970–1999.* Washington, D.C.: Gallaudet University Press.

Barnes, Colin. 1990. *"Cabbage Syndrome": The Social Construction of Dependence.* New York: Falmer.

———. 1992. *Disability Imagery and the Media: An Exploration of the Principles for Media Representations of Disabled People.* Krumlin: British Council of Organisations of Disabled People, and Ryburn Publishing.

Barnes, Colin, Geoff Mercer, and Tom Shakespeare. 1999. *Exploring Disability: A Sociological Introduction*. Malden, Mass.: Polity Press.

Barr, Martin W. 1904. *Mental Defectives: Their History, Treatment, and Training*. Philadelphia: P. Blakiston's Son.

Barth. Karl. 1958. *Church Dogmatics*, vol. 3, pt. 1. Ed. G. W. Bromiley and T. F. Torrance. London: T&T Clark.

———. 1960. *Church Dogmatics*, vol. 3, pt. 2. Ed. G. W. Bromiley and T. F. Torrance. London: T&T Clark.

Bartley, Paula. 2000. *Prostitution: Prevention and Reform in England, 1860–1914*. London: Routledge.

Barton, Len, ed. 1988. *The Politics of Special Educational Needs*. Disability, Handicap, and Life Chances 4. London: Falmer.

Bass, Medora S. 1978. "Surgical Contraception: A Key to Normalization and Prevention." *MR* 16 (6): 399–404.

Batavia, Andrew I. 2001. "The New Paternalism: Portraying People with Disabilities as an Oppressed Minority." *JDPS* 12(2): 107–13.

———. 2004. "Disability and Physician-Assisted Suicide." In Timothy E. Quill and Margaret P. Battin, eds, *Physician-Assisted Dying: The Case for Palliative Care and Patient Choice*, 55–74. Baltimore: The Johns Hopkins University Press.

Baynton, Douglas. 1997. "A Silent Exile on This Earth: The Metaphoric Construction of Deafness in the Nineteenth Century." In Lennard J. Davis, ed., *The Disability Studies Reader*, 128–50. New York: Routledge.

Bazna, Maysaa S., and Tarek A. Hatab. 2005. "Disability in the Qur'an: The Islamic Alternative to Defining, Viewing, and Relating to Disability." *JRDH* 9(1): 5–27.

Beal, Timothy K. 2002. *Religion and Its Monsters*. New York: Routledge.

Beasley-Murray, George R. 1999. *John*. Word Biblical Commentary 36. Nashville: Thomas Nelson.

Beck, Martha N. 1999. *Expecting Adam: A True Story of Birth, Rebirth, and Everyday Magic*. New York: Times Books.

Becker, Laurence, Takashi Mito, Sachio Takashima, and Kazukiyo Onodera. 1991. "Growth and Development of the Brain in Down Syndrome." In Charles J. Epstein, ed., *The Morphogenesis of Down Syndrome: Proceedings of the National Down Syndrome Society Conference on Morphogenesis and Down Syndrome, held in New York,*

January 17 and 18, 1991, 133–52. Progress in Clinical Biological Research 373. New York: Wiley-Liss. ·

Beise, Angela. 2005. "A More Perfect Society: Why I Wouldn't Want to Live There." *Christianity Today* 49(7): 49.

Bellenir, Karen, ed. 1996. *Genetic Disorders Sourcebook.* Detroit: Omnigraphics.

Benjamin, Adam. 2002. *Making an Entrance: Theory and Practice for Disabled and Non-Disabled Dancers.* London: Routledge.

Benton, Janice LaLonde, ed. 1995. *A Loving Justice.* Washington, D.C.: National Catholic Office for Persons with Disabilities.

Berg, J. M., H. Karlinsky, and A. J. Holland. 1993. *Alzheimer Disease, Down Syndrome, and Their Relationship.* New York: Oxford University Press.

Bergant, Dianne. 1994. "'Come, Let Us Go Up to the Mountain of the Lord' (Isa 2:3): Biblical Reflections on the Question of Sacramental Access." In Edward Foley, ed., *Developmental Disabilities and Sacramental Access: New Paradigms for Sacramental Encounters,* 13–32. Collegeville, Minn.: Liturgical Press.

Berkson, Gershon. 2004. "Intellectual and Physical Disabilities in Prehistory and Early Civilization." *MR* 42(3): 195–208.

———. 2006. "Mental Retardation in Western Civilization from Ancient Rome to the Prerogativa Regis." *MR* 44(1): 28–40.

Bernardin, Joseph. 1985. *Access to the Sacraments of Initiation and Reconciliation for Developmentally Disabled Persons: Pastoral Guidelines for the Archdiocese of Chicago.* Chicago: Liturgy Training Publications.

Bérubé, Michael. 1996. *Life as We Know It: A Father, a Family, and an Exceptional Child.* New York: Vintage Books.

Betcher, Sharon. 2000. "Wisdom to Make the World Go On: On Disability and the Cultural Delegitimation of Suffering." In Terence E. Fretheim and Curtis L. Thompson, eds., *God, Evil, and Suffering: Essays in Honor of Paul R. Sponheim,* 87–98. St. Paul: Luther Seminary.

———. 2001. "Rehabilitating Religious Discourse: Bringing Disability Studies to the Theological Venue." *Religious Studies Review* 27(4): 341–48.

———. 2004. "Monstrosities, Miracles, and Mission: Religion and the Politics of Disablement." In Catherine Keller, Michael Nausner, and Mayra Rivera, eds., *Postcolonial Theologies: Divinity and Empire,* 79–99. St. Louis: Chalice.

Betenbaugh, Helen R. 2000. "Disability: A Lived Theology." *Theology Today* 57(2): 203–10.

Betenbaugh, Helen, and Marjorie Procter-Smith. 1998. "Disabling the Lie: Prayers of Truth and Transformation." In Nancy L. Eiesland and Don E. Saliers, eds., *Human Disability and the Service of God: Reassessing Religious Practice*, 281–303. Nashville: Abingdon.

Bijou, Sidney W. 1985. "The Naturalistic View of the Mentally Retarded Person." In *Asian Federation for the Mentally Retarded, Growing in Wisdom: The Mentally Retarded Person in Asia— Proceedings of the 7th Asian Conference on Mental Retardation, Taipei, Republic of China, November 10–15, 1985*, 51–60. Taipei: AFMR.

Bissonnier, Henri. 1962. *Catechetical Pedagogy of the Mentally Deficient Children*. Trans. Mary V. Ouellet. Brussels: International Centre for Studies in Religious Education.

———. 1979. *The Pedagogy of Resurrection: The Christian Formation of the Handicapped*. Trans. Carolyn Frederick. New York: Paulist.

Bittner, Robert. 1994. *Under His Wings: Meeting the Spiritual Needs of the Mentally Disabled*. Wheaton, Ill.: Crossway Books.

Black, Kathy. 1996. *A Healing Homiletic: Preaching and Disability*. Nashville: Abingdon.

———. 1998. "A Perspective of the Disabled: Images of God, Interdependence, and Healing." In Christine Marie Smith, ed., *Preaching Justice: Ethnic and Cultural Perspectives*, 6–25. Cleveland, Ohio: United Church Press.

Blatt, Burton. 1987. *The Conquest of Mental Retardation*. Austin: Pro-Ed.

Blatt, Burton, and Fred Kaplan. 1974. *Christmas in Purgatory: A Photographic Essay on Mental Retardation*. Syracuse: Human Policy Press. (Originally published in 1966).

Blatt, Burton, Andrejs Ozolins, and Joe McNally. 1979. *The Family Papers: A Return to Purgatory*. New York: Longman.

Blau, Joel. 1916. "The Defective in Jewish Law and Literature." In *Jewish Eugenics and Other Essays: Three Papers Read before the New York Board of Jewish Ministers 1915*, 21–50. New York: Bloch.

Blocher, Henri. 1999. *Original Sin: Illuminating the Riddle*. Grand Rapids: Eerdmans.

Block, Jennie Weiss. 2000. *Copious Hosting: A Theology of Access for People with Disabilities*. New York: Continuum.

Block, Martin E., and M. Sherril Moon. 1992. "Orelove, Wehman, and Wood Revisited: An Evaluative Review of Special Olympics Ten Years Later." *ETMR* 27(4): 379–87.

Blumenthal, David R. 1993. *Facing the Abusing God: A Theology of Protest.* Louisville: Westminster John Knox.

Boers, Hendrikus. 1971. *Theology Out of the Ghetto: A New Testament Exegetical Study Concerning Religious Exclusiveness.* Leiden: E. J. Brill.

Boff, Leonardo. 1986. *Ecclesiogenesis: The Base Communities Reinvent the Church.* Trans. Robert R. Barr. Maryknoll: Orbis.

Bogardus, LaDonna. 1969. *Christian Education for Retarded Children.* Rev. ed. Nashville: Abingdon.

Bogdan, Robert. 1988. *Freak Show: Presenting Human Oddities for Amusement and Profile.* Chicago: University of Chicago Press.

———. 1992. "A 'Simple' Farmer Accused of Murder: Community Acceptance and the Meaning of Deviance." *DHS* 7(4): 303–20.

Bogdan, Robert, and Steven J. Taylor. 1992. "The Social Construction of Humanness: Relationships with Severely Disabled People." In Philip Ferguson, Dianne Ferguson, and Steven Taylor, eds., *Interpreting Disability: A Qualitative Reader*, 275–94. New York: Teachers College Press.

———. 1994. *The Social Meaning of Mental Retardation: Two Life Stories—a Reissued Edition of "Inside Out" with a New Postscript.* New York: Teachers College Press.

Bolduc, Kathleen Deyer. 1999. *His Name Is Joel: Searching for God in a Son's Disability.* Louisville: Bridge Resources.

Bonting, Sjoerd L. 2005. *Creation and Double Chaos: Science and Theology in Discussion.* Minneapolis: Fortress.

Borsay, Anne. 2005. *Disability and Social Policy in Britain since 1750: A History of Exclusion.* New York: Palgrave Macmillan.

Bosk, Charles L. 1992. *All God's Mistakes: Genetic Counseling in a Pediatric Hospital.* Chicago: University of Chicago Press.

Bowe, Frank. 1980. *Rehabilitating America: Toward Independence for Disabled and Elderly People.* New York: Harper & Row.

———. 1981. *Comeback: Six Remarkable People Who Triumphed over Disability.* New York: Harper & Row.

———. 2000. *Universal Design in Education: Teaching Nontraditional Students.* Westport, Conn.: Bergin & Garvey.

Bowers, Faith, ed. 1985. *Let Love Be Genuine: Mental Handicap and the Church.* London: Baptist Union.

————. 1988. *Who's This Sitting in My Pew? Mentally Handicapped People in the Church.* London: Triangle.

Boxill, Edith Hillman. 1985. *Music Therapy for the Developmentally Disabled.* Rockville, Md.: Aspen.

Boyce, William, and Seddiq Weera. 1999. "Issues of Disability Assessment in War Zones." In Brigitte Holzer, Arthur Vreede, and Gabriele Weigt, eds., *Disability in Different Cultures: Reflections on Local Concepts,* 332–42. New Brunswick, N.J.: Transaction Publishers.

Boyd, Gregory A. 2003. *Is God to Blame? Moving Beyond Pat Answers to the Problem of Evil.* Downers Grove: InterVarsity.

Boyd, Rosangela. 1997. "Older Adults with Developmental Disabilities: A Brief Examination of Current Knowledge." In Ted Tedrick, ed., *Older Adults with Developmental Disabilities and Leisure: Issues, Policy, and Practice,* 7–27. New York: Haworth.

Braidotti, Rosi. 1999. "Signs of Wonder and Traces of Doubt: On Teratology and Embodied Differences." In Margrit Shildrick and Janet Price, eds., *Feminist Theory and the Body: A Reader,* 290–301. New York: Routledge.

Brandt, Edward N., Jr., and Andrew M. Pope, eds. 1997. *Enabling America: Assessing the Role of Rehabilitation Science and Engineering.* Washington, D.C.: National Academy Press.

Bray, Gerald. 2000. "Adam and Christ (Romans 5:12-21)." *Evangel* 18(1): 4–8.

Brechin, Ann, Penny Liddiard, and John Swain, eds. 1981. *Handicap in a Social World: A Reader.* Sevenoaks, Kent: Hodder & Stoughton.

Bredberg, Elizabeth. 1999. "Writing Disability History: Problems, Perspectives, and Sources." *DS* 14(2): 189–201.

Brett, Jane. 2002. "The Experience of Disability from the Perspective of Parents of Children with Profound Impairment: Is It Time for an Alternative Model of Disability?" *DS* 17(7): 825–43.

Brockley, Janice A. 2001. "Martyred Mothers and Merciful Fathers: Exploring Disability and Motherhood in the Lives of Jerome Greenfield and Raymond Repouille." In Paul K. Longmore and Lauri Umansky, eds., *The New Disability History: American Perspectives,* 293–312. New York: New York University Press.

Brodeur, Scott. 1996. *The Holy Spirit's Agency in the Resurrection of the Dead: An Exegetico-Theological Study of 1 Corinthians 15, 44b-49 and Romans 8, 9-13.* Rome: Gregorian University Press.

Brown, Steven E. 2000. *A Celebration of Diversity: An Annotated Bibliography about Disability Culture*. Las Cruces, N.Mex.: Institute on Disability Culture.

Browne, Elizabeth J. 1997. *The Disabled Disciple: Ministering in a Church without Barriers*. Liguori, Mo.: Liguori Publications.

Browne, Susan E., Debra Connors, and Nanci Stern, eds. 1985. *With the Power of Each Breath: A Disabled Women's Anthology*. Pittsburgh: Cleis Press.

Bryan, Willie V. 1996. *In Search of Freedom: How Persons with Disabilities Have Been Disenfranchised from the Mainstream of American Society*. Springfield, Ill.: Charles C. Thomas.

Buchanan, Allen, Dan W. Brock, Norman Daniels, and Daniel Wikler. 2000. *From Chance to Choice: Genetics and Justice*. Cambridge: Cambridge University Press.

Buck, Pearl S. 1950. *The Child Who Never Grew*. New York: J. Day Co.

Buckley, James J. and David S. Yeago, eds. 2001. *Knowing the Triune God: The Work of the Spirit in the Practices of the Church*. Grand Rapids: Eerdmans.

Bühlmann, Walbert. 1976. *The Coming of the Third Church*. Trans. Ralph Woodhall and A. N. Other. Maryknoll: Orbis.

Burch, Susan. 2001. "Reading between the Signs: Defending Deaf Culture in Early Twentieth-century America." In Paul K. Longmore and Lauri Umansky, eds., *The New Disability History: American Perspectives*, 214–35. New York: New York University Press.

Burke, Chris, and Jo Beth McDaniel. 1991. *A Special Kind of Hero: Chris Burke's Own Story*. New York: Doubleday.

Burrows, William R. 1980. *New Ministries in Global Context*. Maryknoll: Orbis.

Buser, Christella. 1996. *Flowers from the Ark: True Stories from the Homes of L'Arche*. New York: Paulist.

Butler, Ruth, and Hester Parr, eds. 1999. *Mind and Body Spaces: Geographies of Illness, Impairment, and Disability*. London: Routledge.

Bynum, Caroline Walker. 1995. *The Resurrection of the Body in Western Christianity, 200–1336*. Lectures on the History of Religions 15. New York: Columbia University Press.

Byrne, Brendan. 2000. *The Hospitality of God: A Reading of Luke's Gospel*. Collegeville, Minn.: Liturgical Press.

Byrne, Peter. 2000. *Philosophical and Ethical Problems in Mental Handicap*. New York: St. Martin's.

Byrnes, Lynette. 1999. "People with an Intellectual Disability in the Criminal Justice Systems." In Melinda Jones and Lee Ann Basser Marks, eds., *Disability, Divers-Ability and Legal Change*, 313–26. International Studies in Human Rights 56. The Hague: Martinus Nijhoff Publishers.

Cairo, Shelly, with Jasmine Cairo and Tara Cairo. 1985. *Our Brother Has Down's Syndrome*. Toronto: Annick Press.

Calder, Andy. 2004. "'God Has Chosen This for You'—'Really?': A Pastoral and Theological Appraisal of This and Some Other Well-Known Clichés Used in Australia to Support People with Disability." *JRDH* 8(1–2): 5–19.

Callahan, John. 1989. *Don't Worry, He Won't Get Far on Foot: The Autobiography of a Dangerous Man*. New York: William Morrow.

Callahan, Virginia Woods, trans. 1967. *Saint Gregory of Nyssa: Ascetical Works*. Fathers of the Church 58. Washington, D.C.: Catholic University of America Press.

Callender, Dexter E., Jr. 2000. *Adam in Myth and History: Ancient Israelite Perspectives on the Primal Human*. Harvard Semitic Studies 48. Winona Lake, Ind.: Eisenbrauns.

Calnen, Terrence, and Leonard S. Blackman. 1992. "Capital Punishment and Offenders with Mental Retardation: Response to the Penry Brief." *AJMR* 96(6): 557–64.

Calvin, John. 1960. *Institutes of the Christian Religion*. Ed. John T. McNeill. Trans. Ford Lewis Battles. Philadelphia: Westminster Press.

Cameron, Lindsley. 1998. *The Music of Light: The Extraordinary Story of Hikari and Kenzaburo Oe*. New York: Free Press.

Campling, Jo, ed. 1981. *Images of Ourselves: Women with Disabilities Talking*. London: Routledge & Kegan Paul.

Canda, Edward R. 2001. "Transcending through Disability and Death: Transpersonal Themes in Living with Cystic Fibrosis." In Edward R. Canda and Elizabeth D. Smith, eds., *Transpersonal Perspectives on Spirituality in Social Work*, 109–34. New York: Haworth Pastoral.

Capone, George T. 2002. "Down Syndrome and Autistic Spectrum Disorders." In William I. Cohen, Lynn Nadel, and Myra E. Madnick, eds., *Down Syndrome: Visions for the 21st Century*, 327–36. New York: Wiley-Liss.

Carabello, Bernard J., and Joanne F. Siegel. 1996. "Self-Advocacy at the Crossroads." In Gunnar Dybwad and Hank Bersani Jr., eds.,

New Voices: Self-Advocacy by People with Disabilities, 237–39. Cambridge, Mass.: Brookline Books.

Carder, Stan. 1995. *A Committed Mercy: You and Your Church Can Serve the Disabled*. Grand Rapids: Baker Books.

Carey, Allison C. 2003. "Beyond the Medical Model: A Reconsideration of 'Feeblemindedness,' Citizenship, and Eugenic Restrictions." *DS* 18(4): 411–30.

Carey, W. Gregory. 1995. "Excuses, Excuses: The Parable of the Banquet (Luke 14:15-24) within the Larger Context of Luke." *Irish Biblical Studies* 17:177–87.

Carlson, Licia. 2001. "Cognitive Ableism and Disability Studies: Feminist Reflections on the History of Mental Retardation." *Hypatia* 16(4): 124–46.

———. 2003. "Rethinking Normalcy, Normalization, and Cognitive Disability." In Robert Figueroa and Sandra Harding, eds., *Science and Other Cultures: Issues in Philosophies of Science and Technology*, 154–71. New York: Routledge.

Carmeli, Varda, and Eli Carmeli. 2001. "Teaching Jewish Mentally-Retarded Youngsters Holiday Awareness Through Symbols." In William C. Gaventa Jr. and David L. Coulter, eds., *Spirituality and Intellectual Disability: International Perspectives on the Effect of Culture and Religion on Healing Body, Mind, and Soul*, 123–39. New York: Haworth Pastoral.

Carr, Janet. 1995. *Down's Syndrome: Children Growing Up*. Cambridge: Cambridge University Press.

Carroll, Vincent Wayne. 1981. "Theology and Leisure: Implications for the Handicapped." D.Min. thesis, School of Theology at Claremont, 1977. Ann Arbor: University Microfilms International.

Castro-Ponce, Clara. 2003. "*Imitatio Christi* in the Writings of Teresa de Cartagena." *Magistra: A Journal of Women's Spirituality in History* 9(2): 55–65.

Catechism of the Catholic Church. 1995. New York: Image.

Catherine of Genoa. 1979. *Purgation and Purgatory*. Trans. Serge Hughes. New York: Paulist.

Cavallin, Hans Clemens Caesarius. 1974. *Life after Death: Paul's Argument for the Resurrection of the Dead in I Cor 15—Part I; An Enquiry into the Jewish Background*. Lund, Sweden: CWK Gleerup.

Celeste, Richard F. 1992. "Commentary on 'Capital Punishment and Offenders with Mental Retardation.'" *AJMR* 96(6): 565–66.

Ceresko, Anthony R. 2001. "The Identity of 'the Blind and the Lame' (*'iwwēr ûpissēaḥ*) in 2 Samuel 5:8b." *Catholic Biblical Quarterly* 63(1): 23–30.

Chamberlain, Marisha, ed. 1976. *Shout, Applaud: Poems from NorHaven.* St. Paul: COMPAS (Community Programs in the Arts and Sciences).

Chand, Indeera. 1997. *Climb Every Mountain: Radhika's Story.* New Delhi: HarperCollins.

Chapman, Robin S. 1997. "Language Development." In Siegfried M. Pueschel and Maria Sustrová, eds., *Adolescents with Down Syndrome: Toward a More Fulfilling Life*, 99–110. Baltimore: Paul H. Brookes.

———. 2003. "Language and Communication in Individuals with Down Syndrome." In Leonard Abbeduto, ed., *Language and Communication in Mental Retardation*, 1–34. International Review of Research in Mental Retardation 27. Boston: Academic Press.

Charlton, James I. 1998. *Nothing about Us without Us: Disability, Oppression, and Empowerment.* Berkeley and Los Angeles: University of California Press.

Cheatham, Susan Klug, J. David Smith, G. William Lewis, Helen N. Rucker, and Edward A. Polloway. 1995. "Savant Syndrome: Case Studies, Hypotheses, and Implications for Special Education." *ETMRDD* 30(3): 243–53.

Chryssavgis, John. 2002. *The Body of Christ: A Place of Welcome for People with Disabilities.* Minneapolis: Light and Life Publishing.

Cicchetti, Dante, and Marjorie Beeghly. 1990. *Children with Down Syndrome: A Developmental Perspective.* Cambridge: Cambridge University Press.

Claar, Victor. 2006. "Review of Kathryn Tanner, Economy of Grace." *Christian Scholar's Review* 35(3): 416–22.

Clare, Eli. 1999. *Exile and Pride: Disability, Queerness, and Liberation.* Cambridge, Mass.: South End.

Clark, Bill. 1974. *Enough Room for Joy: Jean Vanier's L'Arche—a Message for Our Time.* New York: Paulist.

Clark, Doris C. 2000. *Feed All My Sheep: A Guide and Curriculum for Adults with Developmental Disabilities.* Louisville: Geneva.

Clark, Winfield. 1995. "Buddhism and the Spiritually Challenged." *RE* 9(2–3): 159–62.

Clarke, Andrew D. 2002. "Jew and Greek, Slave and Free, Male and Female: Paul's Theology of Ethnic, Social, and Gender Inclusiveness in Romans 16." In Peter Oakes, ed., *Rome in the Bible and the Early Church*, 103–25. Grand Rapids: Baker Academic.

Clarke, James H. 1973. *L'Arche Journal: A Family's Experience in Jean Vanier's Community*. Toronto: Griffin House.

Claydon, David, ed. 2004. "Ministry among People with Disabilities: Lausanne Occasional Paper No. 35B." N.p.: Lausanne Committee for World Evangelization [http://community.gospelcom.net/lcwe/assets/LOP35B_IG6B.pdf].

Clayton, Philip. 2005. *Mind and Emergence: From Quantum to Consciousness*. Oxford: Oxford University Press.

Clayton, Philip, and Arthur Peacocke, eds. 2004. *In Whom We Live and Move and Have Our Being: Panentheistic Reflections on God's Presence in a Scientific World*. Grand Rapids: Eerdmans.

Cleland, Charles C. 1979. *The Profoundly Mentally Retarded*. Englewood Cliffs, N.J.: Prentice-Hall.

Clements, Luke, and Janet Read. 2003. *Disabled People and European Human Rights: A Review of the Implications of the 1998 Human Rights Act for Disabled Children and Adults in the UK*. Bristol, U.K.: Policy Press.

Clifford, Stephanie. 1984. *Called to Belong: Preparing the Mentally Handicapped Person for Confirmation*. Leigh-on-Sea, U.K.: Kevin Mayhew.

Coakley, Sarah. 2002. *Powers and Submissions: Spirituality, Philosophy, and Gender*. Malden, Mass.: Blackwell.

Cochran, Elizabeth Agnew. 2005. "'The Full *Imago Dei*': The Implications of John Wesley's Scriptural Holiness for Conceptions of Suffering and Disability." *JRDH* 9(3): 21–46.

Cocks, Errol, Charlie Fox, Mark Brogan, and Michael Lee, eds. 1996. *Under Blue Skies: The Social Construction of Intellectual Disability in Western Australia*. Perth: Optima Press and Edith Cowan University Centre for Disability Research and Development.

Cohen, Ian. 1997. "A 'Strange' Vocation." In Frances M. Young, ed., *Encounter with Mystery: Reflections on L'Arche and Living with Disability*, 152–66. London: Darton, Longman & Todd.

Cohen, Jeffrey Jerome, ed. 1996. *Monster Theory: Reading Culture*. Minneapolis: University of Minnesota Press.

Cohen, Marion Deutsche. 1996. *Dirty Details: The Days and Nights of a Well Spouse*. Philadelphia: Temple University Press.

Coleridge, Peter. 1993. *Disability, Liberation, and Development*. Oxford: Oxfam.

Colker, Ruth. 1996. *Hybrid: Bisexuals, Multiracials, and Other Misfits under American Law*. New York: New York University Press.

———. 2005. *The Disability Pendulum: The First Decade of the Americans with Disabilities Act*. New York: New York University Press.

Collins, Kenneth J. 1997. *The Scripture Way of Salvation: The Heart of John Wesley's Theology*. Nashville: Abingdon.

Collins, Raymond F. 1999. *First Corinthians*. Sacra Pagina 7. Collegeville, Minn.: Liturgical Press.

Collins, Robin. 2003. "Evolution and Original Sin." In Keith B. Miller, ed., *Perspectives on an Evolving Creation*, 469–501. Grand Rapids: Eerdmans.

Colón, David M. 1989. "Martin Luther, the Devil and the *teufelchen*: Attitudes toward Mentally Retarded Children in Sixteenth-century Germany." *Proceedings of the PMR Conference* 14:74–85.

Colston, Lowell G. 1978. *Pastoral Care with Handicapped Persons*. Philadelphia: Fortress.

Conley, Ronald W. 1973. *The Economics of Mental Retardation*. Baltimore: The Johns Hopkins University Press.

Conn, Peter. 1996. *Pearl S. Buck: A Cultural Biography*. Cambridge: Cambridge University Press.

Cooley, W. Carl. 2002. "Nonconventional Therapies for Down Syndrome: A Review and Framework for Decision Making." In William I. Cohen, Lynn Nadel, and Myra E. Madnick, eds., *Down Syndrome: Visions for the 21st Century*, 259–73. New York: Wiley-Liss.

Cooper, Burton. 1993. "The Disabled God." In Lewis H. Merrick, ed., *And Show Steadfast Love: A Theological Look at Grace, Hospitality, Disabilities, and the Church*, 56–70. Louisville: Presbyterian Publishing House.

Cooper, John W. 2000. *Body, Soul, and Life Everlasting: Biblical Anthropology and the Monism-Dualism Debate*. 2nd ed. Grand Rapids: Eerdmans.

Corcoran, Kevin J. 2006. *Rethinking Human Nature: A Christian Materialist Alternative to the Soul*. Grand Rapids: Baker Academic.

Corey, Michael A. 2000. *Evolution and the Problem of Natural Evil*. Lanham, Md.: University Press of America.

Corman, Richard. 2003. *I Am Proud: The Athletes of Special Olympics*. New York: Barnes & Noble Books.

Coudroglou, Aliki, and Dennis L. Poole. 1984. *Disability, Work, and*

Social Policy: Models for Social Welfare. Springer Series on Social Work 2. New York: Springer.

Couser, G. Thomas. 1997. *Recovering Bodies: Illness, Disability, and Life Writing.* Madison: University of Wisconsin Press.

———. 1998. "Raising Adam: Ethnicity, Disability, and the Ethics of Life Writing in Michael Dorris's *The Broken Cord.*" *Biography* 21(4): 421–44.

Covey, Herbert C. 1998. *Social Perceptions of People with Disabilities in History.* Springfield, Ill.: Charles C. Thomas.

Cox-Gedmark, Jan. 1980. *Coping with Disability.* Philadelphia: Westminster Press.

Craig, William Lane, and Paul Copan. 2004. *Creation Out of Nothing: Its Biblical, Philosophical, and Scientific Exploration.* Grand Rapids: Baker Academic.

Crane, Lynda. 2002. *Mental Retardation: A Community Integration Approach.* Belmont, Calif.: Wadsworth/Thomson Learning.

Cranefield, Paul F., and Walter Federn. 1967. "The Begetting of Fools: An Annotated Translation of Paracelsus' *De Generatione Stultorum.*" *Bulletin of the History of Medicine* 41: 56–74, 161–74.

———. 1970. "Paulus Zacchias on Mental Deficiency and on Deafness." *Bulletin of the New York Academy of Medicine* 46(1): 3–21.

Crawford, Julie. 2005. *Marvelous Protestantism: Monstrous Births in Post-Reformation England.* Baltimore: The Johns Hopkins University Press.

Creamer, Deborah B. 2004a. "Am I Disabled [Enough]? Disability, Diversity, and Identity Hermeneutics." Paper presented to the Religion and Disability Group of the American Academy of Religion, San Antonio, Tex.

———. 2004b. "The Withered Hand of God: Disability and Theological Reflection." Ph.D. diss., Iliff School of Theology and the University of Denver (Colorado Seminary).

———. 2005. "Including All Bodies in the Body of God: Disability and the Theology of Sallie McFague." *JRDH* 9(4): 55–70.

Crocker, Allen C. 1998. "Exceptionality." *Developmental and Behavioral Pediatrics* 19(4): 300–305.

Crockett, William V., and James G. Sigountos, eds. 1991. *Through No Fault of Their Own? The Fate of Those Who Have Never Heard.* Grand Rapids: Baker Books.

Cropper, William H. 2001. *Great Physicists: The Life and Times of*

Leading Physicists from Galileo to Hawking. New York: Oxford University Press.

Crow, Liz. 1996. "Including All of Our Lives: Renewing the Social Model of Disability." In Jenny Morris, ed., *Encounters with Strangers: Feminism and Disability*, 206–26. London: Women's Press.

Csordas, Thomas J. 1994. *The Sacred Self: A Cultural Phenomenology of Charismatic Healing*. Berkeley and Los Angeles: University of California Press.

Cumberbatch, Guy, and Ralph Negrine. 1992. *Images of Disability and Television*. London: Routledge.

Cunningham, David S. 1998. *These Three Are One: The Practice of Trinitarian Theology*. Malden, Mass.: Blackwell.

Cushing, Pamela, and Tanya Lewis. 2002. "Negotiating Mutuality and Agency in Care-giving Relationships with Women with Intellectual Disabilities." *Hypatia* 17(3): 173–93.

Cuskelly, Monica, Anne Jobling, and Susan Buckley, eds. 2002. *Down Syndrome across the Life Span*. London: Whurr.

Dahl, Murdoch E. 1962. *The Resurrection of the Body: A Study of I Corinthians 15*. Studies in Biblical Theology 36. Naperville, Ill.: Alec R. Allenson.

Daley, Brian E. 1991. *The Hope of the Early Church: A Handbook on Patristic Eschatology*. Cambridge: Cambridge University Press.

Damasio, Antonio R. 1994. *Descartes' Error: Emotion, Reason, and the Human Brain*. New York: G. P. Putnam's Sons.

Danforth, Scot, and Virginia Navarro. 1998. "Speech Acts: Sampling the Social Construction of Mental Retardation in Everyday Life." *MR* 36:31–43.

Das, J. P., Kasturi Jachuck, and T. P. Panda. 1970. "Cultural Deprivation and Cognitive Growth." In H. Carl Haywood, ed., *Social-cultural Aspects of Mental Retardation*, 587–604. New York: Appleton-Century-Crofts.

Daunt, Patrick. 1991. *Meeting Disability: A European Response*. London: Cassell.

Davies, W. D., and Dale C. Allison Jr. 1997. *A Critical and Exegetical Commentary on the Gospel according to Matthew*. Edinburgh: T&T Clark.

Davis, Lennard J. 1995. *Enforcing Normalcy: Disability, Deafness, and the Body*. New York: Verso.

———. 2002. *Bending over Backwards: Disability, Dismodernism, and Other Difficult Positions*. New York: New York University Press.

Dawn, Marva J. 2001. *Powers, Weakness, and the Tabernacling of God.* Grand Rapids: Eerdmans.

——. 2002. *Joy in Our Weakness: A Gift of Hope from the Book of Revelation.* Rev. ed. Grand Rapids: Eerdmans.

Dayton, Donald W. 1987. *Theological Roots of Pentecostalism.* Peabody, Mass.: Hendrickson.

Deegan, Mary Jo, and Nancy A. Brooks, eds. 1985. *Women and Disability: The Double Handicap.* New Brunswick, N.J.: Transaction Books.

de Jongh, Daniëlle. 1996. *A Gift from God: Persons with a Mental Disability in Ovambo.* Utrecht, Netherlands: Utrecht Unitwin Network for Southern Africa.

de la Cruz, Felix F., and Theodore Friedmann. 1995. "Prospects for Human Gene Therapy in Mental Retardation and Developmental Disabilities." *MRDD* 1:2–3.

Deland, Jane S. 1999. "Images of God through the Lens of Disability." *JRDH* 3/2: 47–81.

Delumeau, Jean. 1995. *History of Paradise: The Garden of Eden in Myth and Tradition.* Trans. Matthew O'Connell. New York: Continuum.

DePauw, Karen P., and Susan J. Gavron. 1995. *Disability and Sport.* Champaign, Ill.: Human Kinetics.

DePoy, Elizabeth, and Stephen French Gilson. 2004. *Rethinking Disability: Principles for Professional and Social Change.* Belmont, Calif.: Thomson.

Deutsch, Helen, and Felicity Nussbaum, eds. 2000. *"Defects": Engendering the Modern Body.* Ann Arbor: University of Michigan Press.

Devlieger, Patrick. 2003. "From 'Idiot' to 'Person with Mental Retardation': Defining Difference in an Effort to Dissolve It." In Patrick Devlieger, Frank R. Rusch, and David Pfeiffer, eds., *Rethinking Disability: The Emergence of New Definitions, Concepts, and Communities,* 169–88. Antwerp, Belgium: Garant.

Devlieger, Patrick, Frank R. Rusch, and David Pfeiffer. 2003. "Rethinking Disability as Same and Different! Towards a Cultural Model of Disability." In Patrick Devlieger, Frank R. Rusch, and David Pfeiffer, eds., *Rethinking Disability: The Emergence of New Definitions, Concepts, and Communities,* 9–16. Antwerp, Belgium: Garant.

Devlin, Richard, and Dianne Pothier. 2006. "Introduction: Toward a Critical Theory of Dis-Citizenship." In Dianne Pothier and

Richard Devlin, eds., *Critical Disability Theory: Essays in Philosophy, Politics, Policy, and Law*, 1–22. Vancouver: University of British Columbia Press.

de Vinck, Christopher. 1988. *The Power of the Powerless*. Garden City, N.Y.: Doubleday.

DeVries, Dawn. 1994. "Creation, Handicapism, and the Community of Differing Abilities." In Rebecca S. Chopp and Mark L. Taylor, eds., *Reconstructing Christian Theology*, 124–40. Minneapolis: Fortress.

de Vries-Kryut, T. 1971. *A Special Gift: The Story of Jan*. New York: Peter H. Wyden.

Diamandopoulos, A. A., K. G. Rakatsanis, and N. Diamantopoulos. 1997. "A Neolithic Case of Down Syndrome?" *Journal of the History of the Neurosciences* 6(1): 86–89.

Dikötter, Frank. 1998. *Imperfect Conceptions: Medical Knowledge, Birth Defects, and Eugenics in China*. New York: Columbia University Press.

D'Lil, HolLynn. 2001. "Disability Rights Dare: The 1977 Takeover of the San Francisco Federal Building." In *The Whole World's Watching: Peace and Social Justice Movements of the 1960s and 1970s*, 119–22. Berkeley: Berkeley Arts Center Association.

Dmitriev, Valentine. 1997. *Tears and Triumphs: A Look into the World of Children with Down Syndrome and Other Developmental Delays*. Seattle: Peanut Butter Publishing.

Dobbing, John, et al., eds. 1984. *Scientific Studies in Mental Retardation*. London: Macmillan and Royal Society of Medicine.

Dolmage, Jay. 2005. "Between the Valley and the Field: Metaphor and Disability." *Prose Studies* 27(1–2): 108–19.

Donley, Carol C., and Sheryl Buckley, eds. 1996. *The Tyranny of the Normal: An Anthology*. Kent, Ohio: Kent State University Press.

Dorn, Michael L. 1998. "Beyond Nomadism: The Travel Narratives of a 'Cripple.'" In Heidi J. Nast and Steve Pile, eds., *Places through the Body*, 183–206. New York: Routledge.

Dorris, Michael. 1989. *The Broken Cord: A Family's Ongoing Struggle with Fetal Alcohol Syndrome*. New York: Harper & Row.

Dostoyevsky, Fyodor. 1955. *The Idiot*. Trans. David Magarshack. London: Penguin Books.

Douglas, Mary. 1966. *Purity and Danger: An Analysis of Concepts of Pollution and Taboo*. New York: Praeger.

Down, John L. 1887. *Mental Afflictions of Children and Youth*. London: J&A Churchill.

Downey, Michael. 1986. *A Blessed Weakness: The Spirit of Jean Vanier and l'Arche*. San Francisco: Harper & Row.

———. 2000. *Altogether Gift: A Trinitarian Spirituality*. Maryknoll: Orbis.

Downs, Perry. 1996. "Interventions: An Holistic Approach." In Phyllis Kilbourn, ed., *Children in Crisis: A New Commitment*, 189–203. Monrovia, Calif.: MARC.

Doyal, Lesley. 1983. "Introduction: Poverty and Disability in the Third World—the Crippling Effects of Underdevelopment." In Oliver Shirley, ed., *A Cry for Health: Poverty and Disability in the Third World*, 7–14. Frome, U.K.: Third World Group for Disabled People and Appropriate Health Resources and Technologies Action Group.

Driedger, Dianne L. 1989. *The Last Civil Rights Movement: Disabled Peoples' International*. New York: St. Martin's.

Driedger, Dianne, Irene Feika, and Eileen Girón Batres, eds. 1996. *Across Borders: Women with Disabilities Working Together*. Charlottetown, P.E.I., Canada: Gynergy.

Driedger, Dianne, and Susan Gray, eds. 1992. *Imprinting Our Image: An International Anthology by Women with Disabilities*. Charlottetown, P.E.I., Canada: Gynergy.

Drimmer, Frederick. 1973. *Very Special People: The Struggles, Loves, and Triumphs of Human Oddities*. New York: Amjon Publishers.

Dubarle, A. M. 1967. *The Biblical Doctrine of Original Sin*. Trans. E. M. Stewart. New York: Herder & Herder.

Dudley, James R. 1997. *Confronting the Stigma in Their Lives: Helping People with a Mental Retardation Label*. Springfield, Ill.: Charles C. Thomas.

Duffy, Yvonne. 1979. . . . *All Things Are Possible*. Ann Arbor: A. J. Garvin & Associates.

Dulles, Avery. 1974. *Models of the Church*. Garden City, N.Y.: Doubleday.

Dunn, James D. G. 1988. *Romans 1–8*. Word Biblical Commentary 38. Dallas: Word.

Dupuis, Jacques. 1977. *Jesus and His Spirit: Theological Approaches*. Bangalore, India: Theological Publications.

Durken, Maureen. 2002. "The Epidemiology of Developmental Disabilities in Low-Income Countries." *MRDDRR* 8:206–11.

Dybwad, Rosemary F. 1990. *Perspectives on a Parent Movement: The Revolt of Parents of Children with Intellectual Limitations.* Ed. Peter Mittler. Cambridge, Mass.: Brookline Books.

Easterday, Lois M. 1980. "War Is Hell and Hell Is War: The Autobiography of a Retarded Adult." In Jerry Jacobs, ed., *Mental Retardation: A Phenomenological Approach*, 208–23. Springfield, Ill.: Charles C. Thomas.

Eberly, Susan Schoon. 1991. "Fairies and the Folklore of Disability: Changelings, Hybrids, and the Solitary Fairy." In Peter Narváez, ed., *The Good People: New Fairylore Essays*, 227–50. New York and London: Garland.

Economic and Social Commission for Asia and the Pacific. 1995. *Hidden Sisters: Women and Girls with Disabilities in the Asian and Pacific Region.* New York: United Nations.

Edgerton, Robert B. 1967. *The Cloak of Competence: Stigma in the Lives of the Mentally Retarded.* Berkeley and Los Angeles: University of California Press.

———. 1970. "Mental Retardation in non-Western Societies: Toward a Cross-cultural Perspective on Incompetence." In H. Carl Haywood, ed., *Social-Cultural Aspects of Mental Retardation*, 523–59. New York: Appleton-Century-Crofts.

———. 1979. *Mental Retardation.* Cambridge: Harvard University Press.

———. 1986. "Case of Delabeling: Some Practical and Theoretical Implications." In Lewis L. Langness and Harold G. Levine, eds., *Culture and Retardation: Life Histories of Mildly Mentally Retarded Persons in American Society*, 101–26. Boston: D. Reidel.

———. 1991. "Conclusion." In Robert B. Edgerton and Marcia A. Gaston, eds., *I've Seen It All! Lives of Older Persons with Mental Retardation in the Community*, 268–73. Baltimore: Paul H. Brookes.

Edwards, Jean Parker, and David Dawson. 1983. *My Friend David: A Source Book about Down's Syndrome and a Personal Story about Friendship.* Portland, Ore.: Ednick Communications.

Edwards, Martha. 1996. "Ability and Disability in the Ancient Greek Military Community." In Elaine Makas and Lynn Schlesinger, eds., *End Results and Starting Points: Expanding the Field of Disability Studies*, 29–33. Boston: Society for Disability Studies.

———. 1997. "Deaf and Dumb in Ancient Greece." In Lennard J. Davis, ed., *The Disability Studies Reader*, 29–51. New York: Routledge.

Eiesland, Nancy L. 1994. *The Disabled God: Toward a Liberatory Theology of Disability*. Nashville: Abingdon.

———. 1999. "Changing the Subject: Toward an Interfaith Theology of Disability." *JRDH* 3(1): 55–62.

———. 2001–2002. "Liberation, Inclusion, and Justice: A Faith Response to Persons with Disabilities." *Impact* 14(3): 2–3, 35.

Eiesland, Nancy L., and Don E. Saliers, eds. 1998. *Human Disability and the Service of God: Reassessing Religious Practice*. Nashville: Abingdon.

Eisenberg, Myron G., Cynthia Griggins, and Richard J. Duval, eds. 1982. *Disabled People as Second-Class Citizens*. Springer Series on Rehabilitation 2. New York: Springer.

Eisenberg, Myron G., LaFaye C. Sutkin, and Mary A. Jansen, eds. 1984. *Chronic Illness and Disability through the Life Span: Effects on Self and Family*. New York: Springer.

Elkins, Thomas E. 1995. "Medical Issues Related to Sexuality and Reproduction." In D. C. Van Dyke, Philip Mattheis, Susan Schoon Eberly, and Janet Williams, eds., *Medical and Surgical Care for Children with Down Syndrome: A Guide for Parents*, 253–66. Bethesda, Md.: Woodbine House.

Elks, Martin A. 1993. "The 'Lethal Chamber': Further Evidence for the Euthanasia Option." *MR* 31(4): 201–7.

Elliott, Carl. 2003. "Attitudes, Souls, and Persons: Children with Severe Neurological Impairment." *MRDDRR* 9:16–20.

Elshout, Elly. 1999. "Roundtable Discussion: Women with Disabilities—A Challenge to Feminist Theology." In Alice Bach, ed., *Women in the Hebrew Bible: A Reader*, 429–58. New York: Routledge.

Engel, David M., and Frank W. Munger. 2003. *Rights of Inclusion: Law and Identity in the Life Stories of Americans with Disabilities*. Chicago: University of Chicago Press.

Enns, Ruth. 1999. *A Voice Unheard: The Latimer Case and People with Disabilities*. Halifax, N.S.: Fernwood.

Epstein, Charles J. 1995. "Epilogue: Toward the 21st Century with Down Syndrome—a Personal View of How Far We Have Come and of How Far We Can Reasonably Expect to Go." In Charles J. Epstein, Terry J. Hassold, Ira T. Lott, Lynn Nadel, and David Patterson, eds., *Etiology and Pathogenesis of Down Syndrome: Proceedings of the International Down Syndrome Research Conference*

Sponsored by the National Down Syndrome Society, Held in Charleston, South Carolina, April 11 to 13, 1994, 241–46. Progress in Clinical and Biological Research 393. New York: Wiley-Liss.

Epstein, Charles J., and David Patterson, eds. 1990. *Molecular Genetics of Chromosome 21 and Down Syndrome: Proceedings of the Sixth Annual National Down Syndrome Society Symposium, Held in New York, New York, December 7–8, 1989*. New York: Wiley-Liss.

Epstein, Richard A. 1992. *Forbidden Grounds: The Case against Employment Discrimination Laws*. Cambridge: Harvard University Press.

Erickson, Millard J. 1984. *Christian Theology*. 3 vols. Grand Rapids: Baker Book House.

Ervin, Howard M. 2002. *Healing: Sign of the Kingdom*. Peabody, Mass.: Hendrickson.

Estes, D. Timothy. 1984. *A Humanizing Ministry: A New Direction for Ministry with Persons Who Are Mentally Retarded*. Scottsdale, Penn.: Herald Press.

Evans, Daryl Paul. 1984. "Historical Antecedents of Stereotypes about Mental Retardation." In Stephen C. Hey, Gary Kiger, and John Seidel, eds., *Social Aspects of Chronic Illness, Impairment, and Disability*, 157–96. Salem, Ore.: Willamette University Society for the Study of Chronic Illness, Impairment, and Disability.

Ezeogu, Ernest M. 2003. "'Surely We Are Not Blind, Are We': An African Theological Reading of the Story of the Healing of the Man Born Blind, John 9:1-41." *Society of Biblical Literature 2003 Seminar Papers*, 1–15. Atlanta: Society of Biblical Literature.

Fackre, Gabriel J., Ronald H. Nash, and John Sanders. 1995. *What about Those Who Have Never Heard? Three Views on the Destiny of the Unevangelized*. Downers Grove: InterVarsity.

Fadiman, Anne. 1997. *The Spirit Catches You and You Fall Down: A Hmong Child, Her American Doctor, and the Collision of Two Cultures*. New York: Farrar, Straus & Giroux.

Fahy, Thomas, and Kimball King, eds. 2002. *Peering behind the Curtain: Disability, Illness, and the Extraordinary Body in Contemporary Theater*. New York and London: Routledge.

Falk, Darrel R. 2004. *Coming to Peace with Science: Bridging the Worlds between Faith and Biology*. Downers Grove: InterVarsity.

Falvey, Mary A., Richard L. Rosenberg, and Eileen M. Falvey. 1997. "Inclusive Educational Schooling." In Siegfried M. Pueschel and Maria Sustrová, eds., *Adolescents with Down Syndrome: Toward a More Fulfilling Life*, 145–60. Baltimore: Paul H. Brookes.

Fast, Mary M. 2004. "A Liberation Theology of Disability." M.A. thesis, Luther Seminary.

Fawcett, Barbara. 2000. *Feminist Perspectives on Disability*. New York: Prentice-Hall.

Fee, Gordon D. 1987. *The First Epistle to the Corinthians*. Grand Rapids: Eerdmans.

Fenn, Richard K. 1995. *The Persistence of Purgatory*. Cambridge: Cambridge University Press.

Ferguson, Everett. 1973. "God's Infinity and Man's Mutability: Perpetual Progress according to Gregory of Nyssa." *Greek Orthodox Theological Review* 18(1–2): 59–78.

Ferguson, Philip. 1990. "The Social Construction of Mental Retardation." In Mark Nagler, ed., *Perspectives on Disability: Texts and Readings on Disability*, 203–11. Palo Alto, Calif.: Health Markets Research.

————. 1994. *Abandoned to Their Fate: Social Policy and Practice toward Severely Retarded People in America, 1820–1920*. Philadelphia: Temple University Press.

————. 2003. "Winks, Blinks, Squints, and Twitches: Looking for Disability and Culture through My Son's Left Eye." In Patrick Devlieger, Frank R. Rusch, and David Pfeiffer, eds., *Rethinking Disability: The Emergence of New Definitions, Concepts, and Communities*, 131–47. Antwerp: Garant.

Feuerstein, Reuven, and Yaacov Rand. 1997. *Don't Accept Me as I Am: Helping Retarded Performers Excel*. Rev. ed. Arlington Heights, Ill.: Skylight Training and Publications.

Fiedler, Leslie A. 1978. *Freaks: Myths and Images of the Secret Self*. New York: Simon & Schuster.

————. 1996. *Tyranny of the Normal: Essays on Bioethics, Theology, and Myth*. Boston: David R. Godine.

Field, Martha A. 1992. "Executing with Mental Retardation." *AJMR* 96(6): 567–70.

Field, Martha A, and Valerie A. Sanchez. 1999. *Equal Treatment for People with Mental Retardation: Having and Raising Children*. Cambridge: Harvard University Press.

Fine, Michelle, and Adrienne Asch, eds. 1988. *Women with Disabilities: Essays in Psychology, Culture, and Politics*. Philadelphia: Temple University Press.

————. 2000. "Disability beyond Stigma: Social Interaction, Discrimination, and Activism." In Maurianne Adams, Warren J.

Blumenfeld, Rosie Castañeda, Heather W. Hackman, Madeline L. Peters, and Ximena Zúñiga, eds., *Readings for Diversity and Social Justice*, 330–39. New York: Routledge.

Finger, Anne. 1990. *Past Due: A Story of Disability, Pregnancy, and Birth*. Seattle: Seal.

Fiore, Peter A. 1981. *Milton and Augustine: Patterns of Augustinian Thought in Paradise Lost*. University Park: Pennsylvania State University Press.

Firey, M. J. 1902. *Infant Salvation: The Passivity of Infants, the Key to This Perplexing Subject*. New York: Funk & Wagnalls.

Fiser, Karen. 1994. "Philosophy, Disability, and Essentialism." In Lawrence Foster and Patricia Herzog, eds., *Defending Diversity: Contemporary Philosophical Perspectives on Pluralism and Multiculturalism*, 83–101. Amherst: University of Massachusetts Press.

Fitzmyer, Joseph A. 1993. *Romans: A New Translation with Introduction and Commentary*. New York: Anchor Bible.

Fleischer, Doris Zames, and Frieda Zames. 2001. *The Disability Rights Movement: From Charity to Confrontation*. Philadelphia: Temple University Press.

Fletcher, Joseph. 1979. *Humanhood: Essays in Biomedical Ethics*. Buffalo: Prometheus.

Flynn, Robert J., and Raymond A. Lemay, eds. 1999. *A Quarter-Century of Normalization and Social Role Valorization: Evolution and Impact*. Ottawa: University of Ottawa Press.

Fontaine, Carole R. 1996. "Disabilities and Illness in the Bible: A Feminist Perspective." In Athalya Brenner, ed., *Feminist Companion to the Hebrew Bible in the New Testament*, 286–300. Sheffield, U.K.: Sheffield Academic.

Fox, Matthew, ed. 1987. *Hildegard of Bingen's Book of Divine Works with Letters and Songs*. Santa Fe: Bear.

Francis, Mark R. 1994. "Celebrating the Sacraments with Those with Developmental Disabilities: Sacramental/Liturgical Reflections." In Edward Foley, ed., *Developmental Disabilities and Sacramental Access: New Paradigms for Sacramental Encounters*, 73–93. Collegeville, Minn.: Liturgical Press.

Frank, Arthur W. 1995. *The Wounded Storyteller: Body, Illness, and Ethics*. Chicago: University of Chicago Press.

Frank, Gelya. 2000. *Venus on Wheels: Two Decades of Dialogue on Disability, Biography, and Being Female in America*. Berkeley and Los Angeles: University of California Press.

Franks, Beth. 1996. "Disbar and Fairy Tales: An Analysis." In Elaine Makas and Lynn Schlesinger, eds., *End Results and Starting Points: Expanding the Field of Disability Studies*, 17–22. Boston: Society for Disability Studies.

Fraser, Alistair. 1988. "Traditional Beliefs and Intellectual Disability in Singapore." In Francis C. Chen, Alaistair S. Fraser, Kenneth R. Lyen, David Oon, Doreen Tan, and M. K. Wong, eds., *Intellectual Disability: Proceedings of the 8th Asian Conference on Mental Retardation*, 350–70. Singapore: Asian Federation for the Mentally Retarded, and Unique Image Offset Printing.

French, Sally, ed. 1994. *On Equal Terms: Working with Disabled People*. Oxford: Butterworth-Heinemann.

Freund, Peter. 2005. "Bodies, Disability, and Spaces: The Social Model and Disabling Spatial Organisations." In Miriam Fraser and Monica Greco, eds., *The Body: A Reader*, 182–86. London: Routledge.

Friedman, John Block. 1981. *The Monstrous Races in Medieval Art and Thought*. Cambridge: Harvard University Press.

Fries, Kenny, ed. 1997. *Staring Back: The Disability Experience from the Inside Out*. New York: Plume.

Fritzson, Arne, and Samuel Kabue. 2004. *Interpreting Disability: A Church of All and for All*. Geneva: WCC Publications.

Fulcher, Gillian. 1989. *Disabling Policies? A Comparative Approach to Education Policy and Disability*. London: Falmer.

Fuller, Beth. 2006. "Developing World." In Gary Albrecht, gen. ed., *Encyclopedia of Disability*, 1:386–94. Thousand Oaks, Calif.: Sage.

Gabel, Susan. 1999. "Depressed and Disabled: Some Discursive Problems with Mental Illness." In Mairian Corker and Sally French, eds., *Disability Discourse*, 38–46. Buckingham: Open University Press.

Gadacz, René R. 1994. *Re-thinking Dis-ability: New Structures, New Relationships*. Edmonton: University of Alberta Press.

Gallagher, Hugh Gregory. 1985. *FDR's Splendid Deception*. New York: Dodd, Mead.

———. 1998. *Black Bird Fly Away: Disabled in an Able-Bodied World*. Arlington, Va.: Vandamere.

———. 2001. "What the Nazi 'Euthanasia Program' Can Tell Us about Disability Oppression." *JDPS* 12(2): 96–99.

Gardner, Howard. 1993. *Frames of Mind: The Theory of Multiple Intelligences*. New York: Basic Books.

———. 1999. *Intelligence Reframed: Multiple Intelligences for the 21st Century*. New York: Perseus Books.

Gardner, Jane F. 2002. *Being a Roman Citizen*. London: Routledge.

Gardner, R. J. McKinlay, and Grant R. Sutherland. 1996. *Chromosome Abnormalities and Genetic Counseling*. 2nd ed. Oxford Monographs on Medical Genetics 29. New York: Oxford University Press.

Garland, Robert. 1995. *The Eye of the Beholder: Deformity and Disability in the Graeco-Roman World*. Ithaca: Cornell University Press.

Gartner, Alan, and Tom Joe, eds. 1987. *Images of the Disabled, Disabling Images*. New York: Praeger.

Gause, R. Hollis. 1980. *Living in the Spirit: The Way of Salvation*. Cleveland, Tenn.: Pathway Press.

Gaventa, William C., Jr. 1986. "Religious Ministries and Services with Adults with Developmental Disabilities." In Jean Ann Summers, ed., *Right to Grow Up: An Introduction to Adults with Developmental Disabilities*, 191–226. Baltimore: Paul H. Brookes.

———. 1993. "Gift and Call: Recovering the Spiritual Foundations of Friendships." In Angela Novak Amado, ed., *Friendships and Community Connections between People with and without Developmental Disabilities*, 41–66. Baltimore: Paul H. Brookes.

Gaventa, William C., Jr., and David L. Coulter, eds. 2001a. *Spirituality and Intellectual Disability: International Perspectives on the Effect of Culture and Religion on Healing Body, Mind, and Soul*. New York: Haworth Pastoral.

———, eds. 2001b. *The Theological Voice of Wolf Wolfensberger*. New York: Haworth Pastoral.

———, eds. 2003. *The Pastoral Voice of Robert Perske*. New York: Haworth Pastoral.

Gaventa, William, and Roger K. Peters. 2001. "Spirituality and Self-Actualization: Recognizing Spiritual Needs and Strengths of Individuals with Cognitive Limitations." In Alexander J. Tymchuk, K. Charlie Lakin, and Ruth Luckasson, eds., *The Forgotten Generation: The Status and Challenges of Adults with Mild Cognitive Limitations*, 299–320. Baltimore: Paul H. Brookes.

Gbodossou, Erick V. A. 1999. "Defining the Role of Religion and Spirituality in the Lives of Persons with Disability in the Fatick Regio, Senegal, and the Mono Region, Benin." In Brigitte Holzer, Arthur Vreede, and Gabriele Weigt, eds., *Disability in Different Cultures: Reflections on Local Concepts*, 58–76. New Brunswick, N.J.: Transaction Publishers.

Geisler, Norman. 2004. *Systematic Theology*. Vol. 3, *Sin, Salvation*. Minneapolis: Bethany House.

Gelpi, Donald L. 1998. *The Conversion Experience: A Reflective Process for RCIA Participants and Others*. New York: Paulist.

Gerber, David A. 1990. "Listening to Disabled People: The Problem of Voice and Authority in Robert B. Edgerton's *The Cloak of Competence*." *DHS* 5(1): 3–23.

———. 1992. "Volition and Valorization in the Analysis of the 'Careers' of People in Exhibited Freak Shows." *DHS* 7(1): 53–69.

Gerber, Michael M. 1996. "Reforming Special Education: Beyond 'Inclusion.'" In Carol Christensen and Fazal Rizvi, eds., *Disability and the Dilemmas of Education and Justice*, 156–74. Buckingham: Open University Press.

Gere, Anne Ruggles, and Cynthia Margaret Gere. 2000. "Living with Fetal Alcohol Syndrome/Fetal Alcohol Effect (FAS/FAE)." In Susan Crutchfield and Marcy Epstein, eds., *Points of Contact: Disability, Art, and Culture*, 133–46. Ann Arbor: University of Michigan Press.

Gething, Lindsay. 1997. *Person to Person: A Guide for Professionals Working with People with Disabilities*. 3rd ed. Baltimore: Paul H. Brookes.

Ghai, Anita. 1999. "Disability in the Indian Context: Post-colonial Perspectives." In Mairian Corker and Sally French, eds., *Disability Discourse*, 88–100. Buckingham: Open University Press.

———. 2001. "Marginalisation and Disability: Experiences from the Third World." In Mark Priestley, ed., *Disability and the Life Course: Global Perspectives*, 26–37. Cambridge: Cambridge University Press.

———. 2002. "Disabled Women: An Excluded Agenda of Indian Feminism." *Hypatia* 17(3): 49–66.

———. 2003. *(Dis)Embodied Form: Issues of Disabled Women*. New Delhi: Shakti Books.

Gibbons, Frederick X. 1986. "Stigma and Interpersonal Relationships." In Stephen C. Ainlay, Gaylene Becker, and Lerita M. Coleman, eds., *The Dilemma of Difference: A Multidisciplinary View of Stigma*, 123–44. New York: Plenum.

Gibbs, Eddie, and Ryan K. Bolger. 2005. *Emerging Churches: Creating Christian Community in Postmodern Cultures*. Grand Rapids: Baker Academic.

Gibbs, Kristine. 1981. *Only One Way Up*. London: Darton, Longman & Todd.

Gilkey, Langdon. 1959. *Maker of Heaven and Earth: A Study of the Christian Doctrine of Creation*. Garden City, N.Y.: Doubleday.

Gleeson, Brendan. 1999. *Geographies of Disability*. London: Routledge.

Glidden, Laraine Masters, Jeannette Rogers-Dulan, and Amy E. Hill. 1999. "'The Child That Was Meant?' or 'Punishment for Sin?': Religion, Ethnicity, and Families with Children with Disabilities." *IRRMR* 22:267–88.

Gliedman, John, and William Roth. 1980. *The Unexpected Minority: Handicapped Children in America*. New York: Harcourt Brace Jovanovich.

Goddard, Henry Herbert. 1912. *The Kallikak Family: A Study in the Heredity of Feeble-mindedness*. New York: Macmillan.

Goering, Sara. 2003. "Conformity through Cosmetic Surgery: The Medical Erasure of Race and Disability." In Robert Figueroa and Sandra Harding, eds., *Science and Other Cultures: Issues in Philosophies of Science and Technology*, 172–88. New York and London: Routledge.

Goffman, Erving. 1974. *Stigma: Notes on the Management of Spoiled Identity*. New York: Jason Aronson. (Original publication 1963).

Goggin, Gerard, and Christopher Newell. 2000. "Crippling Paralympics? Media, Disability, and Olympism." *Media International Australia Incorporating Culture and Policy* 97:71–83.

———. 2003. *Digital Disability: The Social Construction of Disability in New Media*. Lanham, Md.: Rowman & Littlefield.

———. 2005. *Disability in Australia: Exposing a Social Apartheid*. Sydney: University of New South Wales Press.

Goh, Jeffrey C. K. 2000. *Christian Tradition Today: A Postliberal Vision of Church and World*. Louvain Theological and Pastoral Monographs 28. Louvain, Belgium: Peeters.

Goldberg, Richard Thayer. 1981. *The Making of Franklin D. Roosevelt: Triumph over Disability*. Cambridge, Mass.: Abt Books.

Golledge, Reginald G. 2004. "Disability, Disadvantage, and Discrimination: An Overview with Special Emphasis on Blindness in the USA." In Antoine Bailly and Lay James Gibson, eds., *Applied Geography: A World Perspective*, 213–32. GeoJournal Library 77. Dordrecht: Kluwer Academic Publishers.

Goode, David A., and James Hogg. 1994. "Towards an Understanding of Holistic Quality of Life in People with Profound Intellectual and Multiple Disabilities." In David A. Goode, ed., *Quality of Life for Persons with Disabilities: International Perspectives and Issues*, 197–207. Cambridge, Mass.: Brookline Books.

Goodey, C. F. 1994. "John Locke's Idiots in the Natural History of Mind." *History of Psychiatry* 5:215–50.

———. 1996. "The Psychopolitics of Learning and Disability in Seventeenth-Century Thought." In David Wright and Anne Digby, eds., *From Idiocy to Mental Deficiency: Historical Perspectives on People with Learning Disabilities*, 93–117. New York: Routledge.

———. 2001. "From Natural Disability to the Moral Man: Calvinism and the History of Psychology." *History of the Human Sciences* 14(3): 1–29.

———. 2004. "'Foolishness' in Early Modern Medicine and the Concept of Intellectual Disability." *Medical History* 48:289–310.

———. 2005. "Blockheads, Roundheads, Pointy Heads: Intellectual Disability and the Brain before Modern Medicine." *Journal of the History of the Behavioral Sciences* 41(2): 165–83.

Goodey, C. F., and Tim Stainton. 2001. "Intellectual Disability and the Myth of the Changeling Myth." *Journal of the History of the Behavioral Sciences* 37(3): 223–40.

Goodley, Dan. 2000. *Self-Advocacy in the Lives of People with Learning Difficulties: The Politics of Resilience*. Buckingham: Open University Press.

Goodley, Dan, and Michele Moore. 2002. *Disability Arts against Exclusion: People with Learning Difficulties and Their Performing Arts*. Kidderminster, U.K.: BILD Publications.

Goodley, Dan, and Geert Van Hove, eds. 2005. *Another Disability Studies Reader? People with Learning Disabilities and a Disabling World*. Antwerp: Garant.

Gordon, Robert A. 1980a. "Examining Labelling Theory: The Case of Mental Retardation." In Walter R. Gove, ed., *The Labelling of Deviance: Evaluating a Perspective*, 111–74. 2nd ed. Beverly Hills, Calif.: Sage.

———. 1980b. "Postscript: Labelling Theory, Mental Retardation, and Public Policy: Larry P. and Other Developments since 1974." In Walter R. Gove, ed., *The Labelling of Deviance: Evaluating a Perspective*, 175–225. 2nd ed. Beverly Hills, Calif.: Sage.

Gorringe, T. J. 2002. *The Education of Desire: Toward a Theology of the Senses*. Harrisburg, Penn.: Trinity Press International.

Gothard, Jan. 2002. "Beyond the Myths: Representing People with Down Syndrome." In Monica Cuskelly, Anne Jobling, and Susan Buckley, eds., *Down Syndrome across the Life Span*, 2–15. New York: Wiley.

Gottlieb, Roger S. 2002a. *Joining Hands: Politics and Religion Together for Social Change*. Boulder, Colo.: Westview.

———. 2002b. "The Tasks of Embodied Love: Moral Problems in Caring for Children with Disabilities." *Hypatia* 17(3): 225–36.

Govig, Stewart D. 1989. *Strong at the Broken Places: Persons with Disabilities and the Church*. Louisville, Ky.: Westminster John Knox.

Graham, Peter W., and Fritz H. Oehlschlaeger. 1992. *Articulating the Elephant Man: Joseph Merrick and His Interpreters*. Baltimore: The Johns Hopkins University Press.

Grandin, Temple. 1996. *Thinking in Pictures and Other Reports from My Life with Autism*. New York: Vintage Books.

Gray, Sherman W. 1989. *The Least of My Brothers: Matthew 25:31-46—A History of Interpretation*. Society of Biblical Literature Dissertation Series 114. Atlanta: Scholars Press.

Greeley, Elizabeth. 1989. *On the Way of the Cross with the Disabled*. Middlegreen, U.K.: St. Paul Publications.

Green, Joel B. 1998. " 'Bodies—That Is, Human Lives': A Re-examination of Human Nature in the Bible." In Warren S. Brown, Nancey Murphy, and H. Newton Malony, eds., *Whatever Happened to the Soul? Scientific and Theological Portraits of Human Nature*, 149–73. Minneapolis: Fortress.

———. 2004. "What Does It Mean to Be Human? Another Chapter in the Ongoing Interaction of Science and Scripture." In Malcolm Jeeves, ed., *From Cells to Souls—and Beyond: Changing Portraits of Human Nature*, 179–98. Grand Rapids: Eerdmans.

Green, Joel B., and Stuart L. Palmer, eds. 2004. *In Search of the Soul: Four Views of the Mind-Body Relation*. Downers Grove: InterVarsity.

Green, Laurie. 1987. *Power to the Powerless: Theology Brought to Life*. Basingstoke, U.K.: Marshall Pickering.

Greene, Richard S. 1991. "P.L. 94-142 and the Retarded Delinquent." In Richard S. Greene, ed., *Mainstreaming Retardation Delinquency*, 113–34. Lancaster, Penn.: Technomic.

Greene-McCreight, Kathryn. 2006. *Darkness Is My Only Companion: A Christian Response to Mental Illness.* Grand Rapids: Brazos.

Greenfeld, Josh. 1972. *A Child Called Noah: A Family Journey.* New York: Holt, Rinehart & Winston.

———. 1978. *A Place for Noah.* New York: Holt, Rinehart & Winston.

Greengross, Wendy. 1976. *Entitled to Love: The Sexual and Emotional Needs of the Handicapped.* London: Malaby Press.

Greer, John G., Robert M. Anderson, and Sara J. Odle, eds. 1982. *Strategies for Helping Severely and Multiply Handicapped Citizens.* Baltimore: University Park Press.

Greer, Rowan A. 2001. *Christian Life and Christian Hope: Raids on the Inarticulate.* New York: Crossroad.

Gregory of Nazianzus. 1954. "To Cledonius against Apollinaris (Epistle 101)." In Edward Rochie Hardy and Cyril C. Richardson, eds., *Christology of the Later Fathers,* 215–24. Philadelphia: Westminster Press.

Gregory of Nyssa. 1987. *Commentary on the Song of Songs.* Trans. Casimir McCambley. Brookline, Mass.: Hellenic College Press.

Grenz, Stanley J. 1994. *Theology for the Community of God.* Nashville: Broadman & Holman.

———. 2001. *The Social God and the Relational Self: A Trinitarian Theology of the Imago Dei.* Louisville: Westminster John Knox.

Groce, Nora Ellen. 1985. *Everyone Here Spoke Sign Language: Hereditary Deafness on Martha's Vineyard.* Cambridge: Harvard University Press.

Gunton, Colin. 1993. *The One, the Three, and the Many: God, Creation, and the Culture of Modernity.* Cambridge: Cambridge University Press.

Gustavson, Karl-Henrik, ed. 1987. *Scientific Studies in Mild Mental Retardation: Epidemiology, Origin, and Prevention.* Uppsala: Swedish Medical Research Council, Sävstaholm Foundation, and Almqvist & Wiksell.

Habel, Norman C. 1981. *Is Christ Disabled? Theological Approaches to Disability: Four Study Guides.* Chicago: Lutheran Campus Ministry Communications and the Synod of Australia's International Year of Disabled Persons Committee.

Hahn, Harlan. 1990. "Can Disability Be Beautiful?" In Mark Nagler, ed., *Perspectives on Disability: Texts and Readings on Disability,* 310–19. Palo Alto, Calif.: Health Markets Research.

————. 1997. "Advertising the Acceptably Employable Image: Disability and Capitalism." In Lennard J. Davis, ed., *The Disability Studies Reader*, 172–86. New York: Routledge.

Haj, Fareed. 1970. *Disability in Antiquity*. New York: Philosophical Library.

Hales, Gerald. 1996. *Beyond Disability: Towards an Enabling Society*. London: Open University.

Hall, Douglas John. 2003. *The Cross in Our Context: Jesus and the Suffering World*. Minneapolis: Fortress.

Hall, Lesley. 1992. "Beauty Quests—A Double Disservice: Beguiled, Beseeched, and Bombarded—Challenging the Concept of Beauty." In Dianne Driedger and Susan Gray, eds., *Imprinting Our Image: An International Anthology by Women with Disabilities*, 134–39. Charlottetown, P.E.I., Canada: Gynergy.

Halpern, Joseph, Karen L. Sackett, Paul R. Binner, and Cynthia B. Mohr. 1980. *The Myths of Deinstitutionalization: Policies for the Mentally Disabled*. Boulder: Westview.

Hambwalula, Constance. 1999. "Attitudes in Zambia." In Michele Wates and Rowen Jade, eds., *Bigger than the Sky: Disabled Women on Parenting*, 118–19. London: Women's Press.

Hand, George W., Amanda B. Clinton, and Jennifer R. Hiemenz. 1999. "The Neuropsychological Basis of Learning Disabilities." In Robert J. Sternberg and Louise Spear-Sweling, eds., *Perspectives on Learning Disabilities: Biological, Cognitive, Contextual*, 60–79. Boulder, Colo.: Westview.

Hans, Asha, and Annie Patri, eds. 2003. *Women, Disability, and Identity*. New Delhi and Thousand Oaks, Calif.: Sage.

Hardesty, Nancy A. 2003. *Faith Cure: Divine Healing in the Holiness and Pentecostal Movements*. Peabody, Mass.: Hendrickson.

Harding, Grace. 1989. "People of the Heart: Initiating Children with Mental Retardation." In Kathy Brown and Frank C. Sokol, eds., *Issues in the Christian Initiation of Children: Catechesis and Liturgy*, 131–40. Chicago: Liturgy Training Publications.

Harrell, David Edwin. 1975. *All Things Are Possible: The Healing and Charismatic Revivals in Modern America*. Bloomington: Indiana University Press.

Harrington, Mary Therese. 1982. "Reflections on Disabled Persons' Participation in Our Sacramental Life." In Suzanne E. Hall, ed., *Into the Christian Community: Religious Education with Disabled*

Persons, 27–45. Washington, D.C.: National Catholic Educational Association.

———. 1992. *A Place for All: Mental Retardation, Catechesis, and Liturgy.* Collegeville, Minn.: Liturgical Press.

———. 1994. "Affectivity and Symbol in the Process of Catechesis." In Edward Foley, ed., *Developmental Disabilities and Sacramental Access: New Paradigms for Sacramental Encounters*, 116–29. Collegeville, Minn.: Liturgical Press.

Harris, James C. 2006. *Intellectual Disability: Understanding Its Development, Causes, Classification, Evaluation, and Treatment.* Oxford: Oxford University Press.

Hasker, William. 1999. *The Emergent Self.* Ithaca: Cornell University Press.

Hassold, Terry J. 1998. "The Incidence and Origin of Human Trisomies." In Terry J. Hassold and David Patterson, eds., *Down Syndrome: A Promising Future, Together*, 67–74. New York: Wiley-Liss.

Hassold, Terry, and Stephanie Sherman. 2002. "The Origin and Etiology of Trisomy 21." In William I. Cohen, Lynn Nadel, and Myra E. Madnick, eds., *Down Syndrome: Visions for the 21st Century*, 295–301. New York: Wiley-Liss.

Hassold, Terry, Stephanie Sherman, and Patricia A. Hunt. 1995. "The Origin of Trisomy in Humans." In Charles J. Epstein, Terry J. Hassold, Ira T. Lott, Lynn Nadel, and David Patterson, eds., *Etiology and Pathogenesis of Down Syndrome: Proceedings of the International Down Syndrome Research Conference Sponsored by the National Down Syndrome Society, Held in Charleston, South Carolina, April 11 to 13, 1994*, 1–12. Progress in Clinical and Biological Research 393. New York: Wiley-Liss.

Hastie, Rachel. 1997. *Disabled Children in a Society at War: A Casebook from Bosnia.* Oxford: Oxfam.

Hauerwas, Stanley. 1981. *Character and the Christian Life: Essays in Christian Ethical Reflection.* Notre Dame, Ind.: Fides Publishers.

———, ed. 1982. *Responsibility for Devalued Persons: Ethical Interactions between Society, the Family, and the Retarded.* Springfield, Ill.: Charles C. Thomas.

———. 1983. *The Peaceable Kingdom: A Primer on Christian Ethics.* Notre Dame, Ind.: University of Notre Dame Press.

————. 1984. "Marginalizing the 'Retarded.'" In Flavian Dougherty, ed., *The Deprived, the Disabled, and the Fullness of Life,* 67–105. Wilmington, Del.: Michael Glazier.

————. 1986. *Suffering Presence: Theological Reflections on Medicine, the Mentally Handicapped, and the Church.* Notre Dame, Ind.: University of Notre Dame Press.

————. 1995a. *In Good Company: The Church as Polis.* Notre Dame, Ind.: University of Notre Dame Press.

————. 1995b. "The Church and Mentally Handicapped Persons: A Continuing Challenge to the Imagination." In Marilyn E. Bishop, ed., *Religion and Disability: Essays in Scripture, Theology, and Ethics,* 46–64. Kansas City: Sheed & Ward.

————. 1998. *Sanctify Them in the Truth: Holiness Exemplified.* Nashville: Abingdon.

Hawkins, Peter W. 2004. "The Buddhist Insight of Emptiness as an Antidote for the Model of Deficient Humanness Contained within the Label 'Intellectually Disabled.'" *JRDH* 8(1–2): 45–54.

Hawley, R. Scott, and Catherine A. Mori. 1999. *The Human Genome: A User's Guide.* San Diego: Academic Press.

Hayes, Susan Carol. 1996. *People with an Intellectual Disability and the Criminal Justice System.* Research Report 5. Sydney: New South Wales Law Reform Commission.

Hayes, Zachary. 1980. *What Are They Saying about Creation?* New York: Paulist.

Hayman, Robert L., Jr. 1998. *The Smart Culture: Society, Intelligence, and Law.* New York: New York University Press.

Hegeman, Mary Theodore. 1984. *Developmental Disability: A Family Challenge.* New York: Paulist.

Helander, Einar. 1999. *Prejudice and Dignity: An Introduction to Community-Based Rehabilitation.* 2nd ed. New York: United Nations Development Programme.

Helm, Paul. 1994. *The Providence of God.* Downers Grove: InterVarsity.

Hendry, George S. 1962. *The Westminster Confession for Today: A Contemporary Interpretation.* Richmond, Va.: John Knox Press.

————. 1980. *Theology of Nature.* Philadelphia: Westminster Press.

Hensel, Elizabeth. 2001. "Is Satisfaction a Valid Concept in the Assessment of Quality of Life of People with Intellectual Disabilities? A Review of the Literature." *JARID* 14:311–26.

Hentoff, Nat. 1987. "The Awful Privacy of Baby Doe." In Alan Gartner and Tom Joe, eds., *Images of the Disabled, Disabling Images*, 161–79. New York: Praeger.

Hentrich, Thomas. 2003. "The 'Lame' in Lev 21, 17-23 and 2 Sam 5, 6-8." *Annual of the Japanese Biblical Institute* 29:5–30.

Herndl, Diane Price. 1993. *Invalid Women: Figuring Feminine Illness in American Fiction and Culture, 1840–1940*. Chapel Hill: University of North Carolina Press.

Hevey, David. 1992. *The Creatures Time Forgot: Photography and Disability Imagery*. London: Routledge.

Hey, Stephen C., Gary Kiger, and John Seidel, ed. 1984. *Social Aspects of Chronic Illness, Impairment, and Disability*. Salem: Willamette University Society for the Study of Chronic Illness, Impairment, and Disability.

Hill, Mildrette. 1994a. "'They Are Not Our Brothers': The Disability Movement and the Black Disability Movement." In Nasa Begum, Mildrette Hill, and Andy Stevens, eds., *Reflections: The Views of Black Disabled People on Their Lives and Community Care*, 68–80. London: Central Council for Education and Training in Social Work.

———. 1994b. "'Burn and Rage': Black Voluntary Organisations as a Source of Social Change." In Nasa Begum, Mildrette Hill, and Andy Stevens, eds., *Reflections: The Views of Black Disabled People on Their Lives and Community Care*, 160–77. London: Central Council for Education and Training in Social Work.

Hillyer, Barbara. 1993. *Feminism and Disability*. Norman: University of Oklahoma Press.

Hingsburger, Dave. 1990. *I to I: Self Concept and People with Developmental Disabilities*. Mountville, Penn.: VIDA Publishing.

———. 1991. *I Contact: Sexuality and People with Developmental Disabilities*. 2nd ed. Mountville, Penn.: VIDA Publishing.

———. 1992. *I Witness: History of a Person with a Developmental Disability*. Mountville, Penn.: VIDA Publishing.

Hinkle, Christopher. 2003. "Smart Enough for the Church? Liberal Protestantism and Cognitive Disability." Paper presented at the American Academy of Religion.

Hirst, David, and Pamela Michael. 2003. "Family, Community, and the 'Idiot' in Mid-nineteenth Century North Wales." *DS* 18(2): 145–63.

Hoche, Alfred, and Karl Binding. 1975. *The Release of the Destruction of Life Devoid of Value: Its Measure and Its Form*. Santa Ana, Calif.: Robert L. Sassone.

Hogenboom, Marga. 2001. *Living with Genetic Syndromes Associated with Intellectual Disability*. London: Jessica Kingsley.

Holcomb, Lillian, and Mary E. Willmuth, eds. 1993. *Women with Disabilities: Found Voices*. Binghamton, N.Y.: Harrington Park.

Holden, Lynn. 1991. *Forms of Deformity*. Sheffield: Journal for Study of the Old Testament Press.

Holeman, Virginia T. 2004. "The Neuroscience of Christian Counseling." In Joel B. Green, ed., *What about the Soul? Neuroscience and Christian Anthropology*, 145–58, 209–12. Nashville: Abingdon.

Holland, Anthony J. 1999. "Down's Syndrome." In Matthew P. Janicki and Arthur J. Dalton, eds., *Dementia, Aging, and Intellectual Disabilities: A Handbook*, 183–97. Philadelphia: Brunner/Mazel.

Hollins, Sheila, Isabel Clare, and Glynis Murphy. 1996a. *You're under Arrest*. London: Gaskell/Royal College of Psychiatrists.

———. 1996b. *You're on Trial*. London: Gaskell/Royal College of Psychiatrists.

Hollins, Sheila, and Margaret Grimer. 1988. *Going Somewhere: People with Mental Handicaps and Their Pastoral Care*. London: SPCK.

Holzer, Brigitte. 1999. " 'We Don't Need to Be Cured First in Order to Live': Self-Help in Oaxaca, Mexico (An Account of an Interview with German Perez Cruz)." In Brigitte Holzer, Arthur Vreede, and Gabriele Weigt, eds., *Disability in Different Cultures: Reflections on Local Concepts*, 268–73. New Brunswick, N.J.: Transaction Publishers.

Holzer, Brigitte, Arthur Vreede, and Gabriele Weigt, eds. 1999. *Disability in Different Cultures: Reflections on Local Concepts*. New Brunswick, N.J.: Transaction Publishers.

Hoogewind, Allen Jay. 1998. *Parables of Hope: Inspiring Truths from People with Disabilities*. Grand Rapids: Zondervan.

Hook, Ernest B. 1982. "Epidemiology of Down Syndrome." In Siegfried M. Pueschel and John E. Rynders, eds., *Down Syndrome: Advances in Biomedicine and the Behavioral Sciences*, 11–88. Cambridge, Mass.: Ware Press.

Hordern, William, and Frederick Dale Bruner. 1984. *The Holy Spirit—Shy Member of the Trinity*. Minneapolis: Augsburg.

Horgan, John. 1997. *The End of Science: Facing the Limits of Knowledge in the Twilight of a Scientific Age*. Boston: Little, Brown.

Houck, Davis W., and Amos Kiewe. 2003. *FDR's Body Politics: The Rhetoric of Disability*. College Station: Texas A&M University Press.

Howe, Kenneth, and Ofelia B. Miramontes. 1992. *The Ethics of Special Education*. New York: Teachers College.

Howe, Michael J. A. 1989. *Fragments of Genius: The Strange Feats of Idiots Savants*. London: Routledge.

Howell, Michael, and Peter Ford. 1980. *The True History of the Elephant Man*. New York: Penguin Books.

Hubbard, Ruth. 1997. "Abortion and Disability: Who Should and Who Should Not Inhabit the World?" In Lennard J. Davis, ed., *The Disability Studies Reader*, 187–200. New York: Routledge.

Hudson, Bob. 1988. "Do People with a Mental Handicap Have Rights?" *DHS* 3(3): 227–37.

Huels, John M. 1994. "Canonical Rights to the Sacraments." In Edward Foley, ed., *Developmental Disabilities and Sacramental Access: New Paradigms for Sacramental Encounters*, 94–115. Collegeville, Minn.: Liturgical Press.

Hughes, Bill, and Kevin Paterson. 1997. "The Social Model of Disability and the Disappearing Body: Towards a Sociology of Impairment." *DS* 12(3): 325–40.

Hull, John M. 2003. "The Broken Body in a Broken World: A Contribution to a Christian Doctrine of the Person from a Disabled Point of View." *JRDH* 7(4): 5–23.

Humphries, Stephen, and Pamela Gordon. 1992. *Out of Sight: The Experience of Disability, 1900–1950*. Plymouth, U.K.: Northcote House.

Hunt, Edward J. 1986. "A Critical Evaluation of the Relationship between Physical Disability and Pastoral Care among Clergy in the PCUSA." D.Min. thesis, San Francisco Theological Seminary.

Hunt, Nigel. 1967. *The World of Nigel Hunt: The Diary of a Mongoloid Youth*. New York: Garrett Publications.

Hunt, Ronald H. 1978. *The Church's Pilgrimage of Pastoral Care in Mental Retardation*. New York: Vantage.

Hurley, Rodger. 1969. *Poverty and Mental Retardation: A Causal Relationship*. New York: Random House.

Hütter, Reinhard. 2000. *Suffering Divine Things: Theology as Church Practice*. Trans. Doug Scott. Grand Rapids: Eerdmans.

Hyun, Younghak. 1985. "The Cripple's Dance and Minjung Theology." *Ching Feng* 28(1): 30–35.

Imrie, Rob. 1996. *Disability and the City: International Perspectives.* New York: St. Martin's.

Ingstad, Benedicte. 1995. "*Mpho ya Modimo*—a Gift from God: Perspectives on 'Attitudes' toward Disabled Persons." In Benedicte Ingstad and Susan Reynolds Whyte, eds., *Disability and Culture*, 246–63. Berkeley and Los Angeles: University of California Press.

———. 1997. *Community-Based Rehabilitation in Botswana: The Myth of the Hidden Disabled.* Studies in African History and Medicine 7. Lewiston, N.Y.: Edwin Mellen.

Iozzio, M. J. 2005a. "The Writing on the Wall . . . Alzheimer's Disease: A Daughter's Look at Mom's Faithful Care for Dad." *JRDH* 9(2): 49–74.

———. 2005b. "Genetic Anomaly or Genetic Diversity: Thinking in the Key of Disability on the Human Genome." *Theological Studies* 66: 862–81.

Iris, Madelyn. 2003. "The Common Agenda of Aging and Disabilities: Stalemate or Progress." In Patrick Devlieger, Frank R. Rusch, and David Pfeiffer, eds., *Rethinking Disability: The Emergence of New Definitions, Concepts, and Communities*, 149–67. Antwerp: Garant.

Isherwood, Lisa, and Elizabeth Stuart. 1998. *Introducing Body Theology.* Sheffield: Sheffield Academic.

Iwakuma, Miho. 2002. "The Body as Embodiment: An Investigation of the Body by Merleau-Ponty." In Mairian Corker and Tom Shakespeare, eds., *Disability/Postmodernity: Embodying Disability Theory*, 76–87. London: Continuum.

Jablow, Martha Moraghan. 1982. *Cara, Growing with a Retarded Child.* Philadelphia: Temple University Press.

Jackson, Mark. 2000. *The Borderland of Imbecility: Medicine, Society, and the Fabrication of the Feeble Mind in Late Victorian and Edwardian England.* Manchester: Manchester University Press.

Jacobson, Denise Sherer. 1999. *The Question of David: A Disabled Mother's Journey through Adoption, Family, and Life.* Berkeley: Creative Arts Book.

Jaeger, Paul T., and Cynthia Ann Bowman. 2002. *Disability Matters: Legal and Pedagogical Issues of Disability in Education.* Westport, Conn.: Bergin & Garvey.

Janssen, Claudia. 2000. "Bodily Resurrection (1 Cor. 15)? The Discussion of the Resurrection in Karl Barth, Rudolf Bultmann, Dorothee Sölle and Contemporary Feminist Theology." *Journal for the Study of the New Testament* 79(1): 61–78.

Jayasooria, Denison. 2000. *Disabled People, Citizenship, and Social Work: The Malaysian Experience*. London: ASEAN Academic Press.

Jeffreys, David, and John Tait. 2000. "Disability, Madness, and Social Exclusion in Dynastic Egypt." In Jane Hubert, ed., *Madness, Disability, and Social Exclusion: The Archaeology and Anthropology of 'Difference,'* 87–95. London: Routledge.

Jeffreys, Mark. 2002. "Visible Cripple (Scars and Other Disfiguring Displays Included)." In Sharon L. Snyder, Brenda Jo Brueggemann, and Rosemarie Garland Thomson, eds., *Disability Studies: Enabling the Humanities*, 31–39. New York: Modern Language Association of America.

Jenkins, Richard, ed. 1998. *Questions of Competence: Culture, Classification, and Intellectual Disability*. Cambridge: Cambridge University Press.

Jenkinson, Josephine C. 1997. *Mainstream or Special? Educating Students with Disabilities*. New York: Routledge.

Jennings, Theodore W., Jr. 2003. "Theological Anthropology and the Human Genome Project." In Susan Brooks Thistlethwaite, ed., *Adam, Eve, and the Genome: The Human Genome Project and Theology*, 93–111. Minneapolis: Fortress.

Jeremiah, Mary, O.P. 1995. *The Secret of the Heart: A Theological Study of Catherine of Siena's Teaching on the Heart of Jesus*. Front Royal, Va.: Christendom.

Joe, Jennie R. 1988. "Government Policies and Disabled People in American Indian Communities." *DSH* 3(3): 253–62.

Joeckel, Samuel. 2006. "A Christian Approach to Disability Studies: A Prolegomenon." *Christian Scholar's Review* 35(3): 323–44.

Johansen, Nancy. 2004. "Voting Rights: A Success Story from Idaho." *Impact* 17(2): 8–9.

Johnson, Allan G. 2006. *Privilege, Power, and Difference*. 2nd ed. New York: McGraw-Hill.

Johnson, Ann Braden. 1990. *Out of Bedlam: The Truth about Deinstitutionalization*. New York: Basic Books.

Johnson, Kelley, and Rannveig Traustadóttir, eds. 2005a. *Deinstitutionalization and People with Intellectual Disabilities*. London: Jessica Kingsley.

———. 2005b. "Introduction: In and Out of Institutions." In Kelley Johnson and Rannveig Traustadóttir, eds., *Deinstitutionalization and People with Intellectual Disabilities*, 13–29. London: Jessica Kingsley.

Johnson, Kelley, and Jan Walmsley. 2003. *Inclusive Research with People with Learning Disabilities: Past, Present, and Futures.* London: Jessica Kingsley.

Johnson, Mary. 2003. *Make Them Go Away: Clint Eastwood, Christopher Reeve, and the Case against Disability Rights.* Louisville, Ky.: Advocado Press.

Johnson, Mary, and Barrett Shaw, ed. 2001. *To Ride the Public's Buses: The Fight That Built a Movement.* Louisville, Ky.: Advocado Press.

Johnson, Roland. 1999. *Roland Johnson's Lost in a Desert World: An Autobiography (as Told to Karl Williams).* Plymouth Meeting, Penn.: Speaking for Ourselves.

Jones, Charles W. 1978. *Saint Nicholas of Myra, Bari, and Manhattan: Biography of a Legend.* Chicago: University of Chicago Press.

Jones, Larry A., and Phyllis A. Barnes. 1987. *Doing Justice: Fifty Years of Parent Advocacy in Mental Retardation.* Olympia: Association for the Retarded Citizens of Washington.

Jones, Philip R., and Ailsa Cregan. 1986. *Sign and Symbol Communication for Mentally Handicapped People.* London: Croom Helm.

Jordan, Shannon M. 1985. *Decision Making for Incompetent Persons: The Law and Morality of Who Shall Decide.* Springfield, Ill.: Charles C. Thomas.

Juarez, Encarnacion. 2002. "Autobiography of the aching body in Teresa de Cartagena's Arboleda de los enfermos." In Sharon L. Snyder, Brenda Jo Brueggemann, and Rosemarie Garland Thomson, eds., *Disability Studies: Enabling the Humanities*, 131–43. New York: Modern Language Association of America.

Judge, Cliff. 1975. *Retarded Australians.* Clayton, Victoria: Melbourne University Press.

———. 1987. *Civilization and Mental Retardation: A History of the Care and Treatment of Mentally Retarded People.* Mulgrave, Victoria: Magenta Press.

Kannann, Kristina. 1987. "Death Dreams and Disability: An Insider's Perspective." In Keith T. Kernan, ed., *Dreams of Death by the Mentally Retarded*, 28–34. Working Papers of the Socio-Behavioral Group 37. Los Angeles: Mental Retardation Research Center of the University of California.

Kanner, Leo. 1964. *A History of the Care and Study of the Mentally Retarded.* Springfield, Ill.: Charles C. Thomas.

Kärkkäinen, Veli-Matti. 2002. *Toward a Pneumatological Theology: Pentecostal and Ecumenical Perspectives on Ecclesiology, Soteriology, and Theology of Mission.* Ed. Amos Yong. Lanham, Md.: University Press of America.

Kass, Leon R. 1988. "Evolution and the Bible: Genesis 1 Revisited." *Commentary* 86:29–39.

Kastner, Janet. 1989. *More than an Average Guy: The Story of Larry Patton.* Canton, Ohio: Daring Publishing Group.

Kasujja, Augustine. 1986. *Polygenism and the Theology of Original Sin Today.* Rome: Urbaniana University Press.

Katz, Irwin. 1981. *Stigma: A Social Psychological Analysis.* Hillsdale, N.J.: Erlbaum.

Katzmann, Robert A. 1986. *Institutional Disability: The Sage of Transportation Policy for the Disabled.* Washington, D.C.: Brookings Institution.

Kaufman, Sandra Z. 1999. *Retarded Isn't Stupid, Mom!* Rev. ed. Baltimore: Paul H. Brookes.

Kaye, Judy, and Senthil Kumar Raghavan. 2002. "Spirituality in Disability and Illness." *JRH* 41(3): 231–42.

Kearney, Richard. 2003. *Strangers, Gods, and Monsters: Interpreting Otherness.* New York: Routledge.

Keck, David. 1996. *Forgetting Whose We Are: Alzheimer's Disease and the Love of God.* Nashville: Abingdon.

Keck, John. 1980. *The Handicapped Experience Christ (HEC Program): A Resource for Ministry to and with the Handicapped and Their Families.* Washington, D.C.: U.S. Catholic Conference, Department of Education.

Keener, Craig. 2003. *The Gospel of John.* Vol. 1. Peabody, Mass.: Hendrickson.

Keifert, Patrick R. 1992. *Welcoming the Stranger: A Public Theology of Worship and Evangelism.* Minneapolis: Fortress.

Keith, Lois, ed. 1994. *Mustn't Grumble . . . : Writing by Disabled Women.* New York: Women's Press.

———, ed. 1996. *"What Happened to You?" Writings by Disabled Women.* New York: New Press.

———. 2001. *Take Up Thy Bed and Walk: Death, Disability, and Cure in Classic Fiction for Girls.* New York: Routledge.

Keller, Catherine. 2003. *Face of the Deep: A Theology of Becoming*. New York: Routledge.

Kelsey, Morton T. 1976. *Healing and Christianity: In Ancient Thought and Modern Times*. New York: Harper & Row.

Kemp, Charles F. 1958. *The Church: The Gifted and the Retarded Child*. St. Louis: Bethany Press.

Kendall, R. T. 2004. *The Thorn in the Flesh*. Lake Mary, Fla.: Charisma House.

Kennedy, Ian. 1988. *Treat Me Right: Essays in Medical Law and Ethics*. Oxford: Clarendon.

Kent, Howard. 1985. *Yoga for the Disabled*. Wellingborough, U.K.: Thorsons Publishing.

Kern, Walter. 1985. *Pastoral Ministry with Disabled Persons*. New York: Alba House.

Khan, Naila, and Maureen Durkin. 1995. "Framework: Prevalence." In Pam Zinkin and Helen McConachie, eds., *Disabled Children and Developing Countries*, 1–9. London: MacKeith.

Khodr, Georges. 1972. "Christianity in a Pluralistic World—the Economy of the Holy Spirit." *Ecumenical Review* 23:118–28.

Kidder, Cynthia S., and Brian Skotko. 2001. *Common Threads: Celebrating Life with Down Syndrome*. Rochester Hills, Mich.: Band of Angels.

Kim, Hong-Deok Daniel. 2001. "A Cultural Understanding of Disability in Regard to Conceptions of Disability and Attitudes toward Disability and toward Persons with Disabilities: A Korean-American Perspective with Biblical, Theological, and Missiological Implications." Ph.D. diss., Reformed Theological Seminary.

Kimball, Dan. 2003. *The Emerging Church: Vintage Christianity for All Generations*. Grand Rapids: Zondervan.

Kingsley, Jason, and Mitchell Levitz. 1994. *Count Us In: Growing Up with Down Syndrome*. New York: Harcourt, Brace.

Kirtley, Donald D. 1975. *The Psychology of Blindness*. Chicago: Nelson-Hall.

Kitchin, Rob. 1999. "Morals and Ethics in Geographical Studies of Disability." In James D. Proctor and David M. Smith, eds., *Geography and Ethics: Journeys in a Moral Terrain*, 223–36. London: Routledge.

Kittay, Eva Feder. 2002. "'Not My Way, Sesha, Your Way, Slowly': 'Maternal Thinking' in the Raising of a Child with Profound Intellectual Disabilities." In Constance L. Mui and Julien S.

Murphy, eds., *Gender Struggles: Practical approaches to Contemporary Feminism*, 95–117. Lanham, Md.: Rowman & Littlefield.

———. 2003. "Disability, Equal Dignity, and Care." In Regina Ammicht-Quinn, Maureen Junker-Kerry, and Elsa Tamez, eds., *The Discourse on Human Dignity*, 105–15. London: SCM Press.

Kittay, Eva Feder, with Leo Kittay. 2000. "On the Expressivity and Ethics of Selective Abortion for Disability: Conversations with My Son." In Erik Parens and Adrienne Asch, eds., *Prenatal Testing and Disability Rights*, 165–95. Washington, D.C.: Georgetown University Press.

Klages, Mary. 1999. *Woeful Afflictions: Disability and Sentimentality in Victorian America*. Philadelphia: University of Pennsylvania Press.

Kliewer, Christopher. 1998. *Schooling Children with Down Syndrome: Toward an Understanding of Possibility*. New York: Teachers College Press.

Klobas, Laurie E. 1988. *Disability Drama in Television and Film*. Jefferson, N.C.: McFarland.

Knitter, Paul F. 2004. "Overcoming Greed: Buddhists and Christians in Consumerist Society." *Buddhist-Christian Studies* 24:65–72.

Kohrman, Matthew. 2005. *Bodies of Difference: Experiences of Disability and Institutional Advocacy in the Making of Modern China*. Berkeley and Los Angeles: University of California Press.

Koop, C. Everett. 1991. *Koop: The Memoirs of America's Family Doctor*. New York: Random House.

Koosed, Jennifer L, and Darla Schumm. 2005. "Out of the Darkness: Examining the Rhetoric of Blindness in the Gospel of John." *DSQ* 25(1), http://www.dsq-sds.org/.

Korsmeyer, Jerry D. 1998. *Evolution and Eden: Balancing Original Sin and Contemporary Science*. New York: Paulist.

Krentel, David Paul. 1986. "The Care of the Geriatric Mentally Retarded." D.Min. thesis, Dallas Theological Seminary.

Kriegel, Leonard. 1964. *The Long Walk Home*. New York: Appleton-Century.

———. 1991. *Falling into Life: Essays*. San Francisco: North Point.

———. 1998. *Flying Solo: Reimagining Manhood, Courage, and Loss*. Boston: Beacon.

Krieger, Linda Hamilton, ed. 2003. *Backlash against the ADA: Reinterpreting Disability Rights*. Ann Arbor: University of Michigan Press.

Krötke, Wolf. 2000. "The Humanity of the Human Person in Karl Barth's Anthropology." In John Webster, ed., *The Cambridge Companion to Karl Barth*, 159–76. Trans. Philip G. Ziegler. Cambridge: Cambridge University Press.

Kuiper, R. B. 1942. *Are Infants Guilty before God? A Doctrinal Discussion*. Grand Rapids: Zondervan.

Kumin, Libby. 1994. *Communication Skills in Children with Down Syndrome: A Guide for Parents*. Rockville, Md.: Woodbine House.

Kupfer, Fern. 1982. *Before and after Zachariah: A Family Story about a Different Kind of Courage*. New York: Delacorte.

Kuppers, Petra, ed. 2001. *Disability and Performance*, special issue of *Contemporary Theatre Review: An International Journal* 11(3–4).

———. 2004. *Disability and Contemporary Performance: Bodies on Edge*. New York: Routledge.

Kutz-Mellem, Sharon, ed. 1998. *Different Members, One Body: Welcoming the Diversity of Abilities in God's Family*. Louisville, Ky.: Witherspoon.

Kydd, Ronald A. N. 1998. *Healing through the Centuries: Models for Understanding*. Peabody, Mass.: Hendrickson.

Laird, Martin. 2003. "Under Solomon's Tutelage: The Education of Desire in the Homilies on the Song of Songs." In Sarah Coakley, ed., *Re-Thinking Gregory of Nyssa*, 77–95. Malden, Mass.: Blackwell.

Lancioni, Giulio E., Mark F. O'Reilly, and Gabriella Basili. 1999. "Review of Strategies for Treating Sleep Problems in Persons with Severe or Profound Mental Retardation or Multiple Handicaps." *AJMR* 104(2): 170–86.

Landes, Scott David. 1997. "God of the Ambulances: Practical Theology and Mental Retardation." M.Div. thesis, Candler School of Theology.

Lane, Harlan. 1997. "Constructions of Deafness." In Lennard J. Davis, ed., *The Disability Studies Reader*, 153–71. New York: Routledge.

Langness, Lewis L., and Harold G. Levine, eds. 1986. *Culture and Retardation: Life Histories of Mildly Mentally Retarded Persons in American Society*. Boston: D. Reidel.

Lanspery, Susan, and Joan Hyde, eds. 1997. *Staying Put: Adapting the Places Instead of the People*. Amityville, N.Y.: Bayville.

Larson, Sheryl, Charlie Lakin, Lynda Anderson, Nohoon Kwak, Jeoung Hak Lee, and Deborah Anderson. 2000. "Prevalence of

Mental Retardation and/or Developmental Disabilities: Analysis of the 1994/1995 NHIS-D." *MRDDDB* 2(1), http://rtc.umn.edu/pub/index.html#brief.

Lauand, Luiz Jean. 2001. "Fools in Aquinas's Analysis." *Quodlibet Online Journal of Christian Theology and Philosophy* 3(3), http://www.quodlibet.net/.

Law, Eric H. F. 2000. *Inclusion: Making Room for Grace.* St. Louis: Chalice.

Laws, Glenda, and John Radford. 1998. "Place, Identity, and Disability: Narratives of Intellectually Disabled People in Toronto." In Robin A. Kearns and Wilbert M. Gesler, eds., *Putting Health into Place: Landscape, Identity, and Well-Being*, 77–101. Syracuse: Syracuse University Press.

Lawson, Anna, and Caroline Gooding, eds. 2004. *Disability Rights in Europe: From Theory to Practice.* Oxford and Portland, Ore.: Hart Publishing.

Lay, Geoffrey. 1998. *Seeking Signs and Missing Wonders: Disability and the Church's Healing Ministry.* Crowborough, U.K.: Monarch.

Lea, Susan J. 1988. "Mental Retardation: Social Construction or Clinical Reality?" *DHS* 3(1): 63–69.

Lee, Carvel. 1961. *Tender Tyrant: The Story of a Mentally Retarded Child.* Minneapolis: Augsburg.

Le Goff, Jacques. 1984. *The Birth of Purgatory.* Trans. Arthur Goldhammer. Chicago: University of Chicago Press.

Leith, John H. 1963. *Creeds of the Churches.* Garden City, N.Y.: Anchor Books/Doubleday.

Leslie, Julia. 1999. "The Implications of the Physical Body: Health, Suffering, and Karma in Hindu Thought." In John R. Hinnells and Roy Porter, eds., *Religion, Health, and Suffering*, 23–45. London: Kegan Paul International.

Levenson, Jon. 1988. *Creation and the Persistence of Evil: The Jewish Drama of Divine Omnipotence.* San Francisco: Harper & Row.

Levin, Faitel. 1987. *Halacha, Medical Science, and Technology: Perspectives on Contemporary Halacha Issues.* New York: Maznaim.

Levitas, Andrew S., and Cheryl S. Reid. 2003. "An Angel with Down Syndrome in a Sixteenth-Century Flemish Nativity Painting." *American Journal of Medical Genetics* 116A: 399–405.

Levy, Michael. 1995. "To Stand on Holy Ground: A Jewish Spiritual Perspective on Disability," *RE* 9(2–3): 163–70.

Levy, Robert M., and Leonard S. Rubenstein. 1996. *The Rights of People with Mental Disabilities*. Carbondale: Southern Illinois University Press.

Lewis, Alan. 1982. "God as Cripple: Disability, Personhood, and the Reign of God." *Pacific Theological Review* 16(11): 13–18.

———. 2003. *Between Cross and Resurrection: A Theology of Holy Saturday*. Grand Rapids: Eerdmans.

Lewis, C. S. 1964. *Letters to Malcolm: Chiefly on Prayer*. New York: Harcourt, Brace & World.

Lewis, Cindy, and Susan Sygall, eds. 1997. *Loud, Proud, and Passionate: Including Women with Disabilities in International Development Programs*. Eugene, Ore.: Mobility International.

Liachowitz, Claire H. 1988. *Disability as a Social Construct: Legislative Roots*. Philadelphia: University of Pennsylvania Press.

Lifshitz, H., and R. Glaubman. 2002. "Religious and Secular Students' Sense of Self-Efficacy and Attitudes towards Inclusion of Pupils with Intellectual Disability and Other Types of Needs." *JIDR* 46(5): 405–18.

Lifshitz, Hefziba, and Joav Merrick. 2001. "Jewish Law and the Definition of Mental Retardation: The Status of People with Intellectual Disability within the Jewish Law in Relation to the 1992 AAMR Definition of Mental Retardation." *JRDH* 5(1): 39–51.

Lindbeck, George. 1984. *The Nature of Doctrine: Religion and Theology in a Postliberal Age*. Philadelphia: Westminster Press.

———. 2002. *The Church in a Postliberal Age*. Ed. James J. Buckley. Grand Rapids: Eerdmans.

Link, Christian. 2002. "Providence: An Unsolved Problem of the Doctrine of Creation." In Henning Graf Reventlow and Yair Hoffman, eds., *Creation in Jewish and Christian Traditions*, 266–76. Journal for the Study of the Old Testament Supplement Series 319. London: Sheffield Academic.

Linton, Simi. 1998. *Claiming Disability: Knowledge and Identity*. New York: New York University Press.

———. 2006. *My Body Politic: A Memoir*. Ann Arbor: University of Michigan Press.

Linton, Simi, Susan Mello, and John O'Neill. 2000. "Disability Studies: Expanding the Parameters of Diversity." In Ira Short and Carline Pari, eds., *Education Is Politics: Critical Teaching across Differences, Postsecondary*, 178–91. Portsmouth, N.H.: Boynton/Cook.

Livneh, Hanoch. 1991. "On the Origins of Negative Attitudes toward People with Disabilities." In Robert P. Marinelli and Arthur E. Dell Orto, eds., *The Psychological and Social Impact of Disability*, 181–98. 3rd ed. New York: Springer.

Loaring, E. I. 2000. "Learning by Heart: Imitation and the Catechetical Process for Children with Disabilities." MTS summative exercise, Toronto School of Theology.

Locke, John. 1965. *Essays on the Law of Nature*. Ed. W. von Leyden. Oxford: Clarendon.

———. 1975. *An Essay Concerning Human Understanding*. Ed. Peter H. Nidditch. Oxford: Clarendon.

Longhurst, Nancy Anne. 1994. *The Self-Advocacy Movement by People with Developmental Disabilities: A Demographic Study and Directory of Self-Advocacy Groups in the United States*. Washington, D.C.: AAMR.

Longmore, Paul K. 2003. *Why I Burned My Book and Other Essays on Disability*. Philadelphia: Temple University Press.

Löning, Karl, and Erich Zenger. 2000. *To Begin with, God Created . . .: Biblical Theologies of Creation*. Trans. Omar Kaste. Collegeville, Minn.: Liturgical Press/Michael Glazier.

Lonsdale, Susan. 1990. *Women and Disability: The Experience of Physical Disability among Women*. New York: St. Martin's Press.

Lott, Ira T., and Ernest E. McCoy, eds. 1992. *Down Syndrome: Advances in Medical Care*. New York: Wiley-Liss.

Louhiala, Pekka. 2004. *Preventing Intellectual Disability: Ethical and Clinical Issues*. Cambridge: Cambridge University Press.

Lovasik, Lawrence G. 1971. *Saint Dymphna: A Saint Who Brings Consoling Light to All—Especially to the Nervous and the Mentally Handicapped*. Tarentum, Penn.: L. G. Lovasik.

Lovering, Robert. 1985. *Out of the Ordinary: A Digest on Disability*. Phoenix: ARCS.

Lubchenco, Lula O., and Allen C. Crocker. 1997. *Bus Girl: Poems by Gretchen Josephson*. Cambridge, Mass.: Brookline Books.

Lubec, Gert, ed. 2003. *Advances in Down Syndrome Research*. New York: Springer-Verlag Wein.

Luckasson, Ruth. 2001. "The Criminal Justice System and People with Mild Cognitive Limitations." In Alexander J. Tymchuk, K. Charlie Lakin, and Ruth Luckasson, eds., *The Forgotten Generation: The Status and Challenges of Adults with Mild Cognitive Limitations*, 347–56. Baltimore: Paul H. Brookes.

———. 2003. "Terminology and Power." In Stanley S. Herr, Lawrence O. Gostin, and Harold Hongju Koh, eds., *The Human Rights of Persons with Intellectual Disabilities: Different but Equal*, 49–58. Oxford: Oxford University Press.

Luckin, Bill. 1986. "Time, Place, and Competence: Society and History in the Writings of Robert Edgerton." *DHS* 1(1): 89–102.

Lull, Timothy F., ed. 1989. *Martin Luther's Basic Theological Writings*. Minneapolis: Fortress.

Luther, Martin. 1964. *Luther's Works*. Vol. 27, *Lectures on Galatians*. Ed. Jaroslav Pelikan. St. Louis: Concordia Publishing House.

———. 1967. *Luther's Works*. Vol. 54, *Table Talk*. Ed. and trans. Theodore G. Tappert. Philadelphia: Fortress.

Lyon, Danny. 1971. *Conversations with the Dead: Photographs of Prison Life with the Letters and Drawings of Billy McCune #122504*. New York: Holt, Rinehart & Winston.

Macchia, Frank D. 1997. "Is Footwashing the Neglected Sacrament? A Theological Response to John Christopher Thomas," *Pneuma: The Journal of the Society for Pentecostal Studies* 19(2): 239–49.

Machuga, Ric. 2002. *In Defense of the Soul: What It Means to Be Human*. Grand Rapids: Brazos Press.

MacIntyre, Alasdair. 1999. *Dependent Rational Animals: Why Human Beings Need the Virtues*. Chicago: Open Court.

———. 2000. "The Need for a Standard of Care." In Leslie Pickering Francis and Anita Silvers, eds., *Americans with Disabilities: Exploring Implications of the Law for Individuals and Institutions*, 81–86. New York: Routledge.

Mackelprang, Romel W., and Richard O. Salsgiver. 1999. *Disability: A Diversity Model Approach in Human Service Practice*. Pacific Grove, Calif.: Brooks/Cole.

Macklin, Ruth, and Willard Gaylin, eds. 1981. *Mental Retardation and Sterilization: A Problem of Competency and Paternalism*. New York: Plenum.

MacNutt, Francis. 1974. *Healing*. Notre Dame, Ind.: Ave Maria Press.

Magid, Shaul. 2002. "Nature, Exile, and Disability in R. Nahman of Bratslav's 'The Seven Beggars.'" In Hava Tirosh-Samuelson, ed., *Judaism and Ecology: Created World and Revealed Word*, 333–68. Cambridge: Harvard University Press, Center for the Study of World Religions.

Mairs, Nancy. 1986. *Plaintext*. Tucson: University of Arizona Press.

———. 1993. *Ordinary Time: Cycles in Marriage, Faith, and Renewal*. Boston: Beacon.

———. 2002. "Sex and Death and the Crippled Body: A Meditation." In Sharon L. Snyder, Brenda Jo Brueggemann, and Rosemarie Garland Thomson, eds., *Disability Studies: Enabling the Humanities*, 156–70. New York: Modern Language Association of America.

Malard, Jeffrey A., ed. 2004. *Focus on Down's Syndrome Research*. New York: Nova Biomedical Books.

Malti-Douglas, Fedwa. 1989. "Mentalités and Marginality: Blindness and Mamlūk Civilization." In C. E. Bosworth, Charles Issawi, Roger Savory, and A. L. Udovitch, eds., *The Islamic World: From Classical to Modern Times*, 211–37. Princeton: Darwin.

Mansell, Jim, and Kent Ericsson, eds. 1996. *Deinstitutionalization and Community Living: Intellectual Disability Services in Britain, Scandinavia, and the USA*. London: Chapman & Hall.

Marino, Bruno, and Siegfried M. Pueschel, eds. 1996. *Heart Disease in Persons with Down Syndrome*. Baltimore: Paul H. Brookes.

Marks, Deborah. 1999. *Disability: Controversial Debates and Psychosocial Perspectives*. London: Routledge.

Marrou, Henri Irénée. 1966. *The Resurrection and Saint Augustine's Theology of Human Values*. Trans. Maria Consolata. Villanova, Penn.: Villanova University Press.

Marthe, E. 1981. "Objectives of Catechetical Instruction of Mentally Handicapped Persons." In Geiko Muller-Fahrenholz, ed., *Partners in Life: The Handicapped and the Church*, 84–96. 2nd ed. Geneva: World Council of Churches.

Martin, Ralph P. 1967. *Carmen Christi: Philippians 2:5-11 in Recent Interpretation and in the Setting of Early Christian Worship*. Society for New Testament Studies Monograph Series 4. London: Cambridge University Press.

Marx, Tzvi C. 2002. *Disability in Jewish Law*. Jewish Law in Context 3. London: Routledge.

Mason, Asiah, Helen D. Pratt, Dilip R. Patel, Donald E. Greydanus, and Kareem Z. Yahya. 2004. "Prejudice toward People with Disabilities." In Jean Lau Chin, ed., *The Psychology of Prejudice and Discrimination*. Vol. 4, *Disability, Religion, Physique, and Other Traits*, 51–92. Westport, Conn.: Praeger.

Massimini, Kathy, ed. 2000. *Genetic Disorders Sourcebook.* 2nd ed. Detroit: Omnigraphics.

Mates, Barbara T. 2000. *Adaptive Technology for the Internet: Making Electronic Resources Accessible to All.* Chicago: American Library Association.

Matisoff, Susan. 1978. *The Legend of Semimaru: Blind Musician of Japan.* Studies in Oriental Culture 14. New York: Columbia University Press.

Mattheis, Phillip. 1995. "Neurology of Children with Down Syndrome." In D. C. Van Dyke, Philip Mattheis, Susan Schoon Eberly, and Janet Willians, eds., *Medical and Surgical Care for Children with Down Syndrome: A Guide for Parents,* 267–87. Bethesda, Md.: Woodbine House.

Mattinson, Janet. 1973. "Marriage and Mental Handicap." In Felix F. de la Cruz and Gerald D. LaVeck, eds., *Human Sexuality and the Mentally Retarded,* 169–85. New York: Brunner/Mazel.

Maxwell, Chris. 2005. *Changing My Mind: A Journey of Disability and Joy.* Franklin Springs, Ga.: LifeSprings.

May, Deborah C. 1988. "Plastic Surgery for Children with Down Syndrome: Normalization or Extremism?" *MR* 26(1): 17–20.

McAfee, James K., and Michele Gural. 1988. "Individuals with Mental Retardation and the Criminal Justice System: The View from States' Attorneys General." *MR* 26(1): 5–12.

McClendon, James William. 1974. *Biography as Theology: How Life Stories Can Remake Today's Theology.* Nashville: Abingdon.

McCloughry, Roy, and Wayne Morris. 2002. *Making a World of Difference: Christian Reflections on Disability.* London: SPCK.

McClure, Harold M., Kathy H. Belden, and W. A. Pieper. 1969. "Autosomal Trisomy in a Chimpanzee: Resemblance to Down's Syndrome." *Science* 165:1010–12.

McCollum, Adele B. 1998. "Tradition, Folklore, and Disability: A Heritage of Inclusion." In William C. Gaventa Jr. and David L. Coulter, eds., *Spirituality and Intellectual Disability: International Perspectives on the Effect of Culture and Religion on Healing Body, Mind, and Soul,* 167–86. New York: Haworth Pastoral.

McConkey, Roy. 1996. "Down's Syndrome and Developing Countries." In Brian Stratford and Pat Gunn, eds., *New Approaches to Down Syndrome,* 451–69. London: Cassell.

———. 1997. "Intellectual Disability: A Psychological Assessment."

In Ray Fuller, Patricia Noonan Walsh, and Patrick McGinley, eds., *A Century of Psychology: Progress, Paradigms, and Prospects for the New Millennium*, 69–84. London: Routledge.

———. 2002. "Creating Positive Lifestyles for People with Down Syndrome in Developing Countries." In Monica Cuskelly, Anne Jobling, and Susan Buckley, eds., *Down Syndrome across the Life Span*, 195–209. London: Whurr.

McCrossan, T. J. 1982. *Bodily Healing and the Atonement*. Ed. Roy Hicks and Kenneth E. Hagin. 2nd ed. Tulsa, Okla.: Faith Library Publications and Kenneth Hagin Ministries.

McCullough, Laurence B. 1984. "The World Gained and the World Lost: Labelling the Mentally Retarded." In Loretta Kopelman and John C. Moskop, eds., *Ethics and Mental Retardation*, 99–118. Dordrecht: D. Reidel and Kluwer Academic Publishers.

McCune, Billy. 1973. *The Autobiography of Billy McCune*. San Francisco: Straight Arrow Books.

McDannell, Colleen, and Bernhard Lang. 1988. *Heaven: A History*. New Haven: Yale University Press.

McDonnell, Kilian, and George T. Montague. 1994. *Christian Initiation and Baptism in the Holy Spirit: Evidence from the First Eight Centuries*. 2nd rev. ed. Collegeville, Minn.: Liturgical Press.

McDonnell, Thomas J. 1992. "Images of Disability—Icons of Beauty: Learning to See the Disabled Person with the Eyes of the Heart." Margaret E. Payne Memorial Lecture, Weston School of Theology, Cambridge, Mass.

McFarland, Ian A. 1998. *Listening to the Least: Doing Theology from the Outside In*. Cleveland, Ohio: Pilgrim Press.

———. 2001. *Difference and Identity: A Theological Anthropology*. Cleveland, Ohio: Pilgrim Press.

———. 2005. *The Divine Image: Envisioning the Invisible God*. Minneapolis: Fortress.

McGrath, Alister E. 1985. *Luther's Theology of the Cross: Martin Luther's Theological Breakthrough*. Oxford: Blackwell.

McKenna, John H. 1975. *Eucharist and Holy Spirit: The Eucharistic Epiclesis in 20th-Century Theology*. Great Wakering, U.K.: Mayhew-McCrimmon.

McKim, Donald K., ed. 1997. *God Never Forgets: Faith, Hope, and Alzheimer's Disease*. Louisville, Ky.: Westminster John Knox Press.

McLaren, Brian D. 2000. *The Church on the Other Side: Doing Ministry in the Postmodern Matrix*. Grand Rapids: Zondervan.

McMurray, Georgia L. 1987. "Easing Everyday Living: Technology for the Physically Disabled." In Alan Gartner and Tom Joe, eds., *Images of the Disabled, Disabling Images*, 143–60. New York: Praeger.

McNair, Jeff, and Heather Kathleen Smith. 2000. "Church Attendance of Adults with Developmental Disabilities." *ETMRDD* 35(2): 222–25.

McNair, Jeff, and Stanley L. Swartz. 1995. "Local Church Support to Individuals with Developmental Disabilities." *ETMRDD* 32(4): 304–12.

Medley, Mark S. 2002. *Imago Trinitatis: Toward a Relational Understanding of Becoming Human*. Lanham, Md.: University Press of America.

Mehta, D. S. 1983. *Handbook of Disabled in India*. New Delhi: Allied Publishers.

Melcher, Sarah J. 1998. "Visualizing the Perfect Cult: The Priestly Rationale for Exclusion." In Nancy L. Eiesland and Don E. Saliers, eds., *Human Disability and the Service of God: Reassessing Religious Practice*, 55–71. Nashville: Abingdon.

———. 2004. "'I Will Lead the Blind by the Road They Do Not Know': Disability in Prophetic Eschatology." Paper presented to the Biblical Scholarship and Disabilities Program Unit, Society of Biblical Literature, November 20–24, http://www.sbl-site.org/congresses/Congresses_AnnualMeeting_SeminarPapers.aspx.

Menolascino, Frank J. 1974. "The Mentally Retarded Offender." *MR* 12(1): 7–11.

Mercer, Jane R. 1973. *Labeling the Mentally Retarded: Clinical and Social System Perspectives on Mental Retardation*. Berkeley and Los Angeles: University of California Press.

Merrick, Joav, Yehuda Gabbay, and Hefziba Lifshitz. 2001. "Judaism and the Person with Intellectual Disability." In William C. Gaventa Jr. and David L. Coulter, eds., *Spirituality and Intellectual Disability: International Perspectives on the Effect of Culture and Religion on Healing Body, Mind, and Soul*, 49–63. New York: Haworth Pastoral.

Merrick, Lewis H., ed. 1993. *And Show Steadfast Love: A Theological Look at Grace, Hospitality, Disabilities, and the Church*. Louisville, Ky.: Presbyterian Publishing House.

Meyer, Luanna, Charles Peck, and Lou Brown, eds. 1990. *Critical Issues in the Lives of People with Severe Disabilities*. Baltimore: Paul H. Brookes.

Meyers, Laura F. 1988. "Using Computers to Teach Children with Down Syndrome Spoken and Written Language Skills." In Lynn Nadel, ed., *The Psychobiology of Down Syndrome*, 247–65. Cambridge: MIT Press.

Michalko, Rod. 2002. *The Difference That Disability Makes*. Philadelphia: Temple University Press.

Middleton, J. Richard. 2005. *The Liberating Image: The Imago Dei in Genesis 1*. Grand Rapids: Brazos.

Migliore, Daniel L. 2004. *Faith Seeking Understanding: An Introduction to Christian Theology*. 2nd ed. Grand Rapids: Eerdmans.

Milam, Lorenzo Wilson. 1984. *The Cripple Liberation Front Marching Band Blues*. San Diego: MHO and MHO Works.

———. 1993. *CripZen: A Manual for Survival*. San Diego: MHO and MHO Works.

Miles, M. 1992. "Concepts of Mental Retardation in Pakistan: Toward Cross-Cultural and Historical Perspectives." *DHS* 7(3): 235–55.

———. 1997. "References to Physical and Mental Disabilities in the Mahabharata (in English Translation)." *Asia Pacific Disability Rehabilitation Journal* 8(2), suppl.: 2–7.

———. 1999a. "Some Influences of Religions on Attitudes towards People with Disabilities." In Ronnie Linda Leavitt, ed., *Cross-Cultural Rehabilitation: An International Perspective*, 49–57. London: W. B. Saunders.

———. 1999b. "Can Formal Disability Services Be Developed with South Asian Historical and Conceptual Foundations?" In Emma Stone, ed., *Disability and Development: Learning from Action and Research on Disability in the Majority World*, 228–56. Leeds: Disability Press.

———. 1999c. "Blindness in South and East Asia: Using History to Inform Development." In Brigitte Holzer, Arthur Vreede, and Gabriele Weigt, eds., *Disability in Different Cultures: Reflections on Local Concepts*, 88–101. New Brunswick, N.J.: Transaction Publishers.

———. 2001. "Martin Luther and Childhood Disability in 16th-Century Germany: What Did He Write? What Did He Say?" *JRDH* 5(4): 5–36.

———. 2002a. "Belief into Practice." *JRDH* 6(2–3): 21–34.

———. 2002b. "Disability in an Eastern Religious Context: Historical Perspectives." *JRDH* 6(2–3): 53–76.

———. 2002c. "Some Historical Texts on Disability in the Classical Muslim World." *JRDH* 6(2–3): 77–88.

———. 2002d. "Disability on a Different Model: Glimpses of an Asian Heritage." *JRDH* 6(2–3): 89–108.

———. 2002e. "Disability in South Asia—Millennium to Millennium." *JRDH* 6(2–3): 109–15.

Miller, Keith B., ed. 2003. *Perspectives on an Evolving Creation*. Grand Rapids: Eerdmans.

Miller, Leon K. 1989. *Musical Savants: Exceptional Skill in the Mentally Retarded*. Hillsdale, N.J.: Erlbaum.

Miner, Madonne. 1997. "'Making up the Stories as We Go Along': Men, Women, and Narratives of Disability." In David T. Mitchell and Sharon L. Snyder, eds., *The Body and Physical Difference: Discourses of Disability*, 283–95. Ann Arbor: University of Michigan Press.

Mitchell, David T. 2003. "Unexpected Adaptations: Disability and Evolution." *DS* 18(5): 691–96.

Mitchell, David T., and Sharon L. Snyder, eds. 1997. *The Body and Physical Difference: Discourses of Disability*. Ann Arbor: University of Michigan Press.

———. 2000. *Narrative Prosthesis: Disability and the Dependencies of Discourse*. Ann Arbor: University of Michigan Press.

Mitchell, Michael, ed. 2002. *Monsters: Human Freaks in America's Gilded Age*. Toronto: ECW.

Mitchell-Innes, James. 1995. *God's Special People: Ministry with the "Handicapped."* Nottingham, U.K.: Grove Books.

Mittelstadt, Martin William. 2004. *The Spirit and Suffering in Luke-Acts: Implications for a Pentecostal Pneumatology*. Journal of Pentecostal Theology Supplement Series 26. London: T&T Clark.

Moede, Gerald F. 1982. "My Power Is Made Perfect in Weakness." In David L. Severe, ed., *Is Our Theology Disabled? A Symposium on Theology and Persons with Handicapping Disabilities*, 13–26. Nashville: United Methodist Church Board of Global Ministries.

———, ed. 1988. . . . *Like Trees, Walking: Biblical Reflections on Healing*. Princeton: Consultation on Church Union.

Moloney, Francis J. 1993. *Belief in the Word: Reading the Fourth Gospel—John 1–4*. Minneapolis: Fortress.

Molsberry, Robert F. 2004. *Blindsided by Grace: Entering the World of Disability*. Minneapolis: Augsburg.

Moltmann, Jürgen. 1974. *The Crucified God: The Cross as the Foundation and Criticism of Christian Theology.* Trans. R. A. Wilson and John Bowden. Philadelphia: Fortress.

———. 1983. *The Power of the Powerless.* Trans. Margaret Kohl. San Francisco: Harper & Row.

———. 1992. *The Spirit of Life: A Universal Affirmation.* Trans. Margaret Kohl. Minneapolis: Fortress.

———. 1993. *God in Creation: A New Theology of Creation and the Spirit of God.* Trans. Margaret Kohl. Minneapolis: Fortress.

———. 1998. "Liberate Yourself by Accepting One Another." In Nancy L. Eiesland and Don E. Saliers, eds., *Human Disability and the Service of God: Reassessing Religious Practice*, 105–22. Nashville: Abingdon.

———. 2000. "Is There Life after Death?" In John Polkinghorne and Michael Welker, eds., *The End of the World and the Ends of God: Science and Theology on Eschatology*, 238–55. Harrisburg, Penn.: Trinity Press.

Moltmann-Wendel, Elisabeth. 1995. *I Am My Body: A Theology of Embodiment.* Trans. John Bowden. New York: Continuum.

Monroe, Doris. 1972. *A Church Ministry to Retarded Persons.* Nashville: Convention.

Montagu, Ashley. 1971. *The Elephant Man: A Study in Human Dignity.* New York: Outerbridge and Dienstfrey.

Monteith, W. Graham. 2005. *Deconstructing Miracles: From Thoughtless Indifference to Honouring Disabled People.* Glasgow: Covenanters.

Monty, Shirlee. 1981. *May's Boy: An Incredible Story of Love.* Nashville: Thomas Nelson.

Moore, Frank. 1990. *Art of a Shaman.* Berkeley: Inter-Relations.

Moore, Michele, Sarah Beazley, and June Maelzer. 1998. *Researching Disability Issues.* Buckingham: Open University Press.

Morad, Mohammed, Yusuf Nasri, and Joav Merrick. 2001. "Islam and the Person with Intellectual Disability." In William C. Gaventa Jr. and David L. Coulter, eds., *Spirituality and Intellectual Disability: International Perspectives on the Effect of Culture and Religion on Healing Body, Mind, and Soul*, 65–71. New York: Haworth Pastoral.

Moreland, J. P., and Scott B. Rae. 2000. *Body and Soul: Human Nature and the Crisis in Ethics.* Downers Grove: InterVarsity.

Morris, Jenny. 1991. *Pride against Prejudice: Transforming Attitudes to Disability.* Philadelphia: New Society Publishers.

————. 1993. *Independent Lives? Community Care and Disabled People*. London: Macmillan.

————, ed. 1995. *Able Lives: Women's Experience of Paralysis*. London: Women's Press. (Originally published 1989.)

————, ed. 1996. *Encounters with Strangers: Feminism and Disability*. London: Women's Press.

Morris, Leon. 1995. *The Gospel according to John*. Rev. ed. Grand Rapids: Eerdmans.

Morris, Pauline. 1969. *Put Away: A Sociological Study of Institutions for the Mentally Retarded*. New York: Atherton.

Moser, Hugo W. 1995. "A Role for Gene Therapy in Mental Retardation." *MRDD* 1:4–6.

————. 2000. "Genetics and Gene Therapies." In Michael L. Wehmeyer and James R. Patton, eds., *Mental Retardation in the 21st Century*, 235–50. Austin: Pro-Ed.

Mosteller, Sue. 1988. *A Place to Hold My Shaky Heart: Reflections from Life in Community*. New York: Crossroad.

Mostert, Mark P. 1991. "The Regular Education Initiative: Strategy for Denial of Handicap and the Perpetuation of Difference." *DHS* 6(2): 91–101.

————. 1999–2000. "A Partial Etiology and Sequelae of Discriminative Disability: Bandwagons and Beliefs." *Exceptionality* 8(2): 117–32.

————. 2002. "Useless Eaters: Disability as Genocidal Marker in Nazi Germany." *Journal of Special Education* 36(3): 155–68.

Mostert, Mark P., James M. Kauffman, and Kenneth A. Kavale. 2003. "Truth or Consequences." *Behavioral Disorders* 28(4): 333–47.

Mostert, Mark P., and Kenneth A. Kavale. 2003. "Rivers of Ideology, Islands of Evidence." *Exceptionality* 11(4): 191–208.

Müller-Hill, Benno. 1988. *Murderous Science: Elimination by Scientific Selection of Jews, Gypsies, and Others, Germany 1933–1945*. Trans. George R. Fraser. New York: Oxford University Press.

Murphy, Glynis, and Maurice A. Feldman. 2002. "Parents with Intellectual Disabilities." *JARID* 15:281–84.

Murphy, Glynis, and Barbara Wilson, eds. 1985. *Self-Injurious Behaviour: A Collection of Published Papers on Prevalence, Causes, and Treatment in People Who Are Mentally Handicapped or Autistic*. Kidderminster: British Institute of Mental Handicap.

Murphy, Nancey. 1997. *Anglo-American Postmodernity: Philosophical Perspectives on Science, Religion, and Ethics*. Boulder: Westview.

Murphy, Robert F. 1987. *The Body Silent.* New York: Henry Holt.

Murray, J. B., and Emily Murray. 1975. *And Say What He Is: The Life of a Special Child.* Cambridge: MIT Press.

Murray-Seegert, Carola. 1989. *Nasty Girls, Thugs, and Humans like Us: Social Relations between Severely Disabled and Nondisabled Students in High School.* Baltimore: Paul H. Brookes.

Musurillo, Herbert, ed. and trans. 1961. *From Glory to Glory: Texts from Gregory of Nyssa's Mystical Writings.* New York: Charles Scribner's Sons.

Nabi, Gene. 1985. *Ministering to Persons with Mental Retardation and Their Families.* Nashville: Convention.

———. 1988. *Teaching Adults with Mental Handicaps in Sunday School.* Nashville: Convention.

Nadel, Lynn. 1986. "Down Syndrome in Neurobiological Perspective." In Charles J. Epstein, ed., *The Neurobiology of Down Syndrome*, 239–51. New York: Raven.

Nagler, Mark, ed. 1990. *Perspectives on Disability: Texts and Readings on Disability.* Palo Alto, Calif.: Health Markets Research.

Nagler, Mark, and Adam Nagler. 1999. *What's Stopping You? Living Successfully with Disability.* Toronto: Stoddart.

Narot, Joseph R. 1973. "The Moral and Ethical Implications of Human Sexuality as They Relate to the Retarded." In Felix F. de la Cruz and Gerald D. LaVeck, eds., *Human Sexuality and the Mentally Retarded*, 195–205. New York: Brunner/Mazel.

Nash, Melissa C. 2005. "Beyond Therapy: 'Performance' Work with People Who Have Profound and Multiple Disabilities." In Philip Auslander and Carrie Sandahl, eds., *Bodies in Commotion: Disability and Performance*, 190–201. Ann Arbor: University of Michigan Press.

National Organization on Disability. 1996. *Loving Justice: The ADA and the Religious Community.* Washington, D.C.: National Organization on Disability.

Nelson, Agnes. 1990. "The New Jerusalem?" In Patrick McGinley and Brian Kelly, eds., *Mental Handicap: Challenge to the Church*, 270–80. Lancashire, U.K.: Lisieux Hall and Brothers of Charity Services.

Nelson, Jack A., ed. 1994. *The Disabled, the Media, and the Information Age.* Contributions to the Study of Mass Media and Communications 42. Westport, Conn.: Greenwood Press.

Nemeth, Sally A. 2000. "Society, Sexuality, and Disabled/Ablebodied Romantic Relationships." In Dawn O. Braithwaite and Teresa L. Thompson, eds., *Handbook of Communication and People with Disabilities: Research and Application*, 37–48. London: Lawrence Erlbaum.

Neville, Robert Cummings. 1996. *The Truth of Broken Symbols.* Albany: State University of New York Press.

Newbigin, Leslie. 1981. "Not Whole without the Handicapped." In Geiko Muller-Fahrenholz, ed., *Partners in Life: The Handicapped and the Church*, 17–25. 2nd ed. Geneva: World Council of Churches.

Newell, Christopher. 2006. "Disability, Bioethics, and Rejected Knowledge." *Journal of Medicine and Philosophy* 31: 269–83.

Newell, Christopher, and Mary Semple. 2002. "Whose Curse? Whose Cure? When Pastoral Care Becomes Abuse." In Christopher Newell, ed., *Exclusion and Embrace: Conversations about Spirituality and Disability*, 108–13. Melbourne: UnitingCare.

Nicholls, Robert W. 1993. "An Examination of Some Traditional African Attitudes towards Disability." In Diane E. Woods, ed., *Traditional and Changing Views of Disability in Developing Societies: Causes, Consequences, Cautions*, 25–40. World Rehabilitation Fund Monograph 53. Durham: University of New Hampshire and World Rehabilitation Fund.

Nind, Melanie. 2003. "Deconstructing Normalisation: Clearing the Way for Inclusion." *JIDD* 28(1): 65–78.

Nirje, Bengt. 1976. "The Normalization Principle." In Robert B. Kugel and Ann Shearer, eds., *Changing Patterns in Residential Services for the Mentally Retarded*, 231–40. Rev. ed. Washington, D.C.: President's Committee on Mental Retardation.

Noble, Vicki. 1993. *Down Is Up for Aaron Eagle: A Mother's Spiritual Journey with Down Syndrome.* New York: HarperCollins.

Noll, Steven. 1995. *Feeble-Minded in Our Midst: Institutions for the Mentally Retarded in the South, 1900–1940.* Chapel Hill: University of North Carolina Press.

Norden, Martin F. 1994. *The Cinema of Isolation: A History of Physical Disability in the Movies.* New Brunswick, N.J.: Rutgers University Press.

Nosek, Margaret A. 1995. "The Defining Light of Vedanta: Personal Reflections on Spirituality and Disability." *RE* 9(2–3): 171–82.

Nosek, Peg. 1982. *A Philosophical Foundation for the Independent Living and Disability Rights Movements*. Houston: Independent Living Research Utilization Project.

Nouwen, Henri J. M. 1972. *The Wounded Healer: Ministry in Contemporary Society*. Garden City, N.Y.: Doubleday.

———. 1990. *The Road to Daybreak: A Spiritual Journey*. New York: Doubleday/Image Books.

———. 1997. *Adam, God's Beloved*. Maryknoll: Orbis.

Nuttall, Mark. 1998. "States and Categories: Indigenous Models of Personhood in Northwest Greenland." In Richard Jenkins, ed., *Questions of Competence: Culture, Classification, and Intellectual Disability*, 176–93. Cambridge: Cambridge University Press.

O'Brien, John, and Connie Lyle O'Brien. 1996. *Members of Each Other: Building Community in Company with People with Developmental Disabilities*. Toronto: Inclusion.

O'Brien, Mark. 1997. "The Unification of Stephen Hawking." In Kenny Fries, ed., *Staring Back: The Disability Experience from the Inside Out*, 74–86. New York: Plume.

O'Brien, Ruth. 2001. *Crippled Justice: The History of Modern Disability Policy in the Workplace*. Chicago: University of Chicago Press.

———, ed. 2004. *Voices from the Edge: Narratives about the Americans with Disabilities Act*. New York: Oxford University Press.

O'Collins, Gerald. 1978. *What Are They Saying about the Resurrection?* New York: Paulist.

———. 1994. "Augustine on the Resurrection." In Fannie LeMoine and Christopher Kleinhenz, eds., *Saint Augustine the Bishop: A Book of Essays*, 65–75. New York: Garland.

O'Connell, Mary. 1988. *The Gift of Hospitality: Opening the Doors of Community Life to People with Disabilities*. Evanston: Center for Urban Affairs and Policy Research, Northwestern University, and State of Illinois Department of Rehabilitation Services.

O'Connor, N., and J. Tizard. 1956. *The Social Problem of Mental Deficiency*. London: Pergamon.

O'Connor, Susan, Ellen Fisher, and Debra Robinson. 2000. "Intersecting Cultures: Women of Color with Intellectual Disabilities." In Kelley Johnson and Rannveig Traustadóttir, eds., *Women with Intellectual Disabilities: Finding a Place in the World*, 228–38. London: Jessica Kingsley.

O'Connor, Thomas St. James, and Elizabeth Meakes. 2001. "Forgiveness and Resentment among People with Disabilities." In

Augustine Meier and Peter Van Katwyk, eds., *The Challenge of Forgiveness*, 297–309. Ottawa: Novalis and St. Paul University.

Oe, Kenzaburo. 1995. *A Personal Matter*. Trans. John Nathan. New York: Book-of-the-Month Club. (Originally published 1969.)

———. 1996. *A Healing Family*. Trans. Stephen Snyder. Tokyo: Kodansha International.

———. 2002. *Rouse Up, O Young Men of the New Age!* Trans. John Nathan. New York: Grove.

Ohsberg, H. Oliver. 1982. *The Church and Persons with Handicaps*. Kitchener, Ont.: Herald.

Okholm, Dennis L., and Timothy R. Phillips, eds. 1995. *Four Views on Salvation in a Pluralistic World*. Grand Rapids: Zondervan.

Okhuijsen, Gijs, and Cees van Opzeeland. 1992. *In Heaven There Are No Thunderstorms: Celebrating the Liturgy with Developmentally Disabled People*. Trans. G. P. A. van Daelen. Collegeville, Minn.: Liturgical Press.

Oliver, Michael. 1990. *The Politics of Disablement: A Sociological Approach*. New York: St. Martin's.

———. 1996a. "A Sociology of Disability or a Disablist Sociology?" In Len Barton, ed., *Disability and Society: Emerging Issues and Insights*, 18–42. London: Longman.

———. 1996b. *Understanding Disability: From Theory to Practice*. New York: St. Martin's Press.

———. 1999a. "Capitalism, Disability, and Ideology: A Materialist Critique of the Normalization Principle." In Robert J. Flynn and Raymond A. LeMay, eds., *A Quarter-Century of Normalization and Social Role Valorization: Evolution and Impact*, 163–73. Ottawa: University of Ottawa Press.

———. 1999b. "Final Accounts and the Parasite People." In Mairian Corker and Sally French, eds., *Disability Discourse*, 183–91. Buckingham.: Open University Press.

Oliver, Mike, and Gerry Zarb. 1993. *Ageing with a Disability: What Do They Expect after All These Years?* London: University of Greenwich.

Olyan, Saul M. 1998. "'Anyone Blind or Lame Shall Not Enter the House': On the Interpretation of Second Samuel 5:8b." *Catholic Biblical Quarterly* 60(2): 218–27.

Oosterveen, Gerald, and Bruce L. Cook. 1983. *Serving Mentally Impaired People: A Resource Guide for Pastors and Church Workers*. Elgin, Ill.: D. C. Cook.

Orelove, Fred P., and Dick Sobsey. 1991. *Educating Children with Multiple Disabilities: A Transdisciplinary Approach.* 2nd ed. Baltimore: Paul H. Brookes.

Orr, William F., and James Arthur Walther. 1976. *The Anchor Bible: I Corinthians—a New Translation.* Garden City, N.Y.: Doubleday.

Orsi, Robert A. 1997. "'Mildred, Is It Fun to Be a Cripple?': The Culture of Suffering in Mid-Twentieth-Century American Catholicism." In Thomas J. Ferraro, ed., *Catholic Lives, Contemporary America*, 19–64. Durham, N.C.: Duke University Press.

Ortberg, John. 2003. *Everybody's Normal till You Get to Know Them.* Grand Rapids: Zondervan.

Oswin, Maureen. 1991. *Am I Allowed to Cry? A Study of Bereavement among People Who Have Learning Difficulties.* London: Souvenir.

O'Toole, Brian, and Roy McConkey. 1995. "Towards the New Millennium." In Brian O'Toole and Roy McConkey, eds., *Innovations in Developing Countries for People with Disabilities*, 3–14. Lancashire, U.K.: Lisieux Hall.

Otto, Bishop of Freising. 1928. *The Two Cities: A Chronicle of Universal History to the Year 1146 A.D.* Ed. Austin P. Evans and Charles Knapp. Trans. Charles Christopher Mierow. New York: Columbia University Press.

Overall, Christine. 2006. "Old Age and Ageism, Impairment and Ableism: Exploring the Conceptual and Material Connections." *NWSA Journal* 18(1): 126–37.

Paciorek, Michael J., and Jeffery A. Jones. 2001. *Disability Sport and Recreation Resources.* Carmel, Ind.: Cooper Publishing Group.

Padgett, Alan G. 2002. "The Body in Resurrection: Science and Scripture on the 'Spiritual Body' (1 Cor 15:35-58)." *Word & World* 22(2): 155–63.

Pailin, David A. 1992. *A Gentle Touch: From a Theology of Handicap to a Theology of Human Being.* London: SPCK.

Pannenberg, Wolfhart. 1985. *Anthropology in Theological Perspective.* Trans. Matthew J. O'Connell. Philadelphia: Westminster Press.

Paré, Ambroise. 1982. *On Monsters and Marvels.* Trans. Janis L. Pallister. Chicago: University of Chicago Press.

Park, Deborah Carter, and John Radford. 1999. "Rhetoric and Place in the 'Mental Deficiency' Asylum." In Ruth Butler and Hester Parr, eds., *Mind and Body Spaces: Geographies of Illness, Impairment, and Disability*, 70–97. London: Routledge.

Parmenter, Trevor R. 1999. "The Role of Science in Advancing the Lives of People with Intellectual Disabilities." In Hank Bersani Jr., ed., *Responding to the Challenge: Current Trends and International Issues in Developmental Disabilities*, 10–22. Cambridge, Mass.: Brookline Books.

———. 2001. "Intellectual Disabilities—Quo Vadis?" In Gary L. Albrecht, Katherine D. Seelman, and Michael Bury, eds., *Handbook of Disability Studies*, 267–96. Thousand Oaks, Calif.: Sage.

Parmet, Wendy E. 2003. "Plain Meaning and Mitigating Measures: Judicial Construction of the Meaning of Disability." In Linda Hamilton Krieger, ed., *Backlash against the ADA: Reinterpreting Disability Rights*, 122–63. Ann Arbor: University of Michigan Press.

Parrey, Ryan C. 2005. "Disability, Embodiment, and Hospitality: A Post-Phenomenological Inquiry." M.A. thesis, University of Toledo.

Parsons, Mikeal C. 2006. *Body and Character in Luke and Acts: The Subversion of Physiognomy in Early Christianity*. Grand Rapids: Baker Academic.

Pasanella, Anne Langstaff, and Cara B. Volkmor. 1981. *Teaching Handicapped Students in the Mainstream: Coming Back or Never Leaving*. 2nd rev. ed. Columbus: Merrill.

Paterson, George W. 1975. *Helping Your Handicapped Child*. Minneapolis: Augsburg.

Paterson, Kevin, and Bill Hughes. 2000. "Disabled Bodies." In Philip Hancock, Bill Hughes, Elizabeth Jagger, Kevin Paterson, Rachel Russell, Emmanuelle Tull-Winton, and Melissa Tyler, *The Body, Culture, and Society: An Introduction*, 29–44. Buckingham, U.K.: Open University Press.

Paton, David M., ed. 1976. *Breaking Barriers, Nairobi, 1975: The Official Report of the Fifth Assembly of the World Council of Churches, Nairobi, 23 November–10 December, 1975*. London: SPCK; and Grand Rapids: Eerdmans.

Patterson, Barbara, A. B. 1998. "Redeemed Bodies: Fullness of Life." In Nancy L. Eiesland and Don E. Saliers, eds., *Human Disability and the Service of God: Reassessing Religious Practice*, 123–43. Nashville: Abingdon.

Patti, Paul, and John Tsiouris. 2003. "Emotional and Behavioral Disturbances in Adults with Down Syndrome." In Vee P. Prasher,

Philip W. Davidson, and Matthew P. Janicki, eds., *Mental Health, Intellectual Disability, and the Aging Process*, 81–93. Malden, Mass.: Blackwell.

Pattison, Stephen. 1994. *Pastoral Care and Liberation Theology.* Cambridge: Cambridge University Press.

Pelka, Fred. 1997. *The ABC-CLIO Companion to the Disability Rights Movement.* Santa Barbara: ABC-CLIO.

Pengra, Lilah Morton. 2000. *Your Values, My Values: Multicultural Services in Developmental Disabilities.* Baltimore: Paul H. Brookes.

Penton, John. 2001. *Widening the Eye of the Needle: Access to Church Buildings for People with Disabilities.* 2nd ed. London: Church House.

Percy, Stephen L. 1989. *Disability, Civil Rights, and Public Policy: The Politics of Implementation.* Tuscaloosa: University of Alabama Press.

Perera, Juan. 1999. "The World Association Movement for Down Syndrome." In Jean A. Rondal, Juan Perera, and Lynn Nadel, eds., *Down Syndrome: A Review of Current Knowledge*, 225–32. London: Whurr.

Pernick, Martin S. 1996. *The Black Stork: Eugenics and the Death of "Defective" Babies in American Medicine and Motion Pictures since 1915.* New York: Oxford University Press.

———. 1997. "Defining the Defective: Eugenics, Aesthetics, and Mass Culture in Early-Twentieth-Century America." In David T. Mitchell and Sharon L. Snyder, eds., *The Body and Physical Difference: Discourses of Disability*, 89–110. Ann Arbor: University of Michigan Press.

Perske, Robert. 1980. *New Life in the Neighborhood: How Persons with Retardation or Other Disabilities Can Help Make a Good Community Better.* Nashville: Abingdon.

———. 1991. *Unequal Justice? What Can Happen When Persons with Retardation or Other Developmental Disabilities Encounter the Criminal Justice System.* Nashville: Abingdon.

———. 1995. *Deadly Innocence?* Nashville: Abingdon.

———. 2000. "Criminal Justice and Mental Retardation: A Journalist's Casebook." In Michael L. Wehmeyer and James R. Patton, eds., *Mental Retardation in the 21st Century*, 395–410. Austin: Pro-Ed.

Perske, Robert, and Shirley Dicks. 1995. "The Mentally Retarded and the Justice System." In Shirley Dicks, ed., *Young Blood: Juvenile*

Justice and the Death Penalty, 75–88. Amherst, N.Y.: Prometheus Books.

Perske, Robert, Andrew Clifton, Barbara M. McLean, and Jean Ishler Stein, eds. 1986. *Mealtimes for Persons with Severe Handicaps*. Baltimore: Paul H. Brookes.

Peters, Susan J., ed. 1993. *Education and Disability in Cross-Cultural Perspective*. New York and London: Garland.

Petersen, Sigurd D. 1960. *Retarded Children, God's Children*. Philadelphia: Westminster Press.

Piachaud, Jack. 1994. "Strengths and Difficulties in Developing Countries: The Case of Zimbabwe." In Nick Bouras, ed., *Mental Health and Mental Retardation: Recent Advances and Practices*, 382–92. Cambridge: Cambridge University Press.

Pierson, James O. 1998. *No Disabled Souls: How to Welcome People with Disabilities into Your Life and Your Church*. Cincinnati: Standard.

Pinnock, Clark H., ed. 1988. *The Grace of God, the Will of Man: A Case for Arminianism*. Grand Rapids: Academie Books.

Pinnock, Sarah Katherine. 2002. *Beyond Theodicy: Jewish and Christian Continental Thinkers Respond to the Holocaust*. Albany: State University of New York Press.

Pius XII, Pope. 1950. *Humani Generis Encyclical Letter*. London: Catholic Truth Society, http://www.papalencyclicals.net/Pius12/P12HUMAN.HTM.

Plumlee, Stephen. 1981. "The Handicapped in the Orthodox Church." In Geiko Muller-Fahrenholz, ed., *Partners in Life: The Handicapped and the Church*, 109–14. 2nd ed. Geneva: World Council of Churches.

Pohl, Christine. 1999. *Making Room: Recovering Hospitality as a Christian Tradition*. Grand Rapids: Eerdmans.

Polani, P. E., and M. Adinolfi. 1980. "Chromosome 21 of Man, 22 of the Great Apes, and 16 of the Mouse." *Developmental Medicine and Child Neurology* 22:223–25.

Polkinghorne, John, ed. 2001. *The Work of Love: Creation as Kenosis*. Grand Rapids: Eerdmans.

———. 2004. *Science and the Trinity: The Christian Encounter with Reality*. New Haven: Yale University Press.

Polkinghorne, John, and Michael Welker. 2000. "Introduction: Science and Theology on the End of the World and the Ends of God." In John Polkinghorne and Michael Welker, eds., *The End of the World and the Ends of God: Science and Theology on Eschatology*, 1–13. Harrisburg, Penn.: Trinity Press.

Poovadan, L. M. 1975. "Value of Yoga for the Mentally Retarded." In Conchita M. Abad, ed., *Hope for the Retarded in Asia: Proceedings of the '73 Asian Conference on Mental Retardation, November 19–23, 1973, Manila, Republic of the Philippines*, 77–79. Manila: National Media Production Center.

Porterfield, Amanda. 2005. *Healing in the History of Christianity*. Oxford: Oxford University Press.

Potter, David C. 1993. *Mental Handicap: Is Anything Wrong?* Eastbourne, U.K.: Kingsway.

Powell, Cynthia M. 2000. "The Current State of Prenatal Genetic Testing in the United States." In Erik Parens and Adrienne Asch, eds., *Prenatal Testing and Disability Rights*, 44–53. Washington, D.C.: Georgetown University Press.

Powell, Samuel M. 2003. *Participating in God: Creation and Trinity*. Minneapolis: Fortress.

Power, David N. 2005. *Love without Calculation: A Reflection on Divine Kenosis*. New York: Crossroad.

Prabhu, G. G. 1983. "The Mentally Retarded and Their Problems." In S. N. Gajendragadkar, ed., *Disabled in India*, 1–18. Bombay: Somaiya Publications.

Preheim-Bartel, Dean A., and Aldred H. Neufeldt. 1986. *Supportive Care in the Congregation: A Congregational Care Plan for Providing a Supportive Care Network for Persons Who Are Disabled or Dependent*. Akron, Penn.: Mennonite Central Committee.

President's Commission for the Study of Ethical Problems in Medicine and Biomedical and Behavioral Research. 1983. *Deciding to Forego Life-Sustaining Treatment: A Report on the Ethical, Medical, and Legal Issues in Treatment Decisions*. Washington, D.C.: U.S. Government Printing Office.

Price, Daniel J. 2002. *Karl Barth's Anthropology in Light of Modern Thought*. Grand Rapids: Eerdmans.

Price, Janet, and Margrit Shildrick. 1998. "Uncertain Thoughts on the Dis/abled Body." In Janet Price and Margrit Shildrick, eds., *Vital Signs: Feminist Reconstructions of the Bio/logical Body*, 224–49. Edinburgh: Edinburgh University Press.

Priestley, Mark. 1999. *Disability Politics and Community Care*. London: Jessica Kingsley.

————, ed. 2001. *Disability and the Life Course: Global Perspectives.* Cambridge: Cambridge University Press.

Prokes, Mary Timothy. 1996. *Toward a Theology of the Body.* Grand Rapids: Eerdmans.

Pueschel, Siegfried M. 2002. "A Personal Account." In William I. Cohen, Lynn Nadel, and Myra E. Madnick, eds., *Down Syndrome: Visions for the 21st Century,* 149–54. New York: Wiley-Liss.

Pueschel, Siegfried M., and Jeanette K. Pueschel, eds. 1992. *Biomedical Concerns in Persons with Down Syndrome.* Baltimore: Paul H. Brookes.

Pueschel, Siegfried M., and John E. Rynders, eds. 1982. *Down Syndrome: Advances in Biomedicine and the Behavioral Sciences.* Cambridge, Mass.: Ware Press.

Quayson, Ato. 2003. *Calibrations: Reading for the Social.* Public Worlds 12. Minneapolis: University of Minnesota Press.

Raessler, Deborah Clement. 1994. "Pearl S. Buck's Writings on Handicapped Children." In Elizabeth J. Lipscomb, Frances E. Webb, and Peter J. Conn, eds., *The Several Worlds of Pearl S. Buck: Essays Presented at a Centennial Symposium, Randolph-Macon Women's College, March 26–28, 1992,* 81–99. Westport, Conn.: Greenwood Press.

Raine, Bonita A. 1982. "Sexuality and the Disabled Christian." In Stanley Hauerwas, ed., *Responsibility for Devalued Persons: Ethical Interactions between Society, the Family, and the Retarded,* 29–39. Springfield, Ill.: Charles C. Thomas.

Ralston, Steven J. 2000. "Reflections from the Trenches: One Doctor's Encounter with Disability Rights Arguments." In Erik Parens and Adrienne Asch, eds., *Prenatal Testing and Disability Rights,* 334–39. Washington, D.C.: Georgetown University Press.

Ram, Eric, ed. 1995. *Transforming Health: Christian Approaches to Healing and Wholeness.* Monrovia, Calif.: MARC.

Ramcharan, Paul, Gordon Grant, and Margaret Flynn. 2004. "Emancipatory and Participatory Research: How Far Have We Come?" In Eric Emerson, Chris Hatton, Travis Thompson, and Trevor R. Parmenter, eds., *The International Handbook of Applied Research in Intellectual Disabilities,* 83–111. West Sussex, U.K.: John Wiley & Sons.

Ramsey, Craig T., and Sharon Landesman Ramey. 1999. "Prevention of Intellectual Disabilities: Early Interventions to Improve Cognitive Development." In Stephen J. Ceci and Wendy M. Williams, eds., *The Nature-Nurture Debate: The Essential Readings*, 148–63. Oxford: Blackwell.

Raphael, Rebecca. 2003. "Images of Disability in Hebrew Prophetic Literature." Paper presented to the American Academy of Religion.

———. 2004. "What Has Biblical Literature to Do with Disability Studies?" Society of Biblical Literature Forum, http://www.sbl-site.org/Article.aspx?ArticleId=250.

———. 2005. "He Who Has Ears to Hear." In Kerry Wynn and Tazim R. Kassan, eds., "Spotlight on Teaching: Embracing Disability in Teaching Religion." *Religious Studies News—AAR Edition* 20(3): i–xii.

Rapley, Mark. 2004. *The Social Construction of Intellectual Disability*. Cambridge: Cambridge University Press.

Rapley, Mark, Patrick Kiernan, and Charles Antaki. 1998. "Invisible to Themselves or Negotiating Identity? The Interactional Management of 'Being Intellectually Disabled.'" *DS* 13(5): 807–27.

Rapp, Rayne, and Faye Ginsburg. 2004. "Enabling Disability: Rewriting Kinship, Reimagining Citizenship." In Joan W. Scott and Debra Keates, eds., *Going Public: Feminism and the Shifting Boundaries of the Private Sphere*, 178–200. Urbana: University of Illinois Press.

Rée, Jonathan. 1999. *I See a Voice: Deafness, Language, and the Senses—a Philosophical History*. New York: Metropolitan Books and Henry Holt.

Reinders, Hans S. 2000. *The Future of the Disabled in Liberal Society: An Ethical Analysis*. Notre Dame, Ind.: University of Notre Dame Press.

———. 2004. "Being Thankful: Parenting the Mentally Disabled." In Stanley Hauerwas and Samuel Wells, eds., *The Blackwell Companion to Christian Ethics*, 427–40. Malden, Mass.: Blackwell.

———. 2005a. "Euthanasia and Disability: Comments on 'What Should We Do for Jay?'" *JRDH* 9(2): 37–48.

———. 2005b. "The Virtue of Writing Appropriately, or Is Stanley Hauerwas Right in Thinking He Should Not Write Anymore on the Mentally Handicapped?" In L. Gregory Jones, Reinhard Hütter, and C. Rosalee Velloso Ewell, eds., *God, Truth, and Witness: Engaging Stanley Hauerwas*, 53–70. Grand Rapids: Brazos.

Reno, Virginia P., Jerry L. Mashaw, and Bill Gradison, eds. 1997. *Disability: Challenges for Social Insurance, Health Care Financing, and Labor Market Policy*. Washington, D.C.: National Academy of Social Insurance.

Reynolds, Thomas E. 2005. "Love without Boundaries: Theological Reflections on Parenting a Child with Disabilities." *Theology Today* 62:193–209.

Richard, Lucien. 2000. *Living the Hospitality of God*. New York: Paulist.

Richard, Pablo. 1987. *Death of Christendoms, Birth of the Church*. Trans. Phillip Berryman. Maryknoll: Orbis.

Richardson, Stephan A., and Helene Koller. 1996. *Twenty-two Years: Causes and Consequences of Mental Retardation*. Cambridge: Harvard University Press.

Ricoeur, Paul. 1969. *The Symbolism of Evil*. Trans. Emerson Buchanan. Boston: Beacon.

Riggar, T. F., and S. W. Riggar. 1980. *Career Education and Rehabilitation for the Mentally Handicapped*. Springfield, Ill.: Charles C. Thomas.

Robinson, Michael D. 2003. *The Storms of Providence: Navigating the Waters of Calvinism, Arminianism, and Open Theism*. Dallas: University Press of America.

Robinson, Nancy M. 1978. "Mild Mental Retardation: Does It Exist in the People's Republic of China?" *MR* 16(4): 295–99.

Rogers, Cheryl. 1987. "The Employment Dilemma for Disabled Persons." In Alan Gartner and Tom Joe, eds., *Images of the Disabled, Disabling Images*, 117–27. New York: Praeger.

Rogers, Dale Evans. 1953. *Angel Unaware*. Westwood, N.J.: Fleming H. Revell.

Rogers, Paul T., and Mary Coleman. 1992. *Medical Care in Down Syndrome: A Preventive Medicine Approach*. New York: Marcel Dekker.

Roizen, Nancy J. 2001. "Down Syndrome: Progress in Research." *MRDDRR* 7:38–44.

Rolfsrud, Erling Nicolai. 1961. *One to One: Communicating the Gospel to the Deaf and the Blind*. Minneapolis: Augsburg.

Rondal, Jean A. 1994. *Exceptional Language Development in Down Syndrome: Implications for the Cognition-Language Relationship*. Cambridge: Cambridge University Press.

———. 2003. Preface to Jean A. Rondal and Sue Buckley, eds., *Speech and Language Intervention in Down Syndrome*, v–vi. London: Whurr.

Rondel, Jean A. 2004. "Intersyndrome and Intrasyndrome Language Differences." In Jean A. Rondal, Robert M. Hodapp, Salvatore Soresi, Elisabeth M. Dykens, and Laura Nota, eds., *Intellectual Disabilities: Genetics, Behaviour, and Inclusion*, 49–113. London: Whurr.

Rondal, Jean A., and Sue Buckley, eds. 2003. *Speech and Language Intervention in Down Syndrome*. London: Whurr.

Rondal, Jean A., and Susan Edwards. 1997. *Language in Mental Retardation*. San Diego: Singular Publishing.

Rondal, Jean A., Robert M. Hodapp, Salvatore Soresi, Elisabeth M. Dykens, and Laura Nota. 2004. *Intellectual Disabilities: Genetics, Behaviour, and Inclusion*. London: Whurr.

Rondet, Henri. 1972. *Original Sin: The Patristic and Theological Background*. Trans. Cajetan Finegan. New York: Alba House.

Rose, Martha L. 2003. *The Staff of Oedipus: Transforming Disability in Ancient Greece*. Ann Arbor: University of Michigan Press.

Rosen, Marvin, Gerald R. Clark, and Marvin S. Kivitz, eds. 1976. *The History of Mental Retardation: Collected Papers*. 2 vols. Baltimore: University Park Press.

Rosner, Fred, trans. and ed. 1978. *Julius Preuss' Biblical and Talmudic Medicine*. London: Sanhedrin Press.

Ross, Lainie Friedman. 2003. "From Peapods to the Human Genome Project: Post-Mendelian Genetics." In Susan Brooks Thistlethwaite, ed., *Adam, Eve, and the Genome: The Human Genome Project and Theology*, 69–89. Minneapolis: Fortress.

Roth, S. John. 1997. *The Blind, the Lame, and the Poor: Character Types in Luke-Acts*. Journal for the Study of the New Testament Supplement Series 144. Sheffield: Sheffield Academic.

Rothman, David J. 1982. "Who Speaks for the Retarded? The Rights and Needs of Devalued Persons." In Stanley Hauerwas, ed., *Responsibility for Devalued Persons: Ethical Interactions between Society, the Family, and the Retarded*, 8–27. Springfield, Ill.: Charles C. Thomas.

Rothman, David J., and Sheila M. Rothman. 1984. *The Willowbrook Wars*. New York: Harper & Row.

Rotholz, James M. 2002. *Chronic Fatigue Syndrome, Christianity, and Culture: Between God and an Illness*. New York: Haworth Medical.

Rothstein, Laura F. 1997. *Disabilities and the Law*. 2nd ed. St. Paul: West Group.

Roulstone, Alan. 1998. *Enabling Technology: Disabled People, Work, and New Technology*. Philadelphia: Open University Press.

Rouner, Leroy S., ed. 1994. *The Changing Face of Friendship*. Notre Dame, Ind.: University of Notre Dame Press.

Rousso, Harilyn. 1993. *Disabled, Female, and Proud! Stories of Ten Women with Disabilities*. Westport, Conn.: Bergin & Garvey.

Rowitz, Louis, ed. 1992. *Mental Retardation in the Year 2000*. New York: Springer-Verlag.

Ruconich, Sandra, and Katherine Standish Schneider. 2001. "Religions and Their Views of Blindness and Visual Impairment." In Madeline Milian and Jane N. Erin, eds., *Diversity and Visual Impairment: The Influence of Race, Gender, Religion, and Ethnicity on the Individual*, 193–222. New York: American Foundation for the Blind Press.

Russell, Marta. 1998. *Beyond Ramps: Disability at the End of the Social Contract—a Warning from an Uppity Crip*. Monroe, Maine: Common Courage Press.

Ryan, Joanna, and Frank Thomas. 1987. *The Politics of Mental Handicap*. Rev. ed. London: Free Association Books.

Sachs, John R. 1993. "Resurrection or Reincarnation? The Christian Doctrine of Purgatory." In Hermann Häring and Johann-Baptist Metz, eds., *Resurrection or Reincarnation?* 81–87. Concilium 1993/5. London: SCM Press.

Samuel, Vinay, and Chris Sugden, eds. 1998. "Biblical and Theological Reflections on Disability." In *Mission as Transformation: A Theology of the Whole Gospel*, 429–37. Oxford: Regnum.

Sanders, Jack T. 1971. *The New Testament Christological Hymns: Their Historical Religious Background*. Cambridge: Cambridge University Press.

Santurri, Edmund N. 1992. "Who Is My Neighbor? Love, Equality, and Profoundly Retarded Humans." In Edmund N. Santurri and William Werpehowski, eds., *The Love Commandments: Essays in Christian Ethics and Moral Philosophy*, 104–37. Washington, D.C.: Georgetown University Press.

Saul, Rebecca, and David Phillips. 1999. "Ghosts and Germs: Cerebral Palsy in Nepal—a Preliminary Exploration of Cosmology and Disability." In Emma Stone, ed., *Disability and Development:*

Learning from Action and Research on Disability in the Majority World, 210–27. Leeds: Disability Press.

Saxton, Marsha. 1997. "Disability Rights and Selective Abortion." In Rickie Solinger, ed., *Abortion Wars: A Half Century of Struggle, 1950–2000*, 374–95. Berkeley and Los Angeles: University of California Press.

————. 2000. "Why Members of the Disability Community Oppose Prenatal Diagnosis and Selective Abortion." In Erik Parens and Adrienne Asch, eds., *Prenatal Testing and Disability Rights*, 145–64. Washington, D.C.: Georgetown University Press.

Saxton, Marsha, and Florence Howe, eds. 1987. *With Wings: An Anthology of Literature by and about Women with Disabilities*. New York: Feminist Press at the City University of New York.

Schalock, Robert L. 1992. "Capital Punishment and the Dilemmas Faced by the Law and Mental Retardation Professionals." *AJMR* 96(6): 570–72.

————. 2004. "The Concept of Quality of Life: What We Know and Do Not Know." *JIDR* 48(3): 203–16.

Scheerenberger, R. C. 1983. *A History of Mental Retardation*. Baltimore: Paul H. Brookes.

Schipper, Jeremy. 2006. *Disability Studies and the Hebrew Bible: Figuring Mephibosheth in the David Story*. Library of Hebrew Bible/Old Testament Studies 441. New York: T&T Clark.

Schneider, Edgar. 1999. *Discovering My Autism: Apologia Pro Vita Sua—with Apologies to Cardinal Newman*. London: Jessica Kingsley.

Schneiders, Sandra M. 2002. "To See or Not to See: John 9 as a Synthesis of the Theology and Spirituality of Discipleship." In John Painter, R. Alan Culpepper, and Fernando F. Segovia, eds., *Word, Theology, and Community in John*, 189–209. St. Louis: Chalice.

Schouppe, F. X., S.J. 1973. *Purgatory: Illustrated by the Lives and Legends of the Saints*. Rockford, Ill.: Tan Books and Publishers.

Schriner, Kay, and Lisa Ochs. 2000. "'No Right Is More Precious': Voting Rights and People with Intellectual and Developmental Disabilities." *Policy Research Brief* 11/1. Minneapolis: University of Minnesota Institute on Community Integration.

Schriner, Kay, and Richard K. Scotch. 2003. "The ADA and the Meaning of Disability." In Linda Hamilton Krieger, ed., *Backlash against the ADA: Reinterpreting Disability Rights*, 164–88. Ann Arbor: University of Michigan Press.

Schur, Lisa. 2004. "Is There Still a 'Double Handicap'? Economic, Social, and Political Disparities Experienced by Women with Disabilities." In Bonnie G. Smith and Beth Hutchison, eds., *Gendering Disability*, 253–71. New Brunswick, N.J.: Rutgers University Press.

Schurter, Dennis D. 2003. "A Mutual Ministry: Theological Reflections and Resources for Ministry with People with Mental Retardation and Other Disabilities." Unpublished manuscript, available by e-mail from the author at dennissandy@juno.com.

Schwartz, Rev. Karl. 1976. "Nature's Corrective Principle in Social Evolution." Journal of Psycho-Asthenics (1908), reprinted in Marvin Rosen, Gerald R. Clark, and Marvin S. Kivitz, eds., *The History of Mental Retardation: Collected Papers*, 2:147–63. Baltimore: University Park Press.

Schwartz, Matthew B., and Kalman J. Kaplan. 2004. *Biblical Stories for Psychotherapy and Counseling: A Sourcebook*. New York: Haworth Pastoral.

Schwier, Karin Melberg. 1990. *Speakeasy: People with Mental Handicaps Talk about Their Lives in Institutions and in the Community*. Austin: Pro-Ed.

———. 1994. *Couples with Intellectual Disabilities Talk about Living and Loving*. Rockville, Md.: Woodbine House.

Schwier, Karin Melberg, and Dave Hingsburger. 2000. *Sexuality: Your Sons and Daughters with Intellectual Disabilities*. Baltimore: Paul H. Brookes.

Schwöbel, Christoph. 1991. "Human Being as Relational Being: Twelve Theses for a Christian Anthropology." In Christoph Schwöbel and Colin E. Gunton, eds., *Persons, Divine and Human: King's College Essays in Theological Anthropology*, 141–65. Edinburgh: T&T Clark.

Scotch, Richard K. 2001. *From Good Will to Civil Rights: Transforming Federal Disability Policy*. 2nd ed. Philadelphia: Temple University Press.

Scotch, Richard K., and Kay Schriner. 1997. "Disability as Human Variation: Implications for Policy." In William G. Johnson, ed., *The Americans with Disabilities Act: Social Contract or Special Privilege?* 148–59. Annals of the American Academy of Political and Social Science 549. Thousand Oaks, Calif.: Sage Periodicals.

Scully, Jackie Leach. 2002. "A Postmodern Disorder: Moral Encounters with Molecular Models of Disability." In Mairian Corker and

Tom Shakespeare, eds., *Disability/Postmodernity: Embodying Disability Theory*, 48–61. London: Continuum.

Seagoe, May V. 1964. *Yesterday Was Tuesday, All Day and All Night: The Story of a Unique Education*. Boston: Little, Brown.

Seidenspinner-Núñez, Dayle, trans. 1998. *The Writings of Teresa de Cartagena*. Cambridge: D. S. Brewer.

Selim, Kumar B. 2006. "Cosmologies of Morality and Origin." In Gary Albrecht, et al., ed., *Encyclopedia of Disability*, 1: 319–20. Thousand Oaks, Calif.: Sage.

Sen, A. K. 1982. *Mental Retardation: An Indian Perspective*. Agra, India: National Psychological Corporation.

Sen, A. K., and S. K. Goel. 1984. *Mental Retardation and Learning*. Bhelupur, India: Rupa Psychological Centre.

Sen, A. K., and Anima Sen. 1984. *Cultural Deprivation and Mental Retardation*. New Delhi: Northern Book Centre.

Sen, Anima. 1988. *Psycho-Social Integration of the Handicapped: A Challenge to the Society*. New Delhi: Mittal Publications.

———. 1992. *Mental Handicap among Rural Indian Children*. New Delhi: Sage.

Senior, Donald. 1995. "Beware the Canaanite Woman: Disability and the Bible." In Marilyn E. Bishop, ed., *Religion and Disability: Essays in Scripture, Theology, and Ethics*, 1–26. Kansas City: Sheed & Ward.

Setzer, Claudia. 2004. *Resurrection of the Body in Early Judaism and Early Christianity*. Boston: Brill Academic.

Shakespeare, Tom. 1999. "Art and Lies? Representations of Disability on Film." In Mairian Corker and Sally French, eds., *Disability Discourse*, 164–72. Buckingham.: Open University Press.

Shakespeare, Tom, Kath Gillespie-Sells, and Dominic Davies. 1996. *The Sexual Politics of Disability: Untold Desires*. New York: Cassell.

Shapiro, Johanna. 2002. "Young Doctors Come to See the Elephant Man." In Thomas Fahy and Kimball King, eds., *Peering behind the Curtain: Disability, Illness, and the Extraordinary Body in Contemporary Theater*, 84–92. New York: Routledge.

Shapiro, Joseph P. 1994. *No Pity: People with Disabilities Forging a New Civil Rights Movement*. New York: Random House/Three Rivers.

———. 1996. "A Separate and Unequal Education for Minorities with Learning Disabilities." In Shirley C. Cramer and William Ellis, eds., *Learning Disabilities: Lifelong Issues*, 109–12. Baltimore: Paul H. Brookes.

Shapiro, R. L. 2003. "Down Syndrome and Associated Congenital Malformations." In Gert Lubec, ed., *Advances in Down Syndrome Research*, 207–14. New York: Springer-Verlag Wein.

Shaywitz, Sally E., and Bennett A. Shaywitz. 1996. "Unlocking Learning Disabilities: The Neurological Basis." In Shirley C. Cramer and William Ellis, eds., *Learning Disabilities: Lifelong Issues*, 255–60. Baltimore: Paul H. Brookes.

Shearer, Ann. 1981. *Disability: Whose Handicap?* Oxford: Blackwell.

Sherrill, Claudine, ed. 1979. *Creative Arts for the Severely Handicapped.* Springfield, Ill.: Thomas.

Sherry, Patrick. 1992. *Spirit and Beauty: An Introduction to Theological Aesthetics.* Oxford: Clarendon.

Shildrick, Margrit. 2002. *Embodying the Monster: Encounters with the Vulnerable Self.* London: Sage.

Shisler, Barbara Esch. 1998. *Blessed Is the Meadow: Stories of the Spiritual Lives of People with Developmental Disability.* Harleysville, Penn.: Indian Creek Foundation.

Shogren, Karrie A., and Mark S. Rye. 2005. "Religion and Intellectual Disabilities: An Exploratory Study of Self-Reported Perspectives." *JRDH* 9(1): 29–53.

Shorter, Edward. 2000. *The Kennedy Family and the Story of Mental Retardation.* Philadelphia: Temple University Press.

Shōshun, Kato. 1998. "'A Lineage of Dullards': Zen Master Tōjū Reisō and His Associates." *Japanese Journal of Religious Studies* 25(1–2): 151–65.

Shults, F. LeRon. 2003. *Reforming Theological Anthropology: After the Philosophical Turn to Relationality.* Grand Rapids: Eerdmans.

Shuman, Joel. 1995. "Beyond Modern Understandings of Care for Persons with Mental Retardation: Toward a Theology Rooted in Friendship." *Journal of Religion in Disability and Rehabilitation* 2(2): 21–44.

———. 1999. *The Body of Compassion: Ethics, Medicine, and the Church.* Boulder: Westview.

Shuman, Joel, and Brian Volck. 2006. *Reclaiming the Body: Christians and the Faith Use of Modern Medicine.* Grand Rapids: Brazos.

Siegel, Morton K. 2001. "Seminal Jewish Attitudes towards People with Disabilities," *JRDH* 5(1): 29–38.

Sienkiewicz-Mercer, Ruth, and Steven B. Kaplan. 1989. *I Raise My Eyes to Say Yes.* Boston: Houghton Mifflin.

Sigelman, Carol K., Edward C. Budd, Cynthia L. Spanhel, and Carol J. Schoenrock. 1981. "When in Doubt, Say Yes: Acquiescence in Interviews with Mentally Retarded Persons." *MR* 19(2): 53–58.

Sigman, Marian, and Ellen Ruskin. 1999. *Continuity and Change in the Social Competence of Children with Autism, Down Syndrome, and Developmental Delays*. Monographs of the Society for Research in Child Development 256. Malden, Mass.: Blackwell Publishers.

Sillanpää, Matti. 1996. "Epilepsy in the Mentally Retarded." In Sheila Wallace, ed., *Epilepsy in Children*, 417–28. London: Chapman and Hall Medical.

Silvers, Anita. 1996. "'Defective' Agents: Equality, Difference, and the Tyranny of the Normal." In Rita C. Manning and René Trujillo, eds., *Social Justice in a Diverse Society*, 224–36. Mountain View, Calif.: Mayfield Publishing.

———. 1998. "Disability." In Alison M. Jaggar and Iris Marion Young, eds., *A Companion to Feminist Philosophy*, 330–40. Malden, Mass.: Blackwell.

———. 1999. "On Not Iterating Women's Disability: A Crossover Perspective on Genetic Dilemmas." In Anne Donchin and Laura M. Purdy, eds., *Embodying Bioethics: Recent Feminist Advances*, 177–202. Lanham, Md.: Rowman & Littlefield.

———. 2002. "The Crooked Timber of Humanity: Disability, Ideology, and the Aesthetic." In Mairian Corker and Tom Shakespeare, eds., *Disability/Postmodernity: Embodying Disability Theory*, 228–44. London: Continuum.

———. 2005. "Predicting Genetic Disability While Commodifying Health." In David Wasserman, Jerome Bickenbach, and Robert Wachbroit, eds., *Quality of Life and Human Difference: Genetic Testing, Health Care, and Disability*, 43–66. Cambridge: Cambridge University Press.

Simmons, William A. 1996. *A Theology of Inclusion in Jesus and Paul: The God of Outcasts and Sinners*. Mellen Biblical Press Series 39. Lewiston, N.Y.: Mellen Biblical Press.

Simon, Barbara Levy. 1988. "Never-Married Old Women and Disability: A Majority Experience." In Michelle Fine and Adrienne Asch, eds., *Women with Disabilities: Essays in Psychology, Culture, and Politics*, 215–25. Philadelphia: Temple University Press.

Simon, Rachel. 2002. *Riding the Bus with My Sister: A True Life Journey*. Boston: Houghton Mifflin.

Simon, Ulrich. 1958. *Heaven in the Christian Tradition*. New York: Harper & Brothers.

Singer, Peter. 1994. *Rethinking Life and Death: The Collapse of Our Traditional Ethics*. New York: St. Martin's.

Singer, Peter, and Helga Kuhse. 1985. *Should the Baby Live? The Problem of Handicapped Infants*. New York: Oxford University Press.

Skrtic, Thomas M., ed. 1995. *Disability and Democracy: Reconstructing (Special) Education for Postmodernity*. New York: Teachers College Press.

Sloan, William, and Harvey A. Stevens. 1976. *A Century of Concern: A History of the American Association on Mental Deficiency, 1876–1976*. Washington, D.C.: American Association on Mental Deficiency.

Smart, Julie. 2001. *Disability, Society, and the Individual*. Gaithersburg, Md.: Aspen.

Smit, Christopher R., and Anthony Enns, eds. 2001. *Screening Disability: Essays on Cinema and Disability*. Lanham, Md.: University Press of America.

Smith, David H. 1987. "Our Religious Traditions and the Treatment of Infants." In Allen Verhey and Stephen E. Lammers, eds., *On Moral Medicine: Theological Perspectives in Medical Ethics*, 511–16. Grand Rapids: Eerdmans.

Smith, George F., and Stephen T. Warren. 1985. "The Biology of Down Syndrome." In George F. Smith, ed., *Molecular Structure of the Number 21 Chromosome and Down Syndrome*, 1–10. Annals of the New York Academy of Sciences 450. New York: New York Academy of Sciences.

Smith, John David. 1985. *Minds Made Feeble: The Myth and Legacy of the Kallikaks*. Rockville, Md.: Aspen.

———. 1995. *Pieces of Purgatory: Mental Retardation in and out of Institutions*. Pacific Grove, Calif.: Brooks/Cole.

———. 2000. "Social Constructions of Mental Retardation: Impersonal Histories and the Hope for Personal Futures." In Michael L. Wehmeyer and James R. Patton, eds., *Mental Retardation in the 21st Century*, 379–93. Austin: Pro-Ed.

———. 2003a. *In Search of Better Angels: Stories of Disability in the Human Family*. Thousand Oaks, Calif.: Corwin.

———. 2003b. "Abandoning the Myth of Mental Retardation." *ETDD* 38(4): 358–61.

Smith, J. David, and K. Ray Nelson. 1989. *The Sterilization of Carrie Buck*. Far Hills, N.J.: New Horizon Press.

Snyder, Sharon L., Brenda Jo Brueggemann, and Rosemarie Garland Thomson, eds. 2002. *Disability Studies: Enabling the Humanities.* New York: Modern Language Association of America.

Snyder, Sharon L, and David T. Mitchell. 2006. *Cultural Locations of Disability.* Chicago: University of Chicago Press.

Sober, Eliot. 2000. "The Meaning of Genetic Causation." In Allen Buchanan, Dan W. Brock, Norman Daniels, and Daniel Wikler, *From Chance to Choice: Genetics and Justice*, 347–70. Cambridge: Cambridge University Press.

Solberg, Mary M. 1997. *Compelling Knowledge: A Feminist Proposal for an Epistemology of the Cross.* Albany: State University of New York Press.

Solomon, Howard M. 1986. "Stigma and Western Culture: A Historical Approach." In Stephen C. Ainlay, Gaylene Becker, and Lerita M. Coleman, eds., *The Dilemma of Difference: A Multidisciplinary View of Stigma*, 59–76. New York: Plenum.

Songster, Thomas B., George Smith, Michelle Evans, Dawn Munson, and David Behen. 1997. "Special Olympics and Athletes with Down Syndrome." In Siegfried M. Pueschel and Maria Sustrová, eds., *Adolescents with Down Syndrome: Toward a More Fulfilling Life*, 341–57. Baltimore: Paul H. Brookes.

Sontag, Susan. 1977. *Illness as Metaphor.* New York: Vintage.

Souter, Alexander, trans. 1922. *Tertullian Concerning the Resurrection of the Flesh.* London: Society for Promoting Christian Knowledge.

Southard, Samuel. 1989. *Theology and Therapy: The Wisdom of God in a Context of Friendship.* Dallas: Word.

Sparks, Richard C. 1985. "The Ethical Criteria Involved in Decisions to Accept or Forego Treatment of Handicapped Newborns." Ph.D. thesis, Catholic University of America.

Spina, Frank Anthony. 2005. *The Faith of the Outsider: Exclusion and Inclusion in the Biblical Story.* Grand Rapids: Eerdmans.

Spink, Kathryn. 1991. *Jean Vanier and l'Arche: A Communion of Love.* New York: Crossroad.

Spufford, Margaret. 1996. *Celebration: A Story of Suffering and Joy.* Cambridge: Cowley.

Stahl, Abraham. 1997. "Beliefs of Jewish-Oriental Mothers Regarding Children Who Are Mentally Retarded." *ETMRDD* 26(4): 361–69.

Stainton, Tim. 2001a. "Reason and Value: The Thought of Plato and Aristotle and the Construction of Intellectual Disability." *MR* 39(6): 452–60.

———. 2001b. "Medieval Charitable Institutions and Intellectual Impairment, c.1066–1600." *Journal on Developmental Disabilities* 8(2): 19–29.

———. 2003. "Identity, Difference, and the Ethical Politics of Prenatal Testing." *JIDR* 47(7): 533–40.

———. 2004. "Reason's Other: The Emergence of the Disabled Subject in the Northern Renaissance." *DS* 19(3): 225–42.

———. "Reason, Grace, and Charity: Augustine and the Impact of Church Doctrine on the Construction of Intellectual Disability." Unpublished manuscript.

Stallings, Gene, and Sally Cook. 1997. *Another Season: A Coach's Story of Raising an Exceptional Son*. Boston: Little, Brown.

Stefan, Susan. 2001. *Unequal Rights: Discrimination against People with Mental Disabilities and the Americans with Disabilities Act*. Washington, D.C.: American Psychological Association.

Steinfeld, Edward, and G. Scott Danford, eds. 1999. *Enabling Environments: Measuring the Impact of Environment on Disability and Rehabilitation*. New York: Kluwer Academic and Plenum Publishers.

Stewart, Houston, Beth Percival, and Elizabeth R. Epperly, eds. 1992. *The More We Get Together . . . : Women and Disability*. Charlottetown, P.E.I., Canada: Gynergy Books and Canadian Research Institute for the Advancement of Women.

Stiker, Henry-Jacques. 1999. *A History of Disability*. Trans. William Sayers. Ann Arbor: University of Michigan Press.

Stone, Deborah A. 1984. *The Disabled State*. Philadelphia: Temple University Press.

Stone, John H., ed. 2005. *Culture and Disability: Providing Culturally Competent Services*. Multicultural Aspects of Counseling 21. Thousand Oaks, Calif.: Sage.

Storey, Keith. 2004. "The Case against the Special Olympics." *JDPS* 15(1): 35–42.

Stratford, Brian. 1982. "Down's Syndrome at the Court of Mantua." *Maternal and Child Health* 7:250–54.

———. 1996. "In the Beginning." In Brian Stratford and Pat Gunn, eds., *New Approaches to Down Syndrome*, 3–11. London: Cassell.

Stroman, Duane F. 1989. *Mental Retardation in Social Context.* Lanham, Md.: University Press of America.

Stromsness, Marilyn M. 1993. "Sexually Abused Women with Mental Retardation: Hidden Victims, Absent Resources." In Lillian Holcomb and Mary E. Willmuth, eds., *Women with Disabilities: Found Voices,* 139–52. Binghamton, N.Y.: Harrington Park.

Stuart, Elizabeth. 2000. "Disruptive Bodies: Disability, Embodiment, and Sexuality." In Lisa Isherwood, ed., *The Good News of the Body: Sexual Theology and Feminism,* 166–84. New York: New York University Press.

Stuart, O. W. 1992. "Race and Disability: Just a Double Oppression?" *DHS* 7(2): 177–88.

———. 1993. "Double Oppression: An Appropriate Starting Point?" In John Swain, Vic Finkelstein, Sally French, and Mike Oliver, eds., *Disabling Barriers—Enabling Environments,* 93–100. London: Open University.

Stubblefield, Harold W. 1965. *The Church's Ministry in Mental Retardation.* Nashville: Broadman.

Stuhlmacher, Peter. 1994. *Paul's Letter to the Romans: A Commentary.* Trans. Scott J. Hafeman. Louisville, Ky.: Westminster John Knox.

Suchocki, Marjorie Hewitt. 1994. *The Fall to Violence: Original Sin in Relational Theology.* New York: Continuum.

Sullivan, Nancy Jo. 2004. *What I've Learned from My Daughter: Blessings from a Special Child.* St. Louis: Ligouri Publications.

Swartley, William M. 1997. "Unexpected Banquet People (Luke 14:16-24)." In V. George Shillington, ed., *Jesus and His Parables: Interpreting the Parables of Jesus Today,* 177–90. Edinburgh: T&T Clark.

Swinburne, Richard. 1986. *The Evolution of the Soul.* Oxford: Clarendon.

Swinton, John. 1997. "Restoring the Image: Spirituality, Faith, and Cognitive Disability." *JRH* 36(1): 21–27.

———. 2000a. *From Bedlam to Shalom: Towards a Practical Theology of Human Nature, Interpersonal Relationships, and Mental Health Care.* New York: Peter Lang.

———. 2000b. *Resurrecting the Person: Friendship and the Care of People with Mental Health Problems.* Nashville: Abingdon.

———. 2001. "Building a Church for Strangers." *JRDH* 4(4): 25–63.

————, ed. 2004. *Critical Reflections on Stanley Hauerwas' Theology of Disability: Disabling Society, Enabling Theology.* Binghamton, N.Y.: The Haworth Pastoral.

Switzer, Jacqueline Vaughn. 2003. *Disabled Rights: American Disability Policy and the Fight for Equality.* Washington, D.C.: Georgetown University Press.

Sykes, Charles J. 1996. *Dumbing Down Our Kids: Why American Children Feel Good about Themselves but Can't Read, Write, or Add.* New York: St. Martin's Griffin.

Tada, Joni Eareckson, and Gene Newman. 1981. *All God's Children: A Handbook to Help Christ's Church Minister to Persons with Disabilities.* Woodland Hills, Calif.: Joni and Friends.

————. 1987. *All God's Children: Ministry to the Disabled.* Grand Rapids: Ministry Resource Library/Zondervan.

————. 1993. *All God's Children: Ministry with Disabled Persons.* Grand Rapids: Ministry Resource Library/Zondervan.

Takahashi, Akihiko. 1999. "Discussion on the Future Design of Residential Care for Persons with Mental Retardation in Japan." In Hank Bersani Jr., ed., *Responding to the Challenge: Current Trends and International Issues in Developmental Disabilities,* 123–26. Cambridge, Mass.: Brookline Books.

Tamez, Elsa. 1993. *The Amnesty of Grace: Justification by Faith from a Latin American Perspective.* Trans. Sharon H. Ringe. Nashville: Abingdon.

Tamler, Julie. 1993. *Perfect Just the Way I Am.* Edina, Minn.: St. John's Publishing.

Tan, Amanda Shao. 1994. "Disability and Christology in the Fourth Gospel, with a Special Reference to John 9:1-7." Ph.D. diss., Westminster Theological Seminary.

Tanner, Kathryn. 2005. *Economy of Grace.* Minneapolis: Fortress.

Taylor, Michael. 1985. "Include Them Out?" In Faith Bowers, ed., *Let Love Be Genuine: Mental Handicap and the Church,* 46–50. London: Baptist Union.

Temkin, Owsei. 1971. *The Falling Sickness: A History of Epilepsy from the Greeks to the Beginnings of Modern Neurology.* 2nd rev. ed. Baltimore: The Johns Hopkins University Press.

Tennant, F. R. 1968. *The Sources of the Doctrines of the Fall and Original Sin.* New York: Schocken Books. (Originally published 1903.)

Thomas, Carol. 1999. *Female Forms: Experiencing and Understanding Disability*. Buckingham: Open University Press.

Thomas, John Christopher. 1991. *Footwashing in John 13 and the Johannine Community*. Sheffield: JSOT Press.

Thompson, Deanna A. 2004. *Crossing the Divide: Luther, Feminism, and the Cross*. Minneapolis: Fortress.

Thomson, John B. 2003. *The Ecclesiology of Stanley Hauerwas: A Christian Theology of Liberation*. Aldershot: Ashgate.

Thomson, Mathew. 1998. *The Problem of Mental Deficiency: Eugenics, Democracy, and Social Policy in Britain, c. 1870–1959*. Oxford: Clarendon.

Thomson, Rosemarie Garland, ed. 1996. *Freakery: Cultural Spectacles of the Extraordinary Body*. New York: New York University Press.

———. 1997. *Extraordinary Bodies: Figuring Physical Disability in American Culture and Literature*. New York: Columbia University Press.

———. 2003. "Making Freaks: Visual Rhetorics and the Spectacle of Julia Pastrana." In Jeffrey Jerome Cohen and Gail Weiss, eds., *Thinking the Limits of the Body*, 129–43. Albany: State University of New York Press.

Thornburgh, Ginny, ed. 1992. *That All May Worship: An Interfaith Welcome to People with Disabilities*. Washington, D.C.: National Organization on Disability.

Thornton, Craig, and Rebecca Maynard. 1989. "The Economics of Transitional Employment and Supported Employment." In Monroe Berkowitz and M. Anne Hill, eds., *Disability and the Labor Market: Economic Problems, Policies, and Programs*, 142–70. Ithaca: ILR Press and New York State School of Industrial and Labor Relations, Cornell University.

Thornton, Sharon G. 2002. *Broken yet Beloved: A Pastoral Theology of the Cross*. St. Louis: Chalice.

Tiessen, Terrence L. 2000. *Providence and Prayer: How Does God Work in the World?* Downers Grove: InterVarsity.

Tilley, Terrence W. 1991. *The Evils of Theodicy*. Washington, D.C.: Georgetown University Press.

Tisera, Guido. 1993. *Universalism according to the Gospel of Matthew*. European University Studies, Series 23, Theology 482. Frankfurt: Peter Lang.

Titchkosky, Tanya. 2003. *Disability, Self, and Society*. Toronto: University of Toronto Press.

Tollifson, Joan. 1997. "Imperfection Is a Beautiful Thing: On Disability and Meditation." In Kenny Fries, ed., *Staring Back: The Disability Experience from the Inside Out*, 105–12. New York: Plume.

Tomlinson, Richard. 1984. *Disability, Theatre, and Education*. Bloomington: Indiana University Press/Midland Book Edition.

Tomlinson, Sally. 1982. *A Sociology of Special Education*. London: Routledge and Kegan Paul.

———. 2004. "Race and Special Education." In Linda Ware, ed., *Ideology and the Politics of (In)Exclusion*, 76–88. Studies in the Postmodern Theory of Education 270. New York: Peter Lang.

Towner, W. Sibley. 1984. "Interpretations and Reinterpretations of the Fall." In Francis A. Eigo, ed., *Modern Biblical Scholarship: Its Impact on Theology and Proclamation*, 53–85. Villanova, Penn.: Villanova University Press.

Towns, Elmer L., and Roberta L. Groff. 1972. *Successful Ministry to the Retarded*. Chicago: Moody.

Townsend, Harvey G., ed. 1972. *The Philosophy of Jonathan Edwards from His Private Notebooks*. Westport, Conn.: Greenwood Press. (Orig. pub. 1955.)

Tracy, David. 2005. "Form and Fragment: The Recovery of the Hidden and Incomprehensible God." In Werner G. Jeanrond and Aasulv Lande, eds., *The Concept of God in Global Dialogue*, 98–114. Maryknoll: Orbis.

Traustadóttir, Rannveig. 1999. "Gender, Disability, and Community Life: Toward a Feminist Analysis." In Hank Bersani Jr., ed., *Responding to the Challenge: Current Trends and International Issues in Developmental Disabilities*, 189–206. Cambridge, Mass.: Brookline Books.

Treffert, Darold A. 1989. *Extraordinary People: Understanding "Idiot Savants."* New York: Harper & Row.

Treloar, Linda L. 1998. "Perceptions of Spiritual Beliefs, Response to Disability, and the Church." Ph.D. diss., Union Institute Graduate School.

Tremain, Shelley. 2001. "On the Government of Disability," *Social Theory and Practice* 27(4): 617–36.

Trembley, Lo-Ann, and David Trembley. 1996. *Emmaus Eyes: Worship with the Mentally Challenged*. The Lakes, Nev.: Eden Publishing.

———. 1999. "God in the Oven: About the Demonstration of Faith and Gifts of Persons Who Have Developmental Disabilities." *JRDH* 5(1): 75–81.

Trent, James W., Jr. 1994. *Inventing the Feeble Mind: A History of Mental Retardation in the United States.* Berkeley and Los Angeles: University of California Press.

Trent, James W., Jr., and Steven Noll, eds. 2004. *Mental Retardation in America: A Historical Reader.* New York: New York University Press.

Trogisch, Jürgen. 1982. "Congenital Subnormality: The Rehabilitation of the Severely Mentally Handicapped." In *God and the Handicapped Child*, 27–46. London: Christian Medical Fellowship.

Trooster, S. 1968. *Evolution and the Doctrine of Original Sin.* Trans. John A. Ter Haar. New York: Newman.

Tse, John W. L. 1993. "The Sexual Abuse of Children with Mental Retardation: Strategies for Intervention." In *Asian Federation for the Mentally Retarded, Global Harmony for Human Equality: Proceedings of the 11th Asian Conference on Mental Retardation, Seoul, Korea, 22–27 August, 1993*, 157–72. Seoul: AFMR.

Turmusani, Majid. 2001. "Disabled Women in Islam: Middle Eastern Perspective." In William C. Gaventa Jr. and David L. Coulter, eds., *Spirituality and Intellectual Disability: International Perspectives on the Effect of Culture and Religion on Healing Body, Mind, and Soul*, 73–85. New York: Haworth Pastoral.

———. 2003. *Disabled People and Economic Needs in the Developing World: A Political Perspective from Jordan.* Burlington, Vt.: Ashgate.

Turnbull, H. Rutherford, III. 2005. "What Should We Do for Jay? The Edges of Life and Cognitive Disability." *JRDH* 9(2): 1–25.

Turnbull, H. Rutherford, III, and Matthew J. Stowe. 2001. "Five Models for Thinking about Disability." *JDPS* 12(3): 198–205.

Turner, Susannah, Chris Hatton, Robina Shah, Julie Stansfield, and Nabela Rahim. 2004. "Religious Expression amongst Adults with Intellectual Disabilities." *JARID* 17:161–71.

Tyor, Peter L., and Leland V. Bell. 1984. *Caring for the Retarded in America: A History.* Westport, Conn.: Greenwood Press.

Üstün, T. Bedirhan, Somnath Chatterji, Jurgen Rehm, Shekhar Saxena, Jerome E. Bickenbach, Robert T. Trotter, and Robin Room, eds. 2001. *Disability and Culture: Universalism and Diversity.* Seattle and Kirkland, Wash.: Hogrefe & Huber and World Health Organization.

Vagaggini, Cipriano. 1969. *The Flesh—Instrument of Salvation: A Theology of the Human Body.* Staten Island: Alba House.

Vail, David J. 1966. *Dehumanization and the Institutional Career.* Springfield, Ill.: Charles C. Thomas.

van Dongen-Garrad, Jessie. 1983. *Invisible Barriers: Pastoral Care with Physically Disabled People.* London: SPCK.

Van Gelder, Craig. 2000. *The Essence of the Church: A Community Created by the Spirit.* Grand Rapids: Baker Books.

van Huyssteen, J. Wentzel. 2004. "Evolution and Human Uniqueness: A Theological Perspective on the Emergence of Human Complexity." In Kees van Kooten Niekerk and Hans Buhl, eds., *The Significance of Complexity: Approaching a Complex World through Science, Theology, and the Humanities,* 195–215. Aldershot: Ashgate.

Vanier, Jean. 1965. *Le bonheur: Principe et fin de la morale aristotélicienne.* Paris: Desclée de Brouwer.

———. 1983. "L'Arche: Its History and Vision." In Griff Hogan, ed., *The Church and Disabled Persons,* 52–61. Springfield, Ill.: Templegate.

———. 1985. *Man and Woman He Made Them.* Mahwah: Paulist.

———. 1988. *The Broken Body.* New York: Paulist.

———. 1992. *From Brokenness to Community.* New York: Paulist.

———. 1995. *An Ark for the Poor: The Story of L'Arche.* Toronto: Novalis.

———. 1997a. *Our Journey Home: Rediscovering a Common Humanity beyond Our Differences.* Trans. Maggie Parham. Ottawa: Novalis.

———. 1997b. "L'Arche—A Place of Communion and Pain." In Frances M. Young, ed., *Encounter with Mystery: Reflections on L'Arche and Living with Disability,* 3–17. London: Darton, Longman & Todd.

———. 1998a. *Becoming Human.* New York: Paulist.

———. 1998b. *The Scandal of Service: Jesus Washes Our Feet.* New York: Continuum: Novalis.

———. 2004. *Drawn into the Mystery of Jesus through the Gospel of John.* New York: Paulist.

van Maastricht, Sylvia. 1998. "Work, Opportunity, and Culture: (In)competence in Greece and Wales." In Richard Jenkins, ed., *Questions of Competence: Culture, Classification, and Intellectual Disability,* 125–52. Cambridge: Cambridge University Press.

van Oorschot, Wim, and Bjørn Hvinden, eds. 2001. *Disability Policies in European Countries.* The Hague: Kluwer Law International.

Vash, Carolyn L. 1981. *The Psychology of Disability*. Springer Series on Rehabilitation 1. New York: Springer.

Veatch, Robert M. 1986. *The Foundations of Justice: Why the Retarded and the Rest of Us Have Claims to Equality*. New York: Oxford University Press.

Verhey, Allen. 1987. "The Death of Infant Doe: Jesus and the Neonates." In Allen Verhey and Stephen E. Lammers, eds., *On Moral Medicine: Theological Perspectives in Medical Ethics*, 708–15. Grand Rapids: Eerdmans.

Vernon, Ayesha. 1996. "Stranger in Many Camps: The Experience of Disabled Black and Ethnic Minority Women." In Jenny Morris, ed., *Encounters with Strangers: Feminism and Disability*, 48–68. London: Women's Press.

Vijay Human Services. 1988. *Teaching Yogasana to the Mentally Retarded Persons*. Madras: Krishnamacharya Yoga Mandiram.

Vlachou, Anastasia D. 1997. *Struggles for Inclusive Education: An Ethnographic Study*. Buckingham: Open University Press.

Vlahogiannis, Nicholas. 2005. "'Curing' Disability." In Helen King, ed., *Health in Antiquity*, 180–91. London: Routledge.

Vogelzang, Anja. 2001. "Liturgical Celebration with People with a Severe Mental Disability: Giving the Gospel Hands and Feet." In William C. Gaventa Jr. and David L. Coulter, eds., *Spirituality and Intellectual Disability: International Perspectives on the Effect of Culture and Religion on Healing Body, Mind, and Soul*, 141–46. New York: Haworth Pastoral.

Volf, Miroslav. 1996. *Exclusion and Embrace: A Theological Exploration of Identity, Otherness, and Reconciliation*. Nashville: Abingdon.

———. 2000. "The Final Reconciliation: Reflections on the Social Dimension of the Eschatological Transition." *Modern Theology* 16(1): 91–113.

Volf, Miroslav, and Dorothy C. Bass, eds. 2002. *Practicing Theology: Beliefs and Practices in Christian Life*. Grand Rapids: Eerdmans.

Vondey, Wolfgang. 2004. Heribert Mühlen: *His Theology and Praxis—a New Profile of the Church*. Lanham, Md.: University Press of America.

Vredeveld, Ronald. 2001. *Caring Relationships: Helping People with Mental Impairments Understand God's Gift of Sexuality*. Grand Rapids: CRC Publications.

Wagner, C. Peter. 1988. *How to Have a Healing Ministry in Any Church*. Ventura, Calif.: Regal Books.

Walker, Martha Lentz, and Robert Burke Walker. 1995. "Mindfulness in Rehabilitation Practice, Education, and Research." *RE* 9(2–3): 201–4.

Walls, Jerry. 2002. *Heaven: The Logic of Eternal Joy*. Oxford: Oxford University Press.

Walls, Jerry L., and Joseph Dongell. 2004. *Why I Am Not a Calvinist*. Downers Grove: InterVarsity.

Walsh, Patricia Noonan, and Tamar Heller, eds. 2002. *Health of Women with Intellectual Disabilities*. Oxford and Malden, Mass.: Blackwell.

Walsh, Patricia Noonan, and Barbara LeRoy. 2004. *Women with Disabilities Aging Well: A Global View*. Baltimore: Paul H. Brookes.

Waltner, Ann. 1995. "Infanticide and Dowry in Mind and Early Qing China." In Anne B. Kinney, ed., *Chinese Views of Childhood*, 193–217. Honolulu: University of Hawaii Press.

Warburg, Mette. 2002. "Visual Impairment." In Vee P. Prasher and Matthew P. Janicki, eds., *Physical Health of Adults with Intellectual Disability*, 88–110. Malden, Mass.: Blackwell.

Ward, David. 1979. *Sing a Rainbow: Musical Activities with Mentally Handicapped Children*. London: Oxford University Press.

Ward, O Conor. 1998. *John Langdon Down, 1828–1896: A Caring Pioneer*. London: Royal Society of Medicine Press.

Warkany, Josef. 1971. *Congenital Malformations: Notes and Comments*. Chicago: Year Book Medical Publishers.

———. 1977. "Congenital Malformations in the Past." In T. V. N. Persaud, ed., *Problems of Birth Defects: From Hippocrates to Thalidomide and After*, 5–17. Baltimore: University Park Press.

Warkany, Josef, Ronald J. Lemire, and M. Michael Cohen. 1981. *Mental Retardation and Congenital Malformations of the Central Nervous System*. Chicago: Year Book Medical Publishers.

Warrington, Keith. 2005. *Healing and Suffering: Biblical and Pastoral Reflections*. Milton Keynes, U.K.: Paternoster.

Wasserman, David, Jerome Bickenbach, and Robert Wachbroit, eds. 2005. *Quality of Life and Human Difference: Genetic Testing, Health Care, and Disability*. Cambridge: Cambridge University Press.

Wates, Michele, and Rowen Jade, eds. 1999. *Bigger than the Sky: Disabled Women on Parenting*. London: Women's Press.

Weaver, Carolyn L., ed. 1991. *Disability and Work: Incentives, Rights, and Opportunities*. Washington, D.C.: AEI [American Enterprise Institute] Press; Lanham, Md.: University Press of America.

Webb, Ruth Cameron. 1994. *Journey into Personhood*. Iowa City: University of Iowa Press.

Webb-Mitchell, Brett. 1993. *God Plays Piano, Too: The Spiritual Lives of Disabled Children*. New York: Crossroad.

———. 1994. *Unexpected Guests at God's Banquet: Welcoming People with Disabilities into the Church*. New York: Crossroad.

———. 1996. *Dancing with Disabilities: Opening the Church to All God's Children*. Cleveland, Ohio: United Church Press.

———. 1998. "Crafting Christians into the Gestures of the Body of Christ." In Nancy L. Eiesland and Don E. Saliers, eds., *Human Disability and the Service of God: Reassessing Religious Practice*, 267–80. Nashville: Abingdon.

Wehman, Paul, Wendy S. Parent, Darlene D. Unger, and Karen E. Gibson. 1997. "Supported Employment: Providing Work in the Community." In Siegfried M. Pueschel and Maria Sustrová, eds., *Adolescents with Down Syndrome: Toward a More Fulfilling Life*, 245–66. Baltimore: Paul H. Brookes.

Weinberg, Joanna K. 1988. "Autonomy as a Different Voice: Women, Disabilities, and Decisions." In Michelle Fine and Adrienne Asch, eds., *Women with Disabilities: Essays in Psychology, Culture, and Politics*, 269–296. Philadelphia: Temple University Press.

Weir, Robert F. 1984. *Selective Nontreatment of Handicapped Newborns: Moral Dilemmas in Neonatal Medicine*. New York: Oxford University Press.

Welborn, Terry, and Stanley Williams. 1973. *Leading the Mentally Retarded in Worship*. St. Louis: Concordia Publishing House.

Wells, Samuel. 2004. *Improvisation: The Drama of Christian Ethics*. Grand Rapids: Brazos.

Wendell, Susan. 1996. *The Rejected Body: Feminist Philosophical Reflections on Disability*. New York: Routledge.

———. 2001. "Unhealthy Disabled: Treating Chronic Illnesses as Disabilities." *Hypatia* 16(4): 17–33.

Werner, David. 1987. *Disabled Village Children: A Guide for Community Health Workers, Rehabilitation Workers, and Families*. 2nd ed. Berkeley: Hesperian Foundation.

Whitney, Barry L. 1989. *What Are They Saying about God and Evil?* New York: Paulist Press.

Whyte, Susan Reynolds. 1995. "Disability between Discourse and Experience." In Benedicte Ingstad and Susan Reynolds Whyte, eds., *Disability and Culture*, 267–91. Berkeley and Los Angeles: University of California Press.

Wickham, Parnel. 2001. "Idiocy and Law in Colonial New England." *MR* 39(2): 104–13.

Wiley, Tatha. 2002. *Original Sin: Origins, Developments, Contemporary Meanings*. New York: Paulist.

Wilke, Harold H. 1980. *Creating the Caring Congregation: Guidelines for Ministering with the Handicapped*. Nashville: Abingdon.

———. 1981. "The Church Responding to Persons with Handicaps." In Geiko Muller-Fahrenholz, ed., *Partners in Life: The Handicapped and the Church*, 146–61. 2nd ed. Geneva: World Council of Churches.

———. 1982. "Response to Gerald Moede." In David L. Severe, ed., *Is Our Theology Disabled? A Symposium on Theology and Persons with Handicapping Disabilities*, 27–31. Nashville: United Methodist Church Board of Global Ministries.

———. 1984. "A Painful Attempt at Autobiography—My 'Marginal Life.'" In Flavian Dougherty, ed., *The Deprived, the Disabled, and the Fullness of Life*, 106–43. Wilmington, Del.: Michael Glazier.

Williams, Gareth. 1996. "Representing Disability: Some Questions of Phenomenology and Politics." In Colin Barnes and Geoffrey Mercer, eds., *Exploring the Divide: Illness and Disability*, 194–212. Leeds: Disability Press.

———. 1998. "The Sociology of Disability: Towards a Materialist Phenomenology." In Tom Shakespeare, ed., *The Disability Reader: Social Science Perspectives*, 234–44. New York: Cassell.

Williams, Patricia A. 2001. *Doing without Adam and Eve: Sociobiology and Original Sin*. Minneapolis: Fortress.

Williams, Paul, and Bonnie Shoultz. 1984. *We Can Speak for Ourselves: Self-Advocacy by Mentally Handicapped People*. Bloomington: Indiana University Press.

Willis, Kimberly Anne. 2001. "The Ritual Procession toward Justice and Transformation: Altering Perceptions of Disability." Ph.D. diss., Garrett Theological Seminary and Northwestern University.

———. 2002. "Claiming the 'Fearsome Possibility': Toward a Contextual Christology of Disability." In Rosemary Radford Ruether, ed., *Gender, Ethnicity, and Religion: Views from the Other Side*, 215–29. Minneapolis: Fortress.

Wilson, Dudley. 1993. *Signs and Portents: Monstrous Births from the Middle Ages to the Enlightenment.* London: Routledge.

Wilson, James C., and Cynthia Lewiecki-Wilson. 2002. "Constructing a Third Space: Disability Studies, the Teaching of English, and Institutional Transformation." In James C. Wilson and Cynthia Lewiecki-Wilson, eds., *Embodied Rhetorics: Disability in Language and Culture,* 296–307. Carbondale: Southern Illinois University Press.

Wilton, Robert D. 2006. "Working at the Margins: Disabled People and the Growth of Precarious Employment." In Dianne Pothier and Richard Devlin, eds., *Critical Disability Theory: Essays in Philosophy, Politics, Policy, and Law,* 129–50. Vancouver: University of British Columbia Press.

Wimber, John, and Kevin Springer. 1987. *Power Healing.* San Francisco: HarperSanFrancisco.

Wishart, Jennifer G. 1995. "Cognitive Abilities in Children with Down Syndrome: Developmental Instability and Motivational Deficits." In Charles J. Epstein, Terry Hassold, Ira T. Lott, Lynn Nadel, and David Patterson, eds., *Etiology and Pathogenesis of Down Syndrome: Proceedings of the International Down Syndrome Research Conference Sponsored by the National Down Syndrome Society, Held in Charleston, South Carolina, April 11 to 13, 1994,* 57–91. Progress in Clinical and Biological Research 393. New York: Wiley-Liss.

Wolfensberger, Wolf. 1972. *The Principle of Normalization in Human Services.* Toronto: National Institute on Mental Retardation.

———. 1982. "Eulogy for a Mentally Retarded Jester." *MR* 20(6): 269–70.

———. 1983. "Social Role Valorization: A Proposed New Term for the Principle of Normalization." *MR* 21(6): 234–39.

———. 1992. *The New Genocide of Handicapped and Afflicted People.* 2nd rev. ed. Syracuse: Syracuse University Training Group.

———. 2005. *A Guideline on Protecting the Health and Lives of Patients in Hospitals, Especially If the Patient Is a Member of a Societally Devalued Class.* 2nd rev. ed. Syracuse: Training Institute for Human Service Planning, Leadership, and Change Agentry (Syracuse University).

Wong, Sophia Isako. 2002. "At Home with Down Syndrome and Gender." *Hypatia* 17(3): 89–117.

World Health Organization (WHO). 1993 [1980]. *International Clas-*

sification of Impairments, Disabilities, and Handicaps. Repr. Geneva: WHO.

World Health Organization and Joint Commission on International Aspects of Mental Retardation (JCIAMR). 1985. *Mental Retardation: Meeting the Challenge.* Geneva: WHO.

Worswick, Marilyn E. 1978. *Thank You Davey; Thank You God.* Minneapolis: Augsburg.

Wright, David. 1996. "'Childlike in His Innocence': Lay Attitudes to 'Idiots' and 'Imbeciles' in Victorian England." In David Wright and Anne Digby, eds., *From Idiocy to Mental Deficiency: Historical Perspectives on People with Learning Disabilities*, 118–33. New York: Routledge.

———. 2001. *Mental Disability in Victorian England: The Earlswood Asylum*, 1847–1901. Oxford: Clarendon.

Wynn, Kerry H. 1999. "Disability versus Sin: A Rereading of Mark 2:1-12." Paper presented to the American Academy of Religion, http://www6.semo.edu/lec/wynn/index.htm.

———. 2003. "PBS at the Jabbok: Genesis 32:22-32." Paper presented to the American Academy of Religion.

———. 2007. "Johannine Healings and the Otherness of Disability." *Perspectives in Religious Studies* 34(1): 61–76.

Yates, James R., Alba A. Ortiz, and Ronald J. Anderson. 1998. "Issues of Race, Ethnicity, Disability, and Culture." In Ronald J. Anderson, Clayton E. Keller, and Joan M. Karp, eds., *Enhancing Diversity: Educators with Disabilities*, 21–37. Washington, D.C.: Gallaudet University Press.

Yelin, Edward H. 1997. "The Employment of People with and without Disabilities in an Age of Insecurity." In William G. Johnson, ed., *The Americans with Disabilities Act: Social Contract or Special Privilege?* 129–47. Annals of the American Academy of Political and Social Science 549. Thousand Oaks, Calif.: Sage Periodicals.

Yong, Amos. 2002. *Spirit-Word-Community: Theological Hermeneutics in Trinitarian Perspective.* Burlington, Vt.: Ashgate.

———. 2003a. *Beyond the Impasse: Toward a Pneumatological Theology of Religions.* Grand Rapids: Baker Academic.

———. 2003b. "Divine Knowledge and Relation to Time." In Thomas Jay Oord, ed., *Philosophy of Religion: Introductory Essays*, 136–52. Kansas City, Mo.: Beacon Hill Press/Nazarene Publishing House.

———. 2005a. *The Spirit Poured Out on All Flesh: Pentecostalism and the Possibility of Global Theology*. Grand Rapids: Baker Academic.

———. 2005b. "Academic Glossolalia? Pentecostal Scholarship, Multidisciplinarity, and the Science-Religion Conversation." *Journal of Pentecostal Theology* 14(1): 63–82.

———. 2005c. "The Spirit and Creation: Possibilities and Challenges for a Dialogue between Pentecostal Theology and the Sciences." *Journal of the European Pentecostal Theological Association* 25:82–110.

———. 2005d. "Christian and Buddhist Perspectives on Neuropsychology and the Human Person: *Pneuma* and *Pratityasamutpada*." *Zygon: Journal of Religion and Science* 40(1): 143–65.

———. 2007a. "God and the Evangelical Laboratory: Recent Conservative Protestant Thinking about Theology and Science." *Theology and Science* 5(2): 203–21.

———. 2007b. "The Spirit of Hospitality: Pentecostal Perspectives toward a Performative Theology of Interreligious Encounter," *Missiology* 35(1): 55–73.

———. 2008. *Hospitality and the Other: Pentecost, Christian Practices, and the Neighbor*. Maryknoll, NY: Orbis Books.

Young, Damon A., and Ruth Quibell. 2000. "Why Rights Are Never Enough: Rights, Intellectual Disability, and Understanding." *DS* 15(5): 747–64.

Young, Frances. 1990. *Face to Face: A Narrative Essay in the Theology of Suffering*. Edinburgh: T&T Clark.

———, ed. 1997. *Encounter with Mystery: Reflections on L'Arche and Living with Disability*. London: Darton, Longman & Todd.

Zaman, Sultana S., Parveen Huq, and Q. S. M. Ilyas. 1990. "Attitudes towards Mental Retardation in Bangladesh." In Sultana S. Zaman, ed., *Research on Mental Retardation in Bangladesh*, 135–61. Dhaka, Bangladesh: Bangladesh Protibondhi Foundation.

Zigler, Edward, and Dianne Bennett-Gates, eds. 1999. *Personality Development in Individuals with Mental Retardation*. Cambridge: Cambridge University Press.

Zola, Irving Kenneth. 1981. *Missing Pieces: A Chronicle of Living with a Disability*. Philadelphia: Temple University Press.

Scripture Index

Note: sustained discussions are indicated by bolded page references

OLD TESTAMENT

Genesis

1:11	160
1:12	160
1:21	160
1:24	160
1:25	160
1:26	172–173, 302n25
2:7	183
3:22	161
18	222

Exodus

4:11	22
22:21-24	40
32:35	23

Leviticus

19:9-10	40
19:14	23
21:16-23	22
22:19	23

Deuteronomy

15:21	23
24:17-18	40
27:18	23
28:15-68	24
30:11-12	143

Job

29:12-17	23
29:15-16	40

Psalms

6	23
32	23
34:20	46
38	23
51	23
51:5	161
102	23
143	23

Song of Solomon

2:8-17	275–276

Isaiah

6:9-10	27
29:18	24
35:5-6	24
42:6b-7	24
43:8	24
53:2b-3	176
55:8	141
56:3-5	23
56:10	27
56:3-5	284

Jeremiah

14:19	23

20:	156
31:8-9	23–24, 284

Ezekiel

47:12	286

Micah

4:6-7	24

Zephaniah

1:17	23
3:19	23, 24

Zechariah

4:6	196

Malachi

1:8	23

NEW TESTAMENT

Matthew

4:24	26
7:21	234
8:16	26
9:32-33	26
9:37-38	294
12:22	26
17:15-18	26
22:30	337n19
23	27
25:31-46	234
25:32	325n49
25:40	188

Mark

1:32-34	26
2:2-12	300n10
9:14-29	26
16:15	82

Luke

4:18-19	204

5:17-26	25
7:11-17	25
7:21	26
7:22b	25
8:51-56	25
9:37-43	25
11:14	26
13:11	26
13:10-13	25
14:7-14	223
14:12-24	27, 175, 222, 284
14:25-33	223
17:11-19	25
18:35-43	25
21:18	263
24:39-40	174

John

3:5	207
3:18	234
5:14	26
5:15	300n10
5:29	234
9:2-3	26
9:3-4	169
9:38	300n10
10:20-21	26
12:40	27
12:24	179
15:14	187
20:23	238
20:24-28	175

Acts

Acts 1:8	218
2:4-11	11
2:17	186, 204, 258, 290
2:17-18	197
2:38	207
8:7	26

10:34	186	2:9-11	179
17:28	286	2:12-13	215
28:26-27	27	3:13	275–276
Romans		1 Thessalonians	
1:4	205	5:23	170
4:25	205	2 Timothy	
5:5	211	3:16	232
5:12-21	**161–165**	Titus	
8:23-25	281–282	3:5	207
8:29-30	230, 231		
10:17	207	Hebrews	
11:7	27	2:12-13	27
11:25	27	2:17	174
		4:12	170
1 Corinthians		9:27	233
1:20–2:4	218	10:12	178
1:25	178	12:4-13	33
3:19	279	13:2a	222
6:19-20	279		
12:4-7	240, 241	James	
12:12-26	204	2:17	231
12:22-24	218, 338n13	2:23	187
15:1-6	262	2:24	231
15:21-22	161	5:14-16	240
15:40-50	**271–274**	1 Peter	
2 Corinthians		2:23	240
3:18	275	2 Peter	
4:4	27	1:9	27
12:9	178, 218, 254	1 John	
13:13	190, 211	2:11	27
Galatians		3:2b	274
3:28	197, 281	Revelation	
Ephesians		3:17	27
2:9	231	21–22	262
4:18	27	21:4	266
4:13	213, 263	22:2	286
Philippians			
2:7	177		

Index of Authors

Note: sustained discussions are indicated by bolded page references

Abraham, William J., 204
Abrams, Judith Z., 142
Albrecht, Gary L., 97
Altmann, Walter, 255
Anderson, Ray S., 312n25
Aquinas, Thomas, 170, 264–266, 303n1, 314n2
Aristotle, 29–30, 36–37, 120, 123, 138, 170–172, 210, 272, 314n2
Asch, Adrienne, 64, 85, 124, 308n31, 314n3
Astor, Carl, 141, 143
Atkinson, Dorothy, 7, 186, 298n6
Augustine, Saint, 30–31, 34, 38, 161, 178, 262–266, 302n21, 318n4, 319n11
Avalos, Hector, 24, 286

Baal Shem Tov, 337n23
Barnes, Colin, 56, 311n2, 311n6
Batavia, Andrew, 310n48
Barth, Karl, 173–174
Bazna, Maysaa, 146, 147
Beasley-Murray, George, 300n10

ben Eliezer, Rabbi Israel, *see* Baal Shem Tov
Bergant, Dianne, 23
Bernardin, Joseph, 210, 219
Bérubé, Michael, 298n4, 308n31, 320n13
Betcher, Sharon, 32, 130, 181, 188–189, 249, 290–291, 329n23
Betenbaugh, Helen R., 218, 318n1
Binet, Alfred, 51–52, 60
Bissonnier, Henri, 208, 209, 213
Black, Kathy, 184, 245
Blatt, Burton, 51, 55–56, 110
Blocher, Henri, 319n11
Block, Jennie, 10, 205, 245, 299n12
Blumenthal, David, 10
Boers, Hendrikus, 326n49
Boff, Leonardo, 326n2
Bogdan, Robert, 19, 40, 85, 107, 185, 193, 303n30, 305n11, 311n3-4
Bonting, Sjoerd L., 166
Bowe, Frank, 99–100, 312n13

Boyd, Gregory A., 318n7
Brett, Jane, 148–149
Brown, Warren, 336n17
Buck, Carrie, 52–53
Buck, Pearl, 6, 55, 297n3, 305n9
Burke, Chris, 298n9
Bynum, Caroline Walker, 262, 265, 274, 335n10
Byrne, Brendan, 330n27
Byrne, Peter, 65, 110, 264–265, 297n1, 334n8

Callender, Dexter Jr., 320n16
Calvin, John, 34
Carlson, Licia, 64, 106
Catherine of Genoa, 287
Catherine of Siena, 175
Charlton, James I., 7
Chryssavgis, John, 330n28
Clayton, Philip, 158, 322n27
Coakley, Sarah, 281
Colker, Ruth, 91, 95, 312n10
Collins, Kenneth J., 331n1, 332n7
Collins, Raymond F., 273
Collins, Robin, 164
Cooper, John W., 170
Corcoran, Kevin J., 322n27
Corey, Michael A., 319n12
Couser, G. Thomas, 298n5, 332n11
Creamer, Deborah, 9, 167, 169, 176, 335n12

Dahl, Murdoch, 189
Damasio, Antonio R., 171
Davis, Lennard J., 86–87, 88, 102, 115, 128

Dawn, Marva J., 250, 333n12
de Cartagena, Teresa, 32–33
de Paul, Vincent, 48, 304n4
de Vries, Jan, 328n15
Descartes, René, 37
Devlieger, Patrick, 89, 313n23
Didymus the Blind, 1
Dorris, Michael, 320n18
Dostoyevsky, Fyodor, 175–176
Dorris, Michael, 320n18
Down, J. Langdon, 1, 49
Downey, Michael, 201, 219, 324n38, 327n5, 327n7
Driedger, Dianne L., 213n9, 316n13
Dubarle, A. M., 319n12
Dunn, James D. G., 321n20
Dybwad, Rosemary F., 298n5
Dymphna, Saint, 31–32

Edgerton, Robert, 74, 103–104, 108, 134, 317n19
Edwards, Jonathan, 335n14
Edwards, Martha, 28
Eiesland, Nancy, 148, **174–176**, 243, 268–270, 282
Epstein, Charles J., 63, 306n19
Epstein, Richard A., 68
Erasmus, Desiderius, 35
Erickson, Millard J., 312n25
Esquirol, Jean Etienne Dominique, 48, 304n4
Ezeogu, Ernest, 300n9

Fawcett, Barbara, 315n6, 315n11
Fenn, Richard, 338n24
Ferguson, Philip, 50, 109, 185, 304n3

Fiedler, Leslie A., 86, 311n4
Fitzmyer, Joseph, 320n17
Fontaine, Carole, 244
Frank, Gelya, 185–186, 187, 206

Gage, Phineas, 171
Gallagher, Hugh Gregory, 54,
    91, 243–244, 311n8
Gardner, Howard, 309n42
Garland, Robert, 29, 301n15
Gaventa, William C., Jr.,
    76, 259, 325n48, 329n21,
    329n24
Gere, Anne, 119
Ghai, Anita, 138
Gleeson, Brendan, 95, 96,
    312n12
Goddard, Henry H., 6, 51
Goggin, Gerard 3314n28,
    333n15
Goffman, Erving, 83–84
Goodey, C. F., 34, 37, 47,
    302n23, 302n27
Goodley, Dan, 90, 298n6
Gordon, Robert A., 110
Gottlieb, Roger S., 108, 251, 254
Green, Joel B., 170, 322n27
Greene-McCreight, Kathryn,
    189–190
Gregory of Nyssa, Saint, 17,
    271–287, 335–336
Grenz, Stanley J., 312n25,
    319n11
Gunton, Colin C., 159, 160

Hahn, Harlan 98, 101
Haiselden, Harry J., 53, 75, 101
Harrington, Mary Therese,
    207–209

Hasker, William, 322n27
Hassold, Terry, 61, 306n20
Hauerwas, Stanley, 3, 4, 187,
    199, 205, 223, 253, 270,
    293–294, 299n12, 326nn3-4
Hawkins, Peter, 147–148
Hephaestus, 29
Herndl, Diane, 315n8
Hildegard of Bingen, 32
Hillyer, Barbara, 117, 125
Hingsburger, Dave, 45, 72, 228,
    309n46, 310n50, 323n30
Holmes, Oliver Wendell, 53
Holzer, Brigitte, 131, 227
Howe, Gridley, 49, 309n42
Hughes, Bill, 102
Hyun, Younghak, 329n20

Ingstad, Benedicte, 132, 133
Irenaeus, Saint, 159, 335n9
Itard, Jean-Marc-Gaspard, 48,
    68, 304n4
Iozzio, M. J., 122, 164

Jerome, Saint, 34
Johnson, Kelley, 10, 57, 155,
    306n15
Johnson, Mary, 95, 312n10

Kanner, Leo, 30, 304n3
Kant, Immanuel, 303n28
Kasujja, Augustine, 319n11
Katz, Irwin, 84
Kaufman, Sandra 305n13
Kearney, Richard, 84–85
Keener, Craig, 300n10
Keller, Catherine, 318n2
Kendall, R. T., 217
Kingsley, Jason, 7–8

Kirtley, Donald, 334n5
Kittay, Eva, 125, 185, 322n28
Korsmeyer, Jerry D., 319n12
Kriegel, Leonard, 319n9, 332n9
Kuppers, Petra, 90–91

Lejeune, Jérôme Jean Louis
    Marie, 61
Levinas, Emmanuel, 183–184,
    202, 325n45
Levitz, Mitchell, 7–8
Lewis, Alan, 178
Lewis, C. S., 337n22, 338n25
Lindbeck, George, 199, 299n14
Linton, Simi, 313n20, 334n4
Locke, John, 37–38, 70, 189,
    302n27, 303n29
Longmore, Paul, 310n48, 311n5
Luther, Martin, 34–35, 177

MacIntyre, Alasdair, 181,
    257–258, 330n30
MacNutt, Fr. Francis, 240–241
Maimonides, Moses, 141
Mairs, Nancy, 178–179, 244–
    245
Mantegna, Andrea, 175
Margaret of Castello, 32,
    268–269
Marx, Tzvi C., 141–143, 331n6
McClendon, James William, 13
McCloughry, Roy, 246–247,
    321n22, 337n20
McCollum, Adele, 42
McConkey, Roy, 60, 136,
    316n16
McCune, Billy, 332n8
McFarland, Ian A., 188, 191,
    324n38

McNair, Jeff, 76, 205
Melcher, Sarah J., 24, 284,
    300n6
Merrick, Joav, 142,143, 146
Merrick, Joseph, 83, 182
Migliore, Daniel L., 159, 326n1
Milam, Lorenzo, 311n8, 317n26
Miles, M., 34, 139, 140, 144,
    146, 147, 302n22, 324n40
Miner, Madonne, 315n9
Mitchell, David T., 164,
    305n12, 313n20
Molsberry, Robert, 40–41, 243
Moltmann, Jürgen, 159,
    286–287, 323n23, 328n14,
    329n23, 329n36, 333n13
Monteith, W. Graham, 74, 176,
    182, 246
Morris, Leon, 300n10
Morris, Jenny, 57, 66, 314n3,
    315n6
Morris, Wayne, 246–247,
    321n22, 337n20
Mostert, Mark P., 54, 69, 110,
    307n27, 308n37
Mother Teresa, 168
Murphy, Nancey, 322n27
Murphy, Robert, 249–250

Nagler, Mark, 309n43, 309n44
Nahman, Rabbi of Bratslav,
    288–289, 337n23
Neumayr, George, 307n27
Newell, Christopher, 242, 255,
    256, 297n2, 314n28, 333n15
Nicholas of Myra, Saint, 302n20
Nicholas Thaumaturgos, Saint,
    30
Nirje, Bengt, 104–105

Noll, Steven, 53, 58, 304n3, 304n7, 305n10
Nouwen, Henri, 219–220, 282–283, 314n1
Nuttall, Mark, 134–135

O'Brien, Ruth, 98, 312n10, 312n11
O'Collins, Gerald, 263, 333n2
Oe, Kenzaburo, 293
Oliver, Michael, 10, 74, 106, 221–222, 311n2
Origen, 161, 274, 336n15
Ortberg, John, 290–291
Otto of Freising, 264–265

Pailin, David A., 250, 252
Paracelsus, 34–37, 302nn23-25
Paré, Ambroise, 34–35
Parmenter, Trevor R., 77, 107
Patterson, Barbara, 284
Pattison, Stephen, 254–255
Pelagius, 161
Pernick, Martin S., 53, 54, 101
Perske, Robert, 9, 113, 252, 314n26, 323n37, 328n18
Peters, Roger, 330n24
Philippe, Fr. Père Thomas, 200
Philo of Alexandria, 275
Pinel, Philipe, 48, 304n4
Pinnock, Clark H., 318n7
Pius XII, Pope, 319n11
Pohl, Christine, 330n27
Polkinghorne, John, 279–280
Pratt, Rosemary, 168
Priestley, Mark, 100, 316n15
Pueschel, Siegfried, 306n19, 306n24, 324n43

Raphael, Rebecca, 19, 24, 303n33
Rapley, Mark, 60, 108
Reinders, Hans, 64, 65, 75, 169, 251, 305n14, 307n28, 325n45, 325n52
Reynolds, Thomas E., 256
Ricoeur, Paul, 298n10
Rogers, Dale Evans, 55
Rondal, Jean A., 61, 62, 308n39, 309n40
Roosevelt, Franklin D., 91
Rose, Martha, 301n15, 301n17
Russell, Marta, 312n18

Santurri, Edmund, 324n41
Saxton, Marsha, 308n31, 314n3
Scheerenberger, R. C., 52, 58, 302n19, 304nn3-4
Schneiders, Sandra M., 300n10
Schwier, Karin Melberg, 45, 46, 72, 79, 309n46, 328n16
Seguin, Edouard, 48–49, 68
Sen, A. K. 137, 138, 317n20
Shakespeare, Tom, 89, 309n44, 311n2
Shapiro, Joseph P., 128, 312n9
Shuman, Joel, 64, 187, 249, 330n31
Sienkiewicz-Mercer, Ruth, 186
Silvers, Anita, 65, 101, 123, 245
Simon, Barbara, 122
Simon, Theodore, 51–52
Singer, Peter, 64
Smith, John David, 6, 53–54, 56, 73, 110, 306n16, 332n10
Snyder, Sharon, 305n12, 313n20

Stainton, Tim, 29, 30, 33, 34,
    37, 302n21, 334n7
Stern, Louis William, 51
Stiker, Henry-Jacques, 29–30,
    248, 301n14
Stratford, Brian, 323n30
Stuart, Elizabeth, 309n44
Stubblefield, Harold, 236–237
Swartley, William, 330n29
Swinburne, Richard, 170
Swinton, John, 187, 189, 225,
    237–238, 334n8

Tada, Joni Eareckson, 38,
    216–217
Tan, Amanda, 300n9
Tanner, Kathryn, 333n14
Taylor, Steven J., 19, 40, 107,
    185, 193, 303n30
Terman, Lewis Madison,
    51–52, 58
Tertullian, 262–263, 266
Theophilus of Antioch, 335n9
Thomson, Rosemarie Garland
    83, 86, 101, 311n3, 311n4,
    313n20
Tilley, Terrence W., 318n7
Tiresius, 42
Titchkosky, Tanya, 293–294
Tracy, David, 336n16
Traustadóttir, Rannveig, 57,
    155, 306n15, 315n10
Tremain, Shelley, 101
Trent, James W., Jr., 52, 53,
    55, 304n3

Trogisch, Jürgen, 326n50
Turmusani, Majid, 127, 145,
    146

Vanier, Jean, 105–106, 156,
    168, 194, 200–203, 211,
    212, 220, 260, 327nn5-7
Volf, Miroslav, 285, 299n14,
    330n27

Walmsley, Jan, 10, 298n6
Walls, Jerry, 283–284, 331n2
Whitehead, Alford North, 30
Waardenburg, Petrus
    Johannes, 61
Webb-Mitchell, Brett, 189,
    212–215, 222–225, 234, 257,
    301n14, 330n26
Wells, Samuel, 267–268
Wendell, Susan, 121, **125–
    127**, 172, 202, 268–269,
    315nn11-12
Wesley, John, 265–266
Wilke, Harold H., 166, 178,
    242, 323n31, 330n28
Williams, Patricia, 319n10
Wolfensberger, Wolf, 30, 75,
    105–107, 220–222, 235
Wynn, Kerry, 41, 300n8,
    301n10, 303n31, 319n8

Young, Frances, 237–238,
    269–270, 327n5, 336n15
Zacchias, Paulus, 34, 36,
    302n26
Zotikos, 30

Subject Index

Note: sustained discussions are indicated by bolded page references

ableism, 10, 64, 89, 100, 110, 115, 127–130, 230, 298–299

abortion, **63–66**, 73, 75, 77, 124, 135, 173, 180, 221, 307n27, 308n31, 334n7

adam, ha, Adam (and Eve), 31, 39, 160–165, 173, 188–190, 272–274, 279, 319nn10–11, 320nn16–17, 321n20, 335n9

adoption, 121, 220, 224, 231, 232

aged, ageing, 28, 97, **74–77**, 122

Allah, 144–146, 317n23, 317n25

Alzheimer's disease, 74, 190, 318n1

American Association on Mental Deficiency, 52

American Association on Mental Retardation, 49, 58

Americans with Disabilities Act (ADA), **92–95**, 257, 312nn10–11, 330n30

annihilationism, 261

anthropology
Cartesian, 208
cultural, 149
dualistic, 235
emergent, 170–174, 181–184, 189–191, 196, 229, 236, 239, 241, 248, 261, 269–271, 279, 325n48, 337n21
holistic, 169
human nature, 321n25, 322n26
relational, **184–187**, 202, 261
spiritual dimension of, 33, 76, 140, 148–149, 170–172, 183–184, **188–191**, 200, 203, 221, 224, 237–238, 240, 262, 266, 272–273, 277–278, 335n14, 336n18
theological, **169–191**, 195–196, 201–202, 229, 264, 274, 285, 321n25, 323n37, 327n6, 327n7

triadic, 201–202, 324n38
Architectural Barriers Act, 92
Arminianism, 16, 37–38,
    165–166, 231–232, 331n1,
    331n2
autism, 62, 297n1, 371, 412, 416
AUTONOMY, Inc., 310n48
Baby Doe, 65, 307n30
blind, blindness, 9, 22, 41,
    42, 141–142, 144–145,
    162, 169, 182, 288, 299n1,
    300n5, 300nn9-10, 301n12,
    317nn23-24, 319n8, 334n5
baptism, Christian, 40, 161,
    203, 207, **209–212**, 232
Buddha, Gautama, 147
Buddhism, 140, **147–148**,
    317n26

Calvinism, 16, 34, 37–38,
    165–166, 231–232, 328n15
caregiver, 8, 10, 39, 62, 108,
    122–125, 184, 223, 286,
    305n14, 315n6, 325n48
catechism, Christian, 17,
    207–212, 219, 287, 321n24
cerebral palsy, 62, 65, 186, 268,
    330n28
Chalcedon, Council of, 167
charisms, 215, **218–225**, 241,
    329n23
China, 135–136, 301n17
Christ, Jesus
    and Down Syndrome, 175
    christology, 157, 167, **174–
    180**, 281
    incarnation, 167, **174–176**,
    219

last Adam, 273–274
life and ministry, 25–26, 40
passion of, suffering, 155,
    176–180, 201–202,
    219–220
Christology, *see* Christ, Jesus
chronic illness, 121
Church, *see* ecclesiology
Civil Rights of Institutionalized
    Persons Act, 92
cognitive disability, *see* intellec-
    tual disability
cosmology, 132, 164, 320n14
creation, doctrine of, 31, 141,
    144, **158–165**, 231, 236,
    258, 264, 267, 284, 318n2,
    319n10, 320n14, 322n29,
    335n12, 338n25
    creation out of nothing, *cre-
    atio ex nihilo* 159, 318n2
    new creation 272, **278–292**,
    335n9, 338n25
criminal justice, **111–114**,
    314n24, 314n25, 332n8
curing 26, **245–247**, 292, 294
    see also healing

deaf, deafness, 19, 26–27, 28,
    34, 36, 114–115, 142, 145,
    172, 207, 288, 291, 299n1,
    300n6, 301n11, 308n37,
    317n23, 317n25, 331n6
Deaf Culture, 12, **87–89**
death, dying, **73–77**, 83–84,
    86, 147, 161–165, 179, 190,
    205, 216, 255, 265–266,
    271, 274–275, 288, 320n17,
    330n31, 337n21

death penalty, 113

deification (*theosis*), 275–278

deinstitutionalization, 15, 48, **55–58**, 67–68, 71–72, 75, 87, 97, 103–104, 200, 215, 303n30, 305n13

dementia, 28

demonic, demonology, 26–27, 34, 82, 118, 235, 240–241, 246

developmental disability, *see* intellectual disability

deviance, deviancy, 50, **82–84**, 86, 95, 105, 256

difference, diversity, 11, 30, 66, 69–70, 74, **84–87**, 89, 101–102, 106–107, 110–111, 125, 141, 146, 159, 164, 168, 181–183, 196, 203, 216, 245, 256, 280–281, 284, 287, 290–291, 336nn15-17

disability
  and culture, **130–140**
  and indigenous cultures, **131–133**
  and politics, 65, 74, **91–95**, 125, 135–136, 149, 174, 217, **253–258**, 281, 285, 333n15
  and race, **128–130**
  and the arts, 89–91
  and women, **120–128**
  in ancient Israel, **22–24**
  in Bangladesh, 316n17
  in Hebrew Bible, Old Testament **22–24**
  in India, **137–140**, 147, 202, 317n20

in New Testament, **25–27**

narratives of, 6–7, 14, 21, 25–27, 39–40, 138, 252

psychology of, 58, 60, 85, 249–250, 310n48

severe or profound, 8, 9, 59–65, 69, 75, 100, 110, 131, 134, 171, 182, 185, 187, 200, 208, 210, 214, 218–219, 224, 232, 234, 265, 267, 301n11, 304n7, 305n11, 307n25, 307n30, 316n16, 328n18, 329n23, 331n4

social model of, **81–90**, 96–97

disability culture, 13, 82, **87–90**, 311n5

disability rights, 9, 81, 92–93, 98, 252, 312nn9–10, 312n16

discipleship, 27, 196, 206, 209, 212–215, 222–224, 232, 239, 263, 295

Donatism, 161

Down Syndrome
  ageing, **74–77**
  and advocacy, 7–8
  and angels, 337n19
  and healing, 245, 334n8
  and heaven, **281–283**
  and christology 175
  and resurrection, 269–270, 282–283
  and salvation, **233–235**
  biographies, authobiographies, 298nn8–9
  biomedical research, **60–63**, 306n19, 306n23, 309n40

chromosomal mutation, 163–165, 180
death and dying, **74–77**, 306n21
early intervention, **67–71**
employment, 71
education, **67–71**, 304n2, 309n42
institutionalization, **48–57**
language development, 308n39
lifespan, 308n33
marriage, 72–73
parenting, 72–73
personality type, 326n51
prenatal testing, abortion, **63–66**, 308n31
trisomy, 21 **61–63**, 163–165, 310n47

Earlswood Asylum, 49
ecclesiology, 174, **193–226**, 326nn1-3, 327n11, 328n12, 330n31, 333n12
  ecclesial practices, **206–215**
  Emerging Church, 198–199
  fellowship of the Spirit, **203–206**
  liturgy, **212–214**
  postliberal, 199
  sacraments, **209–212**
economics, 64–67, **96–99**, 103, 108, 114, 122, 127–138, 182–183, **254–258**, 293–294, 312n15, 313n22, 333n12, 333n14
ecumenism, 206–209, 328n15

Education for All Handicapped Children Act, 68, 92
election, doctrine of, 230–232, 251–252
emancipation, 9–10, 13–14
embodiment, 95, **99–102**, **124–126**, 171–172, **181–184**, 188–189, 201–202, 222, 241, **248–250**, 262, 265, 279–280, 284–285, 315n9
employment, 71–72, 92–94, **96–99**, 122, 127, 137–138, 312nn14-16, 313n18
epectasis, eternal journey, **274–280**
encephalitis, 206
epilepsy, 25–26, 34, 52, 54, 62, 96, 104, 132, 132, 176, 206, 219, 301n11
epistemology, 11, 13–14, 100, 124–126, 152
eschatology, 24–25, 162, 175, 191, 197, **258–292**, 217n22, 320n17, 331n1, 335n9, 335n14, 338nn24-25
eternal life, *see* eschatology
Eucharist, 175, 179, 194, 202, **209–212**
eugenics, 50–54, 135, 305n12
euthanasia, 54, 65, 75, 101, 173, 310n49
evangelism, 212, 235, 239
evil spirits, *see* demonic, demonology
evil, problem of, *see* theodicy

Fair Housing Act, 92

Feminism, 92, **123–126**, 138,
149,172, 315nn6–7, 315n10,
315n12, 322n28, 323n34
fetal alcohol syndrome (FAS),
119, 180, 320n18
footwashing, 203, 211–212
freaks, freakery, **82–86**, 311n3,
311n4
friendship, 8, 57, 69, 71–75, 83,
147, 186–188, 200–202, 206,
225, 233, 240, 250, 253, 258,
305n14, 325nn47-48, 327n7,
335nn47-48

gender, 127–128
see also sex, sexuality
genocide, 53
geography, 20, **95–100**, 103,
312n12
glossolalia, 13–14, 19, 40, 221,
228

healing, 20, **23–27**, 31, 39–40,
43, 220, 230, 236, **239–247**,
267–269, **285–288**, 300n9,
301n10, 317n22, 319n8,
321n22, 334n8
heaven, 210, **259–270**, **281–292**, 294, 330n28, 333n2,
335n9, 336n18, 337n20,
338n25
hermeneutics, 41, 152, 217, 245
handicap, double handicap, 45,
47, 58, 84, 120, 123, 127,
332n9
Holy Spirit, 32, 40, 180–181,
190–191, 195–196, 197–198,
299n13

and charisms, **218–222**
and church, **203–206**
and eschatology, **278–281**,
291–292
and ministry, **215–225**
and salvation, **236–238**
and theological anthropology, **180–191**
see also pneumatological
imagination
hospital, 30–31, 40, 55, 104,
254–255
hospitality, 85, 185, 187, 198,
204–205, 212, **222–225**,
249, 292, 330n27
human genome, Human
Genome Project, 47, 57, 63
humanities, 9, 12, 89, 100

identity politics, 6, 101
illness, 9, 240–241, 315n8
imago Dei, image of God, 39,
141, 155–158, **169–191**,
292, 294, 321n24, 321n25,
324n38, 324n41
impairment, 58–59, 74, 85, 87,
92–93, 101–102, 124, 127,
164, 174–175, 245
inclusion, 20, 31, 42, 47,
99–101, 107, 116, 131, 139,
146, 245, 257, 284, 292,
295, 333n15
ecclesial, 196–225, 290–291,
327n11, 328n12
educational, **68–71**, 110,
308nn35–38
religious, 251
India, *see* disability, in India

Individuals with Disabilities Education Act (IDEA), 68–69

infants, 28, 35, 62, 73, 251, 306n21
baptism of, 34, 161, 207, 210, 233, 318n4
infanticide, 29–30, 37, 53, **63–65**, 301n17
resurrection of, 282
salvation of, **232–235**, 331n3

initiation, Christian, **206–208**, 212, 224

institutionalization, 6, **48–54**, 56–57, 103–105, 108, 112, 114, 297n3, 304n7, 309n46, 310nn49-50, 313n22, 317n19, 328n15, 332n8

intellectual disability, 47, 62, 143, 297n1, 304n3, 306nn22-23, 309n39, 313n23, 334n7
ageing and dying, **74–77**
and religious knowledge, 208, **233–235**
and religious life, 218–222, 250
and the Bible, 21, 299n2
as modern phenomenon, 47
criminal justice, **111–113**
education and early intervention, **67–71**
feeblemindedness, 6, 30, 48–53, 58, 63, 299n2, 304n6, 310n49, 313n23
global context, **133–137**
history of, 28–38, 48
idiocy, 33, 37–38, 48–53, 103, 302nn26-27, 303n29, 304n4, 304n7n, 313n23
imbecility, 48–53, 63, 186, 302n26, 304n4, 304n7, 313n23
marriage and children, 8, **71–73**
mongolism, 49, 67
narratives of, 6–8, 186, 252
normalization, **103–107**
prevention of, 66
social and theoretical construct, **107–111**
social control of, 50–52
stigma of, **103–107**
see also disability, severe and profound
see also mental retardation

intelligence quotient (IQ), 40, 47, 51–52, **57–60**, 77, 108, 297n1, 306n15, 324n43

intermediate state, 286–287, 338n24

Islam, **144–147**

Judaism, 32, **140–143**

justification, 205, 230–232, 238, 252–256, 333n13

kenosis, 179–180, 323n35

L'Arche, 105, 196, **200–203**, 211, 219, 256, 268, 282, 327n9, 328n13, 328n18

learning disability, see intellectual disability

liturgy, 141–142, 203, **212–215**, 219, 225

Lou Gehrig's disease, 283,
    313n19

Martha's Vineyard, 88
media, **87–91**, 115, 121, 198,
    205, 208, 311n6, 313n18
medicine, 20, 36, 43, 47, 62, 77,
    83, 132, 227, 241, 248–249,
    299n3, 312n15
mental health care, 254–255
mental retardation, 4–8, 28, 30,
    34, 45, 48–51, 55, **57–62**,
    66, 70, 73, 75, 79, **104–111**,
    128, 134–137, 173, 176, 205,
    208, 213, 233, 270, 293,
    297nn1-3, 300n4, 302n19,
    303n30, 304n4, 306n15,
    306n17, 306n23, 307n36,
    313nn22-23, 319n19,
    323n37, 327n7, 331n5
    see also intellectual disability
ministry, 40, 196, **215–225**, 246
miracles, 24, 30–33, 180, 182,
    201, 243–245, 247, 268, 285,
    289
monogenism, 319n11
monophysitism, 167
monstrosity, monstrous births,
    see teratology
music, 70, 90, 208, 213–214,
    309n42, 329n19

Nazism, 54, 75, 101, 173
Neoorthodoxy, 173
Neoplatonism, 31, 35, 159, 277,
    280
Nestorianism, 167

normal, normalcy, normate, 41,
    52, 58–59, 74, **84–87**, 90,
    95, 145, 169, 221–222, 245,
    256, 263, 269, 288–291,
    330n26, 331n5, 334n8
    see also ableism
    see also normalization
normalization, **103–107**, 115,
    124–125, 135, 250

Open Theism, 165–166
original sin, **160–165**, 207,
    251, 319nn10-12

paleoanthropology, 163
panentheism, 158–159
pantheism, 158–159
paraplegia, 115, 148, 242–243
parent, parents, parenting, 6,
    8, 29, 64–65, 69, 72–73,
    121–124, 161, 184, 209,
    251, 297n3, 298nn4-5,
    307n26, 308n38, 313n23,
    315n4, 330n26, 336n18
parousia, 158, 191, 257, 261,
    268, 274, 281–286, 290
Pentecost, Day of, and Pente-
    cost narrative, 11–12, 14,
    247, 299n13
Pentecostalism, modern, 40,
    194, 239–243, 246, 268,
    303n30, 331n6
phenomenology of the body,
    99–102, 230, 244
pneuma, *see* Holy Spirit
pneumatological imagination,
    10–14, 152, 158, 195–196

polytheism, 24
postcolonialism, 12, 44, 119, 129–130, 138
postliberal theology, postliberalism, 197, 199–203, 326n3
predestination, 37, 230–232, 251–252
prenatal testing, **63–66**
Prerogativa Regis, 33
providence, doctrine of, 16, **158–169**
Proteus syndrome, 83
purgatory, 235, 286–287, 337n22, 338n24

quadriplegia, 243–244, 270, 310n48

reconciliation, 202, 229, 232, 236, 238, 245, 247, **250–255, 285–288**, 330n27
Rehabilitation Act, 92–93, 311n7
regeneration, 34, 215, 231–232, 252–253
relational ontology, relationality, 60, 87, 96, 123, 141, 147, 159, 171–174, **184–187**, 201–202, 210–211, 229, 237–238, 241, 247, 248, 253, 257, 333n13
see also anthropology, relational
Renaissance, 28, 34–35, 175
resurrection, 170–171, 179–180, 218–220, 224, **259–281**
see also heaven

retardation, *see* intellectual disability
Roman Catholicism, 158, 179, 207, 210, 235, 240, 266–267, 287, 326n2

sacraments, 17, 36, 40, 152, 196, 203, **209–212**, 225, 294, 330n25, 330n31
salvation, 35, 119, 161, 207–208, **230–258**, 260–261, 265, 275, 324n42, 331nn1-2, 332n8
and intellectual disability, **233–235**
eschatological, **281–292**
order of salvation, *ordo salutis*, **230–232**
way of salvation, *via salutis*, **236–239**, 332n7
sanctification, 231–232, 278–279, 284
savant syndrome, 70
science, 12, 13, 67, 70, 77, 83, 100, 110, 149, 320n15
biomedical, 60–63
cognitive neurosciences, 170–171
evolutionary, 163–164, 311n3, 319n12
schizophrenia, 54
self–advocacy, 7–9, 253, 298n6
sex, sexuality, 20, 50, 71–72, 83, 86, 89, 104, 121–122, 124, 144, 161, 182, 202–202, 216, 303n30, 309nn44-46, 315n5, 334n3, 335n10

siblings, 9, 137, 298n4, 330n25
sick, sickness, 24, 30–32, 40,
    75, 97, 132, 147, 240–242,
    245–247
Social Role Valorization,
    106–107
soteriology, *see* salvation
special education, 5, 48–49,
    67–71, 128, 135–136, 205,
    304n2
    see also Down syndrome,
        education
Special Olympics, **114–115**
spina bifida, 65
spirit, human, *see* anthropology,
    spiritual dimension of
spiritual gifts, *see* charisms
stigma, 6, 68, **82–87**, **103–107**,
    109, 114, 125, 127, 134,
    137–138, 148, 177, 254,
    331n6

technology, 9, 12, 43, 47–48,
    61–63, 65–66, 67–68, 71, 87,
    92, 96, 121, 131, 149, 164,
    182, 205, 221, 247–249, 291,
    309n43, 325n46
teratology, 29–33, 35–36,
    82–87, 263
theodicy, 158, **165–169**, 216,
    300n4, 300n9, 318n7, 319n9
theological anthropology, *see*
    anthropology
theological method, 5, 10–11,
    13–14

theology
    and narrative, 6–7, 12–14,
        252, 279, 283, 298nn4-5
    dispensational, 331n6
    evangelical, 38–39, 217, 290,
        318n6, 319n11, 320n15
    feminist, 315n7
    liberal, 251, 336n18
    of children, 336n18
    of nature, 295
    of the cross, **177–180**,
        187, 201, 224, 253, 270,
        323n32, 323n34, 323n35
    performative, 13–14, 195,
        232, 248
    postliberal, 199, 326n3
    systematic, 38–39, 153, 293,
        295
theosis, *see* deification
tongues, speaking in, *see* glos-
    solalia
traducianism, 161–163
Trinity, 157–159, 181, 191,
    201–204, 211, 322n25,
    324n38

universalism, 235, 261

welfare, Welfare State, 73, 94,
    96–97, 136, 149, 312n14
Willowbrook School, 56
witchcraft, 132, 133
World Health Organization,
    58–60

yoga, 139–140